THE intuitive Businesswoman

THE
intuitive
Businesswoman

Achieve Success Through the Power of Your Personality

Judy George
and **Todd Lyon**

CLARKSON POTTER/PUBLISHERS
NEW YORK

FOR Robert George, Simon George, William George, and Jennifer George Cedrone, with love and gratitude for all that I acquired in wisdom, inspiration, and hope. As my children, they taught me the true meaning of life's but a journey! —J.G.

FOR my grandmothers, Margaret "Peg" Wynne and Cecilia "Todd" Lyon, who would have loved this new century. —T.L.

Published by Clarkson N. Potter/Publishers, New York, New York. Member of the Crown Publishing Group.

Random House, Inc. New York, Toronto, London, Sydney, Auckland www.randomhouse.com

CLARKSON N. POTTER is a trademark and POTTER and colophon are registered trademarks of Random House, Inc.

Printed in the United States of America

Design by Jane Treuhaft

Library of Congress Cataloging-in-Publication Data
George, Judy.
    The intuitive businesswoman : achieve success through the power of your personality / by Judy George and Todd Lyon.
    Includes bibliographical references.
    1. Businesswomen.   2. Businesswomen—Job satisfaction.
3. Personality and occupation.   4. Work and family.   I. Lyon, Todd.
II. Title.
HD6054.G46 2000
650.1'082—dc21   99-045742

ISBN 0-609-60433-3
10 9 8 7 6 5 4 3 2 1
First Edition

Acknowledgments

The authors are grateful to the many women and men who put care and energy into this project.

First and foremost, we thank the amazing, inspiring women whose personal stories appear in this book:

Barbara Ashley
Debbie Atkins
Rose Marie Bravo
Meg Brazill
Rev. Margaret Bullitt-Jonas
Lauren Caldwell
Jeanne Cavadini
Claire Criscuolo
Laura Groppe
Susan Hanlon
Barbara Hemingway
Sarah Hoit
Joanna Lau
Shelly Lazarus
Lois Lindauer
Elise Locker
Colleen Mohyde
Ann Moore
Sue Navarretta
Marilyn Carlson Nelson
Lane Nemeth
Shelley Reich
Jennifer Reiley
Ayéssa Rourke
Anne Robinson
Sandra Shea
Susan Sargent
Lois Silverman
Estelle Sobel
Lisa Somers
The Honorable Marie O. Jackson
   Thompson
Cherie Whaples-Elliott
Sharon Whiteley

We also thank the women who allowed us a look into their working lives, and helped inform the Intuitive System:

Lauren Hutton
Francesca Kuglen
Janet Levine
Maggie Melanson
Nancy Seybold

For their professional advice and expertise, we thank:

Vicki Donlan, publisher, *Women's Business*
Anthony F. Rando, CFP, American Express Financial Advisors, Inc.

Our invaluable researchers and assistants:

Barbara Lyon
Lisa Somers
Marisa Queiroz de Vilhena
Lauren Caldwell
Hayward Gatling
Tamara Kruchok

And the hundreds of women who took our Intuitive Quiz, especially:

Suzanne Bates
Brenna Brennan
Barbara Brilliant
Teri Cavanaugh
Evelyn Evans
Kathryn Evans
Marcie Gorfinkle
Denise Hajjar
Karla Jones
Dorothy Langer
Hilda Morrill
Sheila Schechtman
Elaine Taylor-Gordon
Carol Uhrich

Judy George acknowledges:

My mentor in understanding how important it is to know oneself, Janet Levine; my business associates who pushed me to become more involved in women's enterprises, Sheryl Marshall, Dorothy Cunningham, Vicki Donlan, Teri Cavanaugh, Jena Hall, Deborah Naish, Tess Torrey, Molly Wuthridge, Ima Udofia, and Marcie Garfinkle; and my phenomenal partners at Domain, Laura Katz and Jim McCullagh. Special thanks to Sue Beddia, a remarkable woman. Also, my family members, Diane, Barbara, and Joyce.

This book couldn't have happened if I didn't have support from my husband, Simon, who had to be patient throughout the process and give up some of our valuable time together in the evenings.

There are special men who have been coaches, mentors, and supportive friends: Jerry Sprayregan, Larry Crink, George Hamilton, Bob Darvin, Billy Trifone, Mitch Bobkin, Hank Kaminstein, Dan Levy, Jeff Walker, Bob White, Bill Burgin, and Mitt Romney. I'd like to give special thanks to Mark Albion, one of my most compassionate mentors and friends; Nkere Udofia, a great cheerleader and coach; and most of all, my father, who made it possible for me to dream big dreams, and a mother who was gifted with a tenacity and perseverance I believe I inherited.

Finally, Judy and Todd send gratitude and kudos to:

Our Visionary agent, Colleen Mohyde; our Adventurer editor, Katie Workman; and the team at Clarkson Potter, especially Artisan Julia Coblentz.

Contents

Preface
Judy George and the Birth of the Intuitive System

The good news is, I got fired.

That was the day, fifteen years ago, that I launched my career as a solo businesswoman.

A call had come from my boss, the CEO of Scandinavian Design, a modernist furniture store that was the rage for yuppie consumers in the 1980s. When he asked me to meet him at headquarters, I was upbeat. And why not? For ten years, I had worked my way through the company's executive ranks. I became president, and I was negotiating for a bigger compensation package.

I figured I would have great news to tell the guests who were due at my home that evening for a dinner party.

When I walked into his office, my boss got right to the point. It was time for us to go our separate ways, he said. He needed to run his show without any interference.

Shock waves ran through me. I had built a life around my work. I was a successful businessperson, hailed in the press for my accomplishments and featured in books and on TV as a role model. The company was a big part of my identity; I couldn't believe it was being taken away. How could this happen?

At home that evening, surrounded by family and friends, my shock changed to humiliation and sorrow. Then, as light dawned after that long, sleepless night, it became rage. I knew it was time to take control of my life. Like a modern-day Scarlett O'Hara, I stood in the ruined field of ten years of dedicated labor and cried, "With God as my witness, I'll never work for anyone else again!"

Within twenty-four hours I was meeting with bankers and accountants, calling all the people I thought or hoped could help me. Fourteen months later, after raising $3.5 million, I opened the doors to the first Domain stores. I was selling furniture and something else: my own vision.

The Inner Entrepreneur Meets the Cosmic Boot

As it turned out, getting fired was the best career move I could have made. It was a "cosmic boot"—one of those seemingly tragic events that gets things moving and turns out to be a blessing in disguise. Once the unthinkable had happened, I discovered what was really mine. True, I didn't have a college degree, nor did I have great personal wealth. But I had vision, will, perseverance, ambition, and talent. In short, I was—and always had been—an entrepreneur.

Looking back, I can hardly believe it took me so long to see the light. Why hadn't I noticed that the "chain" of lemonade stands I'd started at age six perfectly paralleled the expansion campaign I'd led at Scandinavian? With no training or backing I had launched an interior design service, then a newspaper column, then a TV show. When I entered the workplace in 1975 after rearing four kids, I couldn't land the job I wanted, so I hired a plane to buzz the place. The plane's streamer read, "Hire Judy George. She'll make you money." They did, and I did. What's more entrepreneurial than that?

I'd poured love and energy into Scandinavian Design, never quite understanding that it wasn't my company. Yet my years there were not a loss, because they had given me powerful proof that my ideas worked in the real world. I had anticipated the needs of the marketplace and provided consumers with the right merchandise at the right time.

Once I got in touch with my inner entrepreneur, my own ideas about the furniture industry snapped into focus. I saw that home was evolving into a sanctuary for hardworking people—a feathered nest where stress was banished and creature comforts were indulged. And I saw that I could meet the needs of an emerging population of cocooners.

A Rocket in My Pocket

Domain started small. Two stores, twelve employees. Today, the chain has grown to include twenty-five stores in seven states on the East Coast, and posts annual sales of $60 million.

It's been a snap!

Only kidding.

I think I made every mistake there was. Like positioning the original stores as too upscale. And hiring a partner just like me. I also failed to establish a strong delivery system; I was too controlling when it came to purchasing; and I carried too much inventory.

In the first few years I zigged and zagged around these problems, constantly correcting errors and making adjustments, always learning from my blunders.

But the big lessons came later, when I took stock of myself. I came to understand that I, Judy George, wanted to hit home runs. I liked drama and showmanship, but I was bored with the utilitarian tasks necessary to run a successful business. I tended to project my need for status on the company and to internalize sales figures to the point where, if customers didn't buy a particular line, I was sure it was because they didn't like *me*. Also, I was not a good team player. I didn't know how to organize or lead a team, either.

I suppose I could have spent years in therapy trying to figure out why I wasn't perfect. Instead, I decided to go with my strengths and to hire the best people I could find to manage those aspects of business that baffled, swamped, eluded, or bored me.

It was when I had the courage to look inward and take responsibility for who I was that the road to business success started to smooth out. I stopped trying to be all things to all people. I came to recognize that I couldn't demand love, but I could demand respect. And I learned, slowly, to let go. I became less of a control queen, and turned my energies toward finding talented people and placing them in optimum positions within the company. With the right teams in place, I didn't have to run every aspect of the show. I could trust my people to do their work, just as they could trust me to do mine.

And all things grew.

Enter the Intuitive System

Somewhere along the way, without really meaning to, I became a student of personality. I started to notice patterns of preferences and behaviors among my colleagues and clients. I saw that some people liked to work alone, and others naturally gathered collaborators and teammates around them. Some liked to collect as many facts as possible before making decisions; others relied on gut feelings to guide them.

When I started to take my observations seriously, I was gradually able to formalize them, with the assistance of writer Todd Lyon, into what we now call the Intuitive System. This is essentially a blueprint that divides the world into four broadly drawn archetypes: Visionaries, Artisans, Idealists, and Adventurers.

Looking at the world through these four different lenses was incredibly enlightening. Each type excelled in specific areas. Each had certain ways of getting things done, certain motivating factors, and liked different kinds of environments. (Our first book, *The Domain Book of Intuitive Home Design*, explored the relationship among the four archetypes and their preferred home environments.)

I applied the Intuitive System to management, and I tested every person on the Domain payroll to discover which archetype they most resembled. From this data I was able to gain insights into people's natural impulses and to make changes that increased creativity, productivity, and contentment. I learned to challenge Adventurers with jobs that required guts and paid off in glory. I placed Visionaries in charge of important long-term projects, put Artisans on democratic teams, and charged Idealists with major organizational jobs.

But I was also careful not to pigeonhole people. Most humans are a combination of two, three, or even four archetypes, with one usually dominating the rest.

What has been most useful about the system is that it creates a language with which to better understand and discuss human behavior. In addition to helping people recognize their own natural inclinations, it can really help improve relationships. When you're a hypersensitive Artisan, for example, it's comforting to recognize that the co-worker who avoids office small talk isn't being snobbish—it's just that she's a Visionary. Visionaries are protective of their personal lives, and, though they may be skilled at discussing big concepts, most aren't comfortable exchanging simple pleasantries.

The Intuitive Judy George

Here is my Intuitive Profile: I am a Visionary with a strong streak of Adventurer and a dollop of Artisan.

As such, it's no surprise that I like being visible. (Visionaries tend to establish themselves as figureheads.) It was very Visionary of me to go into a business that put me around luxurious goods (Visionaries are fancy) and beautiful surroundings (in the Visionary world, much depends on visuals).

The Adventurer part of my personality is expressed in my tendency to be flamboyant. There are few gestures more Adventurer than hiring a plane to buzz a company's headquarters! My Adventurer streak is also evident when I take big risks in the hope of big payoffs, rather than making steady, sensible progress.

I take great joy in being a mentor, and I credit that attribute to the Artisan part of my makeup. Artisans also tend to be home-centric and family oriented, and this represents a special part of my personality: I am most content when I'm cooking in the kitchen of the house that my husband built for me nearly thirty years ago.

So, what's missing from this picture? Have you noticed that I don't have one drop of Idealist? Believe me, *I've* noticed. Idealists are ruled by logic. They're the people who lead with their heads and not their hearts. They work everything out on paper, and have an orderliness to most everything they do.

I've learned that Idealists can give me what I lack.

When I first started Domain, I hired creative hotheads like myself. I responded to the passion I saw in others because I was comfortable with it. But if I had looked more closely at the bigger picture, I would have seen an imbalance between my ambition, passion, and creativity, and what I didn't bring to the table: Cool logic and practicality.

I really should have known better. After all, I married an Idealist. Even as a nineteen-year-old bride, I instinctively knew that I needed a stable rudder, a partner who would play tortoise to my hare. My marriage has lasted a long time. Why didn't I notice the success of that partnership and apply it to my business?

Because, back then, I wasn't tuned in to the importance of personality. I was always looking outward, toward the future, money, success, recognition. I forgot to notice what qualities I lacked.

The Intuitive System helped me put together a balanced team and to cover all the bases. It has been a great tool for me and my company, so when I started applying it to fellow businesswomen—many of whom I met through a mentoring program—a "Eureka!" moment happened. I realized that I'd hit upon a set of parameters that could help just about any woman thrive in the career of her dreams—and avoid many bumps on the road to success.

The Intuitive Businesswoman: The Book

We could have written this book for any segment of society. But we decided to focus on working women. Why? Because, with few role models in place, women are inventing their own lives and creating an exciting new chapter in American history.

We have nothing against men. In fact, we love them very much. But women are today's change agents, true pioneers who are shaping the future.

The Intuitive Businesswoman builds a framework within which women can locate themselves in a jungle of working situations. There is a section that deals with employee/employer relations, and another that tells how best to sell to the four archetypes. We look toward the past, observing the career patterns of such historic figures as Josephine Baker (Adventurer), Elizabeth Arden (Visionary), Fannie Farmer (Idealist), and Margaret Sanger (Artisan). We give pointers about big things, like how to raise money to start a business, and little things, like what kind of office space might best suit your personality.

In every chapter you'll find real-life stories of women who have invented themselves. They are the true heroes of this book. Some names you'll recognize, like Ann Moore, president of People, Inc., publishers of People, In Style, and other red-hot publications. And there are names you won't know, like Lisa Somers, who started a home-based company as a way to help heal her postpartum depression. You'll hear from Shelly

Lazarus, who heads Ogilvy & Mather, one of the most powerful ad agencies in the world, and Sue Navarretta, an R.N. who drove across the country with her five-year-old daughter and $6,000 to start her life over again.

All of them are women who have listened to themselves and found the strength, courage, and wisdom not only to survive, but to thrive. It is our hope that their inspiring stories, combined with healthy dollops of hard-headed business advice, will help put you on a path to fulfillment in the workplace. In the words of Oprah Winfrey: "It's not about making a living. It's about making a life."

Or, as Katharine Hepburn once said, "If you have to support yourself, you had bloody well better find some way that is going to be interesting."

Introduction
Making Work Work for You

The future belongs to those who believe in the beauty of their dreams.
— ELEANOR ROOSEVELT

The statistics are marvelous. In 1999 there were 9.1 million women-owned businesses in the U.S., accounting for nearly half of all small businesses in this country. Those businesses employ some 27.5 million people—more than the *Fortune* 500 companies employ worldwide.

Think of it—in our grandmothers' time, the sentence "No wife of mine is going to get a job" actually had some clout. Yet even ambitious women found few business opportunities, to say the least. Now the doors of commerce have opened wide. The range of options has become vast and almost infinite. Which is good, because these days very few women have the luxury of choosing not to work.

But as women continue to create careers for themselves, some sobering statistics also pop up. In 1997, less than 1 percent of women working full-time earned more than $100,000. Women are still earning only about 75 cents for every $1 earned by men; according to U.S. Census figures, women's average salary is only $24,948 (versus $30,854 for men). In 1999, when Carly Fiorina was appointed CEO of Hewlett-Packard Co.—the largest public company ever headed by a female—the grand total of *Fortune* 500 companies headed by people of the female persuasion was brought up to three.

On the brighter side are tales of triumph that would have been aberrations forty years ago. Many of these stories were splashed on the newsstands in October of 1998, when *Fortune* magazine published its list of the fifty most powerful women in American business. The piece was a fascinating snapshot of how women are taking control of our country's economic evolution. Especially interesting was the way in which these women found power from within themselves.

Darla Moore, president of Rainwater, Inc., told *Fortune:* "So many women think their power comes from the outside, from their position in the company. They really aren't powerful if they don't have personal power." Sherry Lansing, Paramount Pictures honcho, commented, "The single most important thing you can do in business is to be yourself."

In the same issue was a story that tracked down the thirty-four women who graduated from Harvard Business School in 1973. The following wisdom is from that group of trailblazers: "The advice is not about how to break the glass ceiling or how to survive a sexist boss. It is instead to know thyself, and then to make your choices accordingly."

The message is clear: If the shoe doesn't fit, don't wear it.

And that is what this book is about.

Right now, 1,600 women start companies in the United States every day. Whether they're inventors, image consultants, contractors, caterers, designers, or software writers, they share certain patterns of success.

The first rule of success is: Know thyself.

The second rule is: Go with your strengths.

Knowing oneself can take a lifetime. But it becomes easier if you have a template, and that's what the Intuitive System provides.

We're not going to teach you how to write a résumé, or tell you which franchises promise the best returns. But we will steer you toward business strategies that suit your soul. With the Intuitive System, you can make decisions that are true to your goals and maximize your strengths—because this book is about that brilliant, maddening, multifaceted, powerful person called you.

The Intuitive Businesswoman begins with a quiz that will help you determine whether you're most like a Visionary, an Artisan, an Idealist, or an Adventurer—or a combination thereof. Then, in learning about the four types, you'll start to recognize people you know—your friends, co-workers, employees, bosses, and, most important, yourself.

Do you plunge into projects with great excitement, then get bored when the show is up and running? Then you're probably an Adventurer. Do you own a company that's named after you? You might be a Visionary. Idealists believe in gathering lots of data before beginning any venture; Artisans are likely to hire friends and family members whenever they can.

No matter what field you're in or what your interests might be, your personality is the best guide you've got for finding your way in the working world.

As *Fortune* notes, the most powerful women in America "tend to bring their whole, multidimensional, emotional, feminine selves to their jobs. . . . these women realize that the 'business' isn't the place where they work. The business is themselves."

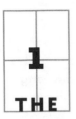

1
THE
Intuitive Quiz
and How to Take It

If you've been to a career counselor (even a high school career counselor), chances are you've taken tests designed to help you find a vocation that suits you.

This is not like those tests.

Oh sure, it seeks to identify your strengths and home in on your preferences. But at the end of it you will not get a neat little printout of jobs that match your profile (for example, bus driver, kindergarten teacher, software CEO who might net $18 mill on her IPO). Rather, it seeks to coax out clues to your personal style and gently group them into a broad category (or two) with which you can identify.

From there, the book concerns itself not with squeaky little job titles but with grand tales and intimate stories of women whose style is much like your own—and who have taken that style, flaws and all, and run with it.

Which is to say: Relax.

Taking this quiz should be a pleasure. In it, you can pretend that you're an entrepreneur, a philanthropist, a boss lady, and a computer whiz—even if you're none of the above. It's so pressure-free that if you come across a question you can't possibly answer, you don't have to. And if you come across a question in which two answers seem equally right to you, you can go ahead and answer twice. Some questions, you'll note, actually invite you to answer twice.

The Intuitive Questionnaire

1 You wake up in the middle of the night to find your fairy godmother standing in your bedroom. She apologizes for her long absence, then offers you one of four gifts. Which do you choose?

■ **a** A portfolio of promising tech stocks

■ **b** Your own syndicated TV show

✗ **c** Choice seats at the entertainment award ceremony of your choice (Academy Awards, Grammys, Tonys, etc.)

△ ■ **d** A house in the country

2 Your employees have an affectionate nickname for you. Which of the following might it be?

■ **a** Dot Com

■ **b** Hurricane _____

(your name here)

△ **c** Your Highness

■ **d** Mother Earth

3 You have a chance to choose one of four mentors. The only information you have about them is listed below. Make your selection as best you can.

■ **a** A technological wizard who has made a fortune in software design

■ **b** A self-made millionaire who has irons in every fire — entertainment, manufacturing, publishing, hospitality, product development, the works

■ **c** An exciting business celebrity who is not just a person but a brand, whose name is licensed to all kinds of consumer products

△ ■ **d** A successful, compassionate, and altruistic mentor who often promotes products for the good they'll do rather than the profits they'll incur

4 You spot an empty storefront in a wonderful neighborhood with a FOR LEASE sign in the window. Of these fleeting thoughts, which would probably cross your mind first?

a I wonder how much they're getting for rent?

b This would make a fabulous apartment.

c I hope somebody opens a great boutique here.

d I could start a sweet little business in this spot.

5 You've interviewed at four companies, and each has returned with a great job offer with virtually identical salaries and benefits. Now you have to make a decision based on each firm's philosophies. Which of the following pitches would most sway you?

a "Your work will be rewarded here. We have a well-defined profit-sharing program as well as generous yearly bonuses based on performance."

b "We think of our company as an incubator for creativity. We want you to bring your whole self to work, take risks, try new approaches, and never be bored or boring."

c "Your take-charge personality is just what we're looking for. We intend to install you as a leader, and will support your vision with all the resources we can muster."

d "Our philosophy is that a person has got to be happy in order to be productive. We offer flexible scheduling and family-friendly policies, and promote wellness on every level."

6 Your one-woman enterprise is really taking off. You need to hire an employee, but the prospect makes you nervous. Why?

a You wonder if the trouble of training someone, in addition to the burden of making payroll, is really justifiable.

b You're not sure you want to maintain a consistent schedule or find things for an employee to do on a daily basis.

△ **c** You doubt you'll be able to find somebody who can live up to your standards.

d You're uncomfortable correcting people or assigning unpleasant tasks to them.

7 **You're throwing a special holiday party for your employees and want to hold it at a memorable place. Assuming money is no object, which one of the following locations would you choose?**

△ **a** An ultramodern hotel dining room with a stunning view

b A campy cocktail lounge, complete with a Vegas-style crooner

 c A beautifully decorated Victorian inn

d A cozy ski lodge, with access to the slopes and a skating pond

8 **You are about to open a high-end department store that emphasizes personal service. How do you outfit your sales associates?**

a You issue classic lab coats with discreet name tags.

b You ask associates to dress stylishly, then assign great-looking "backstage passes" to wear around their necks.

 c You hire a designer to create a wardrobe with tops, trousers, and jackets that employees can coordinate.

d You ask your sales associates to dress casually and assign each attractive aprons that bear the store's logo.

9 **You've held your current job for some time, and, although you're a little bored, you're comfortable and stable. Out of the blue, you get an offer that tempts you to leave. What is it?**

a The federal government asks you to work on an important long-term project, with no change in salary but a promise of a great pension after ten years.

b You have a chance to go on the lecture circuit, traveling around the world to share your knowledge with others in your field, with no change in salary but more free time.

c You've been recruited to do virtually the same job you're doing now, but with higher visibility, more control, a bigger staff, and a 10 percent raise.

d You're invited to take early retirement to the tune of $30,000 (gross) a year for life.

10 **Your eight employees have each given you a birthday present. Though you're delighted by all the gifts, there are two that you secretly like best. Which are they? (Choose two):**

a A state-of-the-art electronic organizer

b A wall calendar that has your face superimposed on famous works of art

c A pair of suede gloves in a delicious color

d A charitable donation made in your name to the local animal shelter

e Tickets to the opera

f An herbal sachet, handmade by the employee

g A deluxe-edition road atlas

h A gift certificate for a parasailing session

11 **You really like the woman you share an office with . . . except for one thing she does that drives you crazy. Which of the following behaviors would bother you most?**

a She has a temper. Though she's never directed it toward you, you've seen her lash out at others.

b Whenever there's a conflict between the two of you, she writes you a memo instead of talking it out.

c Her desk is an absolute mess. She makes piles everywhere and has even spilled coffee on important paperwork.

d She's constantly on the phone with her kids, and will accept calls from them any time, even in the middle of meetings or crucial discussions.

12 You've been contacted by the bank at which you had a savings account as a child. Seems the account is still active and, thanks to compounded interest, you're $6,000 richer. Choose two of the following ways to spend your windfall.

a Pay off debts or outstanding bills.

b Go on vacation.

c Buy stocks, bonds, T-bills, or other financial products.

d Buy a big-ticket item that you've needed or wanted for a long time.

e Take courses toward an advanced degree.

f Do home improvements.

g Throw a big party.

h Have a bit of cosmetic surgery.

13 You're lying in a heap on your sofa, trying to recover from a very bad day. Which one of the following situations is likely to have upset you most?

a You had to let an employee go. She took it so badly that she sobbed in your office.

b A flamboyant presentation you made fell flat on its face.

c You discovered that you made an error that will cost your company time and money.

d A valued client dropped you and hired your number one competitor.

14 You're distressed by the plight of underprivileged teenagers in your community. As a business owner, you want to help. How do you make a difference?

a Create a mentoring program that matches volunteer employees with local teens.

b Fund an after-school art and theater program.

c Select the most ambitious kids to serve as paid summer interns.

d Establish a college scholarship in your company's name.

15 A computer tech from another planet has appeared in your office and offered you one of the following upgrades, free of charge. Which do you pick?

a A special keyboard that, whenever you touch it, makes you feel exactly as if you're lounging outdoors on a beautiful day.

b A design program that allows you to talk about your ideas and have them instantly displayed in full-color 3-D graphics.

c A program that compiles up-to-date data relating to every business decision you have to make.

d A robotic clone that can be programmed to make obligatory phone calls and carry on polite conversations—all in your voice.

16 If you had to fire yourself, which of the following would be your chief reason for letting yourself go?

a Indecisiveness

b Lack of commitment

c Lack of discipline

d Lousy team player

17

You're an established freelance graphic artist. Your best client has invited you to design a print campaign. Unfortunately, it promotes a political stance to which you are fiercely opposed. What do you do?

a You tell your client you can't do the job in good conscience and hope you'll be called back when there are other jobs to bid on.

b You let your client know that you don't agree with the content of the campaign, but accept the job as a favor.

c You take on the job and earmark 20 percent of your fee to donate to your favorite charity.

d You up the price for the job, and secretly hope you'll be turned down.

18

Four invitations have arrived in the mail. Each is for an important business event; unfortunately, they're all scheduled for the same evening. Which one would you be most tempted to attend?

a The one that seems like the most fun

b The one that offers a unique learning experience

c The one that seems the least stressful

d The one that most likely includes meeting influential people

19

Your relationship with your business partner is becoming strained. Which of the following conflicts bothers you most?

a Your partner is pushing for layoffs within the company in order to improve the bottom line instead of examining other options.

b He or she is constantly vetoing your ideas.

c Your partner is doing less than his/her share of the daily work.

d He or she is making decisions without your consent.

20 After a long and fruitful career, you're finally retiring. Just before you're about to go on that celebratory cruise, however, something lures you back into the working world. What is it?

- **a** You're invited to head up a new, nonprofit division of your company that creates grants for needy community groups.

- **b** You're recruited to be a well-paid spokesperson for a product you believe in; the job involves lots of travel and media attention.

- **c** You're tapped to head up the board of directors at your former company.

- **d** You've been asked to be a consultant — with stock options — at a hot new company.

Scoring

On the following lists, make a check mark next to each corresponding answer, then add up your totals to discover where your tendencies fall.

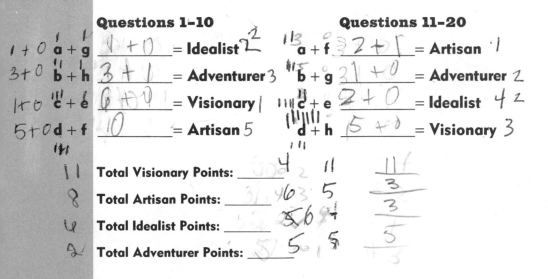

Questions 1–10		Questions 11–20	
a + g ___ = Idealist		a + f ___ = Artisan	
b + h ___ = Adventurer		b + g ___ = Adventurer	
c + e ___ = Visionary		c + e ___ = Idealist	
d + f ___ = Artisan		d + h ___ = Visionary	

Total Visionary Points: ___

Total Artisan Points: ___

Total Idealist Points: ___

Total Adventurer Points: ___

Interpreting the Quiz

The Intuitive System is based on four archetypal personalities: the Vision-ary, the Artisan, the Idealist, and the Adventurer. These are general cate-gories that group people by traits and tendencies. No individual (at least none we've met yet) fits squarely into one category, and that's as it should be. Most people's answers are scattered across three or four categories, with one standing out above the others.

Simply stated, the higher your score in a category, the more you resem-ble that archetype. If you score more than ten points in any category, that's a strong tendency. If your highest scores are split between two types, then you probably share a lot of characteristics with both. If your answers spill more or less evenly between three or even four types, don't fret: this just means that different parts of your personality correspond with different types.

The next four chapters of this book are dedicated to the Visionary, the Artisan, the Idealist, and the Adventurer, in that order. They offer an in-depth look at the types' characteristics, from childhood role models to leadership styles, to favorite industries, to what kinds of offices each type prefers. As you get acquainted with each archetype, you may recognize yourself as something other than what your test results show. There's nothing wrong with that; this, after all, is a book about self-discovery.

Identifying your truest type, the type that feels most like your authen-tic self, is important: it will help you use the more practical business tips offered in the second half of the book.

Enjoy the ride, and may you prosper from it.

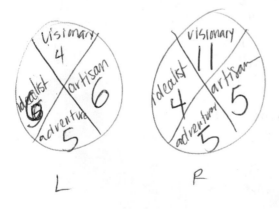

2

THE

Visionary

Determined. Ambitious. Cultured. Courageous. Refined. Competitive. Driven. Independent. Private.

The word **visionary** might suggest a person who is ahead of her time. In the context of the Intuitive System, however, it's more accurate to say that Visionaries have a strong ability to focus on a goal and make it happen—sometimes against all odds.

Unlike the Artisan, who thrives in family-like units, or the Adventurer, who often runs as the leader of a pack, the Visionary stands alone in a role that can only be described as queenly. She is an empire builder who creates her own culture. She sets high goals for herself and the people around her, and she usually has no trouble occupying positions of authority.

Visionaries can be very effective leaders. Because they focus on a goal, they're not bogged down by details. Getting the job done is of supreme importance; the Visionary has places to go and will not be impeded by the ambivalence or faintheartedness of others. Visionary businesswomen tend to follow the shortest path to financial success and are very good at creating demand and building a buzz around their businesses—they excel at marketing and sales.

Yet Visionaries, in their quest for achievement, never neglect what is for them an essential element of success: style. To the Visionary, it is no good moving mountains unless it's done with flair. And since she is likely to be in a business that reflects her personal aesthetics—Visionaries are often found in glamour industries—she's less concerned about how things get done than how they look when they're done.

Visionaries want the best of everything. If the Visionary works as a waitress, it will be at the finest restaurant in town. In business, she will buy from the vendor who offers the highest-quality work, rather than the lowest bidder. She'll vie for the office with the best view and negotiate for sky-high raises, sweetened with extra benefits. In her personal life, the Visionary is equally selective. She's careful about the people she lets in, and usually keeps her private life very, very private.

Because she's independent and has a strong inner vision, the Visionary does her most inspired work when she can control a project from beginning to end. She can tackle ambitious jobs and deliver them on time, with the proverbial cherry on top. But she doesn't take kindly to interference, nor is she much of a team player. The Visionary has her own way of doing things.

A warrior spirit blazes inside Visionaries. Some are blatantly competitive and fit the cliché of the ambitious woman clawing her way to the top. But most only fight to be the best at what they do. They are determined to get straight A's on their report cards, no matter what their classroom might look like.

Inside the Visionary Mind

Visionaries are mistresses of their own fate. Most are blessed with a fierce will to succeed. Many also have a will to secede—to leave their homeland behind.

The archetypal Visionary success story features a strong woman who, determined to distinguish herself, rises from obscurity and becomes a product of her own invention. Throughout history, notable Visionaries have overcome difficult conditions and reached fabulous levels of wealth and fame. Some—including Elizabeth Arden, Madame C. J. Walker, Hattie Carnegie, Estée Lauder, and Lillian Vernon—changed their names to suit their careers, thus cleaving themselves from the past while becoming eponymous with their creations.

Visionaries have, as the title implies, a vision. Often that vision begins with a hunger and develops into a determination to create a life of substance and abundance. As young girls, Visionaries-to-be often dream of a storybook existence. Their picture of perfection may be centered around winning a gold medal in figure skating, operating a four-star hotel in Paris, or becoming president of the United States. But no matter what the particulars, with Visionaries it's all about transformation through accomplishment.

Growing Up Different

When asked about their childhood years, many Visionaries say they felt like misfits; they recall defining themselves against a backdrop of not belonging.

Barbara Ashley, a retail expert and consumer trend forecaster, is a first-generation American born to German parents. She experienced a strict upbringing in an intellectual, politically driven household. When she developed an interest in fashion and design, her family cast her as the "materialistic, superficial black sheep." Today, Barbara admits that anger is still a force in her life. "I am driven every single day to prove to my parents that I am worthy. That's not something I'm proud to say, but I always knew they were wrong. They never gave me the respect and recognition that I've since gained from the rest of the world."

Colleen Mohyde, a Boston-based literary agent, says that growing up in a blue-collar town and working at her family's tobacco shop "felt like someone else's life." She located her true self in the pages of books; her happiest memories are of holing up with Louisa May Alcott novels and Nancy Drew mysteries. Colleen was one of the few people in her extended family to attend college, but because she studied "impractical" subjects—English literature and publishing—she was viewed by her relatives as a hopeless dreamer.

When Colleen graduated and became an editorial assistant at Little, Brown, a prestigious publishing house in Boston, she felt as if she'd "died and gone to heaven." She didn't care that she was underpaid. "I was bringing home less than I had made as a waitress," Colleen recalls, "but I was compensated by working at this beautiful townhouse and picking up the phone and having Lillian Hellman be on the line. I was more than happy to get a sandwich for William Manchester."

Some Visionaries made up perfect identities for themselves. Nancy Friday, author of *My Mother, Myself* and other groundbreaking books, recalls that, in her childhood, "my mother was preoccupied with my older sister and I just couldn't catch her eye. I felt invisible at home," she told *Bust* magazine in 1998. "So I made up this girl—myself—who was an athlete and the president of the class and an A-student."

In classic Visionary style, Barbara, Colleen, and Nancy were compelled to move beyond the comfortable choices laid out by their families. On the road to finding fulfillment, each took her life into her own hands and didn't question the resulting separation from parents, hometowns, and childhood friends.

It should be noted that a great many Visionaries come from homes where they were given plenty of support. Yet virtually every Visionary has a need to make it on her own. Her natural impulse would be to start a business rather than inherit her father's company, or to get on a corporate track even as her siblings were running around being nightclub singers or homemakers.

Independence Is Bliss

> **Many of our readers are rich and powerful. Inevitably, some take trophy husbands.**
>
> — AD FOR *FORTUNE* MAGAZINE

Some Visionaries remember that as children they were in awe of women who made their own money and called their own shots. Gloria Allred, one of the nation's prominent attorneys, looked up to an aunt who was a heart surgeon: "The only woman I knew who didn't get married, didn't have kids, and didn't cook."

Jennifer Reiley, a thirty-six-year-old wine sales representative, says her first role model was her Auntie Ellen. "She worked for a law firm and she painted on the side," Jennifer remembers. "She was the glamour queen of the family, constantly redecorating her home. One of her greatest joys was to put on parties, and there were always lotus dishes filled with peanuts and cocktails being mixed." Jennifer most admired her aunt's independence—her freedom to do just what she wanted, when she wanted. Says Jennifer, "I wanted to be just like Auntie Ellen. I wanted to be an artist. I never imagined myself married, I never imagined myself with children." Auntie Ellen did eventually get married—so did Jennifer—and today Ellen is a full-time artist. Jennifer laughs, "I *still* want to be just like her."

Independence is extremely important to Visionaries. Some opt out of marriage and motherhood in order to concentrate on what Colleen Mohyde calls "the life of the mind." Others maintain their autonomy perfectly well in spite of husbands, parents, siblings, and gaggles of kids—and wouldn't have it any other way.

The Good, the Bad, and the Beautiful

Like cholesterol, there are "good" Visionaries and "bad" Visionaries. Fiction writers have always had a ball with the baddies: they've been immortalized in any number of Joan Crawford movies and have been all over TV shows like *Dallas, Dynasty,* and *Melrose Place.* These dastardly divas always abused their power, and they always looked great doing it.

The quintessential bad-girl Visionary of literature is Scarlett O'Hara. Vain, manipulative, gorgeous, and ruthless, she would do anything to get her way—lie, pitch fits, withhold sex, marry someone else's beau, wear curtains

how to spot
a visionary

In the business arena, it's sometimes hard to separate an authentic Visionary from the rest of the pack because her look is what many businesswomen — whatever their type might be — aspire to. But visual clues can help. Look for:

• **Presence.** No matter what they look like or what they're wearing, true Visionaries are queenly. The most successful of them exude confidence and can fill a room without saying a word. Many are natural leaders, so if you and everyone else in the vicinity start hanging on a stranger's every word and unconsciously doing her bidding, you may have found your Visionary.

• **Makeup.** Visionaries believe in the power of artifice. Few would make an entrance without at least some lipstick and mascara.

• **Great grooming.** Hair and nails professionally done. No roots, no chipped polish. Facials and waxes probably done professionally, too. In older women, look for dazzling teeth and a peculiar absence of wrinkles.

• **Good handbag, briefcase, and shoes.** Many Visionaries consider high-end leather goods to be an investment worth making.

• **An exceptionally pulled-together look.** Some Visionaries are so aesthetically tuned in that they make distinctions between different shades of black. If the tights match the skirt *perfectly,* that's a good clue. Take note: If her clothes are flecked with lint, dust, or dog hair, she's probably not 100 percent Visionary.

• **Writes with a good pen.** No chewed, leaky, or capless ballpoints for these women.

• **Likes accessories, especially scarves.** Visionaries love to sport a silky bit of color at the neck.

• **Wears real jewelry.** Not all Visionaries wear diamonds, but you'll never catch them with an armload of plastic bangles. Look for sterling silver, polished gold, a string of pearls, a good watch, or even a brooch.

• **Power suits.** As investment dressers, Visionaries can often be found in designer suits — or good knockoffs.

• **Reading materials.** Maybe you spied her in your reception area with her nose in a hardcover book. Maybe you spotted a novel or a high-end magazine in her briefcase. Many Visionaries are dedicated readers, and in their spare moments they plug in to the wonders of the written word.

as a dress. Though spoiled beyond belief, Scarlett was, at the core, a stone-cold survivor. She, as a true Visionary, raged against the threat of *not having*.

For Scarlett, hunger was a real enemy. Today, the flesh-and-blood American Visionary is unlikely to physically starve to death, but she does have her own version of hunger, and her rage against it is as powerful as the fictional O'Hara's. Whether she's fighting to overcome poverty, an unhappy home life, political strife—or if she's chasing a dream—Visionaries take control and don't allow others be the boss of them.

With that said, let's remember that most Visionaries fall on the "good" side of the moral scale. Who is Scarlett O'Hara's literary sister? The umbrella-carrying, high-button-shoes–wearing, British nanny known as Mary Poppins.

Now, if you're thinking that Mary Poppins was a canary-voiced goody-goody, it's probably been a long time since you've seen the movie. In fact, Ms. Poppins was attractive, accomplished, flirtatious, magical, kind, wise, powerful, and not shy about it. In the beginning of the film she announces that she is "practically perfect in every way." It's an honest assessment: she spends the rest of the movie solving problems, wrapping people around her little finger, visiting shut-ins, deflating capitalists, championing the working man, and being an independent-minded leader at a time when a leader is needed most.

Nobody was the boss of Mary Poppins. She had no husband, no children, and no family except the families she chose to visit. She arrived unannounced, and when she decided her work was done, left just as abruptly. Nobody even knew where she came from, or where she was headed next. Which is an advantage that many modern Visionaries—good and bad—yearn for.

What Fuels a Visionary?

Sometimes I worry about being a success in a mediocre world.
—**LILY TOMLIN**

It's possible that Visionaries are born powerful. It's equally possible that Visionaries become powerful when circumstances force them to be.

Catalog queen Lillian Vernon started her business in 1951 because she needed to supplement her husband's weekly salary of $75. Mary Kay Ash started her company at the age of forty-eight, after experiencing blatant sexism in the workplace.

Another story that opens a window on the Visionary brand of determination is that of Lois L. Lindauer, the founder of Diet Workshop.

As Lois tells the tale, she was a fat child who felt unloved. After attending Brandeis University, where she met her first husband, she evolved into a fat, unhappy housewife. She was always ambitious, however, with a strong work ethic and a tendency toward perfectionism. "I've done everything to make money that's legal," she says. Since she was twenty years old she wanted to be president of a company, but didn't have a clue as to her specific calling in life.

Then, at thirty-two, Lois made up her mind to lose weight. "I had a real sense of mission," she recalls. "It was a question for me of survival—either live or die. I made the decision to live." She signed up for Weight Watchers and lost forty-two pounds. "I wanted very much to help others enhance the quality of their life and health as I had," says Lois. Yet, when she applied for a job as a Weight Watchers instructor, she was turned down. "It was one of the most devastating experiences of my life," she says.

A friend in Boston who needed to lose weight contacted Lois for help. Nothing could stop Lois, not even her fear of flying. From that weekly counseling, for which she shuttled back and forth between New York and Boston, Lois Lindauer grew the Diet Workshop.

She started the business in 1965 with sixteen members; within two years the Diet Workshop was thriving in five states. Lindauer retooled her company into a franchise operation, and by 1982 revenues had reached $10 million. Her company had become Weight Watchers' chief rival.

Like many Visionaries before her, Lois grew a business that fed her yearning for success and gave her an identity she could be proud of. "I designed

YOU MAY BE A VISIONARY IF . . .

Your company logo is based on your signature.
You're a lousy typist.
You despise fluorescent lighting.
You'd rather be unemployed than work in a cubicle.
You fuss over your outfit almost as much as your presentation when preparing for a meeting.
Your idea of making it includes a personal assistant, a car, and a driver.
Patience is not your greatest virtue.
After hours of shopping you often find yourself refreshed and inspired.
You'd rather be a director than a manager.
You'd rather read books than visit a Web site.
You can't stand it when people write "Xmas" instead of "Christmas."
You discourage your employees from displaying family photos, mugs with slogans, or sports memorabilia in their offices.
More often than not you want to be alone.
You drink expensive coffee.
You're more likely to watch PBS than a sitcom.
You never once have made lunch at home and brought it to the office.
You have a jewelry store–quality fountain pen reserved for signing important letters and documents.
You shrink from "do-it-yourself" projects.
You have your stockbroker, your hairdresser, and your therapist on speed-dial.
Signs, menus, and memos with typos drive you nuts.
You're disinterested in small talk but are always eager for large talk.
You love humankind, but would rather not work directly with the public.
You never let 'em see you sweat.

everything from the control systems to how the diets looked," she confesses. "I got off on this. I wanted people to say, 'Look how clever you are, Lois.' I didn't have a business plan; I was saving my own life."

The Visionary Sense of Privacy

> **A difference of taste in jokes is a great strain on the affections.**
> — GEORGE ELIOT

The Adventurer thinks out loud and would blurt the intimate details of her life to anyone from her stockbroker to her plumber. Visionaries can't imagine such a thing. They are private and establish strong boundaries—especially at the workplace—in order to keep others at arm's length.

Part of this boundary setting is just good business: Visionaries avoid getting close to the people they work with because, on the job, they want to think with their heads, not their hearts. They are very aware of power balances and don't like to blur the borders between "colleague" and "friend." But there is more to it than that: Visionaries resist interference. They don't want other people influencing their decisions or their processes and will ask advice only of the greatest of gurus.

Estelle Sobel, a magazine editor who specializes in launch publications and projects, wrestles with the problem of interference. During her early career, in which she worked as a writer and a public relations rep, she struggled to keep focused on her vision. "I was in situations in which other people's energies took precedence," she says. "My time, rather than being spent on creativity, was spent fending off others' problems and concerns." Things changed as she grew professionally. "I needed to create the structure for myself," she says.

As Estelle well knows, Visionaries are profoundly distracted by clatter and chaos. "I can't stand crowds—those crawling, amorphous crowds—and I don't like people on top of me," she says. "When I'm in a big store, I can only shop one rack at a time. In the street I look straight ahead. I have a friend who sees every celebrity, every old friend, but my tendency is to focus on what I need to do."

Desperately Seeking Sanctuary

> **One of the great hardships of my childhood . . . was that I could never find a decent place to read.**
> — JEAN STAFFORD

Most Visionaries are smart, witty, and great to look at. But you won't catch them yucking it up at crowded parties or joining the gang for a rowdy ski trip. The Visionary's idea of a good time is more likely to involve one-on-one encounters with great conversationalists, or introspective activities like reading, walking, and attending cultural events.

Relationships, families, and a hectic home life can put a crimp in the Visionary's need for solitude. "I think of private and personal time as being by myself," says Jennifer Reiley. "My husband thinks of it as being with me. That's probably why I take so much time in the bathroom." As a wine sales representative, Jennifer often hosts evening wine tastings and calls on restaurants at odd hours. Since she's never quite sure when her day is going to end, she has to create private time for herself. "I try to devise ways to take care of that part of myself that tends to be neglected during the work day," she says. Her favorite soul restorer is making art, so she schedules blocks of time when she can shut out the world, be alone, and paint.

Though most Visionaries find sanctuary at home, some actually find it at the office. When she was working as an editor, Colleen Mohyde's home life was chaotic, with three generations living under one roof. "Work was my refuge," she says, "where I could most be myself. The real me, the life of the mind, the life of ideas—that's what I was always in a hurry to get back to. Home was just a roof over my head, where I was marking time."

How Visionaries Learn

Let me listen to me and not to them.

— GERTRUDE STEIN

When a colleague sincerely requests advice and counsel from a Visionary, the results can be extraordinary. With her laser-beam intelligence, finely tuned intuition, and exquisite sense of business timing, the Visionary can, when she chooses to, dispense guidance that mere money could never buy. If you have eyes to see and ears to hear and you have a Visionary for a mentor, you are truly blessed.

But Visionaries themselves are not prone to seek advice, and prefer to do their learning in private. They'll glean information from books, magazines, documentaries, and the Web, and create their own plan of action, preferably without the assistance of other humans. Visionaries, for the most part, hate being told what to do.

Still, some Visionaries have learned to curb their resistance to advice. Jennifer Reiley, for example, is in an industry in which she constantly has to learn new things. "There's no crash course for knowing wines," she explains. "You have to forgive yourself for what you don't know, go with what you do know and try to build on that." Jennifer admits, "I'm independent in my way of working, but in my way of learning I can't afford to be. I seek out documented stuff—books, mostly—but if I have an urgent question I call somebody. This is a field of growing interest for consumers, so it's not unusual to meet a consumer who knows more than you do."

The archetypal Visionary is intellectually gifted—which may be one reason why she wants to be the one who pulls solutions out of her hat. But as much as she resists asking for help, there are plenty of Visionaries who are lifelong students. College campuses are studded with brainy Visionaries, many of whom have a Ph.D. after their names. A great number of them find joy delving deeply into art, literature, and the humanities.

The Power of Aesthetics, the Aesthetics of Power

> **I've seen the best feminist minds of my generation ogling shoes.**
> **—ELAINE SHOWALTER, "THE PROFESSOR WORE PRADA"**

If the world could be divided into two kinds of people—plain and fancy—Visionaries would fall squarely on the fancy side. Beauty plays an important part in every Visionary's life, and most have a streak of perfectionism when it comes to aesthetics.

Barbara Ashley remembers when, as a young woman, she took a job at Club Med in Guadeloupe. "It was an important turning point in my life," she says, "because it exposed me to an elegant lifestyle. The food was beautifully presented, the environment was gorgeous, the people were beautiful. After six months I returned to New York and made my connections with Bloomingdale's. I had an eye—I bought fashion accessories and then home accessories. I bought creative things."

Visionaries could be described as "lopsided perfectionists." A Visionary could easily spend three hours writing a business letter, polishing grammar and spelling, finding a perfect typeface, and centering it on the page. The same Visionary might have a car that looks like street people have been living in it. But most are meticulous about their professional image. "I'm into looking good," admits Estelle Sobel. "Although I can also dress casually, I like wearing power suits. I have a power coat. It makes me feel good. I like to be the best me I can."

Barbara Ashley must have been born a Visionary, because she remembers, as a child, feeling shoe-deprived. "My parents would never let me get forty-dollar Pappagallos," says Barbara. "I could get the eighteen-dollar Baker's copy. They thought nobody would know. But I knew the difference between the copy and the real thing."

A high-pitched sense of fashion is yet another manifestation of the lofty standards that Visionaries set for themselves. Their lives are multilayered, and they constantly work on perfecting their minds, their skills, their effectiveness, their influence, and their style. Visionaries see the forest *and* the trees; to them, context is just as important as content.

Visionaries in History

Madame C.J. Walker, Hattie Carnegie, *and* **Elizabeth Arden** *had so much in common that it's a shame they weren't friends. Each woman was born financially disadvantaged, educated herself, and dedicated her life to beauty and luxury. As true Visionaries, each was mistress of her own fate; built an empire from virtually nothing; changed her name to suit her business; amassed fabulous personal wealth and fame; never gave up control of her business; and never retired.*

MADAME C.J. WALKER
PIONEER OF BEAUTY

> "I promoted myself. I had to make my own opportunity! But I made it! Don't sit down and wait for the opportunities to come."

The first self-made female millionaire in American history was born in 1867 to former slaves on a Louisiana cotton plantation. At the turn of the century, she and her donkey cart, out of which she sold her "wonderful hair grower," had become familiar figures in the South. By the time of her death in 1919, her $2 million estate included a hair care company, a beauty school, an office and theater complex, and a mansion on the Hudson River "that only Negro money had bought."

Sarah Breedlove's parents were poor, and she didn't have them for long: she was orphaned at age seven. She married at fourteen and had a daughter; by twenty she was a widow. On her own in St. Louis, she worked for nearly two decades as a washerwoman. But Breedlove had Visionary dreams that didn't involve servitude. In her precious spare time, she experimented with potions to help make African-American hair more manageable. By 1905 she developed a regime that utilized a shampoo, a pomade, and

SCORECARD

VISIONARY QUALITIES
- ✔ Leadership-oriented
- ✔ Named business after self
- ✔ Works in glamour industry
- ✔ Made major leaps within industry
- ✔ Master of publicity

heated iron combs that, when skillfully used, resulted in smooth, shining coiffures. With an investment of $1.50 (one week's wages), Breedlove mixed up batches of her innovative hair treatments in her washtub and started peddling them door to door.

Women responded enthusiastically to Breedlove's products. In 1906, already a success in the South, she moved to Denver, married business-man Charles J. Walker, and took on the moniker Madame C.J. Walker. She kept at her business "with a vim." As demand for her products grew, she focused on manufacturing and marketing, and recruited traveling Walker Agents to give at-home demonstrations across the country. She referred to her sales force as "hair and beauty culturists," and in order to properly train them in the Walker Hair Care Method, opened a beauty school.

Madame Walker named her school Lelia College, well aware of the superior tone it suggested. "In the so-called higher walks of life, many were prone to look down on 'hair-dressers,' as they called us," Walker once said. "They didn't have a very high opinion of our calling, so I had to go down and dignify this work." She maintained lofty standards among her trainees, emphasizing such virtues as cleanliness and charitable works. Many of the women trained at Lelia College went on to operate their own salons. In Madame Walker's words: "I am not merely satisfied in making money for myself, for I am endeavoring to provide employment for . . . women of my race."

The Madame C.J. Walker Manufacturing Company transferred its headquarters to Indianapolis in 1910. It was by then the largest black-owned business in the country. At its peak it boasted a sales force of nearly 20,000, and Madame Walker, whose image graced the labels of her prod-ucts, was one of the best-known business figures in America. She lectured extensively, while legions of Walker Agents spread her fame throughout the United States, Central America, and the Caribbean. She was even pop-ular in Europe—thanks, in part, to the star power of Josephine Baker, who sported a Walker System coiffure.

As Walker's empire grew, she helped advance black Americans through gifts to the NAACP (especially its anti-lynching campaign), the Tuskegee Institute, and many community organizations. In 1917 she built Villa Lewaro, a spectacular home in Irvington, New York. It was a Visionary palace through and through, and its significance to Madame Walker was profound: she once said that her home was a monument to "what a lone woman had accomplished."

The business remained in the Walker family after Madame's death at the age of fifty-two. Her daughter, A'Lelia, who was dubbed "Joy Goddess of the Harlem Renaissance" by poet Langston Hughes, moved the company to New York City and ran it until she, in turn, passed it on to her daughter. It was sold in 1985.

HATTIE CARNEGIE
LITTLE SUIT, BIG AMBITIONS

"I've had three husbands, but my romance is my work."

Born in Vienna in 1886 and reared in poverty on the Lower East Side of Manhattan, Henrietta Köningeiser left school at age eleven after the death of her father. In order to help feed her six siblings, she got a job pinning hats in a millinery and continued to support her family for the rest of her life. They were well taken care of: Henrietta made her first million before she was forty and became a fashion legend in her own time.

It all began when Henrietta was a teenager working at R.H. Macy's. Though she was poor, she had beauty and a distinct style that caught the eye of an enterprising neighborhood seamstress named Rose Roth. Rose took Henrietta under her wing, gave her dresses to model, and encouraged her to go into business. With her new mentor's help, Henrietta opened a millinery shop and called it Carnegie—Ladies' Hatter. She'd borrowed the name from the steel tycoon, whose wealth she admired. While she was at it she adopted a new name for herself: Hattie Carnegie.

The women became partners in 1913 and opened the Roth-Carnegie shop near fashionable Riverside Drive. Carnegie designed hats and also modeled the fashions that Roth designed and manufactured. After World War I—and after increasing quarrels between the partners—Carnegie took over the business. "It became a question of my buying her out or her buying me out," Carnegie remembered. Impatient to make a name for herself, she had her former partner/mentor's name removed from the sign and never looked back.

SCORECARD

VISIONARY QUALITIES

- ✔ Leadership-oriented
- ✔ Named business after self
- ✔ Works in glamour industry
- ✔ Made major leaps within industry
- ✔ Master of publicity

INTUITIVE

In 1923 she moved Hattie Carnegie to a townhouse off Park Avenue. Upstairs was a private fitting room, modeled after European couture houses, where live mannequins modeled Carnegie's creations. Many of her designs were interpretations of the Paris fashions that she passionately collected during regular trips abroad. Like Coco Chanel, Carnegie—who was four feet ten inches tall and 104 pounds—showcased her clothes by wearing them to tony clubs and restaurants.

Carnegie's creations were expensive, priced only within the reach of society ladies and celebrities, including Claudette Colbert and the Duchess of Windsor. When business fell off after the market crash in '29, Carnegie didn't miss a beat: she opened a ready-to-wear department where women could buy good copies of couture fashions at a fraction of the price. In 1934 she started a wholesale business called Spectator Sports, which sold affordable lines to shops all over the country. It soon became the most lucrative branch of her business.

In spite of her success with middle-class American women, the luxury-minded Carnegie spent most of her energy developing her high-end fashions and luring wealthy women into her upstairs showroom. By the mid-1940s her shop had some 16,000 charge accounts, with about 6,000 steady customers that Carnegie fawned over. She believed that they alone were the backbone of her business. Of one Social Register lady Carnegie once boasted, "We've made three wedding dresses and three sets of widow's weeds for her."

Four times a year the House of Carnegie introduced a collection of 100 to 150 ensembles, ranging from spangled cocktail suits to mink-trimmed gowns. Carnegie herself never learned to sew, or even draw. But she had an eye for talent and was able to attract top designers to realize her concepts. Every new Hattie Carnegie line was eagerly anticipated, and competitors routinely tried to copy her designs and rush them to market. One season, her entire collection was stolen by her head designer shortly before a show. In three weeks Carnegie and her crew came up with replacement designs and opened on schedule.

By 1945 Carnegie's company was racking up sales of $6.5 million annually, and her "Little Carnegie Suit" had become such a classic that it was, at the government's request, translated into the WAC uniform.

Hattie Carnegie was a stunning woman who loved parties, good restaurants, and gambling—and, incidentally, never wore hats. But in spite of her many interests, she wouldn't be sidelined. Her best-known quip: "I've had three husbands, but my romance is my work."

Like many Visionaries, Carnegie was both revered and feared. "Working with her," said one employee in 1949, "is like sitting on a powder keg. You never know when she's going to blow up." At her upscale salon, Carnegie maintained a bevy of attractive (preferably blond) employees, yet she always remained the star of the show. No designers, sketchers, or fitters became famous under her employ.

At her death in 1956 at the age of seventy, she headed an $8 million fashion, jewelry, perfume, and cosmetics company that employed more than a thousand people. It was an empire built on style, will, and sheer strength of personality. As *Life* magazine commented in 1945, "Hattie Carnegie, Inc., is Hattie Carnegie."

In the decades following her death, Hattie Carnegie's legacy faded to little more than a fashion footnote. Today, however, Carnegie's work is enjoying a revival. Her clothing and jewelry are sought after by collectors, and in 1996 the Fashion Institute of Technology in New York held a retrospective of her work that critics called "magnificent."

ELIZABETH ARDEN
LUXURY, INC.

> **"There's only one Elizabeth like me, and that's the queen."**

Elizabeth Arden got her name in 1909 after taking control of a beauty salon she'd owned with a partner, Elizabeth Hubbard. She wanted to name it after a Tennyson poem called "Enoch Arden," but stopped the sign-maker after he had scraped off *Hubbard* and gold-leafed *Arden*. She then mailed a letter to her new business address, and when the note arrived the next day, she was so pleased by the way "Elizabeth Arden" looked on the envelope that she adopted it for herself then and there.

As every female of makeup-wearing age knows, Elizabeth Arden went on to create one of the best-known cosmetics companies in the world. What many women don't know, however, is that she also introduced the practice of yoga to the general public; owned a stable of racehorses that earned her millions of dollars and a Kentucky Derby crown; that she and Helena Rubinstein had an intense, lifelong rivalry; and that her real name was Florence Nightingale Graham.

Known as Flo to her parents and four siblings, the future Elizabeth Arden was born in 1878 outside of Ontario, Canada. Her father was a produce salesman who sunk his profits into retired thoroughbreds; her mother, who died when Flo was five, arranged to keep the family afloat via a small allowance secretly solicited from a wealthy aunt. The stipend ended when the aunt passed away, forcing Flo to quit high school and go to work.

An ambitious young woman who was determined to be rich, Florence briefly attended nursing school, which was not to her liking. According to one biographer, "She not only wanted to make

INTUITIVE SCORECARD

VISIONARY QUALITIES
- ✔ Leadership-oriented
- ✔ Named business after self
- ✔ Works in glamour industry
- ✔ Made major leaps within industry
- ✔ Master of publicity

people well . . . she wanted to make them beautiful." What followed was a series of jobs in which she discovered her talent for marketing. In her work at a dentist's office, for instance, she increased business 100 percent by sending out letters graphically suggesting what would happen to patients' teeth without regular checkups.

At the age of thirty Florence Graham moved to Manhattan and got a job as a secretary at a Fifth Avenue beauty salon. There she learned how to give facial massages. A novel practice at the time, these early facials consisted of bandaging the client's face and administering a vigorous patting. As a salon's stock in trade, it was far more respectable than "face painting"—in the early 1900s only hussies used makeup. Flo learned that she had "healing hands," and saw her fortune in the wholesome beautification of women. She and Elizabeth Hubbard, who made and sold beauty products, got together and opened a salon nearby.

The partnership was short-lived. Both women were strong-willed, but Florence showed her superior wiles when one month she raced to the landlord ahead of her partner and paid the rent in full. By doing so she was recognized as sole tenant, and Elizabeth Hubbard was out in the cold.

Elizabeth Arden's third order of business—after stealing the business, renaming the company, and adopting the name for herself—was to borrow $6,000 from a relative. This she spent on lavish decorations, including European antiques and the now famous red salon door. The salon was an instant success, and Arden repaid the loan within three months.

Arden's business focused on beauty regimens. Besides facials, she offered innovative treatments such as full-body paraffin dips, yoga sessions (including head-standing), stretching exercises, and diet plans. She worked closely with a laboratory to create face and body products; her first breakthrough was a fluffy face cream that was a great improvement over the heavy, greasy formulas on the market. She went on to make an astringent and a wrinkle cream, and it wasn't long before profits from Elizabeth Arden products outpaced those from the Elizabeth Arden Salon. Within five years she had moved her salon to bigger quarters on Fifth Avenue and had opened her first branch in Washington, D.C. "From the first she was autocratic, exacting, and sustained by an unshakable conviction that her own point of view in any situation was the right one," reported *The New Yorker* in 1935. *Fortune,* for its part, described her in 1938 as "erratic, unpredictable, vague, and tempestuous," and "capable of rages at which strong men turn pale."

She married Thomas Jenkins Lewis, a silk manufacturer, in 1915, and thus gained U.S. citizenship. He managed her business and was general manager of her firm's holdings until their divorce in 1934. "Dear, never forget one little point," she once said to him. "It's my business. You just work here." She married again in 1942, to a Russian prince. That union lasted for two years.

Her relationships with her horses were somewhat more successful. She pampered them as much as she did her clients, and one of her charges, Jet Pilot, won the 1947 Kentucky Derby.

Like so many Visionary women before and since, Elizabeth Arden's anchor in life was her business. At her death in 1966 her company was worth more than $60 million. She was eighty-eight and still the sole owner of Elizabeth Arden Enterprises, which had grown to include more than one hundred salons worldwide, each with her signature red door, two luxury spas, hundreds of cosmetic preparations, and a net worth that made her one of the world's richest women. She, along with her rival, Helena Rubinstein, made cosmetic use respectable for the modern woman, and all along she lived according to the motto that had captivated women all over the world: "Hold fast to life and youth."

The Visionary at Work

Is there a Visionary in your life? If so, she's probably articulate, intelligent, discerning, stylish, direct, and demanding. And you're probably a little bit afraid of her.

It's no wonder. Visionaries are powerful creatures.

There are Visionaries who have grown corporate empires (think of Coco Chanel), and some who have steered entire countries (Queen Elizabeth, Eva Perón, and Madame Chiang Kai-shek come to mind). Like their historical sisters, most contemporary Visionaries focus on a goal, take control, and don't spend much time worrying what other people think.

The Visionary Sense of Leadership

> Stick to three concepts: You can't help everyone. You can't change everything. Not everyone is going to love you.
> —ROBERTA VASKO KRAUS, CENTER FOR CREATIVE LEADERSHIP

The archetypal Visionary is a leader who masterminds brilliant schemes, positions herself as a figurehead, and assembles groups of go-getters to carry out her wishes. She sets high standards for herself and expects the same from those who work with her. Visionaries—most of whom say they don't *feel* intimidating—can seem scary because they have little tolerance for uncommitted or incompetent people. They don't want to make excuses for others or pick up their slack. If you cross a Visionary, watch out: she is not the type to turn the other cheek.

The rewards for working for a Visionary can be great, however. With her eye for talent, she brings out the best in people and challenges them to reach new heights of accomplishment. Visionaries are natural mentors in the sense that they teach—and lead—by example. They are generous with those who give it their all and can foster loyalties that last a lifetime. Anyone who is allied with a Visionary is in for a great ride, because Visionaries make things happen.

Though Visionaries are naturally suited to positions of authority, they can perform brilliantly under a strong, charismatic leader—if the chemistry is right. Sandra Shea, a novelist who has spent nine years as an editor at the *Philadelphia Daily News,* puts it eloquently: "The last thing I want is a manager. But I'll follow a leader anywhere." Sandra defines leaders as those who have a grand vision and a passion, and who "represent the higher ground." As far as Visionaries like Sandra are concerned, true leaders bring meaning to the workplace.

Visionaries are thinkers. They're at their best when they're strategizing, mapping out plans, and putting them into action. When it comes to tasks that don't interest them, especially those that involve organization, maintenance, service, or manual labor, they delegate instantly and easily. Though Visionaries have very definite goals and like exercising a lot of control over their projects, many surround themselves with assistants who take care of everything from cutting checks to picking up the dry cleaning.

Likewise, Visionaries tend to avoid dealing with the "front lines" in business. A Visionary might be quite comfortable running a huge department store, for example, but would be miserable as a clerk (or in current jargon, sales associate) who has to deal with ticketing, writing up sales, or handling rude customers. Though Visionaries have exceptional sales and marketing skills, you'd be hard pressed to find one selling a car off a showroom floor or peddling ad space to a local deli. The Visionary is much more likely to play an overreaching role—creating an ad campaign, for example, or heading up a department of advertising sales.

The Importance of Protocol

> **No matter how bad the manners around us seem to be, most children come to learn that when they grow up, their jobs will depend on how well they behave, not how much they can get away with.**
>
> **— LETITIA BALDRIGE**

The Visionary needs beauty and order. Her aesthetic sense goes beyond visuals, however. She also places a high value on good manners. When business emergencies don't get in her way, it is the Visionary who hand-writes thank-you notes after lunching with clients; she's the one who composes a well-thought-out memo instead of pecking out a quick e-mail. And she appreciates the same level of consideration from her co-workers. A Visionary can't stand it when people barge into her office uninvited, or initiate a complicated conference call without first having made an appointment. She's also annoyed by unclear messages and poorly written correspondence—infractions that might barely be a blip on another type's mental screen.

The Visionary can think on her feet and make quick decisions when necessary. But she is much happier when business moves along in a structured fashion. She likes regular meetings at routine intervals, and often keeps a meticulous schedule of appointments and deadlines. Whether she sticks to her own schedule or not is nobody's business: the Visionary steers her ship through the winds of change with a sturdy rudder called protocol.

Letitia Baldrige, who might just be the queen of protocol, and therefore a double Visionary, wrote a 600-page book about business etiquette. In it, she covers excruciatingly tiny details, like how to fold a letter and insert it into an envelope, and big challenges, like how not to offend your hosts when doing business in other countries. "Success at work does not happen without good human relations," writes Baldrige in *The New Complete Guide to Executive Manners.* "There are many ways in which our knowledge of how to move through life with grace is the key to our happiness on the job." Visionaries couldn't agree more.

When you hear about the importance of first impressions, Visionaries are somewhere on the sidelines, nodding vigorously. Have you sent out a press release with a typo? Visionaries notice, and raise a collective eyebrow. Did your "voice jail" system answer her call with an impossibly complicated menu of options? Visionaries are not amused. ("I refuse to sit through those systems," says Estelle Sobel. "I immediately hit zero to be connected with an operator.")

Visionaries uphold certain standards of business that are apparent in the microcosm as well as the macrocosm. Colleen Mohyde, for instance, says her work is a "gentleman's" profession: "We literary agents tend to be fairly librarianish, or maybe even schoolmarmish," she says. "In spite of Hollywood depictions, in our office we're not fast-talking or hard-sell; it doesn't fit the book world or the product. We're competitive, in an old-fashioned way, but I'm aghast when people go after someone else's author. We don't poach."

Visionaries are tough, and will hold their ground in the most grueling situations. But they never forget their manners.

THE VISIONARY VS. STRESS

Do you remember the film *Broadcast News?* In it, a gold-hearted TV news producer played by Holly Hunter gets up every morning, dons a power suit, perches on the edge of her bed, and cries her eyes out. Then she pulls herself together and by the time she's on the job is utterly in control. Hunter's performance is a perfect portrait of Visionary stress management: the pain is private, ritualized, and contained in a tidy package.

Many a Visionary believes that there is no place for emotions in the business world. She'll set her jaw and plow through tough situations, be they impossible deadlines, political showdowns, or even personal tragedies. If she has to stay in the office until midnight five nights in a row, so be it: she'd much rather take that road than lose face by complaining, pleading her case, or, God forbid, admitting defeat.

But be warned: Visionaries have extra-large anger banks. If a Visionary feels she is being overworked, ignored, or taken advantage of, she'll start her own company and recruit all worthy workers faster than you can say "hostile takeover."

What causes Visionaries to get stressed out in the first place? Like Gulliver, they are vulnerable to lots of Lilliputian problems ganging up and tying them down. When a Visionary is forced to deal with petty squabbles, she is de-powered because it gets in the way of her greater purpose. When it comes to huge problems, however, such as natural disasters or newsmaking tragedies, Visionaries can rise to the occasion. As long as their work is meaningful and they have clear goals, they can survive enormous challenges.

Visionaries focus on things so intensely that small things can seem huge. Most cures for Visionary stress involve anything that restores her perspective. Some suggestions:

1. ESCAPE FROM IT ALL — AT LEAST FOR A WEEKEND. Like privileged women of olden times, modern Visionaries benefit from some version of a sanitorium, a place where they can lose their troubles in the smell of the surf and the blue of the sky. They revel in stolen weekends filled with gourmet food, games of Scrabble, good conversation, and great sex.

2. READ SOMETHING THAT ISN'T WORK-RELATED. Great novels do wonders for the Visionary because she can become blissfully lost in those pages and come away relaxed and inspired — it's like a mini-vacation for her mind.

3. GET THEE TO A SPA. Visionaries need to put themselves in the hands of an excellent masseur, to have their bodies wrapped, scrubbed, and whirlpooled. Why? Spa treatments reconnect them with their bodies — a source of power that Visionaries all too often neglect.

4. WHEN ALL ELSE FAILS, GO SHOPPING. The sensory delight of colors, textures, and fabrics is a true restorative. But beware — Visionaries are the most likely of the four types to become compulsive shoppers. So shop with love, not anger.

The Visionary as Working Mother

Visionaries have a talent for assembling armies of helpers. At no time is this skill more useful than when a baby comes into a Visionary's life. If she can afford it, she'll fill her house with nannies, au pairs, or doulas; later, she'll make great use of day care, pre-K, and even boarding schools.

As Fran Rodgers wrote in her treatise for entreworld .org about balancing business and motherhood, "On the home front, when I could afford it, I hired a housekeeper to clean and eventually even to cook. What required my personal attention, by contrast, was tending to my children's emotional needs. Whenever they needed to 'talk,' no one but I or my husband could listen." Eventually, Fran "gave away" the job of tending day-to-day operations at her headquarters. "I hired a president who is far more management-oriented than I am, so that I could focus on promoting the company and setting its future direction." With her priorities in place, she was able to maximize her effectiveness both as a leader and a mother.

Jane Reynolds, a photographer's rep, had an even more Visionary approach to balancing her professional life with the demands of motherhood. After having her second baby—her first was already in college by that time—she worked at home for months, and none of her clients ever knew it. Her receptionist was instructed to inform callers that Jane was on the phone or in a meeting. Jane would return her calls from a quiet room at home.

Of all the types, Visionaries are most likely to understand the meaning of "quality time." They're well aware that Mommy needs to be happy in order

SOME FAVORITE VISIONARY INDUSTRIES

FASHION
(designer, journalist, buyer, merchandiser)

RETAIL
(company CEO, retail group director)

DESIGN
(interiors, commercial spaces, furnishings, tableware)

PUBLISHING
(magazines, books, limited edition prints, photography)

MARKETING
(national campaigns, branding launches, corporate i.d.)

ADVERTISING
(TV, print)

SALES
(cars, boats, antiques, art)

HOTEL/HOSPITALITY
(executive level)

REAL ESTATE
(luxury properties)

BEAUTY
(spas, salons, cosmetics)

ARTIST MANAGEMENT
(literary agent, record executive)

ENTERTAINMENT
(casting director, programming executive)

THE UPS AND DOWNS OF BEING A VISIONARY

THE UPS

You're comfortable being a leader.
You know how to delegate tasks.
   You establish well-defined boundaries.
You can lock in on a project and bring it home.
   You can ask for what you need or want.
You're motivated to do your best.
   By example, you can bring out the best in others.
You seek meaningful work.
   You have a talent for creating attractive environments.
You're tip-to-toe professional.
   You mind your manners.
You present yourself and your products beautifully.
   You have an iron will.

THE DOWNS

   You can be a bully.
In the workplace, you tend to make yourself emotionally unavailable.
   You're prone to set impossibly high standards for those you hire.
You can be heartless and not value the human side of problems.
   You might put your personal agenda before the group agenda.
You tend to be impatient.
   You can become so focused on a goal that you lose touch with changing realities.
You're prone to playing politics.
   You're easily dazzled by high-powered people or situations.
You sometimes pit yourself against others competitively.
   You can lack or even resist "team spirit."

to be a good parent—and if that means forging on with a career, so be it. Many don't feel the need to be there to change every one of their children's diapers. But like Fran and Jane they do want to influence, guide, and love their children. So they'll plan fascinating family vacations, pay close attention to homework, encourage extracurricular interests, and do their best to keep their children from feeling deprived—of attention, of encouragement, or of all the riches the world has to offer.

The Visionary Work Space

Visionaries can function in hectic environments, but only for so long; like dolphins, they must periodically return to the surface for air. That "surface"—the place where they center themselves, set their priorities, gain their strength—is a quiet place in which they're alone and surrounded by their own stuff.

The most soul-shriveling environment for a Visionary to work in is a prefab cubicle (ditto the Artisan). Polyester-clad half-walls might as well be a prison to her, and not only because they're ugly, they also don't do much to block out noise. The Visionary can be deeply disturbed by the din of machinery and conversation, and especially dislikes open floor plans that allow others to interrupt her whenever they feel like it.

Publishing professional Estelle Sobel recalls certain spaces in her early working life that made her acutely uncomfortable. "I've been in environments where there were ten people crammed into an office," she says. "I could never do that again. I'm extremely territorial, and in certain offices that just doesn't work. You'd round the corner and someone's in your space, playing with your pencils, rifling through your stuff, sitting at your desk—I don't appreciate that." These days, Estelle does much of her work from home, where she has complete control over her environment. "Here I can mute the phone, work on twelve things at once, or relax if I need to. It's extremely productive for me because I'm extremely self-motivated."

• **The ultimate Visionary office** is a large space in a historic building. It has high ceilings and vast windows framed by ornamental wood molding and swathed with fine draperies (to be tied back when the mood strikes). There are floor-to-ceiling bookshelves—built in, of course—an antique mahogany desk, and table lamps instead of overhead and/or fluorescent lighting. Equipment, files, and supplies are stashed out of sight in fine cabinetry. There's an Oriental rug on the floor, framed paintings on the walls, and such niceties as fresh flowers, high-quality paper goods, and at least one old-fashioned letter opener. She has a personal assistant who makes contact via a desktop intercom that doesn't ring or buzz, but silently blinks.

• **The minimum-requirement Visionary office** is quiet and private, with real walls and a door that closes. It features a phone system that discreetly retrieves calls via voice mail, and also has a place to sit and think.

Where to Find the Visionary

I work whenever I'm let.

—KATHERINE ANNE PORTER

Visionaries are attracted to all sorts of enterprises, and not all of them are as grand as corporations, personal empires, or countries. The professor who collects and curates an impressive collection of art books might be a Visionary, as might the dog breeder whose kennel produces prize-winning Chows.

Jennifer Reiley sells wines to restaurateurs and wine shops. Though driving all over a sales territory to make calls is not usually the Visionary's favorite thing, Jennifer has a passion for her product. "I like wine, food, business—that stuff turns me on," she says. "I like to influence a client about a wine list. It's exciting and satisfying when they buy an albariño from Spain instead of a California chardonnay or a comfort brand."

Colleen Mohyde says her favorite thing about being a literary agent is "the thrill of the hunt." The world is her library; every concept, story, and event she runs across has the potential to be turned into a book. "My job is finding new people and new talent. As an agent, there's no one source, you're really beating the bushes. Along the way I get to talk to the very

HOW THE VISIONARY GETS ALONG . . .

. . . WITH ARTISANS

Visionaries and Artisans are somewhat oil-and-waterish. At the meanest extreme, Visionaries can see Artisans as weaklings, dreamers, spaced-out hippies, or granola-eating tree-huggers. Ouch! But when Visionaries really get to know Artisans, all that tends to change.

Remember in *The Sound of Music,* when the Artisan (and Adventurer) Maria lands in the rigid Von Trapp household? Initially, the terribly formal Baron Von Trapp is appalled by Maria's antics. But then she finds his heart for him and brings love into his bitter life. Ah. The hills are alive.

Artisans are reliable and dedicated, and can lend empathy and understanding to the Visionary workplace: as employees, Artisans are steady, stable, and famously loyal, and they can keep the office fires burning while the Visionary goes into battle.

Unfortunately, Visionaries rarely thrive under Artisan leadership. The Visionary tends to be frustrated by the Artisan's slow, careful decisions in which everybody is involved. Artisans, for their part, can have a hard time coping with the Visionary's willful ways.

. . . WITH IDEALISTS

Visionaries and Idealists are both gifted with the ability to focus. Their alliance can be especially good because Idealists naturally gravitate toward numbers and systems, while the Visionary thrives in concept-and-execution situations. Many successful companies have Visionary CEOs and Idealist CFOs.

Visionaries do their best work when there is well-established structure in the workplace, and establishing these systems is right up the Idealist's alley. Though it may infuriate her at times, the Idealist keeps the Visionary in check, especially when it comes to financial feasibility.

Idealists and Visionaries can work for each other with little trouble. But they complement each other best in partner situations, where each takes charge of separate but equal jobs.

. . . WITH ADVENTURERS

Visionaries and Adventurers are natural friends. Remember *The Patty Duke Show,* in which Patty Duke portrayed identical cousins? Kathy's a sophisticated Visionary who adores minuets. Patty the Adventurer loves rock and roll. The two cousins advise, soothe, and amuse each other.

In the workplace, the Visionary can count on the Adventurer's free-wheeling energy without feeling that her authority is threatened. Adventurers are suited for positions on Visionary teams, as long as they are given a particularly long leash.

When Visionaries work for Adventurers, Visionaries may feel that they're "running the store" while the Adventurer is off pursuing her newest passion. This will either cause resentment or can be quite satisfactory, since it offers lots of control and little bottom-line responsibility.

top people in all kinds of fields." How does she feel about pitching books to publishers—that part of the business referred to as "dog and pony shows"? "That can be fun," says Colleen. "I like going in with authors and watching the level of excitement of the publishers go up—you can see the person getting hooked."

Whatever her career path may be, the Visionary needs to have power over her projects. "I need to be involved from start to finish," says magazine developer Estelle Sobel. "I can't just do one little area of a project. I want to mastermind it, implement it, start to finish—like giving birth." It is for this reason that Visionaries sometimes take over projects and end up giving themselves more work than most mortals can handle.

HIRE A VISIONARY TO . . .
DON'T HIRE A VISIONARY TO . . .

Head up public relations.
Deal directly with the public.

Develop cultural programs.
Grow bacterial cultures.

Redecorate your offices.
Redecorate your offices on a low budget.

Launch ad campaigns.
Campaign door-to-door.

Make presentations to clients.
Make cold calls.

Do executive recruitment.
Head up human relations.

Be a hostess.
Bus tables.

On the Net there's a list going around of the top ten signs of work burnout. Number six: "You consider a 40-hour workweek a vacation." Number one: "You think how relaxing it would be if you were in jail right now." For some Visionaries, the truth behind the joke isn't so funny. Because they are so driven and determined to succeed, Visionaries are in danger of becoming textbook-case workaholics and must take extra care to keep their lives in balance.

The Will to Win

> Surviving disaster is one of the great lessons in life. . . . If I had chosen a career where it had all come easily, I don't think I would have had the passion for it.
>
> **— LESLEY STAHL, *60 MINUTES* CORRESPONDENT**

The phrase "fear of success" is virtually meaningless to most Visionaries. But fear of failure is a real presence, especially because Visionaries hate looking foolish. They crave challenges and will rise to meet them, but when they miss the mark—and it does happen now and then—it's not financial setbacks but the fact that they've tried and failed that stings them most deeply. The Visionary can become so invested in her projects that when something goes wrong, it takes all the strength she can muster to hold her head up and carry on in the wake of her mishap.

When her failure is someone else's fault, the Visionary is not likely to be forgiving. Likewise, if she perceives that someone else is trying to thwart her progress or undermine her authority, watch out. Visionaries are competitive creatures, and their "power antennae" are always up. They're acutely aware of interoffice politics and know which relationships to nurture and which to shun. It is very much within the Visionary nature to see competitors as enemies. Some even adopt rivals—people or companies against whom they can gauge themselves. In this scenario, the Visionary actually sets up a race so she can win—or lose, as the case may be.

For the most part, however, losing is not on the Visionary agenda. She protects herself from failure by always having a "Plan B." If a Visionary announces that she either gets a raise or she quits, you can bet she's got another job lined up. If she's making a presentation and the client doesn't like her first idea, she's ready with a second option.

When a Visionary is absolutely committed to succeed, nothing can stand in her way. She'll weather criticism, setbacks, and personal losses, chalk them up to experience, and keep moving forward with guts and determination.

ANN S. MOORE
THE POWER OF PEOPLE

> **"I outlasted all the politics because I did my own work."**

Ann Moore occupies a kind of corporate Olympus. Though she bears witness to a mercurial world of celebrities and newsmakers who come and go in the pages of *People* and *In Style,* she herself has staying power. She believes in building slow, strong relationships. In her personal and professional life she practices the art of pacing, and her long views have resulted in steady growth supported by rock-solid leadership.

The president of People, Inc., is known as a woman who puts down deep roots and grows success. In the volatile world of magazine publishing, her career has been both hugely successful and exceptionally stable: she spent more than twenty years at Time, Inc., holding various key executive positions at *Fortune, Money, Discover,* and, most notably, *Sports Illustrated* and *Sports Illustrated for Kids,* the latter of which she founded.

"When I came to *People* in 1991," recalls Moore, "the *New York Times* picked up a quote that said I had come from a ten-year tour of duty at *Sports Illustrated,* and that I was expecting to start my ten-year tour at *People.* That freaked my staff out because nobody had stayed on that long as publisher of *People!*"

Moore soon graduated from publisher to president of the most successful weekly publication in the world and has gone on to launch *Who* magazine in Australia and three monthly publications: *In Style, People en Español,* and *Teen People.*

Yet Moore claims that after eight years with her management team she's "just getting started." She fervently believes that long-term commitments result in a higher-quality product and a stronger corporation. "We have been able to dig deeper into the layers of building product and serving customers," she says. "When I hire people I ask them about their thoughts on the time horizon. I'm not looking for short-termers. I want people who have the ability to invest in this franchise and not be impatient."

In an era of get-rich-quick corporations, where staffers tend to hit and split, Moore's approach seems both retro and revolutionary: "Everybody on my team gets a year of training before I really expect them to pay back," she says. "I think that's what it takes to get up to speed. Nothing makes me crazier than when somebody wants to make a change after one year—you're still a baby as far as I'm concerned."

Visiting Moore in her executive offices in Manhattan's Rockefeller Center, it's hard to believe that anything could "make her crazy"—or even rock her equilibrium. She is quiet at her core and listens with full attention. When she speaks, in a voice with a wonderful timbre, she is so focused she makes those she connects with feel special, as if they were suddenly worthy of a spread in a magazine.

People really are Moore's passion; she calls her team "the real success of this business" and says that her biggest challenge is to "continually recruit and motivate and keep the team together." To that end, she organizes fun offsite events—including a 1998 sales meeting at a castle in Ireland where "the kids" got a chance to relax and recreate together.

Though she's dedicated to her group and sometimes speaks of her company as a family, Moore keeps her personal feelings out of the workplace. She doesn't, for instance, need to like the people she hires, nor does she need them to like her. "This is professional," she says. "I have some people I don't get personal with, but their performance is breathtaking—I would never want to lose a high performer like that." She recalls that at a leadership conference "someone wrote down that 'Ann plays favorites.' And I said to myself, 'That's not a negative—I do.' But I call that 'pay for performance.' If you are a superstar, I'll do anything for you."

"You'll never have a totally happy and functional family at work," she asserts. "But if you don't have dysfunction at the table, won't you miss opportunities?"

Moore seems to have had a remarkably happy and functional family life herself, and describes her childhood in Virginia as a *Leave It to Beaver* existence. The oldest of five children, she bonded with her father on the basketball court—he taught her to shoot hoops, and she got so good she could "beat any boy." But the man she describes as an "incredibly talented" Air Force pilot was most proud of Ann's mind. "I was smart and he knew it," she says, and recalls with a laugh that he recently brought out her sixth-grade, straight-A report card to show to her son, Brendan.

Ann's mother was, in her words, a "classic, brilliant lady. [Our family] always had dinner together, and she did something to help others every day of her life—the Republican party, the Women's Club, Christmas parties for the elderly. Mom's example rubbed off on most of the kids."

Ann had a special connection with her mother. But when Ann left home to attend Vanderbilt University she balked because she wanted her daughter to get married and have kids. "This was how Mom thought of happiness," says Ann.

Ann did get married, to Donovan Moore, a private banker with whom she shares a home in Brooklyn Heights. But it wasn't until she'd earned an MBA from Harvard Business School and joined Time, Inc., that she had her first and only child. It was a ten-year wait.

Ann Moore didn't follow the path her mother had envisioned, but her mother's influence is evident in Moore's contributions to the greater good. In 1994 she founded People*first,* which raises funds and awareness for such groups as the Pediatric AIDS Foundation. She also serves on the media task force of the National Campaign to Prevent Teen Pregnancy, among other groups.

INTUITIVE SCORECARD
Ann Moore

VISIONARY QUALITIES	ARTISAN QUALITIES
✔ Leadership-oriented	✔ Champions underdog
_ Named business after self	_ Family-centric
✔ Works in glamour industry	_ Outdoorsy
✔ Made major leaps within industry	✔ Produces tangible product
✔ Master of publicity	✔ Treats employees like family

IDEALIST QUALITIES	ADVENTURER QUALITIES
_ Pragmatic	✔ Pioneering
_ Works within systems	_ Unconventional
✔ Holds multiple degrees	_ Socially gregarious
_ Analytical	_ Diversified career path
✔ Long-term commitment to single career	_ Degree unrelated to career

" ANN MOORE ON . . .

TAKING RISKS: "You know about the four magazines that worked, but you don't know about the two I decided to pull the plug on. I never sweated one drop! Get over the fear of failure. My father-in-law told me, 'Ann, remember, you only need fifty-one percent to win.'"

MISTAKES: "I never rehash. Once you've spent the money or made the mistake, the value is zero. Get over it, and don't spend any time worrying about the past."

TIME MANAGEMENT: "Forget the clock. Dump the compass. It's more important to know who you are than where or how fast you're going."

THE ART OF PACING: "Sometimes when you work with other type-A people the team races faster than it should. This is not the hundred-meter. It's more like a long-distance race."

DEALING WITH CRITICS: "I don't worry about them. The world is too big to worry about them. You do have to confront bullies and take the good with the bad—just fix the problem and go on."

HIRING GOOD PEOPLE. "The single thing that keeps me awake at night is worrying about hiring the right person. Everybody is a superstar at something, right? It's like being a detective."

KEEPING GOOD PEOPLE: "That's easy—I pay them really well! I want to keep these brilliant people happy, motivated, and together because that's the real success of this business. In today's marketplace, the burden is on me."

JOB SATISFACTION: "Something is wrong with your work if you don't get a rush—that wave of pure joy. If you don't get it, you need to change jobs. Never stick around to be frustrated." **"**

Moore's charitable projects reflect her personal values. And so, she says, does her company. "The *Fortune* 500 still shortchange women and children. Not my company! When I [introduced] *In Style* they laughed at us. They're not laughing now. Look at *Teen People*. They thought I was crazy. *Teen People* is a grand slam. The *Fortune* 500 has left a lot of money on the table!"

Reflecting on her personal motivations, Moore says, "I'm results-oriented. I'm still proud of that sixth-grade report card, and I get good grades at work—the grades are gross and profits. I measure myself with that."

Moore says she wants the *People* publishing family to have six magazines by 2000. There's little doubt that she'll be there to see them through.

Having survived small failures, wild successes, and unique challenges—including being the boss at the male-dominated *Sports Illustrated*—Moore still maintains the centeredness and independence that are hallmarks of the Visionary spirit. "I just concentrate on my work," she says. "It's more important to know who you are than where you're going. Then you can pick your boss, your company, the industry that's compatible with you. That's why I've been here twenty years. I'm lucky. I outlasted all the politics because I did my own work."

ROSE MARIE BRAVO
REDEFINING TRADITION

"I realize that I've been given a great gift."

Rose Marie Bravo's work ethic is renowned in the world of retail, but according to Bravo her compulsion to achieve started early. As the child of Italian immigrants her perseverance was first tested as a teenager, when she was admitted to the Bronx High School of Science, one of America's most prestigious public schools.

The culture shock was immediate, Bravo recalls, as she went from being a straight-A student in a Catholic girls' school to a largely Jewish male student body and a fiercely competitive academic program. Bravo found herself challenged as never before, and it soon became clear that she would either fail or rise to a new level of performance.

Her decision would cement the tone of her life. She became Rose Marie Bravo, Superachiever, and ended the next year the number-two student in her class. But academia was only a means to an end. Bravo was eager to get on with the business of life, and after graduating from Bronx Science she tore through Fordham University in two and a half years.

And then came the reward—the real world and a life built around work. "I thought I would enjoy working in stores," says Bravo, who grew up doing odd jobs around her dad's hair salon. And so her first day at the New York department store Abraham & Straus was blissful. "I loved it from day one."

Bravo was a natural in the retail environment, and her gifts were challenged with ever-increasing responsibilities, from selling to buying and beyond. And since that first day at A&S in 1971, she has made a broad and indelible mark on the world of style—from department store marketing to prestige retailing, and most recently at the British luxury goods label Burberry.

Along the way, Bravo was noticed far beyond the department store

INTUITIVE SCORECARD

Rose Marie Bravo

VISIONARY QUALITIES	ARTISAN QUALITIES
✔ Leadership-oriented	_ Champions underdog
_ Named business after self	_ Family-centric
✔ Works in glamour industry	_ Outdoorsy
✔ Made major leaps within industry	✔ Produces tangible product
✔ Master of publicity	_ Treats employees like family

IDEALIST QUALITIES	ADVENTURER QUALITIES
_ Pragmatic	_ Pioneering
_ Works within systems	_ Unconventional
_ Holds multiple degrees	_ Socially gregarious
_ Analytical	_ Diversified career path
✔ Long-term commitment to single career	✔ Degree unrelated to career

floor. Her impeccable taste and tireless zeal made her "revered on Seventh Avenue," according to the *Wall Street Journal*, while *Fortune* called her "a brand name herself in the fashion world."

Bravo is quick to note that her rise was primed by a host of mentors in retailing. "I met so many fabulous women and men who were role models, who taught me and nourished my career and set an example in business values. Before I turned thirty I realized that retail was my home. When hard work is great fun, you know you're in the right business."

In 1987, when Macy's parent company acquired I. Magnin, Bravo was asked to become its chairman and CEO. The San Francisco luxury retailer was nothing less than a personal deity to stylish women of the West Coast, and it set the stage for Bravo's move five years later to become president and join the board of directors of Saks Holdings, Inc. Saks Fifth Avenue had lost a bit of its luster; Bravo's job was to put the chain back in the running with luxury leaders like Neiman Marcus and Bergdorf Goodman.

Her success at Saks Fifth Avenue earned her every accolade, as she worked with her team to prepare the company for an initial public offering in 1996. The IPO was followed by a major national expansion of Saks Fifth Avenue.

As president of Saks, Rose Marie Bravo was one of the top fashion retailers in the U.S., with a generous salary and executive perks that included an enviable clothing allowance. Therefore, the industry reacted with shock to the sudden announcement in January 1998 that Ms. Bravo would become worldwide chief executive of the British brand Burberry, best known for its trenchcoats lined with plaid wool. One journalist declared her departure from Saks "a step down. . . . Where she used to pick the best fashion colors, she now has to preside over beige."

The challenge was of course irresistible to Bravo. Burberry was her opportunity to reposition a high-end fashion brand and prepare it to challenge global luxury labels such as Gucci and Prada.

"Her Rolodex," reported *Fortune* in 1998, "is one of her greatest strengths. So is her impeccable taste." Rose Marie Bravo brought both to London. She hired top retail talent from Saks and Barney's, recruited a designer from Jil Sander, and with her marketing team revamped and created a global advertising strategy.

And as she and her new team rediscovered and redefined the company's soul (the 140-year heritage which Bravo calls "the Burberry DNA"), Bravo also addressed the operations side of the business. She closed two factories in Britain, curtailed distribution of a lower-priced line, and cut off "gray market" sales to Asia where Burberry was being sold by off-price retailers. And she invested millions in new computer and manufacturing systems.

Within months of her arrival at Burberry, Bravo and her hand-picked team had transformed the label from a classic and very proper British brand into a fashion collection with instant impact. Designer Roberto Menichetti's first collection, which debuted at the newly renovated Burberry showroom in London, catapulted Burberry into the international spotlight. *Women's Wear Daily* declared the company born again and *Fortune*'s report was prophetic: "Look for the Burberry plaid to start turning up in new places—in nightclubs and *Harper's Bazaar*, on rock stars and runways."

ROSE MARIE BRAVO ON . . .

MANAGEMENT: "I have hired very good people; I try to let everyone define their role. I hand responsibility over to other people and tell them to get back to me on it. But I do like teamwork. I like everyone to stay together."

MAKING DECISIONS: "You have to make decisions. Even if you're sometimes wrong, it's okay. I'd rather have people making decisions than have people be stuck. I like to keep things moving."

LETTING PEOPLE GO: "It's unfortunate, but in the end I feel that if someone isn't going to work out, ultimately you are doing that person a favor. Usually it works out for the best, and he or she goes on to something else."

HANDLING COMPETITION: "You just have to do a better job. You have to work like crazy, do nothing halfway."

THE ONLY JOB SHE EVER HATED: "Housework."

With Burberry's classic heritage, its emergence as a fashion leader is a tribute to Bravo's vision. The company has been a bastion of British tradition since 1856, and the Burberry gabardine raincoat lined in plaid wool has long been the very definition of classic British style.

"I realize that I've been given a great gift," says Bravo. "Burberry is an amazing company. It has history and heritage and authenticity. It's an icon that is world-recognized. It's male and female. It's both accessible *and* aspirational. This combination is rare, and it's our mission to make Burberry relevant and new for the next century."

The first step in Burberry's renaissance has been declared a success. Meanwhile, Bravo's laser-clear focus on the business of Burberry keeps her traveling, putting teams in place, dealing with global issues, and looking to the future. Still, like many Visionaries, she manages to find time for restorative pursuits. "I like to read books, and I try to go to church. I'm not athletic, but a walk in the garden renews me," Bravo says.

She also enjoys visiting her children on Long Island and her extended family in Florida and she is also steadied by quiet time with her husband, who has cheerfully moved with her over the years.

Because her days as Burberry chief executive are so consuming, Bravo deliberately keeps after-hours business engagements to a minimum. And she notes that one of the perks of living in England is that her privacy is respected. "They only care about the royals," she observes with a grin.

Rose Marie Bravo translated Burberry's heritage of authenticity and classic style into something exciting and new. Gabardine has never been so glamorous, and tradition has never been so modern.

LOIS SILVERMAN
FROM COMMON SHARES TO COMMONWEALTH

> **"There's something about waking up and thinking about new vistas and new challenges. That's what gives me a high."**

Lois Silverman's career path seems to have paralleled the rise of the American businesswoman. She started working in the early '60s in a helping profession; entered corporate life in the '70s; founded her own multimillion-dollar company in 1978; and took it public in the '90s. Today she heads a nonprofit organization, The Commonwealth Institute, that helps other women entrepreneurs succeed.

Attractive, poised, beautifully spoken, and impeccably dressed, Lois Silverman is every inch the successful Visionary. Spending an afternoon with her at her drop-dead gorgeous home at an enviable Boston address, it seems hard to believe that Silverman wasn't, as they say, to the manner born. In fact, Silverman was a business pioneer who overcame huge obstacles—personally and professionally—to be where she is today.

Lois lost her mother when she was four years old, and her father eleven years later. "I couldn't have a party dress, or even go out and buy a Coke," she remembers of her impoverished childhood. "I figured out very early I had to be self-sufficient. I started earning money at the age of thirteen." On his deathbed, her father told her that she was the strongest one in her family. "He informed me that I needed to take care of the others."

Lois remembers that her childhood in Providence, Rhode Island, was "a very lonely existence. From a very early age I put a wall around myself and isolated myself from other people." She gained direction in life when she enrolled in the Beth Israel Hospital School of Nursing—an unusual career choice for Visionaries. "I've learned that children who have experienced a lot of illness in their family tend to go into the helping professions," she muses. "I was part of something that would help people. More important, nursing would allow me to support myself and it cost significantly less than college." Lois was determined to do well and not make mistakes. "My tremendous drive to survive helped me throughout my training. And even though I felt a certain isolation during those years, I made friends, and I met and married my husband—so I must have connected with people on some level."

Upon graduating in 1961, one of Silverman's advisors urged her to remain in hospital nursing—not to sell out. "He seemed to recognize I had unusual business talents," she says. But those talents didn't come into play until 1973, when Silverman's two children were still in grade school. That's when she gave up teaching at a proprietary school and LaSalle Junior College. "I went to work for a large insurance company," she recalls. "They asked me to grow a case management business. I had ambition and drive and developed a regional program that proved to be highly profitable, and that earned me a respected name in the industry."

Her program focused on injured employees who were receiving workers' compensation benefits. "Whether in hospitals or at home, I helped people get out of dependent stages and get back to work. It wasn't just for the insurance company, but for the individual's own sense of worth. I helped families regain their ability to earn a living, and saved the taxpayers a lot of money."

Lois Silverman had become a star in her field. But in 1978, the unthinkable happened: "The company brought in new management and my new boss just did not like me. He didn't include me in his high-level meetings, and didn't respect the job I was doing. Within a short period of time we both agreed I should move on."

Silverman was shocked to her core, but quickly regained her footing. "In November of '78, I was walking through a mall and I ran into a friend who asked me what I was doing. Out of nowhere I told him of a new business I was starting." The words poured out, and Silverman got busy backing them up. Within days she founded Comprehensive Rehabilitation Associates (a.k.a. CRA Managed Care, Inc.), which provided services to reduce the cost of workers' compensation, automobile, disability, and health insurance claims. Shortly thereafter she took on a partner. "We were immediately profitable," she says. "I contacted fifty-six insurance companies I knew, and built the concept into a one-hundred-million-dollar business."

Silverman makes it sound easy. But her success came with sacrifices. Unable to get a bank loan to start CRA, she used $20,000 from her severance savings, and for five years she worked from 6 A.M. to 8 P.M. "I have been blessed with a family who supported and loved me and who knew I appreciated them," she says now. "The company grew, and I was courageous enough to know that when I couldn't add value, it was time to bring in a different kind of management."

In 1995, Silverman's company—now known as Concentra Managed Care—went public. At the time, she was one of only three women in Massachusetts to have founded a publicly traded company. "It was a huge success," Silverman recalls. "Everyone profited." With the resulting changes in corporate structure, she gave up her position as CEO and became chairman of the board.

INTUITIVE SCORECARD
Lois Silverman

VISIONARY QUALITIES
- ✔ Leadership-oriented
- _ Named business after self
- _ Works in glamour industry
- ✔ Made major leaps within industry
- _ Master of publicity

ARTISAN QUALITIES
- ✔ Champions underdog
- _ Family-centric
- _ Outdoorsy
- _ Produces tangible product
- _ Treats employees like family

IDEALIST QUALITIES
- _ Pragmatic
- _ Works within systems
- _ Holds multiple degrees
- _ Analytical
- _ Long-term commitment to single career

ADVENTURER QUALITIES
- _ Pioneering
- ✔ Unconventional
- _ Socially gregarious
- ✔ Diversified career path
- _ Degree unrelated to career

Lois Silverman was in her mid-fifties. She was accomplished and afflu-ent and blessed with a happy marriage and healthy children. Like many Visionaries, it had taken a long time for her to feel comfortable with her place in the world. "I don't think I became self-realized until I was in my fifties," she says now. "It was only when the outside world started saying I was a terrific person, a successful businesswoman, that I bought into it."

At that major crossroads, Silverman joined a number of boards of profit and nonprofit organizations. But she wanted something to call her own. "There was this little girl inside of me who had had nothing and had everything, and couldn't be happy unless she could share with others," she explains.

And so, in 1997, Silverman contacted ten businesswomen, and formed The Commonwealth Institute (TCI), a nonprofit group dedicated to help-ing women entrepreneurs in the Boston area. It provides peer-to-peer men-toring, networking, and exposure to female role models. Members attend monthly group meetings and get the benefit of coaching, business referrals, seminars, and special events. Those whose companies gross $1 million or more annually gain entry to a special group called "The Million $ Circle."

In its first year, 100 women participated in TCI's one-year program. Today 250 female entrepreneurs are members. "The Commonwealth Insti-tute has evolved into a wonderful organization," Silverman says. "Every day it brings me joy watching these entrepreneurs grow and flourish with our support."

In addition to serving as president and chair of TCI, Silverman is a partner of *Women's Business,* a monthly regional newspaper focusing on women's accomplishments and opportunities in the working world. She is also a director of Sun Healthcare Group and Immunetics; chair of the board of Community Servings, which provides meals to persons with AIDS; a trustee of the Beth Israel Deaconess Medical Center; an overseer at Tufts University Medical School; a trustee at Simmons College; a mem-ber of the board of the Women's Studies Program at Brandeis University; and a member of the Boston Club, the Committee of 200, and the Inter-national Women's Forum.

Her awards and accolades have been many. But Lois Silverman keeps her eye on the future. "I couldn't have done it without people who dream big dreams," she says. "I love The Commonwealth Institute, and I would like to bring it to all fifty states. I believe in creating opportunities for women."

It isn't surprising that, when asked what her idea of a great time is, Sil-verman answers without hesitation, "Work! There's something about wak-

"

L OIS SILVERMAN ON . . .

WORKING STYLE: "I work at warp speed. I get up at five in the morning, I write down my plan. Sometimes in the middle of the night I
pick up my marker and write down my thoughts."

STRESS MANAGEMENT: "Over the years, stress has caused a lot of
pain in my life. I developed some illnesses . . . yes, I did try the usual
meditation exercises, yoga, spas. But I just thought about the task at
hand and drove myself so hard. Today I'm not taking myself so seriously. I know I've been the best I can be, and that's enough for me."

RISK-TAKING: "Try to be true to your dreams. Don't be afraid to take
risks or try something new."

HIRING GOOD PEOPLE: "I spent a great deal of time interviewing for
the right person and usually that person complemented my skills and
abilities. I didn't need another Lois. I wanted people who could execute my vision and be strong team players."

FIRING PEOPLE: "I've worked at easing into letting people go. If
something didn't work out, most people thanked me afterward. Intuitively they knew I gave them everything I could."

REGRETS: "I wish I were smarter earlier and that I took off the velvet
glove sooner!"

BALANCING FAMILY LIFE AND PROFESSIONAL DEMANDS:
"Work is my life, yet I never forgot my family or friends in the
process. I love my life, and I don't feel the need to change it."

"

ing up and thinking about new vistas and new challenges. That's what gives
me a high. Oh, I like traveling and visiting wonderful places—maybe golf,
and music—but work is my great love."

ADVICE FOR VISIONARIES

- KNOW THE DIFFERENCE BETWEEN STATUS AND SUCCESS. Hob-nobbing with celebrities, seeing your face in the gossip column, being invited to the Inaugural Ball — all are by-products of success. Real success is about sustaining a vision, being the best at what you do, and continuing to evolve. Base your decisions on success — not status.

- TRY TO SHUT OFF YOUR MIND LONG ENOUGH TO LISTEN. Visionaries can become so hell-bent on having all the answers that they mentally lock themselves away. Sure, you're in a hurry. But not listening is a terrible habit that can, in some cases, lead to deadly business decisions. Professional listeners have a trick: they consciously suspend their egos and *become* the person who is speaking. Try it. You may gain profound respect for people you never even noticed before.

- ARE YOU A SCARY BOSS? If so (and let's be honest about this), make sure you have lieutenants who can report what's *really* going on — bad news, good news, low morale, pending wildcat strikes, whatever. If you're intimidating, the rank and file are never going to give you the whole truth — and that can keep you dangerously out of touch.

- BE OPEN TO LEARNING FROM OTHERS. "Forget *Atlas Shrugged*," writes Barnett Helzberg Jr., founder of the Helzberg Entrepreneurial Mentoring Program. He believes that nearly everyone can learn from a mentor. He recommends having more than one mentor, seeking mentors outside of your industry, and considering mentors who are your own age.

- DON'T EXPECT EVERYONE TO BE AS SWIFT AND STYLISH AS YOU. Some people might be slow to act or take a long time to make a decision, have a nonexistent fashion sense, and spend every weekend at Beanie Baby conventions. Okay, it's not your style, but that doesn't mean their contributions aren't valuable. By pushing your co-workers down a predetermined path, you may be squelching qualities that could be beneficial to your project — and stressing them out in the bargain.

- ADMIT DEFEAT WHEN APPROPRIATE. Some Visionaries pride themselves on never backing down. But that's folly if, in the process, you shoot yourself in the foot. When necessary, figure out a way to soften your position while maintaining your self-respect.

- ACCEPT FAILURES WITH GRACE AND HUMOR. You've seen movie stars when the Oscar went to the "sentimental favorite"; they take the moral high ground and bestow blessings on the winner. You can do it, too.

- BE CHEERFUL. Optimism and enthusiasm are key elements of good leadership. Nobody wants to follow a person who is angry, spiteful, or bitter.

- REMEMBER THAT VISIONARIES GET BETTER AS THEY GET OLDER. This is true for many women, but Visionaries especially seem to come into their own in their later years. Take strength from the many Visionaries who started businesses when they were well beyond forty, and the even larger number who never retired.

3

THE
Artisan

Modest. Giving. Personal. Flexible. Physical. Cautious. Socially Aware.

Artisans are not necessarily craftspeople in the strict sense of the word. But if one can define "artisan" as a person who can make something special out of nothing special, then the name is entirely apt. An Artisan can grow almost anything, including kitchen-table start-ups, community organizations, and mighty corporations.

Most Artisans are blessed with an ability to draw people around themselves and create a working unit that looks a lot like family. Artisans are giving of themselves and like to share whatever they can, including power and profits; they are motivated by doing good while doing well.

The Artisan's picture of success extends far beyond the frame of commerce, however. Like a six-armed goddess, the Artisan businesswoman gives her attention to running the store, yet also devotes energy toward her health, her family life, her relationships, her personal growth, and the community at large. If sales are way up and profits are fabulous, the Artisan will not consider herself successful if the effort has left her exhausted and stressed-out. She may yearn for financial rewards, but she refuses to compromise her happiness for the sake of a fat bank account.

Idealists, Adventurers, and especially Visionaries don't mind working alone. But the Artisan likes to feel that she's part of a larger whole, and thrives within stable support systems. With her "all for one and one for all" attitude, she'll offer a hand wherever it's needed, whether that means swinging a hammer, making house calls, or helping proofread documents when deadlines loom.

Artisans are hands-on workers who like to see the fruits of their labors. Satisfaction comes from making things, fixing things, helping others, and healing others. It is the rare Artisan who finds fulfillment by processing data or working with numbers; Artisans are usually more attracted to work that is tangible, personal, and positive.

In her professional and her private life, the Artisan is a diplomat who seeks humane, democratic solutions to problems. She is sensitive to others' feelings; in fact, many Artisans have such strong empathy that they shy from leadership positions that require giving orders or even making corrections. They would rather be part of a team and trust others to fulfill their roles accordingly.

On every level, the Artisan promotes peace. She wants a calm, healthy working environment. She wants to be kind to the earth and to help others in need. As a businesswoman, she focuses on the best interests of everyone involved, and avoids high-risk, kill-or-be-killed situations. Cautious and careful, she prefers to win the race by being steady and consistent—and letting integrity be her guide.

Inside the Artisan Mind

True strength is delicate.

— LOUISE NEVELSON

Artisans run on feelings. While they might be hugely successful in the business world, or may make a lasting difference in society, their deepest yearnings are usually attached to family, home, inner peace, and outdoor life. Everything else is gravy—or, perhaps, roux.

Although she has nothing against riches, fame, and glory, the archetypal Artisan is not motivated by such earthly desires. More often, she is inspired by some greater good—a calling, as it were. Anita Roddick, who founded the Body Shop, wanted standards of beauty to be more realistic and standards of business to be more responsible. Margaret Rudkin, the founder of Pepperidge Farm, started baking whole-wheat bread because she believed it would help her son's asthma. Shamita Das Dasgupta, who was born in India and emigrated to the United States in 1967, formed Manavi, the first South Asian women's group in this country, in order to give a voice to others like herself. Throughout history, Artisans have made their marks not because they needed to be remembered, but because they were compelled to make a better place for themselves and their loved ones.

This is not to suggest that Artisans are a pack of Mother Teresas. But you'd be hard-pressed to find an Artisan who makes money just for the sake of making money. Few Artisans would choose to become defense contractors, bail bondspeople, or insurance industry lobbyists. If you meet an Artisan lawyer, it's certain she's slugging away for the underdog and doing loads of pro bono work. The Artisan financier no doubt invests in environmentally friendly companies; the Artisan fashion designer might campaign against sweatshops; the Artisan physician probably runs a clinic for underserved families.

Artisans can get by with very little, materially speaking, as long as they have health, happiness, and a clear conscience.

What Makes an Artisan?

Be happy. It's one way of being wise.

— COLETTE

Unlike Visionaries, who in childhood usually form a picture of the life they want to make for themselves, most Artisans have a collection of experiences that leads them away from what is superficial and toward what is meaningful. One primary influence is a love of nature. Many Artisans report that as children they were inspired and restored by the earth, the sky, and the sea, and that nature has served as a touchstone throughout their lives.

Ayéssa Rourke, an animal-keeper at the Los Angeles Zoo, grew up in a refurbished fishing shack in the mountains of Vermont. "In the early days, we had no plumbing, no running water," she remembers. "The place was heated with a woodstove. At bath time, my father would chop ice out back and melt it in a galvanized tub." Though such primitive conditions may sound dismal to city folk, Ayéssa found it magical. In the unspoiled woodlands that covered "her" mountain, Ayéssa "ran around like a wild creature. I'd track deer and sneak up on them when they were sleeping. I'd explore caves full of bats; I'd go out with my sketchbook in four feet of snow to draw the birch trees. I always felt there was a secret communication between nature and myself."

Cherie Whaples-Elliott, who now works as an antiques appraiser, found sanctuary in the slow, comfortable rhythms of her grandmother's household. "I remember how it smelled," she says. "I remember her gardens and her birdbaths and her vines growing up lattices, and the gazing balls—everything in her house seemed really old and special. I'd go there and I'd feel instantly comfortable."

Though Cherie also has Adventurer traits, it is typically Artisan that she would give her grandmother an exalted, almost mythic status. The Artisan wants emotional stability and often seeks out grandparent figures—mentors, teachers, wise elders—throughout her life. They make her feel anchored and safe.

"To me, the best things in life are about earthiness, comfort," agrees Lisa Somers, who has a home-based business that supplies breast pumps to new mothers. "I look for what is aesthetically warm, what feels good. Being a stockbroker, that stuff's just not real to me."

In Search of Security

The Artisan's need to find a reliable reality can, in some cases, be traced back to early traumas. Lisa Somers, social worker Debbie Atkins, and Ayéssa Rourke, for instance, are all children of divorced parents. Each woman says her sense of security was shattered when her parents broke up.

"Everything seemed to be falling apart at the seams," recalls Debbie of her parents' divorce. "I was probably fourteen. I made the decision not to go to boarding school, as my father wanted me to, but to stay in this tiny private school where I'd been since kindergarten. That's where I found my support—I had a 'family' of about thirty classmates."

While Ayéssa turned to nature and music for comfort, Lisa held fast to dreams of having her own family. "I always saw myself married and having kids," she says. "I wanted the house with the white picket fence. I didn't have that growing up. It was very important to me and still is." Lisa started forming a clear picture of her future when she met Jack, the man she eventually married, and got to know his family. "They had a white picket fence," she says. "His mom became my role model. She was wonderful—an incredible artist, compassionate, always interested. I'm shy and she's very gentle. It made a big difference."

It's interesting to note that all three women had almost absurdly lengthy relationships with the men they eventually married. Lisa started seeing Jack when she was seventeen and married him ten years later. Last year, Ayéssa sent out announcements that read, "Ray and Ayéssa were married in Las Vegas, February 3rd, 1999, after a scant twelve-year courtship." But Debbie wins the prize: she's known her husband, Rich, since nursery school. By the time she was twenty, her relationship with him had already outlasted her parents' marriage.

Unlike the Adventurer, the Artisan is cautious of making fast moves, taking U-turns, or jumping on bandwagons. Whether she gets it in her personal or her professional life, she will work very hard to own that elusive gift called continuity.

Labors of Love

> **Work is something you can count on, a trusted, lifelong friend who never deserts you.**
>
> **— MARGARET BOURKE-WHITE, PHOTOGRAPHER**

Artisans are drawn to essential tasks that deliver satisfaction. Many of them work with their hands. Others choose to work directly with people (or animals). Though Artisans may do well in business or technology, their happiness will probably be found creating things, fixing things, or healing the sick and the stressed.

The archetypal Artisan takes great pleasure in refinishing her own furniture, painting her own house, and knitting her own sweaters; she's happy to cook dinner for a crowd or bake from scratch. There is an underlying reason for this impulse: the Artisan shows love by doing. To her, actions are far more meaningful than words. You know an Artisan loves you if she crochets an afghan for your birthday, or makes you an herb wreath from her garden. Store-bought baubles (even expensive ones) are not her idea of treasure. Care, effort, and a personal touch make up her highest currency.

It follows that Artisans are dedicated crafters and often find themselves in careers that put their talents to good use. In the fullest definition of the name, many Artisans make their living as potters, picture-framers, landscapers, carpenters, bakers, glass-blowers, and the like.

Claire Criscuolo is one such Artisan. A psychiatric nurse by training, she and her husband opened a restaurant in 1975 to provide local college kids with home cooking. Today she's the author of three cookbooks and an authority on vegetarian cuisine. Yet she continues to cook at her restaurant and still gets a thrill from the sheer sensuality of it. "I often prep my own vegetables, sort my own beans," she says. "I sort of feel jealous if I don't get to do it. Even when I go on TV to cook and people try to set up the demonstration for me, I say, 'Why should you have all the fun?' "

In addition to the satisfaction that comes from making things, Artisans also find the repetition of tasks like weaving, printmaking, and cutting cucumbers to be soothing and meditative. This balm to the spirit is important because, though they may appear calm on the outside, most Artisans are highly sensitive creatures who are terribly susceptible to stress and strife.

how to spot
an artisan

Artisans come in many forms. There are the old-money WASPs, the ex-hippies, the militant environmentalists, the physical elitists, the dedicated moms, and the regular gals just trying to make a living. When it comes to spotting an Artisan, it is usually her lifestyle choices that give her away. Keep an eye out for:

• **A healthy glow.** Most Artisans don't wear makeup, with the possible exception of lip gloss and bronzer. A great many exercise regularly, spend their weekends outdoors, and take a whole bunch of nutritional supplements. Whether or not these rituals translate into natural beauty, it is the rare Artisan who covers her face with artificial color.

• **Comfortable shoes.** Artisans aren't slaves to fashion, especially where footwear is concerned. Featherweight flats, Doc Martens, Birkenstocks, athletic shoes, and even Easy Spirits can be spotted on the Artisan foot.

• **Unstructured clothing.** No form-fitting, shoulder-padded, gut-sucking silhouettes for this gal. If she's being true to herself, the Artisan will wear flowing garments that err on the side of casual. Long cotton dresses, big linen pant suits, and oversized blouses are favorites, and she will don a suit only for the most formal of business events. Some Artisans are fashion-unconscious, and will show up to job interviews in shapeless floral dresses that are a decade out of date. You can bet that these women live in jeans, and keep one or two "ladylike" outfits in their closets for special occasions.

• **Natural fibers and colors.** If it's polyester, an Artisan isn't wearing it. She doesn't like oddball dyes, either. The Artisan palette is natural all the way, and though she might risk a pastel now and then, most Artisan women wear earth tones.

• **One-of-a-kind jewelry.** Some sentimental Artisans wear a simple chain that dangles a gold cross, a star of David, or some other talisman they haven't taken off for fifteen years. For the most part, however, Artisans wear jewelry handmade by craftspeople. They're attracted to raw minerals (turquoise, agate, amber), imperfect beads, and necklaces and bracelets that were not made on an assembly line.

• **Tote bags.** Visionaries and Idealists carry briefcases. Artisans carry totes. Expandable jute bags are a dead giveaway; so are canvas tote bags that sport logos for PBS, independent book stores, or any environmental organization. Younger Artisans may carry backpacks, but beware: if the backpack is made of plastic, or if it looks like a stuffed animal, it's probably an Adventurer accessory.

The Artisan as Rescuer

A penchant for taking in what has been abandoned, neglected, or discarded is visible in all areas of the Artisan's life. She'll breathe life back into dying plants, adopt stray cats, or make an old barn into a wonderful home.

"Even early on I hated the fact that people threw things away," remembers antiques appraiser Cherie Whaples-Elliott. "I've been gathering my whole life. I find warmth and comfort in things that have been used, that have a history. As a kid, I'd see a thing that was old and think, 'You've got to preserve it.'"

It's only natural that in their professional lives Artisans often gravitate toward social work and careers in caretaking—including rehabilitation, physical therapy, counseling, nursing, and medicine. Debbie Atkins was on her way to a career teaching Spanish literature when, after graduating from Georgetown University, she took a year off. "In that year I did a lot of volunteer work," she recalls, "including tutoring disadvantaged kids and working with a blind woman who was a student at the college. Then I took a job with an agency, working with very poor kids in their homes, getting very involved with the families." Debbie says that becoming part of family dynamics was what crystallized her future. "My heart led me to social work," she says. "It didn't even occur to me that I should think financially; my goal was to find satisfaction that wasn't money. It was made very clear to me from early on, money ain't going to make you happy." Helping keep families together did make her happy and inspired a career that continues to give her great satisfaction.

How Artisans Learn

> The truth is that I am enslaved . . . in one vast love affair with seventy children.
>
> —SYLVIA ASHTON-WARNER, *SPINSTER*, 1959

No Artisan is an island. Quite unlike the Visionary, who does her learning, thinking, and decision-making in private, Artisans actively seek out teachers and mentors, and solicit feedback from as many sources as they can tap.

Restaurateur Claire Criscuolo jokes that she needs ninety opinions before she can make a move. Social worker Debbie Atkins has the same syndrome. "I'm baffled by small decisions," says Debbie. "I tend to get dazzled by the details of things. So I ask for a lot of options, I take a poll, a survey. I constantly mull problems over in my head, and ask random people for their opinions." Debbie admits that getting too many views on a subject sometimes leads her off a practical path. "I do it because I over-

YOU MAY BE AN ARTISAN IF . . .

Your office is in a converted carriage house.
You'd rather be a nurse than a medical researcher.
Every day is dress-down Friday.
You often bring your lunch to work.
You cry easily, and wish you didn't.
You're better in the audience than you are onstage.
You love the idea of being an apprentice.
You'd prefer to take a vote than make an autonomous decision.
You have an office cat.
You've owned your stapler since 1978.
When you take "mental health days," you really do work on your mental health.
You have your masseuse, your mentor, your husband, your children, your mother, your naturopath, and your veterinarian on speed dial.
You have separate recycling bins for newspapers, plastics, metals, cardboard, and business papers.
Your office furniture is all reclaimed.
You love doing errands that get you out of the office and into some fresh air.
You keep track of everyone's birthdays—even your co-workers' kids'.
The first thing you do when you get home from work is kick off your shoes and peel off your pantyhose.
You take your dog and/or your baby to work.

think things," she explains, "but I also seek approval. Even for the tiniest decisions, like what color I'm going to paint my walls."

When it comes to big decisions, however, Debbie has no trouble following her gut. "I have more conviction, more confidence," she says. "When I have a strong sense of something I don't question it. When I have faint feelings, I seek out strengthening from others to shore them up."

Artisans love to get inside others' heads and see the world through others' eyes. Many are especially awed by older people who have lots of life experience; words from wise masters feel authentic to Artisans.

Barbara Hemingway, a marketing consultant and an aspiring writer, has a writing teacher she holds in the highest esteem. Though Barbara is primarily an Adventurer, her Artisan qualities become evident when she talks about Hope Hale Davis, a Radcliffe professor who is well into her nineties. "Hope got to know the deepest me through my writing," says Barbara, "and I found myself choosing my thoughts very well because the most perspicacious person was at the other end, evaluating. She really cared. She made me feel like an extraordinary person."

Barbara, Hope, and Hope's husband—also a nonagenarian professor—started meeting for tea. Soon Barbara was helping Hope set up her classes in exchange for free tuition. "I feel like their granddaughter," Barbara says. "I shop for them, run errands, make healthful meals and deliver them on my bicycle." Such a relationship is Artisan to the core.

Artisan-Adventurer Cherie Whaples-Elliott, for her part, found a mentor in the powerful, outspoken Laraine Smith, who owns a respected auction house in Connecticut. "I had heard many stories about Laraine, and I was afraid to meet her," laughs Cherie. In spite of her fear, she signed up for a seminar that Laraine was conducting. "Afterward I walked up to her and said, 'If you ever have an opening, I'll do anything—sweep the floors, clean the toilets.' So she called me to work at an auction, and I loved it. Then she asked me along on an appraisal, and I said yes, yes, yes. I said yes to everything."

In general, Artisans love to learn, which may explain why they are such good teachers. In the role of teacher the Artisan is at once a sympathetic ear, a watchful eye, and a voice of compassion. She is not a master who bangs her ballet stick and barks out criticisms. Rather, she partners with her pupils and becomes part of the learning process.

Debbie Atkins, in her role as a family counselor, has a typically Artisan approach. "I try not to just walk into people's lives—I let them lead the way," she says. "I'm an observer and a reflector, I have to build a relationship with them first, then help them see whatever's causing the problem. I would never dare tell anybody how to live their lives, and anyway reality is so different for every family . . . I probably learn more from them than they ever do from me."

The Artisan Sense of Home

A sense of belonging is important to Artisans. Some find their place within a community, where they involve themselves in grass-roots movements and local politics. Others thrive in companies that function like big families. But most Artisans center themselves in a home they can call their own—a place that may or may not be filled with kids, pets, good smells, family dinners, and a sense of history.

Lisa Somers, the woman who always wanted a white picket fence, knew the importance of home way back when. "I remember when I was growing up, I was really interested in where my family came from," she says. "My great-uncle did our genealogy chart and I remember asking my father over and over when it was going to be done."

Lisa wanted to see how she fit in. It's an Artisan need, and those Artisans who don't have deep family roots are usually compelled to create their own familial structure. Some adopt children, become foster parents, or maintain menageries of stray animals. There are those Artisans whose familial ties extend to classrooms of kids, social-work cases, patients, clients, or employees. As a leader, the Artisan positions herself not at the head of the table, but in the center of a group. Whether she's in a party of two, a company of twelve, or an extended family of thousands, the warm circle of humanity is what makes the Artisan's life worth living.

Artisans in History

The Artisan style is expressed in many ways. In history, we can trace three very different women—one of whom was only marginally involved in business—and find recurring Artisan themes. **Margaret Rudkin,** *founder of Pepperidge Farm, started baking bread to help her son's asthma.* **Margaret Sanger** *became a champion of birth control after observing the plight of poor women with large families. Both women found their calling while seeking to relieve other people's suffering.* **Laura Ashley,** *for her part, created a company based on simple, old-fashioned values, and she worked to preserve the integrity not only of traditional craftsmanship but of ancient cottage industries. All three were socially conscious and became leaders not by the force of their personalities but by the power of their actions.*

MARGARET RUDKIN
THE ACCIDENTAL BAKER

> **"There was no planning, no theory, just: What is necessary to do next? Well, let's do it and see what happens."**

For the first half of her life, Margaret Fogerty was a city girl. Born in 1897, she grew up in Manhattan and attended high school on Long Island, graduating at the top of her class. After school she went to work as a bookkeeper at the Manhattan firm of McClure, Jones & Company, and stayed for six years. There she met Henry Albert Rudkin, who was a partner in the successful brokerage house. The two were married in 1923.

Three years into their marriage, Margaret and Henry had a "whimsical idea" to move to the country and get nearer to nature. So they bought 125 acres of land in Connecticut and built a Tudor-style home there, as well as barns, outbuildings, and a horse stable. They named the estate after a grove of tupelo trees—also known as pepperidges—that grew on the property.

In 1929 the Rudkins moved in to Pepperidge Farm. "We started our country life like babes in the woods," Margaret wrote in 1963, "for neither of us knew anything about country ways." With the help of Department of Agriculture pamphlets that Margaret wrote away for, the Rudkins learned to grow their own vegetables and fruits, and went on to raise turkeys, chickens, capons, cows, pigs—and, incidentally, three sons.

The 1930s brought trying times to the Rudkin family. In 1932, Henry was injured in a polo accident that left him unable to work for six months. In 1937 the couple's youngest son, who suffered from asthma, became increasingly ill. Margaret sought out the advice of an allergist, who suggested she put the boy on a diet of natural foods, and to avoid processed flours in favor of fresh, stone-ground whole wheat. Since whole-wheat products weren't commercially available, Margaret was faced with the challenge of baking her own bread. "I was forty and I had no experience," she recalled. "I turned to the reliable *Boston Cookbook* and started following directions. And then, suddenly, I seemed to remember the way my grandmother did it when I was six years old."

This ancestral memory woke something up inside Margaret. She threw herself into the task, and although she later claimed her first loaf "should have been sent to the Smithsonian Institution as a sample of bread from the Stone Age," she soon achieved delicious results. She gave several loaves to her son's doctor, who in turn distributed it to other patients. It was so popular that he asked her to keep up a steady supply, and Margaret obliged, selling the loaves to asthma patients via mail order.

Though it had started as a labor of love, Margaret realized that her bread might have a more widespread appeal. One day in late 1937, she made extra loaves and placed them with her local grocer. The bread immediately sold out, and soon Margaret was making daily deliveries to stores in Connecticut, while her commuting husband brought as many as fifty loaves each morning on the train to New York.

Margaret's bread was considerably more expensive than breads on the market. No wonder: it was made with heavy creamery butter, fresh whole milk, yeast, water, salt, honey, cane syrup, and, of course, stone-ground wheat flour. The dough was mixed in small batches, kneaded by hand, and sold unsliced. Margaret was committed to these high-quality ingredients and discovered that she had tapped into a market of consumers who were willing to pay more for better bread. Within a year, Margaret's fledgling bakery was turning out 4,000 loaves a week, and she had moved her enterprise into a converted service station.

The New York press picked up on the Pepperidge Farm story. One headline read, "Society Woman Turns Baker to Supply Elite with Healthful Bread." Margaret, a natural beauty, was described in one article as "slim and sophisticated, with gorgeous red hair, green eyes and milk-white skin."

Without the help of advertising, the Pepperidge Farm name had taken on a life of its own. Margaret shifted her energies from baking to product development. She added white bread to her line, as well as melba toast and pound cake, then set her sights on producing a line of cookies. She found the cookies of her dreams at a famous Belgian bakery; obtained the rights to the bakery's recipes and techniques; and shipped a 150-foot oven to her U.S. headquarters. Once again, Margaret insisted on small-batch baking and strict quality controls, and her delicate European cookies became a favorite American indulgence.

From its very beginnings, the Pepperidge Farm Company maintained a family-like atmosphere and garnered lifetime loyalty from many of its employees. Margaret's very first helper stayed with the company for more than twenty-five years. Along the way, Margaret hired that woman's sister, brother, sister-in-law, and cousins. "At one time, ten members of her family were Pepperidge Farm employees," recalled Margaret in 1963. Likewise, the neighbor who stopped in one day and offered to sell bread to a grocer on his way home, remained a valued salesman for twenty-four years.

The Rudkins sold the Pepperidge Farm Company to the Campbell Soup Company in 1960. Margaret served for two years as the director of Campbell Soup, then became the chairman of Pepperidge Farm when Henry died in 1962. Margaret succumbed to breast cancer in 1967.

Today, the home-based bakery started by a forty-year-old city girl employs more than 5,000 workers, and in 1997 reported $825 million in sales.

MARGARET SANGER
REPRODUCTION RIGHTS FOR ALL WOMEN

"The sexual impulse is the strongest force in all living creatures."

Margaret Higgins was born in 1879 in Corning, New York, into an impoverished family of eighteen children, eleven of whom survived childhood. As a girl she developed a passion for social causes, thanks in part to her father, a free-thinking Irish immigrant who preached against orthodox government and orthodox religion. She taught school for a short time, then, after her mother's death, briefly attended nursing school.

In 1902 she married William Sanger, an anarchist architect. The couple reared three children in New York City, where they circulated in a crowd of socialists, radical intellectuals, and writers, including John Reed and Emma Goldman, who for a time became her political mentor.

Though unlicensed, Sanger drew on her nursing skills and hired herself out as a birth attendant to wealthy women. But it was the plight of poor women that more concerned the young Sanger. Having observed dreadful conditions in New York's Lower East Side, she came to realize that much of the poverty among immigrant families was directly linked to their lack of access to birth control (a term she is credited with inventing).

Sanger soon gave up her midwifing practice, and by 1912 had founded the National Birth Control League and launched *The Woman Rebel*, a magazine dedicated to the cause. She began to circulate printed materials in poor neighborhoods that explained the fundamental principles of reproduction. At the time, federal law prohibited the distribution of information about contraception, because it was classified as "obscene matter." Again and again Sanger's pamphlets were confiscated by the U.S. Post Office for their alleged violation of the law.

Sanger was eventually arrested for her postal trespasses and fled to Europe on the eve of her trial. While abroad, she made a study of women's reproduction options and rights. In England, France, and especially Holland—where birth control was not only legal but administered through government agencies—Sanger educated herself thoroughly on the subject. She returned to the United States even more determined to share her knowledge with poverty-stricken women.

It was in October of 1916 that Margaret Sanger and her sister Ethel Byrne, a licensed nurse, opened the nation's first birth control clinic in the Brownsville section of Brooklyn. By this time Sanger had received thousands of letters from desperate women, many of whom had huge families that they couldn't support, begging her for information on contraception. From the minute it opened, the clinic was mobbed with clients, many of whom had suffered annual births, miscarriages, and brutally unskilled abortions. The clinic's primary objective was to fit women with diaphragms. Though the devices themselves were unregulated by law, anti-obscenity laws still forbade physicians and other health practitioners from giving advice about birth control to their patients.

Ten days after the clinic opened, it was raided by police and shut down. A female police officer, posing as a patient, had gotten the necessary evidence: the instructions that Sanger distributed with diaphragms.

The case of the Brownsville clinic gained national attention and eventually forced a change in censorship law. Sanger became the country's best-known birth control advocate.

Margaret Sanger believed that women not only had the right to control reproduction, she also believed they should enjoy sex. She openly cam-

SCORECARD

ARTISAN QUALITIES
- ✔ Champions underdog
- ✔ Family-centric
- _ Outdoorsy
- ✔ Produces tangible product
- _ Treats employees like family

paigned for personal cleanliness, an understanding of the causes of venereal disease, and sex education for all.

Sanger's iron will and seemingly limitless organizational skills were legendary. In 1923 she opened the Margaret Sanger Clinical Research Bureau in lower Manhattan—and shortly thereafter oversaw the manufacturing of diaphragms in a tiny factory nearby. During the '20s and '30s she fought battle after battle with the Roman Catholic hierarchy, congressional conservatives, and medical associations to ensure inexpensive legal access to birth control. True to her father's teachings, she was anything but orthodox: she hired rumrunners to smuggle diaphragms into the country in liquor bottles, once took a swing at an arresting officer, and accused members of Congress of being "bone-heads, spineless and brainless." Along the way she established a number of influential organizations, including the Planned Parenthood Federation.

After living a life at the cutting edge of a cultural, political, and sexual revolution, Margaret Sanger died of leukemia in 1966 in Tucson, Arizona. Throughout the years her credo, originally written in 1920, never wavered: "Women must come to recognize there is some function of womanhood other than being a child-bearing machine."

LAURA ASHLEY
EARTH MOTHER OF THE ALTERNATIVE SOCIETY

> **"I'm only interested in reopening people's eyes to what they have forgotten about."**

Laura Mountney was born in 1925 in South Wales and reared in South London. As the eldest in a family of two rambunctious brothers and a tomboy sister, she found solace with her childless Aunt Elsie, whose fastidious good manners, love of books, and gardening skills made a lifelong impression on the quiet, watchful girl. On holidays, Laura and her sister were packed off to ancestral Wales, where a grandmother and a far more rural set of aunts led a simple life of agricultural domesticity.

Having completed most of her education in London, she and her family were evacuated to Wales in 1938 as Europe moved to the brink of war. Soon, however, Laura was back in the city, keeping house for her father and attending secretarial school. In 1943 she was accepted into the

Women's Royal Naval Service. Just before she left for training, she met handsome, high-spirited Bernard Ashley at a dance. She was eighteen; he was seventeen. "The minute I set eyes on him I knew that this was the man I wanted to spend the rest of my life with," Laura later recalled.

Bernard and Laura were married and settled outside of London. Bernard worked at a small investment firm. Laura was a secretary at the National Federation of Women's Institutes and looked after Bernard with complete devotion.

In 1952 the Women's Institutes organized an exhibit of traditional crafts at the Victoria and Albert Museum, which included hand-printed fabric, patchwork, and quilts. Laura was captivated by the show and wanted to try her hand at patchwork, which she had seen her aunts in Wales assemble, but she could not find fabrics with the small prints and slender stripes that she'd admired in her childhood.

The following year, pregnant for the first time and under doctor's orders to rest, she set about learning how to design her own textiles. Bernard eagerly appropriated Laura's library books on the subject, and within weeks had constructed a printing screen on their kitchen table.

The two began creating simple patterns on squares of fabric in their attic apartment in London—which was 99 steps up from the street. One day, overcoming her natural shyness, Laura walked into a London department store with two dozen homemade scarves. They were put on display and sold out within hours. The store immediately ordered seventy-two more, and the Ashleys worked all night to fulfill the order. Twenty-four hours later, the order was repeated.

In 1954 Laura and Bernard rented a nearby basement and set up the Ashley Mountney Company. Bernard, who by now had quit his job, mixed dyes and worked on developing a continuous printing machine. Laura, for her part, was consumed by the demands of two babies, but managed to design a line of Victorian era–inspired tea towels, which were an immediate success.

Laura's life changed when her growing family rented an ancient stone cottage in the sylvan village of Kent. There she kept goats and grew crops and, because the family's assets were all poured back into the business, became accustomed to drinking out of jam jars and going without shoes. Before and after their third child was born, the Ashleys got in the habit of putting their brood to bed at 4:30 P.M., no matter what the season. That's when Laura would do her business and administrative work. It was her homespun daytime life, however, that informed her best designs, including simple dresses and blouses in cotton prints inspired by eighteenth- and nineteenth-century fabrics. "I didn't set out to be Victorian," Laura later recalled, "but it was a time when people lived straightforward, basic lives, when everything was clear-cut and respectable."

As a designer and a woman, Laura favored flounced, high-necked blouses and long, concealing skirts—quite a contrarian choice in an era when miniskirts, hot pants, and op-art textiles dominated London's boutiques. She considered mod fashions "dreadful," and said, "I sensed that most people wanted to raise families, have gardens and live life as nicely as they can. They don't want to go out to nightclubs every night and get absolutely blotto." One of her most successful styles was a shirred, three-tiered peasant skirt, often paired with a puffy blouse.

In 1963 the Ashleys took over a hundred-year-old railroad station in Wales, which became the international headquarters for their fast-growing business. There, Laura employed local workers and took care of them as if they were family. They, in turn, showed a devotion to her and the company that went far beyond the call of duty.

The first Laura Ashley boutique opened in London in 1968. Over the next twenty years, hundreds more opened in Britain, Europe, and the United States, featuring not only clothing but bed linens, decorative fabrics, wallpapers, and home accessories. The stores maintained the quaint, homey look that Laura favored, and something more: connections with the rural community in Wales. Laura resisted mass production, fearing it would destroy the indigenous cottage-industry model that had inspired and sustained her business.

Over time, the Ashleys became rich and famous. They acquired a yacht, a private plane—which Bernard often piloted—and a series of impressive homes. Laura's skills as an interior designer were coveted worldwide—she helped redecorate the British embassy in Washington, for instance—and she was frequently cited by Prime Minister Margaret Thatcher as an example to British entrepreneurs. Yet Laura herself always remained modest and low-key, more concerned with the welfare of her four children than the state of her multinational corporation. In 1985 the Duchess of Devonshire remarked, upon meeting her: "She was so quiet and absolutely charming in the true sense of the word, so straightforward and without any fuss, the very opposite of what one expected a hugely successful businessperson might look like."

SCORECARD

INTUITIVE ARTISAN QUALITIES

✔ Champions underdog
✔ Family-centric
✔ Outdoorsy
✔ Produces tangible product
✔ Treats employees like family

Tragically, Laura Ashley died in 1985 after a fall down a flight of stairs. Bernard became chairman of the company. Shortly thereafter her company went public, and nearly five thousand Laura Ashley staffers around the world were offered £1.25 million in shares at no cost. As of 1998, more than four hundred Laura Ashley stores were in operation worldwide.

Throughout her life, Laura Ashley sought to create "a kind of scrubbed, simple beauty." That philosophy became the foundation of an empire and could also describe the life of an unlikely style-setter who, in the words of biographer Anne Sebba, maintained "an unshakable belief that there was a moral purpose in what she was doing that transcended mere commercialism."

The Artisan at Work

When you cease to make a contribution, you begin to die.
— ELEANOR ROOSEVELT

Mensch is a word that speaks volumes. In German, it means "human being." In Yiddish, it takes on a more complex definition and describes a person who is upright, trustworthy, and decent, with a character that lives up to the noblest potential of the species.

Of the four archetypes, Artisans tend to be the most *menschlich*. They're the ones most likely to grant a paid leave of absence to the employee who's having family problems. They'll support underdogs and take up ethical causes, even if those causes are unpopular and/or inconvenient. The person who organizes comprehensive office-wide recycling is probably an Artisan, as is the co-worker who solicits contributions to send a disadvantaged neighbor-kid to summer camp.

Menschlike Artisans practically invented the concept of win-win, and practice it as often as they can. Joline Godfrey must have had Artisans in mind when she wrote in *Inc.* magazine: "The new psychology on

SOME FAVORITE ARTISAN INDUSTRIES

HEALTH CARE
  SOCIAL SERVICES
EDUCATION
  AGRICULTURE
ECOLOGY
  NONPROFITS
CHILD CARE
  FOOD SERVICE
CRAFTS
  PHYSICAL FITNESS
REAL ESTATE
  POLITICS (Grass roots)
HOME IMPROVEMENTS/
RENOVATIONS
  HOSPITALITY
BODY WORK (Massage, etc.)
  COUNSELING
GARDENING/LANDSCAPING
  COOKING/CATERING
ELDER CARE
  PHYSICAL THERAPY
SHOPKEEPING
  ANIMAL CARE
MIDWIFERY
  RECRUITMENT
VOLUNTEER COORDINATION

women reveals that relationships are a source of power that women are comfortable nurturing, and that business priorities may be determined as much by family and community imperatives as by a desire to amass wealth or things."

All for One, One for All

Florence Nightingale was one. So was Jane Addams, who tackled the problem of poverty at a time when sweatshops, child labor, and decrepit tenements were the lot of the urban poor. No doubt Rachel Carson, who alerted the public to the dangers of pollution with her 1962 book, *Silent Spring*, was of their ranks; so was Linda McCartney, who used her wealth and fame to promote the vegetarian lifestyle.

These extraordinary women were committed to the common good. Though they made a living (more or less) from their ventures, their goals reached far beyond financial gains.

Contemporary Artisan businesswomen seek to find a balance between giving and taking and are famous for their charitable works and their commitment to community. Within the workplace, they concern themselves with the health and happiness of the entire team, from the executives to the custodians, and seek to create a culture that nurtures the whole person.

Marsha Serlin, founder and president of Illinois United Scrap Metal, applies a very Artisan philosophy to a very industrial environment. "My greatest assets are my people," she told Women's Wire, "and I always listen to them. My door is always open; I am very positive and never discourage an idea." Serlin is committed to advancing her employees, many of whom are immigrants, through the ranks. "Given the labor-intensive work at United Scrap, proficiency in English is not required," she explains. "I offer GED classes for them to take while at work, and they are given financial incentives to pass. It also allows them to break out of the original job they were hired for and move up into sales or working with our computer system."

It Takes a Village

> I view my company as a family. The nurturer in me makes me want to bring out the best in others.
>
> **— DONNA KARAN, FASHION DESIGNER**

In business, as it is in all aspects of their lives, Artisans are most comfortable—and most successful—when they're part of a team. This might be a formal arrangement that includes partnerships, networking groups, mentor/protégée relationships, or advisory boards. Or it may be a more organic circle of friends and loved ones. Artisans are always eager for the insights and opinions of others, to which they give serious respect and consideration.

Deborah Triant, CEO and president of Check Point Software Technologies, Inc., has an Artisan approach to decision-making. "I first kick in to a talkative mode," she told *Fast Company* magazine. "I ask everybody I know to give me an opinion. I get different perspectives—and I listen to them."

To the Artisan, business is a group activity. She's convinced that it takes a village to make things happen, whether it's something as small as an employee birthday party or as big as the launching of a new product, and cherishes all contributions to the cause. She recognizes the importance of the financial mastermind, but is no less grateful to the receptionist who keeps a bottle of aspirin in her upper right-hand drawer.

The Artisan Comfort Level

> **Every woman I know would be so happy if she could . . . work in a place where she could wear a muumuu and no bra, and where there was no desk, and she could sit on the floor with her legs crossed, and there are only couches, and tea is being poured.**
>
> **— CARYN MANDABACH, TV PRODUCER**

You've heard the phrase "comfort level" kicked around, haven't you? The concept of comfort may not mean a great deal to other types, but it is almost always an issue with Artisans. That's because Artisans, who have been known to rely completely on "what feels right" to guide them through difficult circumstances, regard comfort not as a convenience but as an important working condition.

Case in point: Beth Cross and Pam Parker, founders of Ariat International, an athletic riding boot company. The partners are serious about producing blister-free boots for horseback riding, and about being a force in their industry, but they're also dedicated to providing a comfortable workplace. Their headquarters in San Carlos, California, is as flexible as it can be—pets and children are welcome, for instance. "Life is stressful enough," Pam Parker commented to Women's Wire in 1997. "We have the motto that lives come first and jobs come second. We cannot be versatile enough."

Stress reduction also informs the Artisans' general business practices. Guided by an instinctual comfort level, they keep risk to a minimum, and

SEVENTH HEAVEN

"Seventh-generation" is a concept that's Artisan in spirit. It's an approach to business that considers the consequences of any decision through seven future generations.

Kim Schaefer is a 7-G architect; she codirected the design and construction of an eco-friendly home for Habitat for Humanity in Washington, D.C. The energy-efficient structure was built mostly from recycled or salvaged materials from local sources (so as to avoid the ecological impacts of long-distance shipping). The walls were insulated with recycled newspapers; the driveway was made from bricks retrieved from a nearby demolition site; and the rubble and stone from an earlier foundation was used as a drain field in the new foundation.

More and more green-minded companies are taking the 7-G approach. Though right now it's mostly limited to manufacturing concerns, perhaps information-based companies should think about adopting it as well. After all, if programmers had planned for seven future generations, there wouldn't have been a Y2K fiasco.

tend to take small steps rather than great leaps. Most avoid unnecessary gambles, keep expenses low, and weigh options carefully before making a move. In the world of Aesop, Artisans are the tortoises who win the race by being slow, steady, and sensible.

Physical Labor: A Cure for Office Politics

Politics is the process of getting along with the querulous, the garrulous and the congenitally unlovable.

— MARILYN MOATS KENNEDY, RECRUITMENT EXECUTIVE

On its Schedule C tax forms, the IRS asks Jane Q. Business Owner if she "materially participates" in her venture. The question is designed to separate hands-on owners from silent partners and investors. A more efficient question might be, "Are you an Artisan?" If so, then the Feds can be pretty sure that you materially participate in all you do.

Artisans are right in the action, sleeves rolled up and attention fully engaged. Their rewards come from results, whether that means putting up a building, mailing a satisfying stack of letters, or seeing the spark of recognition in a student's eyes. To say that they're not afraid of hard work is an understatement. It's nonwork that bugs Artisans. They especially hate that toxic by-product of wage earning known as office politics.

Cherie Whaples-Elliott is militant about the subject: "As soon as there were politics where I worked, I didn't want to play," she says. "It's one of

THE ARTISAN AS
MENTOR AND/OR PROTÉGÉE

Businesswomen are natural advice-seekers. According to National Foundation of Women Business Owners' statistics, 56 percent of women business owners regularly consult with an outside accountant, versus 47 percent of men. Nearly half regularly consult with a company board (only 36 percent of men do), while 36 percent of women versus 29 percent of men gain frequent input from other business owners.

Of the four types, Artisans are most eager for input, and are perfectly suited for the roles both of mentor and protégée. As eager students and gentle teachers, they benefit from the "talking out" of problems and challenges. Though they sometimes solicit too many opinions and become paralyzed as a result, most Artisans find that good discussion is not only a way to absorb information but to work through emotional issues that can interfere with decision-making.

With that said, here's Barnett Helzberg Jr.'s advice, as told to Entre-World.org, about the art of being mentored:

• SEEK ADVICE FROM MULTIPLE MENTORS. "If you get a good idea from one outsider, namely A, another good idea from B, and a third from C, chances are your solution will be X. Help from at least a couple of mentors outweighs a mantra from a lone guru."

• LOOK FOR MENTORS AMONG YOUR PEERS. "In corporate parlance, mentors are generally older and wiser executives, [but] you needn't be so limited. We encourage young entrepreneurs to serve as advisors to each other's companies."

• ABOVE ALL ELSE, LOOK FOR GOOD CHEMISTRY—EVEN IF IT MEANS FINDING MENTORS OUTSIDE OF YOUR FIELD. "Simpatico has little to do with superficial factors, such as mentor and protégé being in the same industry. That's one reason why most of our pairings aren't industry-specific."

the reasons why I'll never have another nine-to-five job. I hate people's petty natures. It's like being back in ninth grade and I couldn't stand it then. I'll have none of that."

When exposed to bad vibes, head trips, or evil beams of anger shooting across rooms, Artisans wither inside. Their idea of business is based on harmony. They want people to come together to achieve a common goal, and any posturings of power are intensely unpleasant and, for the most part, incomprehensible to them.

Chef Claire Criscuolo says, "Karma is very important in my restaurant. To me this place is utopia, an escape from the real world. I don't like disharmony, I can't work like that. If someone's even in a bad mood it bothers me."

Some sensitive Artisans have sidestepped the pain and suffering of workplace skirmishes by taking on labor-intensive jobs.

Cherie is happy in her current role as an antiques appraiser, and she finds that the physical effort it demands—clearing out estates, moving furniture, going through attics and basements—does wonders for her sense of well-being. "When I worked in a lab, I would come home and couldn't function, I was so depressed. Now when I come home from a day of physical labor my body is tired, but my mind is free. I'm ready to make a big dinner, have some fun."

There is a persistent cultural stigma that women, especially college-educated women, are somehow "above" doing manual labor. But when you look at Martha Stewart, who makes everything by hand, has no problem climbing ladders and operating power tools, and who even raises her own chickens, it's clear that cultural norms are behind the times. There are plenty of women currently sitting behind desks who might be much happier operating campsites, renovating buildings, planting trees, or fixing cars.

It's Lonely at the Top

Ironically, Artisans can become less fulfilled the more successful they get. Why? Because promotions can bump them further and further away from the heart of the action, and place them in lonely posts where they have plenty of power but not enough interaction.

For instance, the Artisan who is happy as a schoolteacher might regret being promoted to school administrator, in spite of better wages, because she's cut off from the joy of seeing kids learn, which is probably why she started teaching in the first place. Likewise, a jewelry designer who hits it big might find herself doing a lot of planning, hiring, selling, and administrating, and virtually no designing.

It happens all the time: graphic designers become art directors, artists become businesspeople, chefs become restaurant owners. These Artisans can easily lose their joy of work and, yearning to return to the trenches, either jump ship and start a different career, or throw themselves into extracurricular activities, such as planting a garden or getting deeply involved in volunteer work.

DO HIRE AN ARTISAN TO . . .
DON'T HIRE AN ARTISAN TO . . .

Fight for justice.
Be a corporate lawyer.

Create an on-site day-care program.
Program computers.

Put together employee benefits packages.
Represent an insurance agency.

Set up your office.
Streamline departments.

Oversee care at a nursing home.
Streamline a nursing home's budget.

Develop plant stock at a nursery.
Pick stocks on Wall Street.

Run a dog-grooming service.
Run a dog track.

STRESS AND THE SENSITIVE ARTISAN

> While I am undeniably happy in my professional life, I am happiest
> of all when I'm sitting on the porch at my cabin in Maine and lis-
> tening to the birds.
> — ELLEN GOODMAN

Let it be said: Artisans and stress don't get along. In fact, Artisans can
be so fearful of the decimating effects of stress that they sometimes
choose careers that offer a low-stress lifestyle rather than picking careers
that might fulfill them.

The Artisan does not function well in competitive work environments
where everyone is jockeying for position and back-stabbing is a spectator sport. She must have harmony in the workplace, and her natural tendency is to try to create it by being a peacemaker. As a result, she can
find herself making decisions based on what will make other people
happy rather than concentrating on her own problems.

One great source of Artisan stress is ethical choices. Are you forced
to choose between hurting someone and advancing your own career? Do
you own a business that will fail unless you employ procedures that are
harmful to the earth? Are you caught between attending a crucial meeting and tending to your sick kid? The Artisan, when faced with such
conundrums, will tear herself apart trying to find a solution. She might
also suffer chronic back pain, stomach troubles, allergic symptoms,
hives, headaches, and ulcers.

But before she goes and hurts herself, the Artisan should try the following stress relievers.

1. LEARN TO SPEAK UP. Artisans aren't complainers and don't like to
draw attention to themselves. Which means their voices can go unheard.
Learning to speak up is no small task for Artisans, however, so they
might do best by talking first with a counselor. The process of airing
problems can greatly reduce the weight that the Artisan bears and untan-
gle her confusion. A trusted friend will do in a pinch, but trained professionals will probably do the Artisan more good in the long run.

2. GIVE YOURSELF REGULAR FIXES OF NATURE. Take a week or two in
a rustic setting—a place where you might have to haul your own water, split
your own logs, and get by without electricity. When the Artisan reconnects
with nature and the rhythms of the earth, life makes a lot more sense to her.
A shack on a deserted beach, a tent in the woods, a campsite in the
desert—these are places where the Artisan can really breathe.

3. EXERCISE OUTDOORS. Skiing, biking, hiking, camping, skateboard-
ing, swimming, kayaking, in-line skating, rock climbing, hula-hooping—
any physical activity done outdoors is excellent medicine for relieving
Artisan stress.

4. DO MEDITATIVE ACTIVITIES. Meditation itself is fine, as are yoga
and tai chi. But don't overlook meditative activities like pottery, calligra-
phy, guitar playing, and bread baking.

The Artisan as Working Mother

Show me a woman who doesn't feel guilty and I'll show you a man.
— ERICA JONG

In Carolyn Jones's *The Family of Women,* Christine Kealy tells a classic '70s tale of life as a newly divorced mother in New York City.

Having never worked before, her first job as a secretary was a disaster. "I spent four months wadding up pieces of stationery and putting them in my bag to take home," she says, so her boss wouldn't know how many mistakes she'd made. She was fired anyway. Then she was fired from her next six jobs in a row. "I'd start a new job and say, 'Oh, my children are no problem.' And then they'd be on the phone—'Ben threw an egg out the window,' 'Sean's at the emergency room, he hurt his ankle'— and I'd be sitting in some office, whispering, 'Do you think it's broken?' Between that and no experience whatsoever. . . . It was totally out of control."

Offices have become more parent-friendly over the last thirty years, but balancing work and motherhood is still a major challenge and a very emotional issue for Artisans. Most are extremely passionate about their children's needs; some choose to abandon their careers for full-time motherhood. Even Brenda Barnes, former CEO of Pepsi-Cola North America, dropped out of the corporate world to spend more time with her kids. "I've had no boredom," she told *Fortune.* "Not a minute. Not a nanosecond."

But most women don't have a choice; they have to work to support their families. And so, recognizing the importance of the home/work balance, more and more companies are offering family-friendly perks. Denise Ilitch has two children and is well aware of the constant worrying that goes along with being a working parent. So she started a child-care program at Little Caesar Enterprises, where she is vice chairwoman. Ilitch reports that the program has been beneficial to both moms and dads, and that productivity is up as a result. She also notes that the child-care option has proven to be a fabulous recruiting tool.

It's definitely the kind of recruiting tool that would lure Artisans. Still, nothing beats staying home, which is one reason why Artisans are so attracted to home-based businesses.

Lisa Somers wouldn't have started a home business if it weren't for the birth of her daughter, Sophie, and the crippling bout of postpartum depression that Lisa suffered. "It was very isolating, very difficult," she remembers. "I thought a lot about what I was doing with my life." Though she still

HOW THE ARTISAN GETS ALONG . . .

. . . WITH VISIONARIES

Remember *Green Acres*, the 1960s sitcom? The fancy, feathery Lisa (played by Eva Gabor), was an über-Visionary. Her husband, Oliver, was a reformed sophisticate who forced her to give up her beloved city life and live a rural Artisan existence. Though the show was cartoonish beyond belief, hard-core Artisans can sometimes view Visionaries like the locals saw Lisa: silly, spoiled, impractical.

Often, however, Visionaries and Artisans can form fruitful alliances. The Visionary respects the Artisan's reliability and down-to-earth viewpoints, while the Artisan admires the Visionary's sophistication and social skills. It is crucial, however, that Artisans learn to stand up to Visionaries — even if the Visionary is the Artisan's boss.

. . . WITH IDEALISTS

At first glance, the Artisan and Idealist styles couldn't be more different. Idealists tend to be modernists who are interested in systems and abstract subjects with concrete answers like math and computer programming. Artisans are animal-vegetable-mineral people who like working with their hands and often resist technological advances. Idealists are digital; Artisans are analog.

But — surprise — Artisans and Idealists usually get along famously. Both value simplicity and pay far more attention to the content of a thing than to the way it's presented. Both also tend to have strong ethics and morals — a real sense of right and wrong. As long as flashier personalities and louder voices don't get in their way, Artisans and Idealists can communicate well in the workplace and respect each other's opinions and input. The Artisan will likely place her faith in the Idealist's planning skills and head for numbers. The Idealist, for her part, will depend on the Artisan's superior people skills, flexibility, and patience.

. . . WITH ADVENTURERS

Adventurers sometimes seem like outrageous characters to Artisans. Depending on how extreme the Adventurer is, or perhaps how low-key the Artisan is, Adventurers can be perceived as either daring and courageous — or downright ludicrous.

When Artisans and Adventurers accept each other, the results can be wonderful. After all, Adventurers are performers and Artisans make great audiences. Also, the Adventurer's wild imagination and free-thinking ways can be liberating to the more timid Artisan.

That corny song "Wind Beneath My Wings" describes another kind of Artisan-Adventurer relationship. In it, the Adventurer gets all the attention while the Artisan hangs in the background, being stable and supportive. However, the Adventurer is not only dependent on the Artisan but is in awe of her steady strength. It really does happen in real life.

worked part-time at her office job, Lisa wanted something of her own. Through a friend she heard about a home-based business opportunity: renting Medela breast pumps to new mothers. "I was like, 'Wait a minute, I want to do this.' I wanted that connection with new moms." She wittily named her new venture Bosom Buddy—"It came to me in the car," she says—placed some ads, and immediately started getting calls.

Lisa is delighted with Bosom Buddy. She makes her own schedule, spends more time at home with Sophie, and has found that helping overwhelmed young mothers is one of the most gratifying jobs she's ever done. But there's been another benefit, too. Chronically shy all her life, Lisa is suddenly able to stand up before rooms full of new parents and give demonstrations, without an ounce of anxiety. "It's a mystery of life," she says.

THE UPS AND DOWNS OF BEING AN ARTISAN

THE UPS
You develop close relationships with colleagues and co-workers.
You're a great listener.
You're nurturing and can draw out the talents of others.
People like and trust you.
You have a holistic viewpoint and can see both the personal and the professional sides of situations.
You're interested in giving back to your community.
You have a hands-on approach to business.
You make democratic decisions.
You're much more of a dolphin than a shark.
You create harmony in the workplace.
You're not afraid of hard work.

THE DOWNS
You can turn yourself inside-out trying to please others.
You're not great at making swift, strong decisions.
You can be too trusting.
You aren't good at asking for what you need or lodging complaints.
You sometimes confuse personal issues with business issues.
You're apt to do things just to avoid stress or to protect others from stress.
You avoid enforcing rules or disciplining others.
You're not so good at setting boundaries.
You sometimes try to compensate for others' failings.
You can have a hard time being direct, especially about money matters.
You're prone to taking on too many responsibilities.
You can resort to passive-aggressive behavior when you don't get the appreciation you deserve.

The Artisan Work Space

The perfect Artisan office isn't an office at all. It's a log cabin on a lake, a cabana by the sea, a hammock stretched between trees. Right now, in cities across America, Artisan women are gazing out the windows of hard-earned corner offices in impressive skyscrapers, wishing they were lying on a forest floor someplace, surrounded by sunlight and butterflies and pine cones.

Artisans, let's remember, are physical creatures, and are best suited to jobs that either (a) get them outside; (b) keep them moving; or (c) let them make stuff. Think of nurses, midwives, and home health workers, who make rounds and visit patients. Picture park rangers, sailing instructors, and tree surgeons, who partner with nature and experience all the seasons. The personal trainer and the tennis pro, the farmer and the choreographer, the building contractor and the field researcher—all of them thrive in what could be described as workplaces-without-walls.

Ayéssa Rourke will never forget the day that she was forever liberated from office life. Having spent years working in deadening jobs and doing music on the side, she signed up for a course in zookeeping at Los Angeles City College. "The course was really hard and I loved it and I passed," she says. Ayéssa started volunteering most weekends at the L.A. Zoo and was so happy there that her nine-to-five life seemed unbearable by comparison. "My office job was sucking the life and soul out of me," she says. "It was so bad that I knew if I was attached to that hateful phone line in that cubicle in that building where the windows didn't even open on my fortieth birthday, I would just kill myself."

With no new job in sight, Ayéssa gave her notice. Days later, the zoo called, interviewed her over the phone and and hired her on her fortieth birthday. "I hadn't felt so free since I was seventeen. Not an ounce of fear. I was liberated."

Ayéssa's job isn't always pretty—feeding and cleaning are her primary tasks. But Artisans don't place much stock in glamour. "I take care of gibbons, fruit bats, a tiger, and Woolly Mountain tapirs. The tapirs will probably be extinct in the wild in five years. We have a breeding pair. They come when called and the baby likes to get kisses on his snout. I feel so honored that they let me be their friend."

Sure beats pushing papers in a cubicle, as far as she's concerned.

• **The ultimate Artisan office** is a converted barn flooded with sunlight. It has giant doors that can be opened onto the garden in good weather and a few friendly cats who visit regularly. The floor plan is more or less open, with office areas loosely defined by half-walls, area rugs, and rows of plants. Lamps are incandescent; furniture is made of wood—even the filing cabinets—and desks are antique country tables. There's a full kitchen on the premises, with real mugs and plates in the cabinets, and plenty of herb tea and spring water for everyone.

• **The minimum-requirement Artisan office** has a window that opens and a plant or two on the sill. There's got to be a chair that offers good back support; a heating/cooling system that can be adjusted for comfort; and reasonably easy access to the outdoors.

SUSAN SARGENT
THE ART OF BUSINESS

"I couldn't have been successful if I couldn't create beautiful products."

Susan Sargent is that rarest of creatures: an artist who has successfully evolved from an independent creator of one-of-a-kind works to a businesswoman who runs a happily thriving company that manufactures and markets her designs.

Ten years ago, Sargent was working in solitude, weaving just a few precious tapestries each year made from wool produced by her own sheep. Now she sells to more than 1,400 wholesale accounts, and her product line includes hand-painted bedding, appliquéd pillows, colorful ceramics, and dozens of rug designs. What's extraordinary is that Sargent's work as an artist has not been diluted or compromised by commercialization; on the contrary, as her company has expanded, her designs have grown in depth, breadth, integrity, quality, beauty, and whimsy.

The Susan Sargent story is a blueprint for Artisan businesswomen. Reared in a New England family with a long Yankee lineage, Sargent was the oldest of six children. As a very young girl she would escape from the crowd by going to her room and illustrating stories with her cherished collection of crayons. That creative impulse grew stronger and deeper with every passing year. "I always wanted to make and not buy anything," she recalls. As well as art, commerce attracted her: in high school she was already selling her creations. "Batik clothing for the Woodstock set," she remembers with a laugh. "I have never been a hobby person. Whatever I made always became a business; everything was made to sell."

Sargent studied at the prestigious Museum School in Boston, but found that a rigid art education didn't satisfy her Artisan spirit. So in 1971 she set off for central Sweden to study textiles at a hundred-year-old workshop. "That's where it all started," she says. "I met all my soul mates there—everyone was making things." She apprenticed at the workshop for four years, learning the ancient arts of dyeing, spinning, and hand weaving. From her primitive timber house she rowed or skated to work each day across the Dal Elven River. She made everything she wore, even her socks, and to survive she wove tapestries and sent them back to America to sell.

Sargent knew that she wanted to earn her living as a full-time artist, which was difficult to do in Sweden. So in 1975 she returned to the United States and camped out on a parcel of family land in Vermont. There, in the

Mettowee Valley, she built herself a house, board by board, while supporting herself first as a part-time curator of a fishing museum, then as a part-time photo editor. As her house took shape she was able to install her loom on the first floor. On the surrounding acres she built an outhouse (her only plumbing for five years) and brought in a small population of sheep and chickens. It was in this bucolic setting that Sargent got to work creating commissioned tapestries. By 1980 she had dropped her outside jobs to concentrate exclusively on her textiles, which were woven from wool that she had sheared from her own livestock.

Nothing is more rewarding to an artist than doing her own work, and Sargent loved her life at the loom. But she was also a success beyond the hand-hewn walls of her Vermont house. Her vibrant tapestries, which have been compared to the work of such diverse artists as Marc Chagall, William Morris, and Grandma Moses, were coveted by collectors and shown in the Albright-Knox Museum, the Boston Athenaeum, and the DeCordova Museum.

In 1990 Sargent got married and was soon presented with the challenge of rearing two children while moving her career forward. "Having children makes you focus on free time," she says. "I didn't spend my free time entertaining, socializing, or cleaning the house. I went to the studio and worked." As her client list grew, Sargent considered expanding her business, but couldn't imagine how she'd do it: training someone would take many years, and she didn't realistically expect that another artist would show up to work alongside her.

A major change came in 1991, when she licensed some rug patterns to a local company. The company was having her designs manufactured overseas; Sargent, not content with a hands-off relationship, traveled there to

INTUITIVE SCORECARD

Susan Sargent

VISIONARY QUALITIES
_ Leadership-oriented
✔ Named business after self
_ Works in glamour industry
✔ Made major leaps within industry
_ Master of publicity

ARTISAN QUALITIES
✔ Champions underdog
✔ Family-centric
✔ Outdoorsy
✔ Produces tangible product
✔ Treats employees like family

IDEALIST QUALITIES
✔ Pragmatic
_ Works within systems
_ Holds multiple degrees
_ Analytical
✔ Long-term commitment to single career

ADVENTURER QUALITIES
✔ Pioneering
✔ Unconventional
_ Socially gregarious
_ Diversified career path
_ Degree unrelated to career

track production. At a women's weaving cooperative in Hungary and a carpet workshop in India, she saw for the first time that her work could be executed by skilled craftspeople and that the voice of her art would not be lost in the translation. "I realized," she says, "that there was great potential in having other people work for you."

Sargent began spending months out of every year at the two factories, painstakingly correcting colors and refining designs. Meanwhile, back home in Vermont, she volunteered to head up a civic organization that was seeking to build a skating rink. Her job was to raise $4.5 million. "I had big businesspeople on board," she recalls, "and I was telling them what to do. It felt great."

Sargent's success at fund-raising so boosted her business confidence that she decided to tackle the biggest of her dreams: to put her art into the hands and the homes of people who never before could afford it. She envisioned a scenario in which overseas artisans would manufacture her products, thereby bringing the prices within reach to consumers. The only question was: where to begin?

"I was sort of a hippie," she confesses. "I was well-read and a news junkie, but I had no experience with business. So I went out and bought a book on how to write a business plan." The resulting document laid the groundwork for what would become her own design, production, and marketing company.

Sargent was prepared for the usual problems associated with start-ups, but first she had to get used to the idea of relinquishing control. "As a solitary artist working in a studio, operations were very predictable," she says. "I knew what I could accomplish, and there weren't any unknowns. But I couldn't grow the business alone. I needed help."

When it came time to hire her first employee, she was nervous. "I had never had one before," she recalls. "So I got lots of advice on how to go about it. I talked to businesspeople who told me all the standard stuff, but the best advice I got was from a fellow artist who said, 'Just hire someone you like.'" She now has what she calls "a great group of employees" and still strives to work only with people she likes.

It was in October of 1995 that she and several partners officially founded Susan Sargent Designs, Inc. Sargent was so liberated by the new venture that she experienced a kind of personal renaissance. Freed from her duties at the loom, her imagination soared. In the words of one of her colleagues, fresh designs "flew from her hand" and into production in India. The new work was supercharged with color and innovative images like spotted ponies, circus performers, cowboy boots, and hand tools. The pub-

"

SUSAN SARGENT ON . . .

DISCOVERING HER INNER ENTREPRENEUR: "I realized that I could work *with* someone but not *for* someone."

GIVING UP THE "I CAN DO IT ALL MYSELF" MENTALITY: "You could learn to weave a scarf in a day and a half. But if you want to do Gobelin tapestry weaving, it's a big commitment of your life—years and years."

FOLLOWING YOUR PASSION: "You have to care about what you are doing. I really cared about creating beautiful things for people—I couldn't have been successful if I couldn't create beautiful products. But there is a lot of compromise and you can't always match realistic results to your passion. It's very hard."

PLANNING A BUSINESS: "You really have to make a plan. Sit down and find out what your mission is. What are you trying to do? Where do you see yourself going? If you're not mature enough to write a business plan then you're not ready to start anything. Keep getting your skills together!"

"

lic was clearly ready for those visual thrills: by 1997 Sargent had more than 1,000 wholesale clients and had opened her own store in Weston, Vermont.

As her company grew, Sargent learned some important lessons. One of them was about pacing her own energy levels. "I get so excited when I do something new that it's hard to keep disciplined," she says. "I get tired of it by the time it's ready to go to market." She finally became accustomed to the long lapse between concept and completion, and has learned to keep a reign on her immediate impulses. "The minute I finish a design I can't just go off and order a hundred and fifty rugs. I have to respect the process and keep the numbers in front."

Today, Sargent is ready to expand the business once again. She's adding dinnerware, mugs, vases, and platters to her line, as well as a few select furnishings. "I feel energized," she says. "I'm ready to take new risks and I have a good perspective and maturity. A few years back, my response to challenge was to isolate myself and hunker down. Now, I take chances I never could have. It completely shakes me up and the rewards are new and exciting."

But the success of Susan Sargent, businesswoman, has not spoiled Susan Sargent, artist. "I couldn't have been successful if I couldn't create beautiful products," she says.

The difference is that now, those beautiful products can be owned by almost anybody with a yearning for what Sargent calls "handmade art for living."

ANNE ROBINSON
MUSIC FOR THE PEOPLE

> **"We did not say, 'We are going to start a record company and get financing and grow this.' Never."**

It's a term she dislikes. Yet Anne Robinson and her former partner, musician Will Ackerman, put New Age music on the map with their home-grown record label, Windham Hill Productions.

It started in 1976 when Robinson and Ackerman, both Stanford dropouts, borrowed $5 from sixty friends to record an album of Ackerman's dreamy guitar solos under the title *In Search of the Turtle's Navel*. But since Ackerman had only about sixty fans, and records had to be pressed in lots of five hundred or more, the two found themselves with 440 spare LPs. Robinson placed them in the bookstore where she worked and also in a health food store on consignment. Then a friend got the album played on radio stations in Portland and Seattle. Encouraged by the subsequent sell-out of his first effort, Ackerman recorded another album, and Windham Hill was more or less on its way.

From these modest beginnings grew an independent record company that by 1996 had annual revenues in the $45 million range and had spawned a New Age music movement that, industry-wide, pulled in more than $200 million a year.

Through it all, Anne Robinson stayed at the helm, nurturing Windham Hill's extraordinary growth and also making sure that the company answered to the music, and not vice versa. Her most important job: "Preserving the mystery, beauty, integrity, and grace of the music."

Like many Artisans, Anne Robinson was a nature girl. Her childhood in Southern California was spent outdoors. "My friends and I had these lives that we spent out in the trees and the gardens—our own little universes." Robinson's world expanded when her father, who worked in the aerospace industry, was transferred to Switzerland. "I went to the U.N. school in Geneva. It drew kids from every country on the planet, people who wore different clothes and spoke different languages. It was an incredibly rich experience that whetted my appetite for life."

Upon returning to the States, Robinson attended Stanford University to study history and art. She was there in the hot eye of the late '60s, when student protests were so intense that the school virtually shut down during her senior year. "I was very troubled by the war, and by

INTUITIVE SCORECARD

Anne Robinson

VISIONARY QUALITIES	ARTISAN QUALITIES
✔ Leadership-oriented	✔ Champions underdog
_ Named business after self	_ Family-centric
_ Works in glamour industry	✔ Outdoorsy
✔ Made major leaps within industry	✔ Produces tangible product
_ Master of publicity	✔ Treats employees like family

IDEALIST QUALITIES	ADVENTURER QUALITIES
_ Pragmatic	✔ Pioneering
_ Works within systems	✔ Unconventional
_ Holds multiple degrees	_ Socially gregarious
_ Analytical	_ Diversified career path
✔ Long-term commitment to single career	✔ Degree unrelated to career

the values emerging in American culture, the materialism. I thought that big business was very hard on people—it was a system I did not subscribe to."

Like so many others of her generation, Robinson dropped out of school, one semester before she was to graduate. After a few forgettable jobs in banks, she went to work at Plowshare, a bookstore in Palo Alto. "I went there to help get them through the Christmas season and I stayed eight years," she says. "There was a community there. It was not just a bookstore but a place for people to exchange information."

Robinson was making very little money but her life was rich. A long-time music aficionado, she was swept away by the revolutionary sounds that were exploding on the West Coast and across the country. "The music was really shaping the culture we were living in," she remembers. "I'd hear Isaac Stern at the symphony one night and Jimi Hendrix at the Fillmore the next. I was immersed in it—my entire body heard the music."

She met Will Ackerman while working on an open-air production of *Romeo and Juliet*. Both were still students at Stanford; she did the costumes and sets and he did the music. The audience liked Ackerman's guitar accompaniment so well that he was repeatedly asked to play it into personal tape recorders. Which is what gave the two—who were later married—the idea for putting his songs on vinyl.

"We did it for fun," Robinson says. "It was about making records and making them available to people." Ackerman's compositions "had a tremendously strong emotional quotient," she says. A few years down the road, Windham Hill's style became "an antidote to disco."

As the duo added other artists to their fledgling roster, Ackerman worked as a carpenter and Robinson stayed on as a bookkeeper at Plowshare. He took care of the musical direction and she did the packaging and looked after money, inventory, and distribution. Soon enough, their labor of love became a bona fide business, and Robinson was challenged with maintaining the integrity of their original vision, even while their company blossomed and branched out.

Windham Hill was nothing like big record companies, most of which were—and still are—obsessed with producing hit singles. "Our goal was to make records that would sell for years," Robinson says, "because they were timeless and of very fine quality." She tells the tale of a gentleman who approached her with a recording of Tibetan monks' chants. "No other record company in their right mind would have touched it with a bargepole," she says. But Windham Hill took it on and released it in 1986, "before it was politically correct to be interested in Tibet. He had this gorgeous recording that really respected that culture. And that kind of record still sells."

As for artist relations, the company adopted a kind of partnership approach. Rather than spending lavishly up front, Robinson and Ackerman chose to be modest with advances and production costs; this ensured that if a record did well the artist would see regular royalty checks quickly

" ANNE ROBINSON ON . . .

INTEGRITY: "Do your work for the love of the product. Not fame or fortune."

DECISION-MAKING: "Many brains have the solution. It's beyond the scope of one person to fix every problem."

STRESS: "The best remedy for me is to take a walk and realize that the sun will still come up in the east."

NEGOTIATING: "There is a pace and every deal is different and sometimes very painful. Know your own comfort level. If you don't know that, you shouldn't be doing the deal."

WOMEN AND POWER: "I think women tend to back-seat themselves, their vision, and their curiosities. They make excuses, they come in and they say, 'Oh, I didn't have enough time,' and their presentation blows away any man's. They don't understand how much they have."

FINDING YOUR PLACE IN THE WORKING WORLD: "It's all about what you really love. If you're seeing it, then there is a business in it for somebody. Before you know it, it's marketable." **"**

after the release. There was psychological value in such an arrangement, and it also served the company well: for twenty-three years it remained privately held and free of debt.

Not many businesses could survive the divorce of its founders, which happened to Windham Hill in 1981. But Robinson believes that she and Ackerman had been better suited as business partners than spouses all along.

The two continued to increase their company's market by keeping in close touch with their customers. "People would call or write letters and say, 'This is so real, this is so wonderful.'" Through conversations with fans, the partners learned where their music was getting airplay and which stores might want to carry Windham Hill records. Robinson believes that their straightforward approach and naive honesty helped them grow. "Will and I didn't try to pretend we had an empire," she told a reporter in 1991. "You can't lie to people; they get it, and it doesn't work."

In 1985 Windham Hill moved into a converted auto shop that included an indoor "tree house" on stilts for Ackerman to escape to. Robinson adopted a typically Artisan management style, involving her employees in decision-making processes, trying to keep her team's spirits high, and deflecting attention from herself. "I'd rather just do my job and have the work speak for itself," she says. It wasn't until 1987 that she hired a consultant, who talked her into developing a business plan.

Over the years, Robinson worked hard to grow her grassroots company into an entity that was strong enough to withstand success. In order to take the company to the next level, she knew she had to find a strategic partner, and so, after three years of research and negotiations, she made a joint venture with Bertelsmann Music Group. "It has strong international distribution and understood the core strength of the company," she explains. In 1992, Ackerman sold his share of Windham Hill to BMG. Four years later, BMG exercised their option to buy Robinson out.

She is philosophical. The deal with BMG, she says, brought "a level of sales, volume, visibility, credibility, and exposure for the artists and their music that I could not have done otherwise."

As for her new role as ex-CEO, Robinson is not only optimistic but energized. "I'm not a one-track person who only cares about music," she says. "I have the rest of my life to pursue all of the other things that fascinate me about the world."

LANE NEMETH
PLAY'S THE THING

"People at Discovery Toys work their jobs around their kids."

When journalists write about Lane Nemeth, they tend to focus on a semi-nal time in 1978 when she went shopping for toys for her baby daughter, Tara. On maternity leave from her position as the director of a children's day-care center, Nemeth was dismayed to learn that, as a consumer, she couldn't buy the kind of high-quality educational toys that were stocked at her workplace.

Where were all the safe, durable, developmental playthings? Nemeth was determined to get her hands on them, and make them available to other concerned mothers. Using the garage of her California home as a ware-house, she started collecting toys from around the world that inspired cre-ative play between parents and children; were not related to war, violence, or commercially generated superheroes; and were genuinely fun for kids.

Nemeth's second idea followed fast on the heels of her first and was as radically practical: instead of selling her newly assembled line of Discov-ery Toys through retail outlets, she would create a network of salespeople to give home demonstrations to small groups of moms and dads.

Her unconventional marketing plan served two purposes. First, it pro-vided a personal touch that was sorely lacking in the land of shoot-'em-up, mass-merchandised toys. Second—and to Nemeth's way of thinking, equally important—it provided a career opportunity for parents who wanted to spend more time at home with their children.

Today, there are more than 40,000 "Educational Consultants" across the United States and Canada who spread the word about Discovery Toys' impressive line of playthings, books, computer programs, kids' personal care products, and home study parenting programs. They must be doing a great job: recent reports put the company's sales at $100 million annually.

As a child growing up in New York City, Lane Perlowin was shy and with-drawn. "I was a loner at school," she recalls, "but I had safety at home, which made it a very okay place to be." Her father was an outgoing busi-nessman who was affectionate and demonstrative; she names him and her first-grade teacher as her first role models. Later, in high school, she found her best friend. "Once I met Nancy, all was right with the world," she says—and it is typically Artisan that Nancy is her best friend to this day.

Yet Lane suffered in her early years with a learning disability—spatial dyslexia—that wasn't identified until she was in her thirties. "I have a strong IQ, but I just couldn't grasp mathematics, and I was always losing things. I was a bit of a mess because I didn't know I had this problem." Her disability impaired her perception of her environment, yet she could "tune into people extraordinarily well."

She further developed her people skills in college and graduate school. At the University of Pittsburgh, where she earned her B.A., Lane says she came into her own intellectually. But it was her years at Seton Hall University, pursuing a master's degree in education, when she really blossomed. "Everything about grad school felt right," she remembers. "I felt very comfortable in those small classes. Professors got to know me quickly and I wanted to be known. I had no fear, I got straight A's." She also met and married Ed Nemeth, who has been a source of confidence ever since.

After graduation, Lane Nemeth floundered, scrabbled, and learned. She moved to Oregon, where her husband was pursuing his master's degree, and got a job at a day-care center that paid $1.50 an hour. She couldn't stand living on food stamps, so she went to work checking on welfare recipients in nursing homes. "I should have learned then that I wasn't a very good employee," she says. "I had no idea what I was doing and I had nightmares." An opportunity came up to recruit foster parents for patients being released from psychiatric institutions, and she volunteered. "I thought anything would be better than the nursing homes." Unfortunately, her new position required her to speak in public—something that the chronically shy Nemeth had no intention of doing. To get around the problem she went to the local university and recruited students to produce a slide show and a brochure.

Nemeth's presentations worked wonders. As a result of her "non-speaking" engagements, she got involved with agencies for disabled and disadvantaged citizens, and came up with a program that placed able-bodied welfare recipients as helpers to home-bound seniors, thus preventing premature nursing home placement. "It's become a big deal in Oregon," she says now. "I learned how to write grants, and my slide show was all over the state. I was feeling very, very successful."

Nemeth was uprooted once again when her husband got a job in San Francisco. There, she briefly worked at a day-care center in an inner-city school and felt as if she "was going completely insane" because her philosophies clashed with the school's idea of appropriate child-rearing. "I thought maybe I was wrong, because I hadn't had years of experience," she recalls. "So I went to take some classes. Before my first class I met a woman in the ladies' room who asked me what was wrong, and I broke out in tears. It turns out she was the head of the early childhood department, and became one of the best mentors I've ever had."

Those classes empowered Nemeth enough that she applied for directorship of a day-care center and got the job. "I had my own school. I could do things my own way. I raised funds for a new building, a bus, outdoor equipment. I ran a conference about child care and people from all over California came." The year was 1975. In the middle of all this success, at the age of twenty-eight, Nemeth had a child. "I had six months' maternity leave, and I never even considered going back to work full-time," she says.

Though she managed to convince her board of directors to let her work part-time, the fact that she wouldn't place her own daughter in day care caused a general deterioration in her leadership role. Nemeth left the center—"Money was never my driving issue," she says with a laugh—and devoted herself to the dream that would become Discovery Toys.

Today, Lane Nemeth oversees an ever-growing company headquartered in Livermore, California. From her corporate offices she watches over the development of toys and games that promote peaceful play and is especially satisfied that thousands of independent "Educational Consultants," who sell Discovery Toys' wares, have prospered as a result of the company's success.

She no longer has trouble speaking in front of crowds; in fact, she does it all the time. She's been honored by the National Association of Business Women and has twice been named as one of *Working Woman*'s Top 50 Business Women. She speaks at child development and leadership seminars all over the country, and serves as a mentor to emerging entrepreneurs.

Yet Lane Nemeth's heroes are close to home. One is her husband, Ed, to whom she's been married for more than thirty years. "He's a real Renaissance man who stays at home," she explains. "He's a fabulous parent—he stopped working when our daughter was in high school." His many intellectual and business activities include designing toys for the company.

INTUITIVE SCORECARD
Lane Nemeth

VISIONARY QUALITIES
- ✔ Leadership-oriented
- _ Named business after self
- _ Works in glamour industry
- _ Made major leaps within industry
- _ Master of publicity

ARTISAN QUALITIES
- ✔ Champions underdog
- ✔ Family-centric
- ✔ Outdoorsy
- ✔ Produces tangible product
- ✔ Treats employees like family

IDEALIST QUALITIES
- _ Pragmatic
- _ Works within systems
- ✔ Holds multiple degrees
- _ Analytical
- ✔ Long-term commitment to single career

ADVENTURER QUALITIES
- ✔ Pioneering
- ✔ Unconventional
- _ Socially gregarious
- _ Diversified career path
- _ Degree unrelated to career

"LANE NEMETH ON . . .

GROWING A COMPANY: "Growth is exciting, stimulating, energizing, and for me it was also like riding an out-of-control bucking bronco. Having had growth years and slow years, I'd take the bronco any day."

MANAGEMENT: "I once heard the great theater director William Ball speak. He said that whenever his actors came to him and asked how they should play a role, what they really meant was, 'I want you to listen and comment on my great idea for how a role should be played.' In management, you create independent people who are able to think through a scenario logically. I like to have an atmosphere, as much as possible, of free speech and debate."

KEEPING GOOD PEOPLE: "Money is never the answer, and rarely why people leave. If they feel they can make a real difference in their jobs, they will give you everything they can."

MAKING MISTAKES: "A mistake is usually a great deal better than no action. As a leader there are decisions you have to make. Use all the known facts combined with your intuition. It usually works."

PUBLIC LIFE: "I'm very glad I'm not a movie star. I admire my sales V.P., who can be in the public eye twenty-four hours a day. I need my privacy and I spend a certain amount of alone time every day."

JUGGLING CAREER AND FAMILY: "I think two parents working is deadly. America is suffering. People at Discovery Toys work their jobs around their kids."

And then there's Tara, whom Nemeth describes as "my girlfriend as well as my daughter." Having grown up with the same spatial dyslexia that plagued her mother, Tara recently graduated from college with honors.

Right now, in between running her company, collecting dolls, knitting, bicycling, and being a wife and mother, Nemeth is celebrating the publication of her first book, *Discovering Another Way: Raising Brighter Children While Having a Meaningful Career.* She wrote it, she says, in order to debunk the overly simplistic choices that are often presented to women today—of either working full-time or staying home full-time. "Things are never really black and white," Nemeth believes. "Either/or is something that happens in math, not in life."

ADVICE FOR ARTISANS

• **TAKE OFF THE WHITE HAT ONCE IN A WHILE.** Ethics are important in any industry. But the Artisan has a tendency to play the Good Guy role to an extent where it can thwart progress and interfere with good decision-making; some even mediate to the point of no action. Taking the moral high road is wonderful, as long as it doesn't put you out of business.

• **BEWARE OF PASSIVE-AGGRESSIVE BEHAVIOR.** Artisans are shy and have trouble speaking up about things that are bothering them. Sometimes they make the mistake of trying to get what they need by being emotionally manipulative—by having sudden hissy fits, for instance, or going stone-cold silent, thereby forcing the other person to call them out. Such behavior is not only ineffective, it can also be damaging to relationships.

• **INSTEAD, SPEAK UP.** It's possible to stand up and speak out about a problem and still respect yourself in the morning. *The Courageous Messenger: How to Successfully Speak Up at Work,* has a few tips:

1. Before you say anything, narrow the problem down so there is a single clear message. Build support for your message, and compose it so that it's not about other people but about work itself.

2. Face your own fears. You can't make people love you, but you can make them respect you; take the risk of airing unpleasantries, and rely on the power of truth to see you through.

3. Be direct. Avoid chit-chat or niceties. Make your point and then stop.

4. If given the chance, lobby hard for what you believe in, but be ready to give up on a losing cause.

• **DON'T INTERNALIZE.** Artisans have a tendency, when business is slow, to think that there is something wrong with them. Take a tip from Idealists and learn to keep your fragile feelings out of any financial equation.

• **AVOID BECOMING TOO FRIENDLY WITH YOUR BUSINESS ASSOCIATES.** While this makes for a pleasant working environment, it has the potential to be troublesome. For instance, the Artisan might become privy to inside information that runs smack up against her ethics. Or, she might have to fire or lay off her friend, which might be even more painful if her friend is in financial straits. It's best to make professional friendships, so that business can continue to run in a businesslike manner and nobody gets mortally wounded.

• **BE CAREFUL ABOUT HIRING FRIENDS AND FAMILY MEMBERS.** For cautionary tales, see above.

• **GET SOMEONE ELSE TO DO YOUR FINANCIAL BIDDING.** Many Artisans are softies when it comes to asking for money. If this describes you, get an agent, a negotiator, or a financial officer for whom financial transactions are a competitive sport.

• **TAKE TIME OFF WHEN YOU NEED IT.** In order to function at their best, the Artisan has to take care of her body, her mind, and her emotional health. Though her work ethic might drive her to keep on going no matter what, too much dedicated labor is ultimately not a good investment.

4

Idealist

Logical. Methodical. Far-sighted. Organized. Analytical. Efficient.

Idealists are the scientists of the business world. They do not answer to passion, ego, or impulse; rather, they let numbers, facts, and logic take the lead, and approach challenges with a cool detachment that is the envy of more mercurial types. Idealists build great careers—and great companies—on solid foundations of research and planning.

Archetypal Idealists like structure. They are comfortable with blueprints, schematics, outlines, and business plans. Give them a spreadsheet, a P&L statement, a set of statistics—the clean world of numbers is one of the Idealist's natural habitats.

They also like maps. In fact, by the time they're in high school, many Idealists have already charted their careers. Each phase of their progress is an investment in the future, and each accomplishment builds toward the next. Most know exactly where they're going and will not be stalled, sidetracked, or distracted.

With their superior diagnostic skills, Idealists can figure out what's broken and fix it or turn sloppy systems into efficient ones. Leave it to them to balance your books, make your investments, invent software, organize your closets, and find cures for disease. If you need a social worker, however, it might be best to look elsewhere. Many Idealists tend to be baffled when it comes to the mucky, unpredictable world of emotions. Though they might be excellent teachers or mentors, they're not usually suited to jobs that demand excellent people skills.

Idealists can be found in any field, from professional sports to film-making. But whether she's the CFO of a multinational corporation, an executive secretary, or a mechanic, the Idealist has the gift of clarity. She stays on top of the game, remains organized, and hitches her wagon to the stars of stability and proven success.

Inside the Idealist Mind

> To wear your heart on your sleeve isn't a very good plan; you should wear it inside, where it functions best.
> —MARGARET THATCHER

The archetypal Idealist is a woman with a plan. She makes her way through life by reaching one goal, and then another; in her head is a gigantic to-do list, which, though it may evolve over the years, serves as a guide through thickets of choices and decisions. Determined and disciplined, the Idealist doesn't wait for life to happen to her. She takes careful but decisive steps, and works to make a life of direction and achievement.

Hers is an orderly existence in which there's a place for everything and everything is in its place . . . theoretically, anyway. She has a wide streak of perfectionism that drives her to do things right, and that means maintaining a fit body, a tidy home, supportive relationships, and a career that keeps her on a path of intellectual and personal growth. She is not impulsive, as Adventurers tend to be, nor is she driven by a need to lead, as Visionaries might. Simply put, Idealists have a destination in mind, and follow the shortest, most reasonable path between A and Success.

Where Idealists Come From

Idealists are planners. But not all of them were born with a map and a compass in their fists. Rather, many modern Idealists developed their methodical ways in order to build a dream. There are Idealists who grew up in chaotic environments, and Idealists who were presented with scant opportunities in their developing years. Some were born into large families or grew up with working parents who had precious little attention to spare; others were only children who bore the brunt of their parents' ambitions. Even in the most idyllic childhood circumstances, however, many grown-up Idealists remember placing their faith in outside systems. School, church, organized sports—any environment with definite rules and roles was where young Idealists did most of their growing.

"During Lent and Advent I went to church every day," recalls Meg Brazill, who is now managing editor of an on-line news service. "I really wanted to be an altar boy. I looked longingly at them up on the altar. . . . As a second choice, I wanted to become a nun."

Like many Idealists, Meg did well in school and loved the atmosphere there. "I looked up to the nuns; I was a good student, so I didn't see their disciplinary nature too much."

Susan Hanlon, a technical manager at Avery Dennison, chose the tomboy route. "Fairly young, I had a gut feeling that I didn't want to go down the traditional path. I didn't see a clear option, but I did know that *Bride's* magazine was exactly what I didn't want." Susan positioned herself counter to the future-wife-and-mother route, and started playing sports. "I was always athletic, and I built on the idea that this was good for me. I expressed my individuality on the courts and the playing fields."

Judge Marie O. Jackson Thompson grew up with a daunting set of challenges. Her hometown was populated by highly educated black people and white immigrants. Even though she was the most academically gifted student in her school, she couldn't swim in the local amusement park or town park pools because of her color. One of a very few black Catholics, and especially dark-skinned, Marie was an outsider everywhere she went. "No one would hang out with me. So I just worked at being smart." It's no surprise that, at thirteen, she knew she wanted to be a lawyer; by then, she had experienced plenty of injustices.

Galvanizing Moments

The quintessential Idealist decides at some point in life to make something of herself. It may come after years of experimentation—first-person research, if you will. Usually, though, it happens at a pivotal moment in which she has to choose a future. Rather than following momentary impulses, she approaches the challenge like a scientist, studying options and developing probability theories.

Pamela Lopker remembers when she had to commit to a career path in college. "While most of my peers were concerned with following their passions, with doing what they 'loved' to do, I was looking for a career that would support me financially over the long run," she told *Fast Company* in 1998. Because she was strong in math and in analytical thinking, she considered doing statistical or actuarial work. "Then I realized that statistics wasn't a booming industry. Computer science seemed like a better long-term bet, so I changed my major." Today she is chairman and president of Qad, Inc., a $172 million software company, and one of the thirty largest public companies to be led by a female CEO.

Technical manager Susan Hanlon, for her part, tells of a galvanizing moment during her second year of college. It was the 1970s, and there was

YOU MAY BE AN IDEALIST IF . . .

You'd rather read a newspaper than a novel.

You have a wireless telephone headset.

You can remember the name of your second-grade teacher, the amount you paid for your first car, and the number of the flight you're taking next Tuesday.

You own the same jacket in two colors.

You're always tempted to clean up your partner's messy desk.

Your family pictures are in JPEG files.

Your handwriting looks either like an architect's or is illegible.

You usually manage to get great deals on airline tickets, hotel rooms, and rental cars.

You'd rather suffer a mild concussion than lose your Palm Pilot.

You belong to a wholesale shopping club.

You believe that for every job worth doing, there's a software program worth learning well.

You know what you're worth—down to the penny.

Your wristwatch has a lifetime warranty.

You know your cholesterol level.

You've never bounced a check.

Given the choice, you'd rather work late or go home than attend an office birthday party.

Your office equipment includes a Soloflex and a TV, silently tuned to CNN.

Your Web site wins awards.

You have your accountant, your stockbroker, and your personal trainer on speed dial.

You haven't played solitaire with a real deck of cards in years.

an explosion of opportunities for women in engineering. As a student she did well in math and science, so she put two and two together and decided to pursue a degree in chemical engineering. Her announcement was not met with resounding support, however. "One of my professors actually discouraged me," she recalls, "but I just dismissed it. There was no way I was taking his advice." When she broke the news to her "hateful" boyfriend, "He looked at me and said, 'You're never going to make it, you'll never pass physical chemistry.' I didn't even acknowledge it, but in my mind I said, 'You'd better *believe* I'm going to pass. You'd better *believe* I'm going to finish.' It just drove me more. I was determined."

Susan did get her degree, and it has taken her all over the world. "I was a woman in a traditionally man's field," she says, "and it was hard. But that was important— proving that I was smart. That need to prove myself and to be respected is still with me. It's a lifelong thing."

For on-line editor Meg Brazill, independence was a key goal in early life, and she clung to it against all odds. To this day she's upset about the path that her best friend in high school chose. "We were special people who were going places," Meg recalls. "We weren't going to stick around Buffalo like the rest of these dweebs." Then her friend met a man, built her world around him, and enrolled at a local Catholic women's college. "I just did not see this as the course of our lives," Meg says. She recalls coming home from her faraway school and talking about the new worlds she'd discovered. "My roommates at college were modern dancers who'd introduced me to Merce Cunningham, John Cage, Andy Warhol. I thought this stuff was so cool. She didn't approve.

But it was like, well, I don't approve of your lifestyle, either." Meg was determined to find what was right for her, even if it meant breaking away from all that was safe and familiar.

Joanna Lau made that break, too—but her stakes were much higher. Having emigrated from China at age seventeen and finding herself working in a Chinatown sweatshop, she had no choice but to set out on her own. Joanna wasn't out for glory; she was just committed to doing her best. She left her family, learned to speak English, graduated from high school, earned an undergraduate degree and two graduate degrees, worked a number of thankless jobs, and now heads up a multimillion-dollar company.

Success hasn't gone to her head, however. Like most Idealists, Joanna seems immune to the dangerous egotism that can come with major triumphs. She's still clear-eyed and realistic, and takes each day as it comes.

A Black-and-White World

> You can't go around hoping that most people have sterling moral characters. The most you can hope for is that people will pretend they do.
> —FRAN LEBOWITZ

Adventurers make up their own rules as they go along; Visionaries believe that ends justify almost any means; Artisans seek out random acts of kindness to commit.

But Idealists are a breed apart: they believe in right and wrong. Idealist judges analyze and uphold laws; Idealist cops represent Good in contrast to criminals' Bad. A number of Idealists are genuinely pious and try to live according to religious doctrine. But no matter what her beliefs or her vocation, the quintessential Idealist has at her core a basic honesty. Professionally, she has to: how could a serious mathematician fudge numbers? Why would a medical researcher fiddle with the results of a study? Idealists are truth-tellers.

And yet, some business situations call for Idealists to spin facts and tell tales that aren't 100 percent accurate. At the same time, they might have to decide who is or isn't telling them the truth. Both circumstances can be deeply painful for them.

With enough practice, Idealists can, like everybody else, learn to detect others' falsehoods and even become pretty wily themselves. But it's not natural to them. Worse, such worldliness can undermine the Idealist's faith in humankind. Few things upset her more than spin-doctoring, empty promises, and inaccurate statements. When it comes to trusting others, the best she can do is be 100 percent honest herself, and hope for the same consideration from others.

The Essence of Idealism

> My philosophy, in essence, is the concept of man as heroic
> being . . . with productive achievement as his noblest activity, and
> reason as his only absolute.
>
> —AYN RAND

Writer Ayn Rand developed a philosophy called Objectivism, which posited individual effort and ability as the sole source of all genuine achievement. Rand, who abhorred "groupthink" and fiercely believed that each person is responsible for his or her fate, was no doubt an Idealist. But there is a central Idealist characteristic that Rand didn't dwell on: deflection of glory.

Most Adventurers, some Visionaries, and more than a few Artisans need shovelsful of approval and encouragement in order to carry on. Idealists are the least needy. They can put their energies into a worthy project and, as long as things go according to plan, never even notice if fans are applauding at the sidelines. Like Rand, the Idealist sees purity in accomplishment. She'll be thrilled and genuinely proud of herself when she isolates and identifies a troublesome virus. If the Nobel committee happens to take note of her work, lovely—but that's icing on the cake. Though she places a value on self-respect, she doesn't do things to get attention. In fact, the average Idealist is uncomfortable in the hot spotlight of celebrity and prefers a low-key life of prudent yet significant achievement.

Most Idealists see themselves as part of a greater whole, which is one reason why their egos are so admirably in check. The Idealist basketball player values her assists as much as her points; the Idealist CEO is only as good as her team. Idealist mathematicians, scientists, researchers, computer code writers, and engineers usually have such deep respect for the significance of their fields that they see themselves as mere atoms in a giant organism.

Elise Locker, who works with a company that acquires defense systems for the U.S. Air Force, has a long history of not only succeeding in her chosen field, but also serving others in her work in the armed forces. In college she joined ROTC on the advice of her father, who wanted her to be a pilot. "It was only one day a week, so I gave it a shot," she says. Two years later she was offered an ROTC scholarship in math. Her major was music, but she made the decision to stay with ROTC and switch her major to suit her scholarship. "The air force paid for my education, then I got to spend four years serving my country. It may sound corny, but that's what I wanted to do." It suited her well; she ended up staying in the military for six years.

how to spot
an idealist

When it comes to personal appearance, Idealists fall into two general camps: those who are fastidious about their look and those who think as little about it as possible. Both groups have two things in common: they don't like fussy clothes and they tend to adopt uniforms. Do you have an Idealist in your midst? Look for:

• **Simple garments.** No ruffles, bows, blousy sleeves, poufy skirts, teeny buttons, twee embroidery, or do-nothing detail for these gals. They're comfortable in classic clothes and simple cuts, which can translate into ensembles ranging from the perennial blazer and oxford shirt to a Prada suit.

• **Serious shoes.** To the Idealist, shoes are not toys — they're tools. They've got to be practical, attractive, and versatile. She'll gladly part with good money for well-made flats, pumps, and loafers, but she has no interest in suede platforms, pointy-toed ankle boots, dyed-to-match mules, or any shoe that's only kidding.

• **Minimal accessories.** If she's wearing big, shiny, complicated earrings, you can be sure she's not an Idealist. The Idealist's taste in jewelry runs from muted metals in simple, clean shapes to modest diamond studs.

• **Plain hair.** Stylish cuts that require no extra fussing are just what Idealists want, especially since so many of them are also athletic and don't have time for 'dos that call for appliances and products.

• **Uniform dressing.** Idealists like outfits that don't give them any trouble. Fashionable Idealists might have a wardrobe of beautiful suits, jackets, trousers, and skirts, all of which more-or-less coordinate. As for Idealists who don't give a hoot about fashion, they too tend to adopt uniforms. This Idealist might own the exact same blazer in three colors (black, navy, gray), a bunch of identical white shirts, and simple trousers or skirts that she can rely on to get her through the week.

• **A classic trench coat.** High-quality trenches are an Idealist staple. And yes, she might even go for a zip-out lining.

• **Good business accessories.** Idealists consider briefcases, luggage, and pocketbooks to be business investments worth spending money on. She'll likely take good care of her leather goods and hang on to them for years.

• **And keep an eye out for . . .** understated makeup . . . small handbags (Idealists are organized) . . . chic eyeglasses (an item they'll splurge on) . . . a practical watch that's easy to read . . . and short, buffed nails.

Photographer Annie Leibovitz is another fine example of Idealist ego-lessness. She's famous for her images of celebrities, yet few people even know what she looks like. Her M.O. has been to spend lots of comfortable, daily-life time with her subjects. It's a feat she's pulled off with a combination of natural shyness and an absence of awe in the presence of icons. Leibovitz thinks of her photographic portraits as collaborations between herself and her subjects. With characteristic Idealist modesty she has said, "I'm not the people I photograph. It's more of a service I perform."

When the legendary Abby Joseph Cohen, co-chair of the Investment Policy Committee at Goldman Sachs, was named ninth most powerful woman in American business by *Fortune,* she responded by saying, "The power belongs to the analysis." The magazine called her "the Atlas who held up the Dow for so long," and commented that she is a "friendly, modest, elfin woman who rides the bus to work each morning." Cohen accurately predicted that the Dow would reach 9,300 by the end of 1998, but she didn't make a fuss about her forecast or her reasons for believing in bullishness: "I'm not creating those reasons," she told *Fortune.* "I'm just recognizing and summarizing them."

Out with the Old

> I wear my sort of clothes to save me the trouble of deciding which clothes to wear.
>
> — KATHARINE HEPBURN

Idealists dislike clutter. They throw away the newspaper the minute they're finished reading it. They wash pans and utensils while they cook, file papers as soon as they've reviewed them, and record every debit card purchase in their checkbooks, right at the counter. Why? Because Idealists value something called clarity of mind, and they want their surroundings to reflect and support that mental state.

Idealists have little use for what is merely decorative; they work toward sustaining a minimalist existence. Every object in their lives must earn its keep and ask little in return. When it comes to her wardrobe, for instance, the Idealist prefers "uniforms" that require no extra thought or advance preparation. She's likely to own a reliable car, sensible shoes, and a foolproof computer. As a consumer, she's cautious and hugely practical: to her, shopping is not a sport but an exercise in good research and informed selectivity. Same goes if she's choosing a career, negotiating a salary, responding to a party invitation, taking on a business partner, or subscribing to a magazine.

In day-to-day life, the Idealist functions best when she's right on schedule. She likes to get up at the same time every day, go for a run, eat her favorite cereal, take a shower with her preferred shampoo, put on a perfectly appropriate outfit, and make it to the office at exactly the right time. Simple things, like getting a ding in her car bumper or receiving a stack of smeared photocopies, can resonate throughout her day. It's not just because of the minor crises that she's upset, but because her routine's been thrown off.

Other types might be puzzled as to why unforeseen circumstances can be so perturbing to Idealists. An Adventurer, for instance, would probably be perfectly willing—and even eager—to run out for an unscheduled meeting. The Idealist could be hugely irritated by the same request. Such an interruption could cause her to have to cancel a phone conference, be late for her Page Maker class, and lose a great parking space. It's doubtful that any of these inconveniences would be bothersome to an Adventurer, but to some Idealists, they could add up to a day gone awry—a day off track.

Digital *vs.* Analog

Do you recall the name of the town where you went to summer camp? Idealists do. Can you remember phone numbers, sports stats, state capitals? Idealists can. They're natural-born *Jeopardy!* contestants. Once they memorize something, it stays memorized.

The rest of the types might cover their desks with Post-it notes, panic when they recognize a face and can't come up with a name, and freak out when the prosecutor says, "Where were you on the night of June 12, 1991?" That's because they're analog people, and their memory function is dependent on associations, visualizations, and the relationships between objects, time, emotions, and space. Idealists, on the other hand, are digital people. They know the interest rate on the CD they opened five years ago. They can quote sales figures off the tops of their heads. If you say a quote is by Keats, and an Idealist says she believes it's by Yeats, you'd better back down.

Idealists pride themselves on knowing what they know—and they can't stand it when they make mistakes. When the Idealist misses a cue, stumbles on a detail, or forgets to carry the seven, she can be almost inconsolable. Her tendency is to beat herself up for a while, swear she'll never forgive herself, then work doubly hard to ensure that it never happens again. In her working life as well as her personal life, no one is as hard on the Idealist as she is on herself.

Says engineer Susan Hanlon, "I make decisions based on data and information. It's not one hundred percent natural; I'm data-driven because

THE UPS AND DOWNS OF BEING AN IDEALIST

THE UPS
You are 100 percent reliable.
> **You gather hard data before making a decision.**

You have a natural affinity for science, mathematics, and technology.
> **You're organized, methodical, tidy, and detail-oriented.**

You uphold rules and the "right" way of doing things.
> **You're meticulously accurate in your communications.**

You respect procedures, even if they're tedious.
> **You're an excellent team player.**

You recognize the long-term effects of virtually every action.
> **You love to keep learning new things and perfecting your skills.**

You're great with money and investments.
> **You only take highly calculated risks.**

You're a minimalist at heart.

THE DOWNS
You resist "spin-doctoring" to the point that you sometimes can't make effective sales pitches.
> **You get nervous in loose, "whatever works" situations.**

You can't stand making mistakes and don't get over them easily.
> **You tend to be unforgiving when it comes to others' sloppiness or inconsistencies.**

You aren't usually comfortable making presentations or speaking in public.
> **You tend to micromanage yourself and others.**

You can lack flexibility.
> **You only take highly calculated risks, and can be perceived as "risk-averse."**

You're a minimalist at heart.

I've been burned. If there's data out there I didn't see or didn't use, I don't like that feeling.

"It's traumatic when I make mistakes," she continues. "Especially in the workplace, to the point that I'm overly cautious. I'll write an e-mail to a senior manager and spend twenty minutes checking it. I don't take mistakes easily."

Judge Marie O. Jackson Thompson echoes Susan's sentiments. After graduating from Harvard Law School she went to work for Cambridge Legal Services, defending what she calls "poverty cases."

"I was very successful," she admits, "but I can tell you every case I lost and why. It was traumatic for me to lose. I just hate being wrong."

Susan Hanlon says that her errors embarrass her, but she's learning to cope. "When I made a mistake I just wanted to hide my face . . . but I have learned that what I need to do in most cases is acknowledge the mistake and take corrective action." Yet she remains diligent. "I'm always amazed by people who make mistakes and just get on with life. They make a decision based on the wrong information and they're not looking back, they're moving on to the next thing. Part of me is jealous. And, I'll admit, part of me is disgusted."

Most non-Idealists would agree that Idealists are meticulous, disciplined creatures. But bring up the subject of discipline with an Idealist and she'll be the first to roll her eyes, shake her head, and say, "I have no discipline at all!"

Which just goes to show that Idealists set high standards for themselves, and most of them take full responsibility for their actions. When the Idealist burns her finger on a hot stove, she admonishes herself, saying it was a dumb blunder. When the bases are loaded and she strikes out, she's ready to crack herself on the head. But if someone else does something that causes the Idealist to make a mistake, beware. The receptionist who "loses" an important call, the co-worker who forgets to relay a crucial message, the cab driver who gets lost on the way to a business function . . . Ms. Idealist doesn't have much of a sense of humor about acts of incompetence and is likely to take measures to ensure they don't happen again.

What Idealists Want

> I cannot and will not cut my conscience to fit this year's fashions.
> — LILLIAN HELLMAN, LETTER TO HOUSE COMMITTEE ON UN-AMERICAN ACTIVITIES, 1952

Idealists aren't easily seduced. They don't need the bells and whistles of marketing to sell them on something; they see through fancy trappings and concern themselves with the bottom line. When buying supplies for their home, they'll make one efficient trip to a wholesale warehouse and buy towers of toilet paper and gallons of olive oil. When reading a proposal, they'll skip the verbiage and go right to the bottom line. With their scientific minds, they're always trying to separate the wheat from the chaff; substance is what they're looking for, even if it's in the form of molecules, laser beams, atoms, or space dust. It follows that to them, equality is much more than a word, and ethics are not just a pretty dress put on in the name of good public relations. Most have a deeply held code of conduct that signifies true order; a tidy work space and a freshly vacuumed car are just superficial expressions of a profound need for rightness in the world.

"I've quit jobs because the people I worked with didn't stand up for the principles I believed in," says Judge Marie O. Jackson Thompson. "I've walked away from great salaries. I won't be window-dressing. I have been offered corporate positions, money positions, there have been numerous executive positions that I've run away from, knowing they weren't right for me."

The archetypal Idealist believes in healthy living, cleanliness of mind and body, and constant learning. She might drive the best-built car money can buy and dwell in a penthouse furnished with classic modern treasures. Perhaps she holds a number of advanced degrees and has masterminded IPOs that have made her a millionaire many times over. But underneath it all, what the Idealist really wants is a world that makes sense, and a life for which she never has to apologize.

Idealists in History

Idealists seem to be slightly ahead of their time. Maybe that's why **Christine McGaffey Frederick** *and* **Grace Hopper** *aren't yet household names. They should be: each woman made contributions that changed the way we live.* **Fannie Farmer,** *for her part, is an American icon; perhaps that's because she wedded Idealist sensibilities with the sensual—and practical—subject of cooking.*

CHRISTINE MCGAFFEY FREDERICK
THE SCIENCE OF HOMES

> **"A new concept of glory which is neither male nor female but *human* is being substituted by the American man, in which the prize is the lifting of living standards. . . . That it makes Mrs. Consumer the pivotal center of modern life is simply the logic of nature."**

Christine Campbell was born in 1883 in Boston, an only child whose parents divorced when she was a baby. Her mother took her to Russia, where she was reared for a number of years by relatives in Moscow. At the age of seven, mother and child returned to the States; in 1894 her mother married Wyatt MacGaffey, a Chicago lawyer, who adopted Christine. After high school, Christine attended Northwestern University, where she earned a bachelor of science degree and graduated Phi Beta Kappa—quite an accomplishment for a woman in 1906.

The following year, Christine McGaffey (the spelling she preferred) married Justus George Frederick, a business executive, writer, and editor active in advertising and market research. They moved to Long Island, New York, where Christine gave birth to four children. That's when her penchant for science started to resurface.

As a mother and a homemaker, Mrs. Frederick found her house to be ill-suited to the challenges of family life. Drawing upon the experiments of Frederick Winslow Taylor, who worked toward increasing factory production by standardizing workers' actions and machinery, she rearranged her kitchen and laundry in order to make housekeeping easier, and adapted Tay-

SCORECARD

INTUITIVE IDEALIST QUALITIES
- ✔ Pragmatic
- ✔ Works within systems
- – Holds multiple degrees
- ✔ Analytical
- ✔ Long-term commitment to single career

lor's twelve principles of efficiency for the science she dubbed "household engineering." Over time, she transformed several rooms of her house into the Applecroft Home Experiment Station, where she tested household equipment and products.

The results of Frederick's experiments were published in the *Ladies' Home Journal*, of which she became household editor in 1912. Soon manufacturers were sending products to Frederick for testing and subsequently ran her endorsements in their advertising.

Frederick believed that running a home was a serious job, and she encouraged housewives to think of themselves as business managers. In her columns she preached the importance of modern surroundings and the latest equipment, and focused on ways to make housework less straining and less time-consuming. Over the years she contributed to the standardization of sinks and working surfaces; compiled child-friendly food charts and recipes; made a film about housekeeping; and lectured about home management.

Her books include *The New Housekeeping: Efficiency Studies in Home Management* (1913); *Household Engineering: Scientific Management in the Home* (1915); and *Selling Mrs. Consumer* (1925), based on a survey she'd conducted—one of the first of its kind—on the buying habits of women. Besides counseling manufacturers on how to reach women in the marketplace, the book espoused many of Frederick's vigorously modern ideas about American consumerism. In it she defends what she calls "creative waste" and blasts thrifty, penny-pinching housekeeping practices, calling them "medieval."

"There isn't the slightest reason in the world," she wrote, "why, for instance, bread crusts and left over portions of breadloaves, should be on the conscience of Mrs. Consumer because she doesn't make a bread pudding or French toast out of them. . . . Or hash out of yesterday's roast of beef. Or dust cloths out of old undergarments; or pantaloons for son out of father's cast-off suits—and so on *ad infinitum*."

She also espoused spending habits that today sound distinctly yuppie, encouraging women to "apply a very large share of one's income, even if it pinches savings, to the acquisition of the new goods or services or way of living." Frederick was convinced that "progressive obsolescence," as she called it, was healthy not only for women, but for the economy at large. "We have more because we spend more—this is our American paradox."

Frederick was an advocate of all things modern, including art, architecture, and business. She founded the League of Advertising Women in New York; testified before a House committee in support of a law against unfair competition between businesses; and served as household editor for *American Weekly,* an advertising trade publication.

Frederick lectured extensively and gave popular radio talks in the United States and Europe. She was a dramatic speaker who blasted archaic attitudes toward housekeeping, architecture, and women's roles. Later in life she became increasingly interested in interior design, and devised innovative ways to create compact, useful working spaces. She and her husband separated in the early 1940s, and she went on to start an interior consulting service that focused on the functional planning of space in the home.

Christine Frederick retired in 1957, having empowered a generation of homemakers. She died in 1970 at the age of eighty-seven.

FANNIE FARMER MERRITT
MEASURE FOR MEASURE

"Progress in civilization has been accompanied by progress in cookery."

Before Fannie Farmer started her School of Cookery in 1902, much of meal preparation was based on guesswork. Recipes called for vague measurements like "one teacup of flour" and "butter the size of an egg." It was she who introduced standard volumes for teaspoons, tablespoons, and cups, and thus ensured that even inexperienced home chefs would turn out palate-pleasing dishes that were well spiced, nutritionally balanced, and uniformly cooked.

Born in Boston in 1857, the teenaged Fannie suffered a paralytic stroke that forced her to drop out of high school. During her recovery she developed an interest in food and its preparation, and eventually enrolled in the Boston Cooking School. She graduated in 1889, and had done so well in her studies that she was asked to stay on as assistant director. Five years later she became head of the institution.

Though she was essentially shy and reticent, Farmer's step-by-step, no-nonsense teachings proved so powerful that she became sought after as a lecturer. She also became something of a celebrity when, in 1896, she penned the *Boston Cooking School Cookbook,* which is now known as *The Fannie Farmer Cookbook.* It's since sold upward of four million copies, but the book had tentative beginnings: Farmer's publisher, Little, Brown and Company,

SCORECARD

INTUITIVE

IDEALIST
QUALITIES
✔ Pragmatic
✔ Works within systems
_ Holds multiple degrees
✔ Analytical
✔ Long-term commitment to
   single career

considered the project so risky that it published an initial three thousand copies only on the condition that the author would pay for the printing. That author, upon becoming the best friend of fledgling cooks across the country, left her administrative post in 1902 to open Miss Farmer's School of Cooking.

Culinary institutes of the day were mostly designed to train teachers, professional cooks, or servants, but Fannie Farmer's school was dedicated to the education of housewives. As such, her teachings included instruction on formal entertaining, management of the home, use of kitchen equipment, and etiquette. She also extolled the virtues of oven thermometers and wrote recipes that specified baking times and temperatures, which was a major innovation at the time. In addition to standard measurements, heating levels, and timing, it was Farmer who introduced the cupcake. In classic Idealist style, this future birthday party staple was named not for its charming personal portion but for its recipe measurements—one cup butter, two cups sugar, three cups flour, and so on.

In the introduction to the twelfth edition of *The Fannie Farmer Cookbook,* James Beard wrote: "Today more than ever one is proud to be a good cook, and the time [is] ripe for the true spirit of Fannie Farmer to reemerge, teaching young people the right way to deal with simple, fresh foods and offering them basic, dependable American recipes that provide a grounding in good cooking and offer opportunity for embellishment in creative ways."

To Farmer's mind, her most important contribution to cookery was her virtually unprecedented foray into the science of nutrition. Of the six cookbooks she wrote in her lifetime, the one she considered to be of long-term significance was *Food and Cookery for the Sick and Convalescent* (1904). She stressed the "knowledge of the principles of diet [as an] essential part of one's education," and believed that a well-balanced intake of foods was crucial to good health and, therefore, a good life. "Mankind will eat to live, will be able to do better mental and physical work, and disease will be less frequent," she wrote. Farmer espoused her theories in a course she taught at Harvard and a column she and her sister, Cora Farmer Perkins, wrote for *Women's Home Companion.*

There is no doubt that Fannie Farmer Merritt was "the mother of the level measurement," as she is often called today. But at the time of her death in 1915, she was also recognized as a woman who transformed home cooking from a "by guess and by golly" process to a sane system that guaranteed nutritious—and delicious—results in kitchens across America.

GRACE HOPPER
MOTHER OF THE COMPUTER

> **"Life was simple before World War II. After that, we had systems."**

Grace Murray was blessed with parents who believed in higher education for girls. Born in New York City in 1906 and influenced by her father's love of literature, her mother's love of mathematics, and her grandfather's career in the U.S. Navy (he was a rear admiral, a rank that Grace herself would one day achieve), Grace was an excellent student with a natural curiosity about machines. She graduated Phi Beta Kappa from Vassar in 1928, with a B.A. in mathematics and physics. She promptly joined the Vassar faculty, then earned both an M.A. and a Ph.D. from Yale University.

While in graduate school she met and married Vincent Foster Hopper, an English teacher at New York University. He was soon fighting overseas, and Mrs. Hopper enlisted in the WAVES (Women Accepted for Voluntary Emergency Service). Never mind that she did not meet the height and weight requirements; she got a waiver, took a leave of absence from Vassar, and was soon enrolled in the Midshipman's School for Women. She graduated first in her class as Lieutenant Junior Grade Grace Murray Hopper. From there she was assigned to work at the Bureau of Ordnance Computation Project at Harvard University. Her job was to learn how to communicate with Mark I, the great-grandfather of today's computers. Working under Commander Howard Aiken, Lieutenant Hopper's first mission was "to have the coefficients for the interpolation of the arc tangents by next Thursday."

She succeeded, and went on to create many important "firsts" in the fast-developing world of computing. At Harvard, she devised a compiling system that served as the first translator between human and machine. "I had a running compiler and nobody would touch it," she recalls of that breakthrough. "They told me computers could only do arithmetic." At around the same time, Hopper also invented the term "bug" to describe computer glitches. Her inspiration was an actual moth that she had found in the workings of the Mark II.

SCORECARD

IDEALIST QUALITIES
- ✔ Pragmatic
- ✔ Works within systems
- ✔ Holds multiple degrees
- ✔ Analytical
- ✔ Long-term commitment to single career

In 1949, retired from active naval duty, she joined the corporation that was building UNIVAC I, the first large-scale electronic digital computer. That company eventually became Sperry-Univac, and it was during her years there that Hopper devised the FLOW-MATIC system, which allowed computers to execute typical business tasks like automatic billing and payroll calculation using commands in English. From FLOW-MATIC came COBOL (Common Business-Oriented Language), the first widely used computer language that allowed commands to be written in English, rather than code.

"I seem to do a lot of retiring," Hopper recalled in 1987. Indeed, she officially retired from the navy in 1966 and was called back to active duty in 1967 to oversee the standardization of the navy's computer languages. She retired from Sperry-Univac in 1971; in 1982 she became the oldest officer on active duty in the armed services; in 1983 President Ronald Reagan promoted her to the rank of commodore, which was elevated to rear admiral in 1985.

"Salty" is a word that pops up in descriptions of Grace Hopper. A tiny, wizened woman, she smoked unfiltered cigarettes and had a blunt, unorthodox way of expressing herself. (She once referred to the women's movement as "tommyrot and nonsense.") Yet, unlike most Idealists, she was an inspiring lecturer who loved to teach. After all her pioneering achievements and all her awards, including honorary doctorates, a National Medal of Technology, and the Data Processing Management Association's "Man of the Year" award, presented in 1969, Hopper believed that her greatest reward was "all the young people I've trained."

To Hopper's mind, "young people" was defined as "anybody half my age." To these students she brought a new clarity to the difficult subject of computers. One of her famous teaching tools was a piece of wire about a foot long. This, she said, represented a nanosecond, because it was the maximum distance electricity could travel in wire in one-billionth of a second. Then she contrasted it with a microsecond, representing one-millionth of a second, by displaying a coil of wire nearly a thousand feet long. Her message to her students was not technical but philosophical: "Don't waste even a microsecond."

Admiral Grace Murray Hopper died in her sleep on New Year's Day in 1992. The impact of her work, which spanned programming languages, software development concepts, compiler verification, and data processing, continues to grow and to benefit millions of people—even those who are still computer-shy.

Idealists at Work

Success is more a function of consistent common sense than it is of genius.

—AN WANG, FOUNDER OF WANG LABORATORIES

The ancient Greeks eschewed emotion and personal passion in favor of order and logic. Architecture was based on mathematical formulas to

DO HIRE AN IDEALIST TO . . .
      DON'T HIRE AN IDEALIST TO . . .

Clean up a fiscal mess.
      Settle employee disputes.

Write program code.
      Write greeting cards.

Discover a cure for M.S.
      Be a school nurse.

Design an inspiring Web site.
      Make motivational speeches.

Serve on the Supreme Court.
      Court new employees.

Be an architect.
      Cut corners.

Create special effects.
      Create publicity stunts.

ensure harmonious proportions; sculpture celebrated ideal bodies. Plato wrote about the rational relationship between the soul, the state, and the cosmos. His philosophies embraced law, mathematics, and science, and he taught that the universe of ideas assured order, intelligence, and design in a world in constant flux.

Like followers of Greek teachings, Idealists are classicists. They work within the context of a greater whole (vs. Romantics, who place emotion over reason). The Idealist has no need to wave her personality like a flag, nor does she have dreams of personal glory; she is not driven by passionate urges or visions of grandeur but by the promise of sensible success based on rational decisions.

Archetypal Idealists are emotionally and intellectually suited to working within predetermined structures. They like well-defined boundaries and clear goals, and thrive within broad systems like law, mathematics, and science. You can find Idealists working as stockbrokers, medical researchers, attorneys, financial analysts, software writers, engineers, surgeons, and technicians. Idealists have a special talent for analyzing situations, diagnosing problems, and turning chaos into order. Of all the types, it is the Idealist who is most likely to invent a groundbreaking communication system, isolate a gene, or discover a moon on a distant planet. Idealists are marathon runners, astronauts, professors, graphic designers, and inventors; their lives are marked by tenacity and by a need for steady intellectual, personal, and professional growth.

Safe and Secure

Elise Locker is one Idealist whose entire career has been about establishing and following standard procedures. After years in the air force, she took a position at a company that developed Internet systems. "My job was to develop and implement a project management system," she explains. "It was a chaotic atmosphere because they were trying to develop and launch products in a short period of time. We had to establish a process, then teach it to the employees, then ensure they followed the process. Once we got that rolling, I taught Total Quality Management tools. It was a very

THE ANXIOUS IDEALIST

Idealists tend to be taciturn. They don't usually act out or complain (unless they're one of a rare breed of hypochondriac Idealists). But in their quiet way they do get very, very tense.

What upsets Idealists more than anything is uncertainty. They place their faith in facts — data, numbers, spreadsheets — and when uncontrollable influences like unstable foreign markets or NASDAQ nose-dives cause those numbers to tremble, Idealists get freaked out. Equally stressful for Idealists is other people's irrational behavior. When her assistant starts making excuses, her best client abruptly cancels a meeting, or her boss starts having an affair with a co-worker, the Idealist's foundation can be rocked off its hinges.

Idealists must have order to feel relaxed. Chaotic work and/or home environments in which nobody's quite sure what anyone else is doing can cause them chronic stomach knots and many sleepless nights.

To assuage her stress, Idealists might try the following:

1. MAKE DISTINCTIONS BETWEEN WHAT IS WITHIN YOUR CONTROL AND WHAT ISN'T. Idealists can work themselves into a frenzy over impossible problems like crime, traffic jams, and secondhand smoke. Anxious Idealists should memorize the Serenity Prayer and take it to heart: "God, give us the serenity to accept the things that cannot be changed, the courage to change the things that can be changed, and the wisdom to know the difference."

2. ESTABLISH AS MANY ROUTINES IN YOUR LIFE AS POSSIBLE. When life gets crazy, it's good to know that, every Tuesday night at 7 P.M., you will take that yoga class; at nine the next night you'll watch your favorite show; you'll go biking every Thursday like clockwork; and you'll go to the movies with your husband every Friday no matter what.

Regular routines may seem like a rut to other types, but they can anchor Idealists and give them a sense of stability when it seems that everything else is falling to pieces.

3. PLAY SPORTS. Join a team and have some fun. Whether it's softball, bowling, or rugby, Idealists can work out their aggressions and enjoy a little healthy competition within the framework of organized sports. This isn't just about getting some exercise, mind you. Though an hour on the treadmill might be good for your cardiovascular system, a whole different set of benefits can be gained from playing on a team in a game that has rules and regulations. To Idealists, team sports are at once exhilarating, stimulating, and stress-free. After all, virtually any questions or disputes can be settled by a ref or a rule book.

4. DO SOME MAINTENANCE. Clean the house. Mow the lawn. Balance your checkbook. Though the tasks themselves might be tedious, Idealists feel much, much better when their home lives are tidy and organized. And they function better at work, too.

rigid system—step one, step two, step three, and so forth. And you do not deviate from those steps."

Free-wheeling Adventurers would last about ten minutes in such an intensely structured environment. But Idealists like Elise would rather have too many rules than not enough. In fact, Idealists can become very uncomfortable if a project is disorganized and lacks a clear direction. Although she'll do whatever it takes to make a deadline, she doesn't want her time to be wasted while other people are making up their minds, nor does she want to expend her energy on work that amounts to nothing.

Engineer Susan Hanlon recalls a short period in her life when her future was subject to the whims of others. Having briefly left engineering to pursue her dream of becoming a chef, she worked lackey jobs in kitchens of top L.A. restaurants, and then became a hostess. But the industry just didn't suit her. "It's such an unstructured environment," she says. "One of the things I found out about myself was that I need rules and regulations, I need things to be spelled out, how to reach goals, and get recognition for achieving them. In restaurant work, the boundaries are all over the place. The owner dates one of the waitresses and then promotes her to manager? I couldn't deal with it. I knew I had to get back to the corporate world."

Like Susan, most Idealists feel at home within established schedules (i.e., nine to five). They want to count on their vacation time and their days off, and they don't appreciate having to pinch-hit or make schedule adjustments to accommodate others. It's not that Idealists aren't generous, it's just that they're careful and very organized, and other people's emergencies put a crimp in their plans.

When Caution Doesn't Pay

The Idealist's methodical approach to problem-solving isn't always appreciated in go-go environments. Elise Locker once worked at a manufacturing company where she was charged with ensuring that quality procedures were being followed. "I was process-oriented, which was a requirement of the job, but the company was rewarding people who were letting a lot of details fall through the cracks," she says. "It drove me crazy. We'd be assigned to come to a meeting with our thoughts on a particular subject, and I'd put in time thinking about it, typing it all up, putting certain segments in boldface. Other people would do something verbally, or hand-write their ideas. And they were the ones who would get promoted."

Elise's company perceived her as being "risk-averse" because her approach—gathering data, examining differentials, producing solid research—caused her to be slower in making decisions than some of her jackrabbit co-workers. In fact, her analytical abilities actually held her back.

She's much happier in her current position because, besides working on the same air base where she spent her military years, she is appreciated for her data-driven approach. Of approximately 250 people in her division, Elise is one of two women on her company's "high-potential list"— quite an honor for someone who's been with the firm for only two years. "It's my boss and me," Elise says with pride. "And she was the one who recruited me."

Order in the Court

> You are hired for your judgment, not your stamina.
> — DONNA SHALALA

In the working world, Idealists are known for creating efficient systems for virtually every task that's set before them. In the course of a day, the Idealist might utilize a half-dozen of her own devices, including a neighborhood car pool; an office-wide e-mail system; an idiot-proof filing system; a lunchtime schedule rotation; a customized Internet search engine; and a cost-saving long-distance phone service. Idealists want to work in "smart" environments and can be deeply annoyed by messy, archaic, inefficient offices in which systems, equipment, and/or personnel don't suit the tasks at hand.

One Idealist who's always had the gift of organization is on-line editor Meg Brazill. When she worked in nonprofit arts management in New York, she made the most of low-rent offices with shoestring budgets and few supplies. Then she moved to Los Angeles and eventually found herself in an arts foundation that was anything but underfunded.

"The place was set up like a dream," she remembers. "The mailing room was easy to work in; the counter was set up at the perfect height for women. Supplies were well laid out and organized, and the whole aesthetic was gorgeous. It was such a pleasure. Everything we needed was there— nicer scissors than I've ever used, the deluxe postage machine that closed the envelopes, a high-speed copier. The office kitchen was like that, too. *Way* nicer than our kitchen at home."

Meg recognized that the money spent for top-notch equipment could have been supporting starving artists. "It was almost decadent," she reflects. "But I believed in the goals of the organization and came to appreciate that working in dignity did not have to be exclusive of those goals."

The Idealist as Working Mother

There is a distinct Idealist approach to working motherhood. It is: schedule, schedule, schedule. Though it's a hugely emotional demand, many Idealists are damn good at it. Executive Idealists will fly home for recitals and traumatic orthodontist appointments; less international moms will carefully juggle their Filofaxes so that a parent is there when a parent needs to be there.

However, Idealists are unlikely to coddle their offspring or to be overindulgent or overprotective. It's rare to find an Idealist mom on the phone in the middle of the day talking her nine-year-old through the steps of How to Make Toast. In fact, many Idealist moms have a pact with their kids: they don't bother Mommy unless it's really important, and Mommy rewards them with privileges. These can range from a loose curfew, to sending them to the best summer camp in the country.

An unusual ratio of Idealist moms depend on their husbands for child-care support. Elise Locker, for instance, says that she could not have accomplished what she has without her husband Al, a systems engineer. "Whatever job I had, he said he'd follow me. He believes that my career has more potential than his, and he always told me he could find a job wherever I went. Our jobs have always required quite a lot of travel, and when either one of us is away, the other takes on the role of single parent. It's tough for both of us, but it's a sacrifice we're willing to make."

To some Idealist parents, good scheduling means micromanaging their kids' time. It is well within the Idealist nature to sign her child up for extracurricular sports, dance classes, math rodeos, canoe trips, Girl Scouts, and Junior Mensa—to the extent that the kid needs a Palm Pilot of her own.

On a bigger scale, Idealists are, like Artisans, very concerned with providing for their children's health, education, and welfare. They are eternally grateful to companies that provide infant immunization programs, on-site day care, special college funds, after-school programs, internships, or even take-your-daughter-to-work days. Idealists are, after all, practical, and will take all the help they can get.

The Idealist Work Space

Inside every Idealist is an efficiency expert. She likes great equipment that works on demand, and wants a place for everything and everything in its place. The Idealist is interested in convenient parking, fast elevators, clean offices, adequate bathrooms, good lighting, and good security. Most of all, she covets a designated space that offers plenty of invisible storage (drawers and cabinets), enough electrical outlets to power all her gizmos, and vast, clean surfaces upon which she can gaze in satisfaction and reflection.

Since other people's clutter and messy work habits can drive her to distraction, the Idealist is convinced that she can only reach peak performance in an office that's private, secure, tidy, and organized according to her high standards. And she's probably right.

STRENGTH THROUGH STRUCTURE
IDEALIST INDUSTRIES

The Idealist's affinity for structure can be manifested in a thousand ways. Idealists can be quite content serving in the military, for instance, and function well within that strictly defined hierarchy and in minutely planned operations. Other professions that are based on structure include:

• MEDICINE. Idealists can thrive in those fields of medicine that deal with the human body as a closed system. Their natural talents for restoring order, as well as their diagnostic skills, are well used in specialized fields such as endocrinology, dermatology, forensic medicine, and all kinds of surgery. Medical research, too, is an area in which Idealists shine.

• SCIENCE. Chemistry, biology, physics, geology, meteorology, entomology, astronomy, archeology . . . the wide world of science is appealing to most Idealists because it involves identifying and cataloging. Again, it places phenomena within a logical system.

• SPORTS. Many Idealists are big sports fans. They love the stats, the play-by-plays, the analysis, the strategies, and the surprises — all enacted within that big structure known as The Game. There are plenty of Idealists who also like to play, yet it is more within the Idealist nature to be an informed spectator — or, perhaps, a professional announcer, sports journalist, or team owner.

• TECHNOLOGY. Though that elastic term *technology* stretches wider by the hour, all technology is based on systems. Electricity, electronics, microchips, sine waves: these invisible systems can be tackled and mastered by Idealists, resulting not only in the maintenance and improvement of existing technologies, but in the invention of new ones.

• MATHEMATICS. Accounting is something that most Idealists do well. So is bookkeeping, auditing, actuarial work, underwriting, statistics, and economic projections. The dispassionate world of numbers is one of the Idealist's natural habitats.

• ENGINEERING. Whether it be structural, chemical, environmental, electrical, civil, or nuclear, Idealists are likely to find satisfaction in virtually any field of engineering.

• FINANCE. When you want your dollars to shut up and start performing, it's time to call an Idealist. She can analyze all the variables and can make well-informed money decisions better than any other type. Idealists can thrive in virtually any kind of financial career.

• BUILDING. Many architects are Idealists. It is not just the challenge of creating an aesthetically pleasing building that fascinates them; they also love solving the puzzles of heating and cooling, electrical systems, land surveying, weather issues, and building codes. Likewise, Idealists can be happy doing building maintenance.

• ENTERTAINMENT. Cinematographer, sound mixer, lighting technician, technical director, gaffer, best boy, and FX expert are all Idealist job titles. Which just goes to show that you don't have to be an Adventurer to be a success in "the Industry."

• **The ultimate Idealist office** is a brilliantly designed space in a high-rise building with a fabulous view. It has a modernist aesthetic and features state-of-the-art computer equipment, a media center, push-button everything, and a private bathroom with a shower. All the furnishings are brand-new, ergonomically correct, and perfectly coordinated. Even the treadmill, stationed in front of the window for maximum viewing pleasure, and the under-counter refrigerator, stocked with favorite snacks, look as though they belong there. As for filing cabinets, there aren't any—it's a paperless office.

• **The minimum-requirement Idealist office** has all the equipment necessary for the Idealist to do her job. Computer modems are fast enough for speedy Internet access; the copier doesn't put black streaks on every page; and faxes come through legibly. Also, she has her own space—whether it's an office, a cubicle, or just a desk—that she can keep clean and organized.

Fascination with What's Difficult

What's *fun* in life is knowing you're not good at something, and then making yourself good at it.

—**LESLEY STAHL**

For all their methodical ways, many an Idealist is drawn toward professional challenges and will take career risks when given the chance. Why? Because Idealists love to learn. Of all the types, it is the Idealist who is most likely to take advantage of company tuition reimbursements and earn advanced degrees and certifications. But her education doesn't have to be formal: Idealists will jump on opportunities to broaden their knowledge or intensify their expertise—on or off company time.

Of all the jobs that Meg Brazill ever had (and there have been plenty), the one she speaks most enthusiastically about was at the Oakland Feminist Women's Health Center. "That was a hugely important job for me because they had everybody take turns in rotation at all the different positions in the company. There was administration, phone counseling; in the clinic itself there was medical assistance. There was this strong philosophy about women controlling health care and women controlling their bodies. It was all about information. I loved the idea that I could come in, not know something, then was given the training, the confidence, the autonomy to go forward and do well."

Elise Locker has taken a profoundly different path, yet she, like Meg, has been attracted to growth opportunities. She graduated from Ithaca College with a math degree and a minor in music. ("I should have been a computer science minor—I'd probably be doing Internet start-ups by now—but I love my music," she reflects.) She then served in the air force for six years before entering the civilian working world. Since that time she's earned a master of science degree in systems management. But it was a trade-off, because her coursework kept her from another of her passions: volleyball. "I kept asking myself, volleyball or my masters?" Today, she's torn between going for her M.B.A. or spending more time with her two children. "The kids are winning out so far," she laughs, "but I've taken lots of classes—in math, and in quality assurance—and I always read self-improvement books and listen to motivational tapes in my car. If the opportunity for education is there, I'll take it."

The Idealist Order

> Math is the great equalizer. If you can do the numbers, the boys have to respect you.
> — AUDREY MACLEAN, SILICON VALLEY INVESTOR

Idealists rule with their heads. They can be strong leaders who stay cool and focused in good times and bad, and tend to create formalized business structures with strong departmental direction. The Idealist's approach is to compartmentalize tasks; in this way she can create an organization that functions like a well-oiled machine, in which risks are kept at a minimum and little is left to chance.

The danger of the Idealist approach is that she can sometimes focus too closely on rules and not have the vision or flexibility to get the best out of people. By overdefining jobs, she runs the risk of quelling creativity. Idealists like things to run smoothly; in their effort to stick with the prescribed program, they might forget to change with the times, strategize, and see unexpected opportunities as they arise. Likewise, they might be blind to personal problems within their ranks.

Most Idealists truly shine not when they're managing unruly individuals but when they're pushing around bytes, pixels, abstract numbers, and, especially, information—which gives them a distinct advantage in the current business climate.

Women like Carly Fiorina, CEO of Hewlett-Packard, and techie guru Esther Dyson, CEO of EDventure Holdings, are bringing Idealist sensibilities to the workplace, with brilliant results. Yet not all successful Idealists are aligned with mouses and modems.

Sarah Hoit, for example, took an Idealist approach and applied it to a low-tech, Artisan-like project. She started Explore, a community-based after-school program for kids that focuses on learning projects. Her years of careful planning included an M.B.A. from Harvard; work in national

HOW THE IDEALIST GETS ALONG . . .

. . . WITH VISIONARIES

If Visionaries were a political regime, they'd be a monarchy. Within their royal court, Idealists would be the information officers. Given the right chemistry, Idealists and Visionaries can form partnerships so powerful that they could take over the world. With the Visionary steering the ship and the Idealist fueling it with know-how—look out!

On a personal level, there's no reason why Idealists and Visionaries can't get along. The two respect each other's privacy as well as each other's talents. Both are intensely serious about their work. Idealists don't usually have power issues, so they're not likely to interfere with the Visionary's style of leadership. True, the Visionary's tendency to think hierarchically might rub Idealists the wrong way now and then, but that's small potatoes compared to the greatness these two can achieve when they're well matched.

. . . WITH ARTISANS

The Idealist and the Artisan tend to like each other. Idealists appreciate the Artisan's warmth and personal touch; Artisans appreciate the Idealist's cool head and clear thinking. The two make terrific teammates and can have a great time being in cahoots, finding solutions to problems, and getting tons of work done.

As leaders, however, the Idealist/Artisan partnership lacks one important element: the ability to confidently "present." Both types tend to be shy, and speaking in front of groups can be agonizing for them. Needless to say, neither type possesses a natural dramatic flair—which can be a major handicap when it comes to selling concepts or products.

. . . WITH ADVENTURERS

Desk Set is a fabulous old Katharine Hepburn–Spencer Tracy vehicle, in which Hepburn plays a wildly efficient newsroom librarian—totally Idealist—and Tracy plays a hotheaded, slightly bumbling Adventurer attempting to install a room-sized computer meant to take over Hepburn's job. Of course, Hepburn proves to be more of a computer than the computer is, and Tracy, who is an alleged "efficiency expert," is anything but.

The movie is a great study in Idealist/Adventurer relationships. In the real world, however, the two don't always fall in love. The Adventurer tends to make a big noise, build castles in the air, and get lots of attention for it. This can irritate the hell out of methodical, conscientious Idealists. Worse, the Adventurer can end up making all the speeches and getting all the glory while the Idealist does all the work. Unless they can find a Hepburn-Tracy chemistry, the two types are not natural as partners. But they make fine co-workers and even, sometimes, friends.

service for the White House; a stint as Deputy Director for Americorps Domestic Peace Corps; and a job researching environmental science for "Gore's camp" (Al, that is). While making powerful contacts, she did her homework and discovered that there was a time of day when "we were really losing kids": the gap between the end of the school day and when parents got home from work.

In order to fill that dead zone with meaningful educational experience, Sarah raised $4 million from "heavy hitters" and piloted the Explore programs at twenty schools in seven states. Kids, who ranged from kindergarteners to eighth-graders, responded so well to the curriculum that their scores on national tests literally doubled. In 1998, Explore was in 75 schools, and in 1999, 100-plus locations participated—with 500 more waiting in the wings. Says Sarah, "My team loves the rationality of the business sector, and we love children."

Making It on Her Own

> We didn't have to do the minuets of diplomacy. We got down to business.
> **—MARGARET THATCHER, ON MEETING WITH MIKHAIL GORBACHEV**

Both Idealists and Visionaries get a certain thrill from succeeding in traditionally male business territory.

Cathy Clay, a floor manager for Timber Hill, LLC, and a floor official for the Pacific Exchange, knows what it takes to excel at her Idealist job. She told *Bust* magazine: "You must have the ability to think of many things at one time; be cool-headed because having emotions is considered a weakness; be quick with numbers; have a love for the market, economics, and trading; be a good listener because you need to hear one important voice amidst a sea of others." And what are the rewards, besides financial gains? "The best part of the job is the thrill of winning and wanting to succeed in a competitive situation. Men are used to being in a physically demanding environment. A lot of women who come in have never had to push, shove, get spit upon. . . . But it's all part of the job."

Elise Locker admits that she got a certain thrill when, at the age of twenty-three, her air force job allowed her a level of power that some older, more experienced colleagues could only dream of. "I could tell the contractors to jump and they'd say, 'How high?'," she recalls. "It was a great responsibility, and yes, a bit of a power trip."

In 1980, Marie O. Jackson Thompson was appointed district court judge to the Cambridge [Massachusetts] District Court. "It was a plum of a court and I walked in as the youngest full-time appointment ever made," she remembers. "I was black, I was thirty-two years old, and I was female. Back then it was very significant. Being all those things made it very difficult for me." Yet she succeeded brilliantly, and why? "I guess it was my ability to step back and look objectively at each and every situation. I've had a reputation for being fair, single-minded, and independent over the years. Each and every person has a specialness and uniqueness all their own."

The irony is not lost on Judge Thompson when she says, "I don't judge."

SHELLY LAZARUS
IDEALIST MIND, ARTISAN HEART

> "It's not that I wanted to get ahead, it's that I really thought Herbal Essence Shampoo was the greatest product that ever came along."

It was a business coup heard 'round the world: Shelly Lazarus, in her first year as CEO of Ogilvy & Mather Worldwide, landed the IBM account—worth an estimated $500 to $700 million.

The move was a big one for IBM, which was pulling its accounts from a number of smaller advertising agencies worldwide and consolidating its market image. The transaction was facilitated in part by Abby Kohnstamm, IBM's vice president for corporate marketing, who had worked with Lazarus when Kohnstamm was at American Express. The final deal was built, to a great extent, on the strength of the two women's working relationship—their trust in each other.

The headline-making event was a perfect illustration of the Shelly Lazarus style. She's warm and unpretentious, and equally at ease with the nonconformist "creative" crew at O&M and with top executives of the blue chip clients she serves—including American Express, Kodak, Ford, Mattel, Kraft, and Unilever. When she took over the top spot at O&M in 1997, she chose to stay in her familiar, less-imposing office rather than move into the CEO suite. That same office is cluttered with frog figurines that she and her husband, George, a pediatrician, have collected—or, more often, been given—over the course of their thirty-year marriage. And, oh yes: she is unapologetically devoted to her three children, and makes it clear that being a mother is more important to her than being a CEO.

But for all her modest ways, the woman with the clipped ash blond hair and the signature strand of pearls is a fiercely intelligent strategist who is fascinated with process and totally committed to substance, quality, and, especially, content. She is given credit for laying the groundwork for the

INTUITIVE SCORECARD

Shelly Lazarus

VISIONARY QUALITIES	ARTISAN QUALITIES
✔ Leadership-oriented	_ Champions underdog
_ Named business after self	✔ Family-centric
✔ Works in glamour industry	_ Outdoorsy
✔ Made major leaps within industry	_ Produces tangible product
_ Master of publicity	_ Treats employees like family

IDEALIST QUALITIES	ADVENTURER QUALITIES
✔ Pragmatic	_ Pioneering
_ Works within systems	_ Unconventional
✔ Holds multiple degrees	_ Socially gregarious
✔ Analytical	_ Diversified career path
✔ Long-term commitment to single career	_ Degree unrelated to career

IBM deal, and so much more: before taking over as CEO following the retirement of the charismatic Charlotte Beers (marking the first time one woman succeeded another at a major advertising agency), she steered the company through rough times at its flagship New York City office, helping reverse client and staff losses.

Lazarus deflects glory, however. Though she doesn't come right out and say, "Aw shucks, it was nothing," she talks as if remarkable events simply happen, with little interference from her. "Things just come fast to me," she says. "I'm not an intellectual—I just get it."

Shelly Lazarus was born Rochelle Braff to a CPA father and a homemaker mother. She describes her childhood in suburban Oceanside, New York, where she was reared with two brothers, as "happy, loving, and secure. I had a lot of friends and did well in school—I never thought I could not achieve anything because I was a girl." Though she says she had no goals besides being a wife and mother, she does admit that her father got her interested in stocks at an early age.

After graduating from Midwood High in Brooklyn, where the family moved in 1960, she went to Smith College and majored in psychology. She became interested in advertising in her senior year, when she accompanied a friend to a lecture sponsored by the Advertising Women of New York. "I was amazed you could do something that fun and make a living."

Lazarus got married in 1970 to the Yale man she'd fallen in love with while at Smith. He went on to Columbia Medical School. "I needed to work, but I couldn't type," she recalls. "So I went for my M.B.A. at Columbia so I could get a job that didn't require typing. I just wanted that piece of paper and also wanted to be near George, so I took marketing courses."

While at Columbia, she was recruited by Clairol. "At that time it wasn't illegal for companies to say, 'We just don't take women.' But Clairol was perfectly willing to talk to a woman, and it was one of the very few places that actually had one female product manager. I was completely taken by her—she told me how fabulous her job was, and that she wanted some company because she was the only woman there."

Lazarus became a product manager at Clairol, and found herself among a group of people who were excited about ideas. "This was the cosmetics part of the industry," remembers Lazarus. "There was a lot of product activity, experimentation, and people held themselves accountable for results. It was a terrific environment."

Lazarus soon discovered her own talent for driving a project to completion. "I wouldn't stop till it got to market." Lazarus emphasizes that she focused on the product, not on her own career agenda. "It's not that I wanted to get ahead," she says, "it's that I really thought Herbal Essence Shampoo was the greatest product that ever came along."

After two years, Lazarus was approached by Ogilvy & Mather, a company she'd become acquainted with during her time as an intern at General Foods. Though she had no plans to leave Clairol—"It could have been a job for life"—she thought carefully about the most exciting aspects of her job and came to realize that she was turned on by interacting with

SHELLY LAZARUS ON . . .

ENEMY-FREE LIVING: "When it's not about your personal agenda, when it's not about getting ahead, when it's not about your winning over another human being, but about believing passionately in the content of whatever it is you're doing, it's hard for people to dislike you."

LIFE SKILLS: "There are two trump cards everyone should have in life: writing and speaking."

FEAR OF BEING FIRED: "I was never afraid to express my family-first priorities. The worst thing they can do is fire you—they can't take your children!"

BEING THE PIED PIPER: "The whole idea is to engage people in your mission, make them see things as you do, make them care about it more than anything else."

A TWO-CAREER MARRIAGE: "I have a partnership with George. When people ask him if it bothers him that I make more money than he does, his response is, 'I hope she'll continue to make even more money!'"

advertising agencies. "I was less interested in manufacturing and those kinds of things, so I thought, maybe I should just spend all my time at the agency."

Lazarus has been at Ogilvy & Mather for more than twenty-five years, starting out as a junior account executive and working her way up to chairman and CEO. Today she has offices in Latin America, Asia, Europe, and around North America. Two years in a row, 1998 and 1999, she was named the fourth most powerful woman in American business by *Fortune,* which described her as "pragmatic and famously unpretentious."

Indeed, when asked about her long-time loyalty to O&M, Lazarus once told *Forbes* the story of when she was having a difficult pregnancy and was ordered to stay in bed. "After two weeks I couldn't take it anymore and went back to work," she recalls, but the president of the agency wouldn't let her ride the subway. Instead, he sent his car to drive her back and forth to work. "At that moment I became a lifetime employee of Ogilvy."

Over the years, it has been that kind of down-to-earth, reality-based thinking that has made Shelly Lazarus a shining star in the hotheaded world of advertising. Her business philosophy: "We build brands by building the relationship with the consumers. So at its heart, our business is all about respect for the consumers, for their intelligence, and for their values and emotions—it's about connecting with them in ways that are insightful, meaningful, and real. It's just that simple."

JOANNA LAU
MAKING AMERICA WORK

> *"My advice? Just learn and learn."*

When Joanna Lau emigrated to the United States from Hong Kong, her first job was running a sewing machine in a New York City sweatshop. It was a cruel welcome for the seventeen-year-old Lau, who had been a brilliant high school student in her native country and had never worked, much less sewn in a cramped, noisy factory. After three days on the job she told her mother, "This is not what I want."

Joanna's mother, a widow with eight children, knew little of life outside the tight Chinese community into which she had settled. So Joanna set out on her own, encountering language barriers, sexism, and "invisibility" along the way. Today she is president and chairman of LAU Technologies, a multimillion-dollar company specializing in defense work.

INTUITIVE SCORECARD

Joanna Lau

VISIONARY QUALITIES	ARTISAN QUALITIES
✔ Leadership-oriented	_ Champions underdog
✔ Named business after self	_ Family-centric
_ Works in glamour industry	_ Outdoorsy
✔ Made major leaps within industry	✔ Produces tangible product
_ Master of publicity	_ Treats employees like family

IDEALIST QUALITIES	ADVENTURER QUALITIES
✔ Pragmatic	✔ Pioneering
✔ Works within systems	_ Unconventional
✔ Holds multiple degrees	_ Socially gregarious
✔ Analytical	_ Diversified career path
✔ Long-term commitment to single career	_ Degree unrelated to career

Lau's life has been a learning journey in which she has constantly moved away from what she didn't want and studied hard to find out what she did want—and then taught herself how to get it.

In two decades of brave moves, the first seems to have been the hardest: earning her high school diploma. In unfamiliar America, while her mother and sisters stayed behind and sewed in the garment district, Lau secured herself a minority scholarship and enrolled in boarding school. "The first day," Lau recalls, "I had to take a hygiene exam. I had no clue what the word meant." She didn't like the school and barely spoke the language, but she did what she had to do: she lowered her head and plowed through, graduating in the top ten of her class.

Again on a scholarship, Lau went to the State University of New York at Stony Brook, on Long Island. There she studied computer science and mathematics, and also worked as a disc jockey at the college radio station. Upon graduation she took a job at General Electric in Binghamton, New York. She was twenty-three years old, the only woman in her group, and the only one without an engineering degree, which was a handicap because her job was centered on Boeing commercial aircraft.

Lau took advantage of GE's tuition reimbursement program and studied for her master's degree in engineering. "I was one of thirteen students, again the only woman, and I ranked second to last in my class," she remembers. "I struggled through. I stuck it out. Then I was transferred to an even more male-dominated department." For three months, says Lau, she felt invisible. Then she took a weekend seminar in how to dress for success—this was in the early '80s—and abandoned her jeans-and-sneakers garb. "I went shopping," she says, "and I came in with a suit. This guy looked at me and said, 'Are you new?' I learned that to get noticed you have to send a message."

Though she was no longer completely invisible, Lau was treated like a gofer by many of her colleagues. After two years she transferred to a GE plant in Virginia where she was exposed to marketing. "I really liked the marketing side, the glamour, so I went to the marketing director and told him I'd like to move to his department. He told me I'd have to start over at entry level and get an M.B.A. I didn't do that."

Instead, Lau got married and moved to Massachusetts, where she took a job working on "the factory of the future" with GE. "It was a different culture—thirty-five young people, energetic, ready to go, everything 'can do.' I planted myself in that factory, trained eighteen guys who never shaved." Her interaction with factory workers would prove invaluable.

When Lau was passed over for a promotion that she was squarely in line for, she knew it was again time to move on. She got an attractive offer from computer giant Digital Equipment. Lau devised a rock-solid plan to help the company improve its product delivery. However, her proposal, which would reduce the size of certain departments, proved to be too threatening to the top-heavy company and was met not only with rejection but with veiled hostility. Frustrated, Lau packed her bags once again.

JOANNA LAU ON . . .

CHANGING JOBS: "Do a self-inventory. Look at what you've done. Are you learning anything, moving forward? You have to make yourself marketable."

LABOR-MANAGEMENT RELATIONS: "I learned so much dealing with union people. When you're in an office, you only think of P&L and scheduling; you think people are not working hard enough on the floor. These people work really hard and are not listened to—they're the ones who have an idea of how the shop should be run."

FAMILY: "I asked my husband, should I go for my M.B.A. or have a kid? He said, 'It's cheaper to get an M.B.A.' A few years later he said, 'No Ph.D., please!' So now we have a little girl."

INCLUSIVE MANAGEMENT: "When you come from a family of eight, you learn to be inclusive. My receptionist, my front line, my custodian . . . they're the most important people, in my opinion. I treat everybody with respect."

SELF-IMPROVEMENT: "Learning is a great part of life. My advice? Just learn and learn."

Lau next took a consulting job with Phoenix-based Bowmar Industries, which had been making circuit and control boards for Bradley fighting vehicles for nearly two decades. The company was in trouble; quality had slipped and deadlines were being missed. Meanwhile, defense spending had been reduced, so in 1989 Bowmar put its Acton, Massachusetts, division up for sale. Lau saw an opportunity.

"I looked at the system they were running—it was obsolete. I analyzed it and knew how I could keep it going." Lau got to work creating a business plan with the help of financial experts, including her husband. She scraped together more than $400,000 of her own money, raised another $450,000 from twenty-four employees, and got a loan from Shawmut Bank. "There was a story in the newspaper saying that banks don't support minority-owned businesses," she recalls of her loan process. "So I went after them. It was great." She led the bid for the company and acquired it in March 1990 for $3.1 million.

Lau wasted no time getting the company back on track: she got on a plane and personally visited every one of its customers and vendors. She outlined her new plans and gave her personal guarantee that product would be delivered to specifications and on time. The company hasn't missed a deadline since.

LAU Technologies has done so well that it was presented with the Contractor Excellence Award from the U.S. Army for its part in Operation Desert Storm. "That put us on the map," says Lau. "We were the choice provider." Lau herself was recognized as *Inc.* magazine's National Entrepreneur of the Year in 1995 and has also been honored by the U.S. Small Business Administration for her participation in the Department of Defense's Mentor-Protégé program.

As her company grows, Joanna Lau continues to keep her eye on the big picture and to take things one step at a time. "We've built an important reputation," she says. "We're not a megamillions company. As a corporation we can spin off, take earnings, reinvest. But if we got too big, we couldn't be personal."

"Being personal" is a big issue for Lau; she firmly believes that much of her success has to do with customer communications. She has no tolerance for middlemen and makes it a point to have end users deal directly with the engineers and designers who are working on a project.

As for her executive team, Lau admits that she's made mistakes— "Finding good partners is tough," she says—but is happy with her current setup. "My husband is now the COO," she says. "He is my strength. He is interested in negotiations, bidding, Wall Street, and my specialty is operations, the quality side of the world. The two of us do very well together."

THE REVEREND MARGARET BULLITT-JONAS
FULFILLING A HOLY HUNGER

> **"I was created with an infinite longing that only the infinite can satisfy."**

Margaret Bullitt, born in 1951, faced a life of privilege and demand. She had a lot to live up to: her father was a highly respected professor at Harvard, and her mother was a wealthy trustee of Radcliffe. She and her family grew up in a spacious home on the Harvard campus, and she spent a year attending a Swiss boarding school.

So who was Margaret's childhood hero? Not a character out of classic children's literature, but one from a TV cartoon: Mighty Mouse. "He was powerful and his job was to rescue people," she recalls. "I was fascinated by that image; I had fantasies of being the one who would come to the rescue."

Ultimately, Margaret did come to the rescue—of herself and her family. But that wasn't until she was in her thirties. First, as a brilliant student, she earned a B.A. with honors in Russian literature from Stanford University; worked as a VISTA volunteer in downtown Philadelphia; earned a doctorate in comparative literature from Harvard; and, along the way, developed a secret eating disorder that nearly killed her.

Most of Margaret Bullitt's life was marked by outward accomplishment and inward turmoil—an all-too-typical Idealist state. "I grew up feeling that it was important to be the best," she recalls. "There was very much an ethic of achievement, of excellence. I also grew up being taught that it was important to be kind and nice and generous, so I had somewhat competing value systems going on."

It seemed that Bullitt managed to keep the balance between being a top-ranked student and a decent person. In the mid-1970s her life looked like the perfect picture of an academic star: she was fulfilling her doctoral requirements, was assisting in teaching college courses, and had won a fellowship. But privately Bullitt was bingeing, stuffing herself with whole pies, stacks of pancakes, and entire jars of peanut butter. She could gain ten pounds in four days, but then would furiously exercise and diet to mask her trespasses. "I used to numb myself with food, using food as a way of swallowing anger and sadness. I remember how isolated and ashamed I felt. . . . But of course food addicts are people who have lost control of their eating, and no amount of willpower or good intentions is enough to get it back."

Her life reached a crisis point while studying at Harvard. "Being caught up in addiction is like being caught in a war zone," she recalls. "I had almost no energy for anything but trying to stave off the irresistible crav-

INTUITIVE SCORECARD

Margaret Bullitt-Jonas

VISIONARY QUALITIES
- ✔ Leadership-oriented
- _ Named business after self
- _ Works in glamour industry
- _ Made major leaps within industry
- _ Master of publicity

ARTISAN QUALITIES
- ✔ Champions underdog
- ✔ Family-centric
- ✔ Outdoorsy
- _ Produces tangible product
- _ Treats employees like family

IDEALIST QUALITIES
- _ Pragmatic
- ✔ Works within systems
- ✔ Holds multiple degrees
- ✔ Analytical
- _ Long-term commitment to single career

ADVENTURER QUALITIES
- _ Pioneering
- _ Unconventional
- _ Socially gregarious
- ✔ Diversified career path
- ✔ Degree unrelated to career

ings that had taken hold of me." So she took a break from academia and went to work as a residential coordinator for a group of schizophrenic men. Her interaction with them opened a window to her self-perception; she started to recognize her own deep loneliness, her mother's ongoing depression, and the effects of her father's alcoholism. Eventually she helped to organize a family intervention on behalf of her father, yet she herself remained trapped in addiction and pain.

In 1982, at the age of thirty-one and after years of futile therapy, diet workshops, and hospital-sponsored programs, Bullitt joined Overeaters Anonymous. "That's when I really took hold of my life," she remembers. "I changed the work I was doing, I changed my friends, I found a man I instantly adored and eventually married—everything just kind of turned around and took off. In the process of getting into recovery I began to take seriously my spiritual longing."

Following her burgeoning faith, Margaret Bullitt-Jonas entered a seminary, and graduated four years later from Episcopal Divinity School. "In one way it was a complete surprise to me because that was not a dream I had when I was little," she says. "I did consider becoming a nun. But I was so in love with my husband-to-be I decided that wasn't for me." Bullitt-Jonas was ordained as an Episcopal priest in 1989, and shortly thereafter gave birth to a son, Sam. "I was infertile, so this was a miracle birth," she says. "What a gift!"

Bullitt-Jonas was serving at a parish in the Boston area, teaching at the seminary, and leading retreats and conferences throughout the United States and Canada, when another event changed the shape of her life: she decided to write a book.

Already fifteen years into recovery, she set out to create an account of her past experiences that was both "loving and true." What she hadn't expected was that the writing process itself would inspire her to find a deeper level of healing. She found that "until I learned to tell the story of my life with compassion for everyone in it, for every single character, then I would never learn to be fully compassionate toward myself."

Holy Hunger: A Memoir of Desire was published by Knopf in 1999. The *New York Times Book Review* reported that the book's "emphasis on communicative relationships (with humans and God) and on individual responsibility seems to have allowed Bullitt-Jonas not just to forgive her parents but to accept partial responsibility for her disease." *Kirkus Reviews* commented, "Recovering her own identity is the memoir's

MARGARET BULLITT-JONAS ON . . .

LISTENING: "I think we struggle in this country to listen to each other. We are all the beloved. It's just that we look different, we sound different, we come from different countries. The challenge is, how can we create a community where we can honor the best in each other?"

SETTING BOUNDARIES: "Saying no is like exercising a muscle. As a Lenten discipline a couple of years ago I decided to say no to every single request for those forty days. I wanted to notice what ego issues made me keep saying yes. I learned a lot about my fears; I learned about the fear of being forgotten, and the wish to be at the center of things—all that ego stuff."

FAMILY LIFE: "My family is one of my great joys. If I were single I'd be a workaholic and traveling around. . . . When I come home they hold me and tell me they love me."

GETTING THINGS DONE: "I like order. I have an appointment book and everything is in that. Some things I tend to want to do right away. Then I make lists—I could not survive without my lists!"

MANAGING STRESS: "I guess I believe that some level of stress is necessary and healthy—you need it just to be alive. But as far as excess stress, the key for me is getting exercise regularly. I run several times a week, somewhere between five and seven miles."

ADVICE FOR WOMEN: "Trust the longing of your heart. Trust your desire to be loved—because you *are* loved. Trust that there is a presence in you that longs to be expressed. Trust yourself."

goal. . . . She clears a space she can live in. An encouraging testimonial to the rewards of following a wise suggestion: 'Heal thyself.'"

Holy Hunger has had an impact on many levels. Besides its effect on Bullitt-Jonas's mental and spiritual health, it has become a touchstone for many people recovering from, or in the throes of, eating disorders. Though she does not host seminars about eating disorders, she does draw followers across the country to her sermons about loneliness, love, and addiction. "Going numb is a popular way of handling pain," she told a Cleveland parish in 1999. "We live in a very addictive culture. Feel a little uncomfortable? Buy something. Take a little drink. Have a little bite. If we aren't sensitive to what we are really looking for, searching for, hungry for, the culture around us will tell us in a heartbeat."

Bullitt-Jonas now lives happily with her son and husband in a Boston suburb. Her mother, who teaches Buddhist meditation, occupies an upstairs apartment. "It has worked out wonderfully," she says. "It's very grounding." What has become a challenge is Bullitt-Jonas's increasingly public life. Last year, she was appointed as one of the two chaplains to the Episcopal Church's House of Bishops—the first woman to receive such an honor. As her recognition builds, she is learning to manage her time more closely. "I'm trying not to pick up the phone every time it rings," she says with a smile.

One of her focal points continues to be the courses she teaches about prayer at the Episcopal Divinity School. "That is really my passion," she says. "In God's eyes I am number one and you are number one. To learn to sit there in that place where you are completely the apple of God's eye, that is what prayer is all about. Then we are free to go out in the world, and it's okay to be number ten and number twenty. But," reminds Margaret Bullitt-Jonas, "that's not where one's ultimate identity is found. Everyone is number one."

ADVICE FOR IDEALISTS

- **LEARN THE POWER OF FLEXIBILITY.** As a leader, try not to overschedule or micromanage others; it will probably result in a loss of productivity. For instance, an Adventurer might work best after hours, while an Artisan might turn into a star performer with the help of telecommuting or flextime. Likewise, make allowances for social interaction among your team members. It does wonders for morale.

- **GIVE YOURSELF UNSTRUCTURED DAYS NOW AND THEN.** Idealists tend to follow a set plan, day after day and week after week. Whenever there's an opening in their schedules, they immediately fill it with *something* — be it an afternoon spent catching up on paperwork, fifteen minutes returning phone calls, or an hour at the gym. By not scheduling yourself, you open yourself up to the unexpected, and that, in turn, can wake up your creativity and your deepest thoughts.

- **GET HELP WITH TASKS THAT ARE DIFFICULT FOR YOU.** Idealists, when presented with challenges, tend to want to conquer them on their own — but that's not always the best approach. When writing a letter, for instance, recruit the help of someone who has a way with words. He or she might have the perfect phrase to get your point across, or see flaws in your work that you wouldn't have noticed. Likewise, if you have a people problem, don't keep it all to yourself. Others may have insights or actual information that can help you to understand puzzling situations.

- **DON'T JUDGE A PERSON BY ONE OR TWO ISOLATED INCIDENTS.** If a new co-worker is late to an important meeting, it doesn't automatically mean that he's a flake. If a recent hire makes a mistake on a report, it's not necessarily because she's incompetent. Look at the big picture, and reserve judgment until you can make a full, balanced assessment.

- **PARTICIPATE.** Do you hate mandatory staff meetings? Rather than sit through them, watching the clock, bring something to the table — even if it's just an announcement or an observation. Are you completely bored by water-cooler chat? Rather than shun the socializing entirely, butt in with a well-timed joke once in a while, then be on your way.

- **FORGIVE YOURSELF YOUR TRESPASSES.** Idealists beat themselves up when they make a mistake, or even a minor blunder. This is not only a waste of energy, but over time it can create a fear of taking risks and can even result in a distaste for your job in general. Lighten up, fix the problem, forgive yourself, move on.

- **LET YOUR SENSE OF PLAY COME OUT.** Idealists generally have wonderful senses of humor, and love a good prank now and then. Have some fun.

9

THE Adventurer

Flamboyant. Unpredictable.
Unconventional.
Free-spirited. Dynamic.

Back in the 1960s, a study was done that determined that entrepreneurs and juvenile delinquents had nearly identical personality traits. Both groups proved to have little respect for authority and showed a willingness to take enormous risks, in spite of the possibility of bad consequences. They tested as self-starters who did things on their own time; rebelled against outside structure and discipline; and believed that rules and regulations were for other people.

More than anything, the study suggested that each group had an intense inner voice that needed to be heard above the harmonious drone of the crowd. In the case of juvenile delinquents, that voice was expressed in destructive ways. In the case of entrepreneurs, it was made into something positive, creative, and constructive.

Adventurers are born entrepreneurs. Whether or not they start their own businesses, they want to take their impulses and run with them. Like juvenile delinquents, Adventurers are not interested in methodical, sensible ways of getting ahead: they want to think big, to leap-frog over conventional, conservative teachings, and hit the jackpot—and they want plenty of attention along the way. When successful, Adventurers are the rock-and-roll stars of the business world.

Inside the Adventurer's Mind

Adventurers are courageous creatures who dare to try, dare to fail, and dare to win. They run on passion; their idea of success is not a stable position or a secure retirement but an epic life filled with interesting chapters.

In history books, you'll know the Adventurer by the risks she takes. Think of near-mythic figures like Isadora Duncan and Annie Oakley. Picture Nellie Bly, the girl reporter who in 1889 circled the globe in seventy-two days. She wrote daily dispatches about the perils of her journey; published on page one of the *New York World*, her stories were a national sensation.

Clare Boothe Luce was an Adventurer who made her own challenges. In her teens she was a crusader for women's rights; in her twenties she was a magazine editor; in her thirties she wrote three hit plays. At the age of forty she became a congresswoman, and then served as a U.S. ambassador. Luce's life was "full of double dares," and the same could be said about most Adventurers. Whether running a company, playing professional sports, or chasing down an illusive microorganism, the Adventurer is in her glory when she's at the edge of new frontiers.

Where Adventurers Come From

> It is vain to say human beings ought to be satisfied with tranquillity:
> they must have action, and they will make it if they cannot find it.
> — GEORGE ELIOT

Are Adventurers born or made? Is their spirited, unconventional approach to life a product of nature or nurture? Perhaps Auntie Mame can shed some light on the subject. In all of literature there is no better example of the Adventurer spirit than she. Though she's been heavily mythicized over the years (she even got her own musical comedy), the real Mame Dennis, if her nephew Patrick's account is to be believed, had a brother who was her exact opposite. He was cold and conservative, while Mame was as madcap, daredevilish, and liberal as they come. During Prohibition (and beyond), she hosted fantastic parties that were the very model of multiculturalism at a time when the concept didn't even exist. She sent her nephew Patrick to a school so progressive that clothing was optional. And nothing angered her more than lock-jawed "Aryans from Darien" who valued their "restricted" neighborhoods where Jews and blacks were not welcome.

During the Depression, when Mame lost everything but her grand apartment on Astor Place, she was fired from a slew of menial jobs. Her last was at Macy's, where she was dismissed because she couldn't remember how to write up a cash sale. Yet Mame traveled the world, climbed mountains, sailed seas, absorbed art, culture, music, and language—and wrote a book about it all.

All of which suggests that certain women may be born with an Adventurer streak.

Shelley Reich, founder and CEO of Royal Heirlooms Home Collections, Inc., says that as a child she "always liked the opposite of what everyone else liked." She grew up in California, a place that suited her. When her parents moved the family to Idaho, Shelley learned the depth of her independent spirit: at the age of fourteen she made up her mind to get out as soon as possible. She started taking night classes, graduated high school three semesters early, and enrolled at the University of California at sixteen. By the time she was twenty-one she had already had a career in computers and was working as a runway model in Japan, pulling down $30,000 a month. From there she bicycled through Europe for a year; worked in sales at Dean Witter; became an interior designer; and then started a company that creates sophisticated home furnishings. "It's been a wild ride," she admits, "and I'd have it no other way."

Cherie Whaples-Elliot, a Connecticut antiques appraiser (who also has Artisan qualities) always had a taste for action. Of her childhood she says, "I was stimulated by mayhem. I wanted to cause trouble. If there was nothing to do I would just find somebody and beat them up. If I could pop somebody's tooth out that was the most satisfying thing I could do in a day. I'd be grounded for a month but behind my parents' backs I was like, 'Whee! That was fun.'" Cherie no longer bullies others for kicks. "But I do crave action," she says, "in more positive ways."

The Walls Come Tumbling Down

> **Women have the feeling that since they didn't make the rules, the rules have nothing to do with them.**
>
> **— DIANE JOHNSON**

Adventurers don't want to be fenced in. That essential truth translates into a tendency to bust through barriers and boundaries. Lots of Adventurer women in history have been the first of their gender to accomplish something that only men had done before. In the arts, Adventurer women trailblaze new forms; in business, they ignore hierarchies and unwritten rules. Many have no respect for protocol and refuse to believe that anyone is "better" than anyone else. The Adventurer practices a kind of unstudied omniculturalism and an attitude that is inclusive, rather than exclusive.

Josephine Baker, for instance, fought against racial segregation her whole life. It wasn't enough that she successfully integrated nightclubs and theaters across America; she also created a "rainbow tribe" by adopting twelve children of different races and religions.

Categories, divisions, and conformity are the Adventurer's enemies. She has a kind of buffet mentality and likes to pick and choose her favorite dishes from life's smorgasbord. Some Adventurers go one step further and actually reinvent themselves throughout their careers and their lives. When you look at Madonna, you can see an extreme version of the Adventurer style: she's looked like Marilyn Monroe, Eva Perón, and a geisha girl, all in the course of a few years.

Jane Fonda's Adventurer spirit is more than skin deep. She started her career as a Barbarella sex kitten; became a Vietnam war protester; triumphed as a serious actress; made millions as a workout guru; and is now a ranch-residing philanthropist.

It's no wonder that many Adventurers still don't know what they want to be when they grow up—even if they're forty. The idea of sticking with one thing is against her nature; the Adventurer reserves the right to change her mind.

The Meaning of Travel

> She dreamed, lulled by the train, of getting off at heaven or New York City, whichever she got to first.
>
> —MARY LEE SETTLE, THE SCAPEGOAT

The lure of travel, whether armchair or actual, fills many an Adventurer's dreams. Adventurers are not merely itchy to observe landmarks and lifestyles in faraway places; they are freestyle anthropologists who yearn to immerse themselves in other cultures and experience life from different perspectives.

Adventurers will live among Buddhist nuns in Tibet, work as card dealers in Monaco, spend a season surfing in Australia—anything that allows them to be not a tourist but a participant. Some take short-term jobs just so they can save enough money to hit the road, then do it again when they run out of funds. Lauren Hutton was the first model to work with a contract; it allowed her months of time off to travel. At last count she'd visited Africa twenty-six times and now scuba dives in remote coral reefs all over the world.

Sue Navarretta has an unusual career for an Adventurer: she's a registered nurse. Born not-wealthy in an affluent New England town, Sue's "ticket out of mediocrity" came when she was twenty and married a talented chef who whisked her away to California. He opened a successful restaurant there, but Sue, who had gotten pregnant almost immediately after taking her vows and

how to spot
an adventurer

No matter how professionally she's dressed, the Adventurer's strong sense of style usually gives her away. Look for:

• **Unusual accessories.** When an Adventurer suits up in business gear, she'll often let her personality come through in her jewelry, shoes, scarf, and handbag. Note, however, that though they are accessory queens, Adventurers have little feeling for "good" jewelry or pedigree leather goods; they'd rather have dramatic, unexpected pieces, whether they cost $9,000 or 99 cents.

• **Contrasting colors.** Adventurers like colors that play off one another and are unlikely to wear muted or monochromatic outfits. Look for strong, contrasting hues — mustard-colored beads against a black dress, for instance, or a spring green shirt with a plum suit.

• **Cutting-edge style.** Adventurers love being ahead of trends, and especially relish wearing new pieces by hot designers (or cheap knockoffs). When given the chance, the Adventurer will always choose the extreme over the conservative. She likes very pointy/square-toed shoes; very short/long skirts; and very big/small handbags.

• **Hair with personality.** No anchorwoman 'dos for this gal. If she's a spiky blonde or a cascading redhead, or if she's got her black hair lacquered into a complex arrangement, she's probably an Adventurer. Note: Some Adventurers change their hair color as often as Visionaries change their nail polish.

• **Good stories.** If you compliment a woman on one of her accessories, and she launches into a lively story about the piece, it's 90 percent certain she's the Adventurer type.

had given birth to a baby girl, wasn't cut out to keep the home fires burning. "Within six months of having my daughter I woke up one day and wanted to be free. He supported us for a while, then I got a job as a waitress." Sue soon learned that motherhood and restaurant life didn't mix, so she started taking courses at a local college in order to qualify for nursing school. She was accepted at an East Coast university. "I packed the car and drove across the country with this angel, my daughter—she was five years old—and $6,000 in cash, all the money I had in the world."

Sue graduated knowing that her degree was an open-ended ticket to anywhere. She moved to Oregon and worked in a drug rehab facility and as a home care nurse. Then she came back east and got a job at a prestigious, big-city hospital. She's still there—for now—but she's changed assignments a number of times, always seeking a more challenging position. Today she's head of the neurosurgical operating room. It's a high-stress job that could give ulcers to some women, but Sue loves being at the cutting edge (no pun intended) of innovative surgical procedures and relishes the challenge of working with new patients and new problems every day.

The Social Butterfly

"I have a huge capacity for new people." That's how Lauren Caldwell explains her astounding social energy. Lauren, a New York City stylist, surrounds herself with crowds of interesting characters. "I'm a pickup artist," she says. "I love people who love what they're doing—I'm attracted to their energy." It doesn't stop there: Lauren is a natural-born networker who makes little separation between her personal life and her professional life (a trait that is alien to most Visionaries). "I'm constantly introducing people to each other," she says. "There's a silver thread—I connect them all. Whether a person likes to collect something or make something or do something, there's always someone else I know who would be interested." Lauren has literally hundreds of friends. She is selective, however: "I like people who bounce off each other—what I'm looking for is combustion. And enjoyment."

YOU MAY BE AN ADVENTURER IF . . .

You've never had a real job.
Your filing system consists of bulletin boards, Post-it notes, and stacks of papers on the desk and floor.
You'd rather figure it out yourself than read the instructions.
You're a brilliant procrastinator.
The last time you were on time for a meeting, your co-workers gave you a standing ovation.
You use a Mystic 8-Ball and a pair of dice to help you make executive decisions.
You once hired an efficiency expert to organize your office and couldn't find anything for six months.
Your address is "The Road Less Traveled."
The office Christmas parties you organize are actually fun.
You delegate dull tasks, even if they're important, and keep all the juicy jobs to yourself, even if they aren't that important.
You own a VW Beetle and/or an iMac.
When you announce that you have a fabulous new idea, everybody groans.
You truly believe that the only bad publicity is no publicity at all.

Adventurers don't usually sit still long enough to be mentors or protégées, and they lack the patience to be apprentices. However, like Lauren, they can be great matchmakers. When an Adventurer is fired up she'll work the phone like a madwoman and in the course of an hour arrange a job interview for one friend, find a resource for another, and introduce two interested parties to each other. Adventurers are the ones to call when you don't know who else to call—say, when you need to find plastic sushi for a party, a hip phrase to describe baby boomers, or a helper who can photocopy your proposal and deliver it—tonight.

Once again, this networking/matchmaking talent is evidence of an intellectual agility. No connection is an island; the Adventurer finds commonalities between all kinds of people.

How Adventurers Learn

School was hard—I think it's not there to teach, but to smooth down the edges so you fit into the round hole.

— CHER

Adventurers don't learn by rote. They're not interested in studying formulas or memorizing data; they would much rather learn by doing. It's unusual to find an Adventurer who has a string of degrees after her name, because she studies at the University of the Streets. She embraces new experiences and will take on interesting challenges even if the financial rewards aren't particularly promising.

One hallmark of the college graduate Adventurer is that her degree often has no relation to her career. Her interests evolve over her lifetime and she runs with them, while drawing from past experiences.

The Adventurer likes the challenge of figuring things out for herself and would rather invent new ways of doing things than follow standard procedures. She throws away the road map, ignores case histories, and avoids following instructions. However, she will seek out inspiration wherever she can find it. In the kitchen, for instance, she might browse through cookbooks but will rarely follow recipes.

Obviously, Adventure-style procedures can be disastrous at, say, a nuclear power plant. However, the Adventurer approach works well in creative pursuits such as writing a novel or masterminding a runway fashion show.

One warning note to managers: Adventurers don't want to do the same thing twice and, in fact, often can't achieve consistent results. This is because, like the cook riffing in the kitchen, she doesn't always remember exactly how she got from A to Z—or what combinations of ingredients made her fajitas taste so good.

Fear of Boredom

Life is short. Eat dessert first.

— ANONYMOUS

Some people fear financial failure, personal disasters, ill health, or isolation. Adventurers fear boredom.

"I'd rather be starving and broke than go through a routine," says Lauren Caldwell. "Whenever I took a full-time job and it got too mundane, I quit. Even on boring freelance jobs, I've taken different routes to and from the site just to see what I could discover. I need that visual stimulation."

Lauren's a talented artist whose styling work is in demand. Even so, she's sometimes tempted to take a break and go work the counter at a coffee bar. "To me that's interesting because I've never done it before. I'd like to watch all the people, see the comings and goings." As Lauren well knows, the Adventurer must keep herself stimulated, engaged, and entertained. "I am my own class of third-graders," she says.

Though fear of boredom may seem a frivolous motivation, there is a real reason why boredom is poisonous to Adventurers: many have a self-destructive streak. When the hungry Adventurer spirit is not being properly fed, the Adventurer easily falls into negative behavior patterns, which can range from depression to various forms of self-abuse.

When handed a project, the Adventurer usually drums up excitement about it right away. Even before a lick of work gets done she creates a buzz, and can make even minor projects seem special and important. The reason for this M.O. is twofold: on one hand, the Adventurer has a real talent for P.R. and likes putting a bit of P.T. Barnum into everything she does. It's fun for her to make a splash. On the other hand, by making a big deal of things the Adventurer assures herself that her talents and energies aren't going to waste.

Adventurers in History

It's hard to imagine three more exciting Adventurers than editor **Diana Vreeland,** *Renaissance woman* **Clare Booth Luce,** *and entertainer* **Josephine Baker.** *Their backgrounds and their professional lives were very different, yet each woman was self-taught; each had a flamboyant and public persona; and each lived a life that glittered with unconventional style, variety, outrageous daring, grand ambition, and a refusal to recognize limitations. And isn't it interesting to know that Baker and Vreeland actually met one day, quite accidentally, in a Paris movie theater?*

DIANA VREELAND
STYLE MEETS SUBSTANCE

> **"I've always had an abhorrence of *popularity*. In fashion, you have to be one step ahead of the public."**

"I'm sure I chose to be born in Paris," wrote Diana Vreeland in 1984. "I'm sure I chose my parents. I'm sure I chose to be called Diana. And I'm sure I chose to have a nurse called Pink."

Besides having a childhood caretaker named Pink, Diana Vreeland led a life that could scarcely have been more colorful.

Born Diana Dalziel in 1903 (or thereabouts) to a privileged family, the young Diana studied ballet and hobnobbed via her parents with artists and intellectuals, including Diaghilev and Nijinsky. The Dalziels moved to New York City to escape World War I, and there Diana began to show her stunning personal style. Influenced by the Ballet Russe, whose flamboyance enchanted the young student of dance, she chose to emphasize her dramatic features, including her gaunt body and her long, prominent nose. At thirteen she took up the then-scandalous habit of painting her fingernails with bright red lacquer; at her coming-out party in 1923, she covered her face and her arms in dead-white makeup and wore a dress adorned with fringe.

Diana married handsome banker Reed Vreeland in 1924 and kept up a globe-trotting romance with him that lasted until his death forty-six years later. The couple lived for a short time in Albany, where Diana bore the first of two sons. Then it was off to London, where the Vreelands lived—in between lavish trips to faraway lands—for nearly ten years.

In London, Vreeland opened a lingerie shop, an enterprise that she referred to as her "first job." She got her design ideas from Paris and hired nuns in convents to do the fine handiwork. Most of Vreeland's time, however, was taken up with being a *mannequin du monde*. She loved to dance and made such a dramatic impression at posh nightclubs that couture designers gave her gowns just so their creations could be seen on her.

When the Vreelands relocated to New York, Diana caught the eye of Carmel Snow, editor-in-chief of *Harper's Bazaar*. Though Vreeland knew nothing of the publishing world, she took up Snow's invitation to contribute to the magazine and created a column called "Why don't you . . . ?" which gave readers outrageous suggestions for creating their own personal style. Her recommendations for 1936 included covering the bathroom floor in fake leopard skin; wearing bright yellow shantung pajamas with carved coral bracelets; and clipping bushes into the shapes of peacocks and poodles.

In time Vreeland was appointed fashion editor and then editor-in-chief of *Harper's Bazaar,* a position she held for twenty-three years. She became known as an international tastemaker with a fashion view that was informed as much by the runway in Paris as the harems of Morocco, the royal courts of Russia, and the streets of Bombay. ("Pink is the navy blue of India," she once declared.) Richard Avedon observed, "Vreeland invented the fashion editor. Before, it was society ladies who put hats on other society ladies."

Vreeland's indelible mark was made when she became editor-in-chief of *Vogue.* The year was 1963, and Vreeland recognized that the Sixties were a pivotal time not only in fashion but in all of culture. Her work emphasized the youthful, the eccentric, and the wild. It was she who turned Twiggy, Verushka, Marisa Berenson, Edie Sedgwick, and Lauren Hutton into top models, and presented imperfect celebrities like Cher and Mick Jagger as fashion icons.

For eight heady years, Vreeland ruled *Vogue* in her own Adventurer way. She was capricious and exciting, and known for outbursts such as, "I want everybody to write with quill pens!" Tied down to her demanding job, she satisfied her wanderlust in the pages of her magazine. "I couldn't take off for a few weeks to see, say, a bit of India," she wrote in *D.V.,* "but I could send groups of photographers, editors, and models." Vreeland always had a strong idea of what images she wanted. "It wasn't what they *might* find, it was what they *had* to find. And if they couldn't find it, fake it."

Diana Vreeland wore rouge on her ears. Truman Capote said she looked like a cross between the Red Queen and a flamingo. She had her Manhattan apartment designed to look like "a garden in hell." And she was very particular about her rituals. "I had a bridge table brought in with my lunch on it—a peanut butter and marmalade sandwich. And a shot of scotch. Never took anyone out to lunch. Never, ever. The business lunch destroys the work of the day. It's got to go."

In 1971, Vreeland was dismissed from *Vogue* because her vision—as well as her spending habits—were deemed too excessive for the new era. But another opportunity immediately unfolded: she was appointed special consultant to the Costume Institute of the Metropolitan Museum of Art. It was a bold move on the part of the museum, but not much of a gamble: Jackie Onassis and a group of other supporters had raised enough money to pay Vreeland's salary for two years.

Vreeland mounted exhibitions that put the Met's 30,000-piece costume collection on the map and drew millions of visitors. By the time of her death in 1989, Vreeland was known as "The High Priestess of Style." In 1993 an exhibit was mounted at the Metropolitan Museum in her honor; in their exhibition notes, curators Richard Martin and Harod Koda wrote, "Diana Vreeland's sense of style was not simply a rarefied, fashion-oriented one, but a force that enthralled the entire visual and creative world."

Vreeland's impact on culture and her thrilling way with words ("God, I miss fringe!") continue to resonate via a one-woman show, *Full Gallop*, that was an Off-Broadway hit in 1997. Mary Louise Wilson, who coscripted and starred in the play, wrote about Vreeland, "She nourishes the soul. We tune in to laugh and end up obeying her commands never to go to bed tired . . . always keep our shoes shined . . . never look back . . . go all the way all the time . . . and to dream."

CLARE BOOTHE LUCE
A LIFE OF DOUBLE DARES

> **"What rage for fame attends both great and small."**

She was a crusader for women's rights, a prominent magazine editor, a playwright, a congresswoman, and an ambassador. Married twice, and known to flirt with both men and women, she was accused at various times in her life of being a gold digger and a sexpot, while envious writers wondered out loud if she had penned her plays all by herself. This much is true: Clare Boothe Luce was a zealous Catholic, a late-life feminist, a Republican, a capitalist, and, according to friend Gore Vidal, "easily the most hated woman of her time." Why? "She was too beautiful, too successful in the theater, in politics, in marriage."

An early biographer wrote that Luce lived a life "full of double dares." Her first challenge was her birthright: she was born in 1903 in New York City to a mother who worked as a call girl. Though she eventually married a doctor, Mrs. Boothe had a lifelong affair with a man she wouldn't marry because he was Jewish. Neither man was Clare's father; that distinction was held by a musician who never quite made a living at it.

In her childhood, Clare moved from New York to Memphis to Chicago, and eventually ended up back east to attend The Castle, a school in Tarrytown, New York. In her yearbook she wrote, "What rage for fame attends both great and small."

Clare raged not only for fame, but for love and money. She studied drama for a time, and also worked for Alva Vanderbilt Belmont, a women's rights activist. At the age of twenty she married George T.

Brokaw, a man in his mid-forties who brought her standard of living up to dizzying heights. The couple had a daughter and divorced in 1929.

The following year, Mrs. Brokaw decided she wanted to work at *Vogue* magazine. She was told that there was nothing available, but she wasn't interested in taking no for an answer. In classic Adventurer style, she simply arrived at headquarters one day and appropriated a desk. She was put to work writing photo captions. A year later she was transferred to *Vanity Fair* where, in addition to polishing her writing skills, she had affairs with Condé Nast's wife, Leslie, and with Donald Freeman, the managing editor of the magazine. When Freeman killed himself in 1933, she took over his job. Clare Boothe Brokaw, managing editor of *Vanity Fair*, was by then all of twenty-nine years old.

Publisher Henry R. Luce had just launched *Fortune* magazine when he met Mrs. Brokaw at a party. For him it was love at first sight. Within an hour he decided to divorce his wife of eleven years. The two married, and Clare's idea for a picture magazine soon blossomed in the form of *Life,* but husband Harry, as he was called, kept her at arm's length from his publishing ventures. So she set her literary talents to play writing.

Luce's first play, *Abide with Me,* flopped on Broadway. Her second, the deliciously bitchy *The Women,* was a smash on stage and screen. Luce had written the first draft in three days in 1936. It was followed by *Kiss the Boys Good-bye* in 1938, and the anti-Nazi play *Margin for Error* in 1940.

Flush with success, Luce could have gone on writing scripts and seeing her name in lights. But she was becoming increasingly political. In 1938 she had visited Hitler's Germany and was horrified by the rampant anti-Semitism she witnessed. So in 1939 she walked into the editorial offices at *Life* and announced that she wanted to be a war correspondent. Though her husband protested, she was dispatched to Europe. Her reports were well received; in 1940 they were anthologized and published as *Europe in the Spring.* Of the book, the notoriously cruel Dorothy Parker had kind words: "While it is never said that the teller is the bravest of all those present, it comes through."

Luce entered politics almost accidentally. A backer of Wendell Willkie, Roosevelt's presidential challenger, she spoke on his behalf at Madison Square Garden, and the crowds loved her. Of the event, H. L. Mencken wrote: "Slim, beautiful and charming . . . when she began to unload her speech, it appeared at once that she was also a fluent and effective talker." In 1942 she was elected as a Republican to Congress from the 4th District of Connecticut

INTUITIVE

SCORECARD
ADVENTURER QUALITIES
✔ Pioneering
✔ Unconventional
✔ Socially gregarious
✔ Diversified career path
_ Degree unrelated to career

and served two terms. In 1944 she delivered the keynote address at the Republican National Convention—the first woman to do so—and in 1953 became U.S. ambassador to Italy under President Dwight D. Eisenhower—the first woman named to a major U.S. embassy.

Gore Vidal wrote, "She had been Eisenhower's turbulent ambassador, single-handedly saving Italy from Communism. . . . Clare was a fierce professional warrior for God and the deserving rich." Politics remained central to Luce's life until the end. "If I fail," she said upon beginning her life as a public servant, "they will say women don't have what it takes. Success by a woman makes it easier for other able women." She didn't fail. She sat on boards under Presidents Nixon, Ford, and Reagan, and was awarded the Presidential Medal of Freedom in 1983.

Luce never stopped writing, either. A frequent contributor to newspapers and magazines, she returned to the theatrical world in 1971 with a feminist play, *Slam the Door Softly*. In her older years she spent her free time swimming, snorkeling, water-skiing, and, according to Gore Vidal, occasionally dropping a bit of acid. "Clare was endlessly seductive," he wrote. "She was often compared to a Dresden doll because of her yellow hair, blue eyes, and chiseled features. . . .[But] 'Dresden doll' suggests a delicate figurine easily broken. Clare was not breakable."

JOSEPHINE BAKER
BEAUTIFUL DREAMER

> **"I would like to meet the woman who has the courage even to play my life story."**

Her signature outfit was a bunch of bananas—and little else. Yet there was much more to Josephine Baker than she revealed in her uninhibited stage shows.

Baker was born Freda Josephine McDonald in 1906. As a very young girl she danced and clowned in amateur theatrical productions in her native St. Louis. But behind the scenes, reality was grim. Her family was desperately poor, and in 1917 the eleven-year-old Baker witnessed riots in which white thugs roamed her neighborhood, burning buildings and killing thirty-nine black people—an experience that affected her deeply.

At sixteen, Baker ran away with a traveling dance troupe, and within three years was performing on Broadway and in Harlem. In 1925, the height of the Jazz Age, she traveled to Paris with a show called *La Revue Nègre*. In spite of the group's high hopes, Parisians couldn't stand the raucousness of tap dancing. The show closed and Baker, who was then nine-teen years old, found herself stranded. Yet she was just where she wanted to be. "The first time a white waiter served me and called me 'ma'am' I nearly died," said Baker. "I fell in love with Paris that day."

It wasn't long before Baker landed a spot with the Folies Bergère, Paris's source of high-toned, lavishly produced burlesque shows. She was hired to do a dance number in a new, all-black segment. On opening night, how-ever, the audience's thrilled reaction to her exotic look—including the string of bananas around her waist—inspired Baker to burst into a spon-taneous one-woman show. She danced, scatted, and jumped into a prop palm tree. Her career was launched, and for decades she reigned as France's living symbol of "le jazz hot."

Baker embraced her celebrity in true Adventurer style. She lived like a madcap queen, dressed in the height of fashion, caroused with smitten men and, in her professional life, never did the same show twice. She opened her own Paris club in 1926, and appeared in several French films.

At one point, Baker briefly crossed paths with another notorious Adventurer, Diana Vreeland. In her autobiography, Vreeland tells of watching a silent movie at a theater in Paris. When the lights came up there was a movement under her seat. It was a live cheetah—attached by a lead to La Baker, who had been sitting next to her the whole time. "Josephine, with those *long* black legs, was *dragged* down three flights of stairs as fast as she could go," wrote Vreeland. "Out in the street there was an enormous white-and-silver Rolls-Royce waiting for her. The driver opened the door; she let go of the lead; the cheetah *whooped,* took *one* leap into the back of the Rolls. . . . I've never seen anything like it."

Josephine Baker's antics made good copy. But behind the public image of the irrepressible flapper was a courageous woman who was deeply commit-ted to the cause of human rights. She first showed her true colors during World War II when she became a spy for the French Resistance. Baker gath-ered intelligence and smuggled information even as she frolicked among European society and entertained troops in Africa and the Middle East. In appreciation for her help in defeating the Nazis, she was awarded the Legion of Honor, the Croix de Guerre, and the Rosette de la Résistance—France's highest military honors.

The entertainer/war hero relished her fame, but with passing years yearned intensely to settle down and raise a family. In the Thirties she was briefly married to a French industrialist—subse-quently converting to Judaism and becoming a French citizen—but remained childless.

SCORECARD

INTUITIVE

ADVENTURER QUALITIES
- ✔ Pioneeering
- ✔ Unconventional
- ✔ Socially gregarious
- ✔ Diversified career path
- _ Degree unrelated to career

When she married again in 1947, she and her husband, a successful band leader, had a vision of a "rainbow tribe." Their plan was to adopt children of all races and religions, and to turn Baker's castle in the south of France into a World Village with accommodations for hundreds of visitors. They adopted twelve children in all, as well as a slew of animals, but the World Village project became so costly that in order to keep the family afloat Baker had to gather up her costumes and go on tour.

This time, Baker stormed the theaters of America. Her performances were a great success, and she was the talk of the society pages. But it wasn't long before Baker's tour turned into a personal cause. Already appalled at the segregationist practices in her homeland, she was, in 1951, refused service at New York's high-toned Stork Club. Outraged, Baker took on the problem of racial segregation and refused to perform in any venue to which blacks were not admitted. As a result of her protests, clubs and theaters from New York to Miami became integrated. During the March on Washington in 1963, Baker stood shoulder to shoulder with Martin Luther King Jr. and spoke passionately to the huge crowd.

But back in France, all was not well. Baker's husband had left her, and in his wake were crushing debts. The last scraps of her dream came crashing down in 1968, when her estate was seized in lieu of back taxes and every bit of her personal property was sold. The auction was so badly run that most of Baker's possessions went for a fraction of their worth; a silver-framed letter from Charles de Gaulle, for instance, which Baker had treasured, was auctioned off for one franc.

When the castle was finally emptied out, Baker refused to leave and barricaded herself in the kitchen. Her protest had little effect, however. She was physically evicted—literally thrown out the door into the rain, where she sat, wrapped in a blanket and clutching a kitten, for seven hours, until she was finally taken to a hospital.

Baker moved her twelve children into a two-room apartment in Paris. She was broke and despairing, with no relief in sight. What Baker didn't know was that she had a champion in the form of Princess Grace of Monaco, who, back when she was Grace Kelly, had been dining at the Stork Club on the very evening that Baker was turned away. The princess had long admired Baker's campaign for civil rights and invited Baker to perform at a special Red Cross benefit in Monaco.

The performance was a triumph, and Baker was besieged with contracts and offers. Princess Grace convinced the Red Cross to give Baker a down payment on a seaside villa in Monaco, where the rainbow tribe happily settled in. Baker, once again a star, proceeded to perform in sold-out concert halls all over the world.

In 1975 she celebrated the fiftieth anniversary of her debut in the City of Lights with a show in Paris that reviewed her Adventurer life in story and song. The evening-length performance featured La Baker driving across the stage on a motorcycle, remembering her war years from the seat of a dusty Jeep, and appearing in one fabulous costume after another. It was a smashing success, and her encore performance of Bob Dylan's "The Times They Are A-Changin'"—sung in her unmistakable chanteuse style—brought the house down.

Sadly, the performance proved to be her last. Two days later, after retreating to her room to take a nap, she quietly died of a stroke. She had been found in bed, surrounded by glowing reviews of her show; one friend said that Josephine Baker had "died of joy."

The memory of Josephine Baker—performer, activist, patriot—was honored at a lavish state funeral. Paris came to a standstill as twenty thousand fans said good-bye to a legend.

Adventurers at Work

Real success is being totally indulgent about your own trip.
— BETSEY JOHNSON, FASHION DESIGNER

The term *Adventurer* implies one who circles the globe in search of challenges, high jinks, and capers. Don't take it too literally: there are many, many Adventurers who get their kicks in the pages of books, on the Internet, and in stay-put careers that offer intellectual excitement and visual variety.

Adventurer journalists are challenged every day with new stories to research and write. Adventurer photographers get assignments that may take them to high-fashion runways or disaster areas wracked with destruction. Actresses, designers, and veterinarians may keep the same job title for years, but their day-to-day lives are full of surprises because they're constantly presented with unpredictable sets of challenges.

Where you won't find Adventurers is in careers, jobs, or projects that require long-term continuity. Their best talents are creative; they can raise the bar, think outside the box, invent and reinvent. The Adventurer is stimulated by theories and possibilities, and shuns that which is conventional, concrete, or "proven."

Adventurers have tremendous start-up energy and are electrified by the

THE OVERWORKED ADVENTURER

Adventurers like high-energy working environments. They perform quite well when faced with difficult deadlines and overwhelming challenges; they'll pull all-nighters to get the job done, and secretly enjoy the drama.

There are certain problems, however, that can make Adventurers' blood pressure go through the roof. Personality clashes are one. Money troubles are another. Finally, there's boredom. When an Adventurer isn't challenged her anxiety level can be just as bad as when she's swamped. She can become depressed, lethargic, sloppy in her work habits, forgetful, and chronically late — all stress reactions that don't look like the classic, pull-your-hair-out symptoms of anxiousness.

For Adventurers, perhaps the most dangerous by-product of stress is burnout. Because she's a project-oriented creature who tends to respond to one emergency after another, the Adventurer can become a victim of too much intensity. This might present itself as clinical exhaustion.

Some tips to keep stress under control:

1. OFFSET HUGE CHALLENGES WITH EASY JOBS. Many Adventurers are freelancers or sole proprietors who, because of money worries, take on too many difficult jobs at once. Rather than say yes because something's interesting, the Adventurer should look at the big picture. When you're making decisions, take the stress factor into consideration and give yourself periodic "treats" in the form of laid-back, no-brainer gigs.

2. DON'T BE SEDUCED INTO HEROISM. The archetypal Adventurer has a secret Superwoman costume that she just loves to change into when extraordinarily difficult challenges arise. Though it's okay to respond to the call once in a while, it can lead not only to burnout, but to a lack of perspective about what's really important.

3. SHAKE YOUR BOOTY. Regular exercise is something every Adventurer knows she needs, but doesn't always get — unless her vocation is tied in to physical activity. Adventurers should sign up for interesting classes — tae kwon do, horseback riding, tap dancing — and change the curriculum every season. Keep in mind that Adventurers do best when there's some kind of reward at the end of a course. This may be a tap recital, a martial arts demonstration, or a climbing expedition.

4. FIND YOUR ZEN ZONE. Though most Adventurers are too impatient to actually meditate, they really do need to be alone with their thoughts in a neutral space with no distractions. Some Adventurers report that driving long distances by themselves is a form of mental hygiene. Other Adventurers might try rowing, bead-stringing, golfing, or any soothing-yet-concentrated activity that gets you into a Zen-like state.

5. TAKE AN ADVENTURE VACATION. The Adventurer wants to be a participant, not a spectator. Standard vacations don't make her heart go pit-a-pat; as such, she should hook up with an action-based travel company and try her hand at white-water rafting, or salmon fishing in Scotland, or trekking through Nepal.

thrill of new beginnings; they often take on seemingly impossible challenges and are deeply satisfied when they succeed against all odds.

They do tend to have short attention spans, however, and will lose interest after a project is up and running, when duties shift to maintenance or slow growth. As a result, the Adventurer's business life tends to be a work-in-progress that undergoes constant reinvention.

It is the Adventurer's lot to be restless and perpetually looking for the next most interesting thing—no matter how successful her current venture might be.

Making It Up as They Go Along

A woman's life can really be a succession of lives, each revolving around some emotionally compelling situation or challenge, and each marked off by some intense experience.
— WALLIS SIMPSON, THE DUCHESS OF WINDSOR

A number of Adventurers, instead of following a career plan, let fate take the lead. They tend to pounce on intriguing opportunities with all faith that they'll end up in a place where they want to be. As a result, many have crazy-quilt careers that incorporate an array of unrelated interests and pursuits that somehow add up to a whole picture.

Carolyn Myss, author of *Anatomy of the Spirit* and other books about power and healing, may seem at first to be an Artisan. After all, she takes a mystical approach to health, and her books are filed in the "self-help" section. Yet Myss has the mind of an Adventurer. Her background is in newspaper journalism, and, though she holds a master's degree in theology, when she first started writing about alternative healing, she did it because she needed a job.

"I had no desire to meet any healers myself," Myss writes of her early days. "I refused to meditate. I developed an absolute aversion to wind chimes [and] New Age music. . . . I smoked while drinking coffee by the gallon." Her hard-boiled rejection of the alternative healing culture is a distinctly Adventurer reaction: Adventurers are not joiners and fiercely protect their individuality, even if their reactions may be on the self-destructive side.

But a small miracle happened in Myss's life when she discovered that she was a "medical intuit" who could accurately perceive other people's illness. When she finally embraced her gift, she made sense of human wellness and unwellness by integrating Judaic, Christian, Hindu, and Buddhist concepts. From the teachings of these major religions she was able to describe "seven universal spiritual truths." Hers is a perfect example of the

SOME FAVORITE ADVENTURER INDUSTRIES

FILM
TELEVISION
ENTERTAINMENT
THEATER
NEWSPAPER/MAGAZINE
PUBLISHING
FASHION
SALES
MARKETING
MUSIC
ADVERTISING
PUBLIC RELATIONS
PROMOTION
DESIGN
POLITICS
JOURNALISM
THE ARTS
TRAVEL
HOSPITALITY
NIGHTLIFE
THE MEDIA

Adventurer's talents: she pulls what she needs from a broad spectrum of knowledge to create a new school of thought.

Bach Nguyen definitely makes up her working life as she goes along. She fled war-torn Vietnam in 1975 with her four children. Thanks to the sponsorship of a church in Guilford, Connecticut, she was able to leave the California refugee camp where she had been detained for three months and begin a new life with her family. Wanting to repay Guilford's townspeople for their many kindnesses, she took the only thing she'd rescued from Vietnam—a stack of recipes—and cooked seven-course meals for fifty people at a time in her home. The reaction to her native cuisine was overwhelmingly positive, and she was convinced by her new fans to go into the restaurant business. Chez Bach was opened in 1980 to major acclaim, and Nguyen eventually opened three additional restaurants in Connecticut, Massachusetts, and Washington, D.C. Her success led to a collaboration on the first Vietnamese cookbook printed in the U.S., *The Classic Cuisine of Vietnam,* which has since won international fame.

By 1997 Nguyen had sold her restaurants and rekindled her lifetime love of art—her own and her countrymen's—and sponsored an exhibit in New York. While carrying three of her lacquered vases that were to be displayed, she ran into a designer who wanted to buy her work. Soon, Nguyen was turning out furniture, trays, boxes, bowls, and jewelry that wedded the ancient art of lacquering with contemporary designs. She reached out to artists and craftspeople in her home country and helped start two companies—one in North Vietnam, one in South Vietnam—that produce traditional and contemporary artworks.

Today, Nguyen runs a gallery that showcases work from overseas collectives as well as pieces by underrepresented artists from Vietnam. She also makes time to act as a liaison between American companies and businesspeople in her homeland.

Chef, restaurateur, cookbook author, artist, gallery owner, importer, international business liaison—Nguyen's path is about as Adventurer as it can get, and she continues to grow in new ways.

Fulfilling a Destiny

> It's not enough to have talent. You have to have a talent for having talent.
>
> —RUTH GORDON, ACTRESS AND SCREENWRITER

Some Adventurers are born with special gifts, and know almost from toddlerhood that they have a destiny to fulfill. It's doubtful that Madonna ever visited a career counselor, for example. And can you imagine Dolly Parton questioning her ambitions?

Rap star Missy Elliot always knew where she was headed. When her mother urged her to go to college, she said, "I'm not going. I'm going to be a star." Missy's mom retorted, "Until you're a star, you're going to college." But true to her instincts, Missy got a record deal shortly after graduating from high school. Now she has Grammy nominations, MTV Video Awards, Soul Train awards, a record company, and a cosmetics line. She told *Bust,* "I just feel like I was supposed to be in the industry no matter what."

Dolly Parton is a true Adventurer who grew up in a dirt-floor cabin with eleven brothers and sisters in Locust Ridge, Tennessee. In spite of zero opportunities and grinding poverty—she made her first guitar out of an old mandolin and two bass guitar strings—Dolly put herself in the spotlight, singing on a local TV show at age eleven and talking her way onto the stage at the Grand Ole Opry at thirteen. On the day she graduated from high school (the first in her family to do so) she got on a bus to Nashville, where, three years later, Porter Wagoner signed her on as his "girl singer." Today, sixty-four albums, six films, and one theme park later, she says, "Every day I count my blessings. Then I count my money."

Though certainly not all Adventurers have Parton's clarity of vision, many have an extraordinary confidence in themselves. Parton speaks for many Adventurers when she says, "I got more guts than I got talent, but I got enough talent to back it up."

A Matter of (No) Degrees

> Don't wait too long to do a few other things with your life. Be open to new opportunities.
>
> —CAROL BELLAMY, EXECUTIVE DIRECTOR, UNICEF

Adventurers are famous for learning as they earn, and many of them do very well in life without the benefit of a college degree. Sometimes their lack of higher education is due to circumstances, but it's just as likely, when speaking of Adventurers, that they either didn't know what to study or had such a strong idea of what they wanted to do in life that they didn't need to.

HOW THE ADVENTURER GETS ALONG . . .

. . . WITH VISIONARIES

In the movie *Harold and Maude,* starring Ruth Gordon and Bud Cort, Harold is an unhappy Visionary, a poor little rich boy trapped in his mother's world. Then he meets über-Adventurer Maude, an elderly concentration camp survivor who introduces him to all the sensual pleasures of the world and teaches him to enjoy life. Which just goes to show that, at least in Hollywood, Adventurers and Visionaries can be excellent allies, and can even be enriched by each other's qualities.

Though both types tend to be strong-willed, Adventurers are not classically competitive (except with themselves) and pose little threat to the positioning-conscious Visionary. Adventurer-Visionary partnerships do lack something — that is, a willingness to do the dirty and/or boring work — but as part of a leadership team they're well matched.

. . . WITH ARTISANS

Adventurers and Artisans usually get along famously. While the Adventurer dances her dance and goes off on tangents, the Artisan stays grounded in reality and maintains the steady rhythms of day-to-day life.

The two can form very fruitful partnerships and working relationships. Perhaps the nicest thing about Adventurer-Artisan alliances is that the two are often each other's biggest fans. If you can stand the corny analogy, Artisans can be the wind beneath Adventurers' wings, and also the Adventurers' heroes.

. . . WITH IDEALISTS

Whoops. This potentially disastrous pairing can threaten the Adventurer and drive the Idealist crazy. Why? Because Adventurers don't like rules, while Idealists believe that good rules make good order. Also, Idealists want to identify and enforce boundaries while Adventurers want to bust through them. Also, Idealists value tidiness and Adventurers do not. Also, Idealists aren't responsive and/or expressive enough for the Adventurer's taste (remember, Adventurers need applause).

Once in a while, though, Idealists and Adventurers do forge terrific, long-term partnerships in which the Adventurer thinks up thrilling possibilities and the Idealist provides the financial and practical smarts to back them up. In Anne Tyler's *The Accidental Tourist,* an Idealist travel writer hooks up with an extra-ditzy Adventurer who has a way with dogs. Once the two get over their horror of each other's style, they get along quite well. Very well, in fact. The Idealist anchors the Adventurer, and the Adventurer liberates the Idealist. Which really can happen in real life.

Shelley Reich, who fled to California at the age of seventeen, worked hard to get into U.C. San Diego and had to pay her own way. But she soon decided that the life of a college student wasn't for her. She dematriculated in order to direct her own studies, and in the meantime decided to get a "real" job: setting up a computer system for a surf shop. Never mind that she had no computer experience: Shelley convinced the shop owners that she could do it, and, with the help of manuals that she crammed with at night, was true to her word.

DO HIRE AN ADVENTURER TO . . .
DON'T HIRE AN ADVENTURER TO . . .

Work on short-term projects.
Be a committed employee for life.

Organize a photo shoot.
Organize your office.

Inspire your team to think outside the box.
Teach your team to be efficient.

Be a great communicator.
Install a communications system.

Be an art director.
Create a financial portfolio.

When Leslie Hindman dropped out of Indiana University, she filled out an exit form and gave a single reason for leaving: "Boredom." Boredom also drove Hindman out of her office manager job at Sotheby's. At age twenty-seven she left and opened Leslie Hindman Auctioneers; fifteen years later, when Hindman's annual sales had hit the $15 million mark, Sotheby's turned around and bought her company.

Adventurers do have fierce intellectual curiosity, and some are driven to earn multiple degrees in various—and sometimes unrelated—fields. Others earn a degree and then follow a dream that has nothing to do with their education. Usually, though, Adventurers meet challenges as they arise, and not a minute sooner.

How Cherie Got Her Job: A Tale of Adventurism

Cherie Whaples-Elliott was happily living an artist's life in San Francisco when the earthquake of 1989 wiped out her place of employment and decimated the job market. With zero dollars in her bank account and a rising panic, Cherie borrowed enough money to get to the East Coast. There she started looking for work in the sciences, which she had studied in high school and college.

"The only job I could find was in a chemistry lab," she says. "I put on my résumé that I had a degree in biological sciences, which wasn't true—I never actually graduated from college." Cherie was called for an interview on the strength of her highly embellished résumé. "I was nervous as all sin," she recalls. "But these people were pushovers, I must say. A fifth-grader could have handled the questions they asked me. They gave me a tour of all the equipment, and asked if I knew how to run these machines and I said, 'Yes.' I had never seen these machines before in my life. But they didn't ask me to prove it."

Cherie got the job and spent the next few days at the library, cramming with every chemistry book she could get her hands on. "I went in Monday morning and there was a guy there who was going to 'reacquaint me' with the equipment. I told him, 'Pretend I'm in kindergarten.' A week later I had to run my first experiment, and I found that there is an actual bible for chemistry people, filled with standard experiments, step by step. So I slipped into the ladies' room with this book. It's laid out like a cookbook, and there was the experiment! From then on I knew that as long as I had the book I'd be free and clear."

A few years down the road, Cherie was asked to be the assistant laboratory director. "By then I'd accepted the fact that I'd done really well, I could keep going with this. Then I found out I had to be certified, they'd be looking at my transcripts from college, and I'd have to take a test."

Cherie told her employers that she needed to brush up on her math before taking on such a big responsibility. "They were thrilled," she recalls. "I even got them to pay for my classes. They were the classes I needed to complete my college degree, but they didn't need to know that. I got all A's, sent in my paperwork, and got my degree by mail." Cherie also passed the certification test, got a substantial raise, and worked at the lab until her interests in antiques eclipsed her life.

Acting for Fun and Profit

> My maiden name is Dalziel. . . . It means in old Gaelic, "I dare." That's me.
>
> — DIANA VREELAND

Of all the archetypes, Adventurers win the award for best actors. They can act as if they know what they're talking about, and do a damn good job of it. They also have an ability to look like they belong—although many a corporate Adventurer refers to wearing conservative suits and pumps as being "in drag."

Jennifer Reiley, a successful wine rep, is essentially a Visionary but has a strong streak of Adventurer. This becomes evident when she's on the road selling. "In college I was called a chameleon by one of my professors," she recalls. "He hit it right on the head. I didn't know if that was negative or not, but I agreed with him. It's served me well. In sales, you put on a different hat for a different person. Some days I look like an insurance executive. Other days I wear purple and a lot of makeup. It's about pulling off an act."

There is something inherently theatrical about Adventurers. In some cases it's blatant, like when designer Betsey Johnson, dressed in a tutu and high heels, opens her runway shows by doing cartwheels down the catwalk. Jill Barad, CEO of Mattel, is also a drama queen; she and her top managers sometimes put on skits on a makeshift stage in the company's cafeteria. Barad has played a beatnik, a rapper, and a *Star Trek* officer to get various messages across. When the company made every day Casual Day, she and other senior execs showed up in bathrobes, leather jackets, and the like to demonstrate casual do's and don'ts.

Adventurers also have an affinity for pulling off stunts. You already know that Judy George hired a plane to buzz the headquarters of Hamilton's when she was trying to get a job there. You probably don't know about Tanya Styblo Beder, head of Capital Market Risk Advisors. In 1998 she brought the first male partner into her firm, and to publicize the event, she mailed out cards decorated with blue ribbons that announced, "It's a Boy."

One Adventurer of our acquaintance, whom we'll call "Betty" (she chooses to remain anonymous), once had a job interview in which she and her potential employer acknowledged that she was a risky candidate. The day after, Betty sent her interviewer a package. In it were two oversized dice with her photo pasted on every side, and a simple note: "Throw them."

Actress Camryn Manheim pulled off an Adventurer coup that changed her life. She was being considered for a lead in a new TV show called *The Practice*, directed by David E. Kelley. After viewing her clips, the legendary director said she was "too conservative" for the part. Manheim was shocked, not only because she has multiple piercings, a tattoo, and drives a motorcycle, but because she felt in her heart that she was going to get the role. Spying a cribbage board in David's office, she made a proposition: if she beat him at cribbage he'd give her an audition. He was so impressed by her gutsiness, she didn't have to play *or* audition. He rewrote the part for her, and the following year Manheim snagged a Best Supporting Actress Emmy.

The Adventurer Working Style

Adventurers are creatures of great extremes. They thrive on action and change, and like nothing better than big, complicated projects that call their best talents into play. They work in terrific bursts of energy, which are usually followed by serious stretches of downtime that can sometimes resemble actual hibernation.

Because Adventurers have maverick energies, they're not easily managed. When presented with menial or uninteresting tasks, the Adventurer is sometimes compelled to create her own dramas. That means complicating simple

THE UPS AND DOWNS OF BEING AN ADVENTURER

THE UPS
You're a self-starter who can come up with her own ideas and run with them.
> You shine when it comes to recruiting others, whipping up group enthusiasm, and garnering support for your ideas.

You have a talent for anticipating trends.
> You maintain your sense of humor in even the most tense situations.

You feel comfortable interacting with all kinds of people.
> You rarely back down from a challenge.

You're willing to work crazy hours and pull off heroic accomplishments when necessary.
> You can think on your feet, and function well in high-pressure situations.

You're socially gifted and make friends easily.
> You have a talent for public speaking and publicity in general.

You respond to good leadership but need very little supervision.

THE DOWNS
You're easily bored.
> You have a tendency to dominate conversations and try to impress others rather than listen to them.

You're not detail-oriented.
> You resist doing routine, repetitive, or maintenance-related tasks.

You can set unrealistic goals for yourself and others.
> You're not good at sticking to schedules, especially self-imposed schedules and deadlines.

You're so fun-loving that you might enjoy yourself at the expense of the bottom line.
> You're easily distracted.

You can be undependable or irresponsible.
> You're overly sensitive to criticism and can be easily discouraged.

tasks, making small jobs into big jobs, or procrastinating until a project becomes an emergency.

The smartest way to handle an Adventurer is to treat her as a "positive deviant." This handy phrase is used by Barbara Waugh, who is a "change agent" at Hewlett-Packard Worldwide. Her job, she told *Fast Company* magazine, is to make change by making connections. Rather than squelching the voices of unsatisfied or frustrated employees, she solicits their feedback and—if it's valid— puts a value on their criticisms. "You seek out the positive deviants and support them," she says. "You feed them; you give them resources and visibility."

Adventurers need to be matched with their assignments. Consistency, reliability, and endless stamina are not their best qualities. But when projects call for improvisation, invention, and great infusions of energy, the Adventurer will boldly go where no woman has gone before.

As leaders, Adventurers can be charming, magnanimous, and inspiring, and can draw workers into a magic circle that feels like a delicious conspiracy. Flamboyant and fun-loving, they do all they can to keep the business day from feeling routine or stale. They're not well suited to managing, however, because they are not usually interested in the details of day-to-day operations. Therefore, they are most successful when they surround themselves with competent helpers who can keep matters organized and moving in a constructive direction.

The Adventurer Work Space

The Adventurer sees her life as an ongoing series of experiments, and her office space reflects this. She often works on multiple projects and has materials stacked on desks, windowsills, chairs, and floors to prove it. She likes visual stimulation—her decorating credo is, "anything but boring"—and is an action-oriented creature who thrives in atmospheres that are supercharged with energy.

Unlike Idealists, who are apt to create some version of a filing system for everything from Zip discs to paper clips, the Adventurer likes her stuff out where she can see it. In the Adventurer's world, when something is put away, she's likely to forget that it exists. The result? A chaotic-looking work space dotted with Post-its and scribbled reminders.

To complicate matters, Adventurers are likely to cover their walls and bulletin boards with festive postcards, pages ripped from magazines, swatches of fabric, and anything else that might inspire them. As Betsey Johnson says, "I need a lot of junk around me."

• **The ultimate Adventurer office** is a large loft space with "floating walls" that can be reconfigured as needed. These walls not only serve as temporary dividers but as bulletin boards and working surfaces where the Adventurer can plot out plans of action. There is color everywhere, and eclectic collections of oddball furnishings and decorative accessories. Besides permanent storage areas, she has rolling files and bookcases on casters that can be zoomed to center stage when they're needed, or pushed out of the way when they're not. Finally, there is a big, round table where the Adventurer can meet, eat, muse, and socialize.

• **The minimum-requirement Adventurer office** isn't isolated or shut away. It doesn't need a door or even walls, but it does need at least one large bulletin board and plenty of open shelves where she can stack her works-in-progress.

LAURA GROPPE
GIRL GURU

> "I can't sit in charted territory. Going down a new and untrodden path — that's my comfort zone."

It's pretty easy to bet that the CEO of a company called Girl Games would be an Adventurer. When you consider that this same woman co-produced an Oscar-winning film, shared four MTV Video Awards, and garnered honors at the prestigious Sundance film festival, the odds increase. The big payoff comes when you have a conversation with the tall, blond, Texas-born Laura Groppe, and find out that her achievements are part of a life-long pattern of Adventurism. Her thirty-six years on this earth have been distinguished by gutsy moves, daredevil decisions, and enough unconventional wisdom to launch an entire industry.

Groppe's Adventurer tendencies became apparent in pre-school. "When I was finished finger painting, napping, or whatever, regardless of the time of day, I would decide that I was done," she recalls in a voice as accent-free as an anchorwoman's. "I'd then gather my belongings and sit in the teacher's chair and wait for my mom to come and get me. This was my mother's first indication that I was going to be my own boss."

Fast-forward to the twenty-one-year-old Groppe holding a brand-new philosophy degree from Sweet Briar College, an all-female college in Virginia. Though she didn't have a clear direction, she did have a plan: "I figured if I moved as many time zones away from my parents as I could, they wouldn't be able to question me." She chose Tokyo as her destination because of her interest in Shintoism, Taoism, and Buddhism, and incidentally, because "it was 1985 and the Pacific Rim was the total hot spot on the globe." It didn't faze Groppe that she didn't know a soul there, had no job prospects, and didn't speak Japanese. "I built my network by talking to anybody—people in elevators, friends of friends of friends," she explains. Once in Japan she hooked up with three French Canadian roommates who were fluent in five languages—Japanese included—which proved to be a real lifesaver. "I couldn't even order food," Groppe laughs. "I'd be starving, waiting for them to come home."

With time, Groppe's finances grew thin and she needed to find work. No problem: one evening at a party in the Roppongi district in Tokyo, Groppe met a Canadian real estate developer who was building a new health club and desperately needed an aerobics instructor. "I said, 'That's what I do!' My girlfriend kicked me, because I had never even taken an aerobics class. But I figured, how hard can it be?" Groppe was hired, and at the end of the interview she was photographed. "I thought it was for my employee file. The next day, when I got off the train to start my new job, I saw that the whole station was plastered with purple flyers—with my photo on them. I couldn't read the writing, but I think it said something like 'giant American woman teaches aerobics.'"

While raking in bucks from her popular classes—which, she notes, were full of men suddenly interested in feeling the burn—Groppe became intrigued with the idea of making films. "I would skip my language class and go to the movies with one of my roommates, who was studying Japanese cinema," she recalls. "That was the spark." After eighteen action-

"

LAURA GROPPE ON . . .

REJECTION: "The first time you get fired it's really devastating, but each time after it gets easier. It's a very clear signal that you're going down the wrong path. For me it wasn't that I couldn't do a job, it's that the job and I didn't see eye to eye."

HER ADVENTURER HERITAGE: "My dad has so many interests, he is always surrounded by huge stacks of papers. One day a table in his office actually collapsed under the weight of the piles. As for my mom, I was visiting recently and opened the fridge, and there among the milk and the pickles was a dead bluebird. She said it had broken its neck flying into the window and was such a beautiful color she just couldn't throw it out. I definitely come from a long strand of Adventurer DNA."

THE ADVENTURER SPIRIT: "You need it to get through even one day on a movie set. If your director wants seventeen pygmies on Harley-Davidsons before sunset, you get creative. You have to be blind to barriers."

THE ADVENTURER AS CEO: "The jury's still out on how the role of an Adventurer plays as your company matures. Having an unconventional approach can tend to be not positive when you're hitting certain growth thresholds of an organization. Never will I give up that spirit, but it's my job to find the people who can operate around me."

THE TEEN GIRL MARKET: "They're interested in having products developed for them, but industries are not paying attention. Why not have women involved in the design and technology of telephones? It's a perfect fit. We try to drive that market. Boy, is it moving mountains to get it done."

ADVICE FOR FLEDGLING ENTREPRENEURS: "I recommend that you color outside the lines. And understand that 'no' means 'come back later with a different perspective.' 'No' doesn't mean much to me—never has. My poor mother, it must have been hell raising me.**"**

packed months in Japan, which included side trips to Burma and Thailand, Groppe moved back to the States. In Los Angeles she found a mentor, June Guterman, who took her on as an assistant director. It was a fruitful relationship: in 1992, Guterman's production group won an Academy Award for Best Short Film for *Session Man*, a Showtime cable-network movie that Groppe co-produced. She went on to co-produce music videos, and in 1994 shared four MTV Video Awards for the moody, atmospheric video of R.E.M.'s "Everybody Hurts." In the meantime, Groppe co-produced an independent film called *Suture*, which won best Cinematography at Sundance and was a nominee at Cannes.

Flush with success, the thirty-year-old Laura Groppe was perfectly positioned for Hollywood's fast track. But her heart wasn't in it. "What I was doing in the film business was not necessarily continuing to be stimulating and challenging," she recalls. Standing at a career crossroads, she turned to her family for guidance. "My father asked me to look at other women in the industry and see if they had a life I could emulate," says Groppe. "Not a career, but a life. It was so provocative. I packed my bags, left L.A., and went back to Texas."

In her hometown of Houston, Groppe explored her options. "I knew I wanted to start my own company, and I wanted to leverage the entertainment industry experience I had," she says. Interactive entertainment was an emerging industry at the time, and Groppe observed that most—if not all—computer games were directed toward boys, complete with intergalactic wars and shoot-'em-up thrills. Within this gaping void in the CD-ROM market, Groppe saw her future: she was going to pioneer a new kind of entertainment for girls in the seven- to seventeen-year-old range. With a portion of her savings and an extra desk in her dad's office, she launched Girl Games.

Groppe's first challenge was to understand the inner workings of teen girls. With a grant from the National Science Foundation, she went directly to the source, sitting in on high school classes and making friends with her demographic. "I wanted to know eveything," she told *Forbes* in 1998. "I

INTUITIVE SCORECARD
Laura Groppe

VISIONARY QUALITIES
- ✔ Leadership-oriented
- _ Named business after self
- _ Works in glamour industry
- ✔ Made major leaps within industry
- ✔ Master of publicity

ARTISAN QUALITIES
- ✔ Champions underdog
- _ Family-centric
- ✔ Outdoorsy
- ✔ Produces tangible product
- ✔ Treats employees like family

IDEALIST QUALITIES
- _ Pragmatic
- ✔ Works within systems
- _ Holds multiple degrees
- ✔ Analytical
- _ Long-term commitment to single career

ADVENTURER QUALITIES
- ✔ Pioneering
- ✔ Unconventional
- ✔ Socially gregarious
- ✔ Diversified career path
- ✔ Degree unrelated to career

wanted to know what one girl had written on a note she was passing to the other girl in math class." She then rounded up sixty girls and let them loose on interactive games at Rice University's PC labs. The results didn't surprise Groppe: the girls were bored with the games on the market. Next question: What did girls want? What could technology give them that they weren't getting anywhere else?

Groppe knew just how to find out: host pajama parties. At these soirees, she learned that teenage girls still make crank calls, paint their toenails, do each other's hair, and something else: log on to chat lines. Technology was a pipeline to personal interaction, as far as these girls were concerned.

Armed with reams of first-person data, Groppe and her growing crew developed Girl Games' first CD-ROM, "Let's Talk About ME!" Released in 1996, its noncompetitive video environment features interactive horoscopes, a diary, a virtual wardrobe, funky graphics, and a "panic button" that makes the screen go dark in case a parent or pesty sibling walks in unannounced. Groppe says that it's still her favorite product, and she is particularly proud of a segment that, via a quiz, leads the player to one of twenty mentors. These successful career women were taped in advance to answer a galaxy of questions. "No matter who they hook up with—a biologist, a lawyer—most girls want to know, 'Did you get along with your sister when you were my age? When was your first kiss? How was it?' They ask personal questions that relate to themselves. They're self obsessed, and that's okay—it's their job."

Girl Games has since released a number of titles that are "wired to the minds of teenage girls." But she continues to struggle with inherent prejudices in the computer games industry. "There is this academic understanding that fifty-one percent of the population isn't being sold to, yet there is also this fear of change," she says. "If point-and-shoot works, why change it, right?"

The landscape is indeed changing, albeit slowly. One harbinger of the future is the fact that Girl Games' research lab—the one that initiated pajama parties and gang game-testing—is now one of the most valuable components of the company. It generates an ever-evolving portrait of a notoriously fickle yet hugely significant group. As CEO, Groppe finds herself constantly monitoring two moving targets: teenage girls and technology. "We have to reinvent ourselves all the time," she says. "We're building business models in a lava lamp."

Not that she's daunted by the challenge. Quite the opposite. "I can't sit in charted territory," says the intrepid Groppe. "Going down a new and untrodden path—that's my comfort zone. It's a critical component in our industry, because we're having to invent business models, and design and create new content from nothing."

Groppe, in true Adventurer fashion, has also gone outside the parameters of her industry. When in-house research revealed that 80 percent of her demographic carried beepers, she called Motorola with the news. Her company was signed on as a consultant, and has subsequently become a teen touchstone to Fox, Hallmark, Procter & Gamble, Mattel, and other corporations eager to wake the sleeping giant of pubescent female consumers.

Yet Groppe remains dedicated to her original vision. "I think that we have the opportunity and the talent to be *the* entertainment company for teenage girls," she says. "We've managed to develop some of the most original content out there, so our challenge now is to build meaningful partnerships. We have a tremendous amount of responsibility to deliver products that are not only entertaining but supportive." Pausing for a moment, Laura Groppe puts a finger on the pulse of her labors: "We're providing girls with the tools to grow up opinionated and full of self-expression—without them knowing it."

SHARON WHITELEY
ETERNAL ENTREPRENEUR

> **"I have this beginner's mind. . . . I love learning."**

How many companies can one woman start and grow in a lifetime? If you're Sharon Whiteley, the answer is five. And counting.

"My path has been a series of happy accidents," she says. First, it was shopping centers. Back when she was the principal of Sharon P. Cavanaugh & Associates, she was integral to the success of a number of innovative complexes, including the famous Faneuil Hall Marketplace in Boston. It was she who dreamed up and executed the "pushcart vendor" concept that is now a familiar feature of urban malls. Next, as a partner in Williams Jackson Cavanaugh, she developed major retail centers. From there she moved on to confections and co-founded Sweet Stuff, a chain of upscale candy stores. In 1982 she launched Peacock Papers, a fast-growth company that created contemporary gifts, party products, and paper goods. "That was a really meaningful fourteen years of my life," recalls Sharon. "Our product was, in a nutshell, my heart and soul on paper." Following in 1984 was Peacock Retail, a specialty store primarily showcasing Peacock products.

Her most recent project was perhaps her riskiest: Crimson Solutions, an Internet start-up that streamlines the job-finding and recruiting process for students and employers at colleges and universities. "I didn't even own a computer until four months before becoming CEO," Sharon muses.

Sharon Pfau grew up in Connecticut with an identical twin sister named Sheila, also an entrepreneur who has just launched her third venture. "I don't think I ever thought individually then," she recalls of her childhood. "It would be 'Sheila/Sharon, Sharon/Sheila, what difference does it make?' We were so identical that the only differentiation was who wore pink or who wore blue."

With time, the twins gained separate identities. In high school, for instance, Sharon became a bit of a rebel, while Sheila remained the more conservative sister. In spite of their changing roles, the two girls chose to attend the same college (Skidmore); spent their junior year in England; and got engaged within one month of each other, right after graduation.

Sharon majored in American studies. "It was the most liberal arts major," she explains. "I really didn't know what I wanted to do, and certainly wasn't thinking in terms of a career." After college, she dabbled in art and photography and studied interior architecture. She and her twin started working together as freelance photographers in the early seventies; from there, Sheila went into advertising, while Sharon began to recognize and honor her entrepreneurial spirit.

"My first real encounter with creating a business was when I was twenty-one and working at a clothing store during the holidays," she remembers. "The shop had no evening wear at the time—a big miss. My dad was in the textile business, so I took a bunch of velvet and stitched up elastic-waistband skirts and sold them to the store at a nice profit." Sharon says she learned a lot. "One big lesson was that women need slits in long dresses," she laughs.

Shortly thereafter, Sharon got involved in a specialty shopping center project. "It was a lot of money for me at the time, and I liked to shop, so I said, 'Why not!' I got incredible encouragement and support from the project's developer. I learned to appreciate what my talents and capabilities were, and came to know the value of a true mentor."

After a successful one-year stint as a sales manager for the real estate division of Aetna, she was approached by the Rouse Company, a leading national developer, to work on the refiguration of Boston's historic Faneuil Hall. Back in 1976, the melding of tourism and retail was a risky new concept; the three-year project proved to be both a challenge and a triumph for the state, the city, and Sharon herself. "I remember the day before the grand opening of the Quincy Market building, walking through with Jim

INTUITIVE SCORECARD
Sharon Whiteley

VISIONARY QUALITIES	ARTISAN QUALITIES
✔ Leadership-oriented	_ Champions underdog
_ Named business after self	_ Family-centric
_ Works in glamour industry	_ Outdoorsy
✔ Made major leaps within industry	_ Produces tangible product
_ Master of publicity	✔ Treats employees like family

IDEALIST QUALITIES	ADVENTURER QUALITIES
_ Pragmatic	✔ Pioneering
_ Works within systems	✔ Unconventional
_ Holds multiple degrees	_ Socially gregarious
_ Analytical	✔ Diversified career path
_ Long-term commitment to single career	✔ Degree unrelated to career

Rouse and using chalk to outline the tiny areas where pushcart merchants could stash their goods," she recalls. "And the following two years, when the South and North Market buildings opened . . . I knew I had contributed significantly and I was extremely proud."

It wasn't long before she got together with two former Rouse employees and formed Williams Jackson Cavanaugh. From 1978 to 1984, she and her partners developed imaginative retail centers in the United States and Canada, including Queen's Quay Terminal, which led to the revitalization of Toronto's waterfront, and Suburban Square, the country's oldest shopping center, on Philadelphia's Main Line. In 1982 her firm won a national competition to redevelop Union Square in Washington, D.C., a landmark urban project.

It was at the point when Sharon's passion for shopping centers started to wane that a new love walked into her life: future husband Richard Whiteley, whom she met at a United Airlines baggage claim area. "I used to joke that the operative words were 'united' and 'baggage claim,'" she says. "He's been my most valued mentor ever since. He's not only a very smart man, but also a very wise one, and on top of that, a loving man, too." He is also, it should be noted, a shaman who does his healing work in the corporate arena. "We're wired the same way," Sharon says, "true soul mates."

The next phase of Sharon Whiteley's entrepreneurial life revolved around products much smaller than 250,000-square-foot malls. In 1978, she and two partners started Sweet Stuff, a regional chain of trendy shops that sold endorphin-producing treats. Its decor, featuring black walls, floor-to-ceiling Plexiglas cylinders brimming with candy, and pink neon signs, was pure Adventurer.

"

SHARON WHITELEY ON...

EMBRACING CHANGE: "I'm an evolutionary thinker. I've never had a specific goal in my life. If I'm starting out at A and I'm aiming to get to Z, there's no way that I could map out that road because somewhere along the way something's going to happen that's going to make Z look very different. If you don't change, you're going to become extinct. I embrace change. That's where innovation comes from."

TEAMWORK: "I believe in different minds working together. When engaged people share ideas, they cross-fertilize and contribute to thinking in other areas. It's about creating situations and the environment where people's true genius can emerge. To be successful, all of us need to function in an interdependent way."

SPIRITUALITY IN THE WORKPLACE: "With downsizing and re-engineering, a lot of workplaces have become soul-less. A great company is one where a person can bring their heart and soul to work, in addition to their brain, their feet, and their hands."

STAYING ENERGIZED: "The intensity is at such a pitch in my life, and pretty much always has been. I take retreats. I've been to Bali on a two-week trip led by a spiritual teacher. We meditated and interpreted dreams; one of the highlights was a nine-and-a-half-hour hike up and down a volcano. I've trekked in the hills of Thailand, I spent a week with a Zen Buddhist group at Auschwitz. This summer I'm going to the Amazon to visit indigenous shamans."

ADVICE FOR ENTREPRENEURS: "If you truly believe in an idea, and if you are passionate, purposeful, and persistent—even in the face of adversity—then you can achieve whatever it is you want. I say, go for your dream. You can make it happen, and don't let anyone tell you otherwise."

"

It was in 1982 that Sharon launched the company she calls her "biggest birth." "It all started when I read somewhere that 'a peacock that sits on its tail feathers is just another turkey,'" she recalls. "It was at a time when I was really bored, and the phrase struck me, especially since my maiden name means 'peacock' in a number of languages. I was inspired, and I wanted to do the same for others." Sharon started Peacock Papers with an opening product line of just a hundred message postcards, and grew it into a leading manufacturer of specialty gifts, silk-screened apparel, paper products, and party goods with more than five thousand items. "I built Peacock from the ground up," she says, "and I created the entire product line from scratch, too." She and Richard opened a Peacock store in Boston in 1984, which thrived for ten years; in 1996, her firm acquired Beach Products, an international party goods manufacturer. They merged and became Contempo Colours, Inc., a $50 million company of which Sharon served as president and chief creative officer.

Sharon was anything but a traditional executive; she believed then, as she does now, that individuals should be able to bring their whole selves to work. "At Peacock, I had scholarships for people who wanted to pursue personal development—what I call 'heart-centered consciousness work,'" she says. "If somebody wanted to enroll in that sort of program, the company would pay half." Considering that she had an in-house staff of 125, it was a most generous offer.

When Sharon sold her significant share of Contempo in 1998, it was to be her first real break in twenty-eight years. "I wondered if I could really stay put and just wait and see what came in," she remembers. "Creating, for me, has always been so fulfilling, a real magnet."

During her so-called respite, she served as a coach to a group of emerging entrepreneurs. Though she'd approached the job with purely philanthropic intent, a new project took root. "I met a young man at one of my coaching sessions," Sharon recounts. "We beelined for each other at the end of the talk because he had been involved in Internet start-ups and he'd heard that I'd grown a number of companies. We had lunch. He liked me and I sort of took him under my wing and encouraged him. A month later he called me and asked me if I would be CEO of a new company he was investing in."

Sharon was flattered, but turned him down. "My dream in life then was not to be a CEO and operate a company," she explains. "I like creating, motivating, inspiring—that, and taking great care of customers. I'm an entrepreneur."

But business moves in mysterious ways. In spite of her initial resistance, Sharon became president and CEO of Crimson Solutions, working with three techie founders still in their early twenties.

"As the lone executive I needed to wear a lot of hats, and there were many weeks when I worked over eighty hours," she confesses. To Sharon Whiteley, the reward of such intensely focused energy is "to be part of an environment where you can create a spirited, enthusiastic, and positive culture and a place where people can truly flourish." There has been another reward, as well: "I have this beginner's mind—I love learning. And right now I am learning a ton."

MARILYN CARLSON NELSON
ONE FLAG, 141 COUNTRIES

> **"I like to bring the best, most fun people together — we do more as a group than anyone could do by themselves."**

When *BusinessWeek* named its top twenty-five executives for 1998, Marilyn Carlson Nelson was one of only two women on the list. She heads up the mammoth Carlson Companies, a multibillion-dollar family business based in Minnesota. The company's holdings include the Radisson and Regent hotels, Country Inns & Suites By Carlson, TGI Friday's, Radisson Seven Seas Cruises, Carlson Wagonlit Travel, and Carlson Marketing Group, to name a few. But that's not the only reason Nelson made the short list: it's because she thinks big, and has a *joie de business* that electrifies everything she does and unifies a network of 160,000 people around the world.

If business savvy runs in families, then Nelson's inheritance is rich in more ways than one. Her father, Curtis L. Carlson, was a business legend who started the Gold Bond Stamp Company in 1938 with $55 and a dream. He introduced the concept of trading stamps—which had been used in department stores since the 1800s—to grocery stores, gas stations, and the like. After enormous success in the 1950s and 1960s, Carlson diversified into the hotel, travel, and restaurant industries. By 1977, the newly renamed Carlson Companies' revenues had hit $1 billion.

Marilyn Carlson Nelson joined her father's company in 1968 as director of community relations. But she was by no means a carbon copy of her dad. To the Carlson table she brought an international outlook she'd developed at the Sorbonne and Smith College, as well as a taste for adventure, a fluency in French, an interest in technology, and a sense of multiculturalism that seems to have been built into her nature.

"Celebrations have always been part of my life," says Nelson. Her childhood, she says, was marked by "intense, unconditional love" amid a big extended family that still brings as many as seventy people together on holidays. "Our gatherings were so inclusive that I think they defined my sense of inclusivity," she reflects. "From the time I was little I went out of my way to make sure everybody was invited to my birthday parties."

Besides living abroad in Paris and Geneva, where she studied political science and international economics, Nelson's years at Smith opened her eyes to the global community. "I loved working with people from different countries," she recalls. "I had seminars with people from Japan and Iran

INTUITIVE SCORECARD

Marilyn Carlson Nelson

VISIONARY QUALITIES
- ✔ Leadership-oriented
- _ Named business after self
- ✔ Works in glamour industry
- ✔ Master of publicity

IDEALIST QUALITIES
- _ Pragmatic
- ✔ Works within systems
- _ Holds multiple degrees
- _ Analytical
- ✔ Long-term commitment to single career

ARTISAN QUALITIES
- _ Champions underdog
- ✔ Family-centric
- ✔ Outdoorsy
- ✔ Produces tangible product
- ✔ Treats employees like family

ADVENTURER QUALITIES
- ✔ Pioneering
- ✔ Unconventional
- ✔ Socially gregarious
- ✔ Diversified career path
- _ Degree unrelated to career

and Turkey and Africa. It was so stimulating to understand and value the differences."

Nelson brought the first African-American woman into the Junior League in 1964. "Minnesota led the way," she says. "She was a lawyer, a perfect candidate. I was asked by members from the South how I could dream of such a thing, but the National Junior League did accept her."

Nelson herself faced a different sort of discrimination in her early business days. After graduation, she worked as a securities analyst at PaineWebber in Minneapolis, where she was asked to use the abbreviation "M. C. Nelson" on her correspondence in order to mask her gender. More than ten years later she was the first woman to take a place on the board of First Trust Company. "The boardroom was in this skyscraper," she recalls, "and I had to go down two floors to use the ladies' room. That was sort of symbolic to me—there was no thought of women being there."

But Nelson was never one to back down from a challenge. Even as she worked her way through the ranks at Carlson Companies, she and her younger sister, Barbara Gage, bought a bank—the Citizens State Bank of Waterville, Minnesota—and took an active management role in its operations for three decades.

For two women to buy a bank in 1971 is pretty astonishing. But Nelson explains that in a family without brothers "there were no girl jobs and boy jobs. We shoveled the walk. We got a speedboat, and my father taught me to spell him and wind the ropes. As I became more engaged and he could see that I was intellectually curious, he'd use his sales and marketing skills to urge me to set goals. If I was elected vice president he'd ask me when I was going to be president."

MARILYN CARLSON NELSON ON . . .

GLOBAL PARTNERSHIPS: "The American way is not the only way, and it may not always be the best way. . . . We're finding that once we go into a partnership or a joint venture that our objective is to create a new culture using, ideally, the best of each culture."

DIVERSITY: "Inclusivity has been a hallmark of my life. We forget how much society's changed. We forget that there were times in history when Catholics and Protestants were seldom married, let alone the diversity we enjoy now."

HER ADVENTURER ENERGIES: "I love to organize people, and to do things that have never been done before. I'm not a particularly good maintainer. I like to start things, and I like to create memorable experiences. We're going into the experience economy—people are looking for experiences, and they're looking for relationships, two themes of my life. And it's on a global basis—that makes three. I'm so excited to be where I am."

HER IDEALIST HUSBAND: "Glen is the best partner in the world. We're yin and yang. He's a scientist, and has actually stimulated me to combine sales and marketing with measurement and precision."

ADVICE FOR WOMEN: "There's a Carlson credo: 'Whatever you do, do with integrity. Wherever you go, go as a leader. Whomever you serve, serve with caring. Whenever you dream, dream with your all. And never, ever give up.'"

Nelson worked side by side with her powerful, demanding father for thirty years. On March 23, 1998, in front of 5,000 Carlson employees assembled at the MGM Grand in Las Vegas and a panel of special guests, including George Bush, the eighty-three-year-old Curt Carlson handed over the reins of the company he'd been building for sixty years. Marilyn Carlson Nelson was now CEO. To celebrate the occasion, she climbed into an F-16 fighter jet and took a little spin—at nine g's—above the Nevada desert.

"I like to go fast," Nelson says with a laugh. "I like to ski—it's as close as you can get to flying—and water ski, and I love to dance." She also loves in-line skating, as she once proved at a business meeting. "We were trying to get people to take risks," she explains. To underscore her point, she decided to Rollerblade into the 4,000-strong meeting. "I got really nervous, even my daughter was worried for me. She asked, 'Is this executive behavior?' Before going in I bladed up and down the hallways, in this enormous hotel in Vegas, to practice."

Of course, the stunt was a hit. Nelson also brought the house down when she showed up at a party for one of her groups that was being held at a nightclub called the Glam Slam. "They had asked me to give a welcoming speech," she says. "And I thought, I can't go down there in a designer suit, it's a party! So I got motorcycle boots, old jeans, flip-up shades, and I wrote a rap song and came out and performed it. At first they didn't know it was me, then someone caught on, and they went crazy."

One of the most spectacular performances Nelson ever pulled off was outside the corporate realm entirely: she brought Super Bowl '92 to Minnesota, in the dead of the Twin Cities' legendary winter. It was a huge job to which she applied astounding energy and creativity; the night before the final site selection vote, she sent toy bathtub ducks to each NFL owner's room, with a message: "For a great game and wildlife, play indoors in Minnesota!" (a reference to the Minneapolis Metrodome). The resulting event, which included citywide celebrations, brought more than $100 million into the state.

Super Bowl '92 is just one of the many civic and community events that Nelson has hosted in her home state. But what occupies most of her energy is her company's continued growth and its worldwide presence.

The CEO's goals are multilayered: on one hand, she wants to double the size of the company every five years. (Anyone who has noticed TGI Friday's two-stores-a-week growth won't doubt that she can make it happen.) She plans to continue to forge partnerships all over the world, in order to create win-win situations in new markets. She wants her company to be data-driven and relationship-driven—she has said that "we are as much a technology company as a service company"—and that her objective is never having to ask customers the same question twice. Ever forward-thinking, Nelson ultimately wants to take on a holistic, lifetime view of customers and customer relations—an idea that was nurtured by her husband, a surgeon who is vice chairman of Meditronic, Inc.

Throughout it all, however, Marilyn Nelson beats the drum of global consciousness. "I have a profound sense of interdependence," she says. "I believe we can do things together that we can't do alone. I like to bring the best, most fun people together—we do more as a group than anyone could do by themselves.

"We're a family business, but it's important to me that my children and grandchildren and nieces and nephews understand that we have 160,000 people in 141 countries working under our flag. I'm passionate about building a truly global company, one that has voices at the table from all over the world."

ADVICE FOR ADVENTURERS

• **TRY, TRY, TRY TO SIMPLIFY.** If you're like most Adventurers, you have a tendency to turn one-act plays into epic costume dramas. If you need to make boring jobs more interesting, challenge yourself to be as efficient as possible, and pit yourself against the clock to see if you can complete them in record time.

• **FEED YOUR HEAD.** While you're taking over the world, don't forget to sign up for a course here and there, visit a museum, see a really good play — and for God's sake, take a vacation. When Adventurers get too tired to work they tend to just lie down and tune the world out — which doesn't exactly refill their creative well. Plan recreational activities for yourself that recharge your batteries with intellectual and visual stimulation.

• **DON'T LET YOUR SOCIAL LIFE OVERWHELM YOUR PROFESSIONAL LIFE.** The Adventurer can easily become friends with her co-workers and clients, and so runs the risk of having her personal relationships eclipse her business relationships. The best way to guard against this is to set stringent standards for yourself, and don't relax them in the presence of friendship. Just because your friend/associate understands why you're late for a meeting doesn't mean it's okay.

• **AVOID ACTING OUT.** As an Adventurer, it might feel perfectly natural for you to rant dramatically about whatever's on your mind, whether it's market conditions, Bob in Accounting, or the traffic that morning. But what you might see as a perfectly healthy blast of steam-letting might make other people acutely uncomfortable. Sure, you don't take your own rantings seriously, but others might — especially sensitive Artisans and fact-centered Idealists.

• **REMEMBER TO LISTEN.** Adventurers have large personalities and can easily dominate conversations, meetings, and projects. Make the effort to quiet yourself and tune in to what others are saying. You'll probably learn a lot — and it will help you keep a grip on reality.

• **FINISH ONE THING BEFORE YOU START THE NEXT.** Yes, projects do get boring after the honeymoon is over. You have to finish them anyway, or no dessert for you.

• **WHEN CHOOSING A CAREER, THINK OF THE LONG-TERM.** Do you really want to be an astronaut, or do you just want to float weightlessly? Do you really want to be a radio disc jockey, or do you just want strangers to call you in the middle of the night? Do you really want to be a beekeeper, or do you just like the outfit? Adventurers sometimes don't know the difference between having a calling and having the urge to play a role.

• **KEEP IN TOUCH WITH YOUR INNER FABULOUSNESS.** Don't let dull tasks, drab surroundings, or cranky co-workers get you down. Bring your cheerful, creative self to work every day, and seek social approval elsewhere.

What Have You Learned?

TEST YOUR INTUITIVE KNOW-HOW:
MATCH THE POCKETBOOKS WITH THEIR OWNERS' TYPES

1. I am a canvas backpack that once belonged to a Boy Scout in 1962. Inside of me are pencils, a spiral-bound notepad, Chap Stick, a Swiss Army knife, and a water bottle. **To whom do I belong?**

2. I am a sleek aluminum-clad evening bag. I am carrying one Clinique lipstick, two keys on a ring, a credit card, a $10 bill, and a very small cell phone. **Who is my mistress?**

3. I am a red leather tote. I'm filled with an overstuffed Filofax, an overstuffed makeup bag, a passport, an overstuffed wallet, a checkbook, the newest Archie McPhee catalog, old newspaper clippings, a copy of *Bridget Jones's Diary,* four books of matches, ten pens, Post-it notes, a bag of M&M's, tissues, an address book, stray business cards, a cocktail napkin with phone numbers written on it, a broken earring, and a well of paper clips, hair clips, hair ties, and bobby pins. **On whose shoulder am I swinging?**

4. I am a black leather handbag with a discreet monogram. I am housing a jeweled compact and lipstick case, a small hair brush, a slim wallet, a Mont Blanc fountain pen, sunglasses in a case, a nail file, and a purse-sized spray of Giorgio Armani's Red. **Whom do I belong to?**

5. I am a featherweight leather briefcase neatly packed with a calculator, a laptop computer, a train schedule, a comb, a pair of running shoes, today's crossword puzzle, and a tube of deodorant. **Who owns me?**

6. I am a pink microfiber handbag. Inside of me is a date book, a cell phone, a beeper, sunglasses without their case, a bottle of aspirin, wads of cash, and three shades of MAC lipstick. **Who is carrying me around?**

7. I am a green velvet shoulder bag. I am toting a copy of *Martha Stewart Living,* a vial of valerian, reading glasses, knitting equipment, a change purse, a small bottle of hand cream, family photos, and an expandable mesh tote bag. **On whose shoulder do I rest?**

8. I am a soft leather briefcase with a shoulder strap. Inside of me is a sheaf of CVs printed on very good paper, a letter of introduction from a well-known CEO, a hardcover novel, and a boarding pass. **Whom do I belong to?**

ANSWERS: 1. Artisan **2.** Idealist **3.** Adventurer **4.** Visionary **5.** Idealist **6.** Adventurer **7.** Artisan **8.** Visionary

6

Intuitive Finances

Your best friend bought a house, all by herself, when she was still in her twenties and earning less than $30,000 a year. Your other best friend makes more than you do, yet she has terrible credit and no savings to speak of. Your sister announced last week that she's buying a Miata with her annual bonus—and paying cash. Your closest co-worker brings her lunch to work every day and looks at you funny when you pay $1.50 for a latte.

Do these circumstances baffle you? That may be because women, who are so tuned in to relationships with their loved ones, their careers, their homes, and their bodies, tend to clam up when it comes to their relationship with money. It seems to be a far more intimate subject than sex, cigarettes, or even food.

Only in recent history have women been given the power to control their personal finances, and the permission to discuss their financial facts of life with people other than their husbands or their dads. The fact is, every woman has her own financial style, and each is as valid as the next. Her challenge, in these revolutionary times, is to understand her own attitudes and impulses toward saving, investing, earning, and spending the green stuff. After all, knowing one's money habits is yet another way of knowing oneself.

The Visionary and Money:
More Is More

I've been poor and I've been rich. Rich is better.

— BESSIE SMITH

"To me, success is about taking charge of your own destiny, serving others, and making tons of money." So announced Carol Szatkowski to the *Boston Globe* upon her nomination for 1998's Business Woman of the Year, an award sponsored by New England Women Business Owners. "I craved a job that would recognize me if I worked hard and smart. I wanted a house and Caribbean vacations."

Carol's attitude is typical of many Visionaries. When it comes to money, they are not apt to stretch and save it, as a good number of Artisans do, or meticulously invest most of it, as Idealists might. To the Visionary, money is the ticket to a better life. Her ideal is to have plenty of cash to enjoy in the here and now, while keeping enough in a portfolio to provide for a comfortable retirement.

Financially, Visionaries are not major risk-takers. ("You won't find me in Vegas," says one.) They're unlikely to take a second mortgage on their house to start a business; they'd rather romance outside investors to take that risk for them. When it comes to personal finances, the archetypal Visionary hires a financial advisor or a broker to quietly make conservative investments, that is, blue-chip stocks.

The Visionary's day-to-day spending habits are a different story. Because Visionaries are material girls who crave the best of everything, they'll go ahead and splurge on a really nice car or an expensive vacation. Visionaries tend to spend freely on personal items like clothes, haircuts, and dinners in good restaurants. "I love shopping, I love makeup," announces magazine developer Estelle Sobel. "I love massages, facials, manicures, pedicures, spas. I can't do regular traveling anymore because I'm so used to press trips; I expect someone to greet me at the door with an itinerary and treat me like a VIP."

There is a method behind the Visionary's madness: for one thing, life's niceties cheer her and keep her motivated. For another, she believes that money attracts money. And, since she's always looking to reach the next financial rung, it is important to her to maintain the most luxurious lifestyle she can afford.

Although there are those rare Visionaries who are indifferent about money and what it can buy, these Visionaries probably (a) never had to worry about money; or (b) have a different kind of currency that they care about. Visionaries in academia, for instance, might focus their ambitions on earning degrees, writing books, and getting tenure. They don't expect to get rich, but they do expect to gain respectability, security, a certain status, and, most important, knowledge.

Colleen Mohyde is one Visionary for whom money is a secondary concern. When she first got into publishing, earning $11,000 a year as an editorial assistant, she remembers that her father was appalled. "He didn't think all the free books I could read were much of an incentive," she says. "Having a new car every two years was his idea of success. How much money you made was one of his yardsticks of being smart."

At one point, when her salary was still in the teens, Colleen was offered a job from the Speaker of the House in Massachusetts for $25,000 a year. "I wrestled and wrestled with it, and I ended up turning him down," she says. "You think you make a difference in politics, but you end up trying to get someone reelected. The issues you deal with are superficial. Literature and books felt more substantial, I felt that my work at Little, Brown was in the grand scheme of things more important—it was much more powerful to be working with ideas."

These days, Colleen is still working with ideas as a literary agent. It's interesting to note, however, that her hobby is playing the stock market. "I do a lot of shopping, depending on how the market's doing," she confesses. "Alan Greenspan controls my shopping sprees. I have about one hundred pairs of shoes now . . . do same ones in different colors count?"

Anything Worth Doing Well Is Worth Being Paid Well For

Visionaries can't stand being underpaid. They're well aware of what their contributions are worth, and it's deeply painful for them to fall behind the high end of the pay curve. If you are a Visionary, you're probably familiar with the tightening in your chest when you read about someone who makes twice what you do for the same work.

It's no wonder that so many Visionaries become "bail-out" entrepreneurs—those who leave the corporate world to start their own businesses. Carol Szatkowski is one: she started her working life as a nurse. She left to take on a higher-paying job in recruitment, then quit that position for a gig that had no earnings ceiling: CEO of Clear Point Consultants, her own company, which provides temporary placement of specialized employees. In 1998 the firm grossed about $8.5 million—definitely enough for a house and Caribbean vacations.

Mary Kay also set off on her own in pursuit of higher earnings. In 1952, she found herself stuck in a male-dominated company with no promise of advancement. An excellent saleswoman, she was training men who would then be promoted and given salaries higher than hers. When one of her trainees became her supervisor at twice the money she was making, she quit and started her own company, Mary Kay Cosmetics. By 1968 she was a millionaire; in 1995 her personal worth was estimated at $320 million.

Inexpensive Riches

Visionaries like beautiful things of lasting quality. But what about Visionaries who can barely buy Kraft's macaroni and cheese, much less blue-chip stocks and $300 shoes? They have to use more ingenuity, but their commitment to quality remains the same. You can find not-rich Visionaries snapping up gorgeous drapes in Goodwill stores, buying sets of china at yard sales, working out barters and trades whenever possible, and exhibiting spectacular chutzpah when needed.

Estelle Sobel laughs when she describes her early days as a lowly administrative assistant in New York. "I was twenty-three, I had no money, and I decided I wanted a doorman apartment. My friends said, 'You'll never get it, Estelle!' I went to a roommate-finding service, they had a place I loved, but the woman wanted a roommate who was at least twenty-five. I went and met her, confessed I was twenty-three but very mature, and talked her out of the other candidate. I knew I was going to get that apartment. I walked around singing, *'I'm moving on up, to the East Side, to a deeelux apartment in the sky. . . .'* It was gorgeous, there was a pool on the roof, I had my own room—and a doorman, of course."

Like many Visionaries, Estelle had a clear picture of how she wanted her life to look, right down to the fashion details. "I went and bought myself a Joan Collins hat, a little power outfit, and I had a briefcase—with nothing in it but my lunch! I was so into it. Of course I was too big for my britches. My first assignment, which was to get doughnuts and pastries for a meeting, I botched totally. I didn't have the experience to back up my look."

Spend/Not Spend

Of two evils choose the prettier.

— CAROLYN WELLS

Visionaries—with or without a fat salary—are anything but cheap. In fact, they usually err on the side of extravagance. In the workplace as well as in their homes, they believe wholeheartedly in spending money on services. Many Visionaries choose to work extra hours to afford hiring others

FINANCIAL ADVICE FOR VISIONARIES

- **CONTROL YOUR MONEY.** Visionaries tend to be very focused on certain areas of their lives (e.g., their jobs) and delegate the hell out of everything else. Though delegation might be smart and practical, be very careful when putting your finances in the hands of bookkeepers, accountants, investment counselors, stockbrokers, and the like. Work only with professionals, and keep a close watch on what they're doing. Though it may not be your area of expertise and might distract you from your pressing day-to-day duties, take time to look after your finances. Insist on regular reports and make sure that you understand them fully — and that you fully approve of how your money is being handled.

- **SHOP FOR THE BEST SERVICES.** It is typically Visionary to find a good service and stick with it. Visionaries tend to be loyal to a single bank, for instance, or to always buy their cars at the same dealership. While this may save the Visionary time and mental energy, it's not such a good financial habit. For instance, your stuffy accounting firm with the impressive offices might keep you square with the IRS, but could be missing loopholes and restructuring that could increase your bottom line. Shopping for financial services should be an ongoing project. Keep your eye open for a better broker, a better banker, a better rate on your credit card. It's your money, and it's up to you to make it perform.

- **AVOID OVERSPENDING.** Visionaries are self-confident and are prone to betting on themselves. While this is a fine quality in business, it can mean trouble when it's applied to lines of credit and purchases that really are out of your price range.

- **KNOW THAT SOME THINGS CAN'T BE BOUGHT.** Go ahead and join a country club if you want to play golf, swim laps, or have a place to bring your dinner guests when you don't feel like cooking. *Don't* join a country club if you think it's going to boost your social ranking and therefore magically improve your bottom line. Some Visionaries are enamored with how they look "on paper," and will spend ridiculous amounts of money on designer clothes, cars, vacations, etc., in order to gain prestige. This is folly. Your personal choices — especially when it comes to recreation — should please you, down deep in your soul. Other people's opinions should never enter the picture.

- **KEEP FINANCIAL ISSUES IN PERSPECTIVE.** Visionaries can focus too hard on money and drain the joy out of their work and even their lives. In her book *The 9 Steps to Financial Freedom,* Suze Orman describes going through phases where she'd obsess about money and throw herself first into panic, and then depression. That is, until she discovered a cure for her financial freak-outs: she'd give money to charity. "With each check I wrote, whether it was for $5 or $500, I felt more powerful," she writes. "I was able to extinguish the feeling of poverty that had been burning at me. That act, for me, was worth its weight in gold."

to clean, do taxes, mow the lawn, and maintain the computer system—though in a pinch they could probably do it themselves.

Even if she's a CEO with a multimillion-dollar budget, the Visionary will resent earmarking funds for mundane stuff like paper towels, vacuum cleaner bags, and utility bills. That's because the Visionary gets no pleasure from workhorse staples. She'd much rather splurge on a high-priced consultant or launch a lavish ad campaign.

Though Visionaries are very energetic workers, they hate to waste their energies on anything that somebody else could do just as well—if not better. But hiring all those helper services can get expensive and cut into the budget for what Visionaries really want: tangible gains.

Artisans and Money:
An Uneasy Alliance

> I didn't want to be rich, I just wanted enough to get the couch reupholstered.
>
> — KATE MOSTEL

In the Artisan's world, "happiness" and "financial success" are not locked arm in arm. In fact, they barely know each other. When the Artisan thinks of success, she doesn't envision a two-comma income, but a rich life filled with love, joy, discovery, and personal fulfillment. Though many Artisans recognize that life might be easier with a bottomless well of assets, they are far too spiritual to believe that making money is a worthy goal in and of itself.

Caroline Hirsch, owner and CEO of Caroline's Comedy Club and Comedy Nation Restaurant, knows this lesson well: "Money doesn't buy happiness," she told *Bust* magazine. "Money doesn't buy love. . . . Your life has to be fuller than that. You can really only shop a certain number of days."

Most Artisans do have financial goals. They are practical creatures and will do whatever it takes to survive and thrive. But their long-term ambitions are rarely about accumulating fabulous wealth. More often, the Artisan only wants three things: a house, enough money to comfortably provide for her family, and a little left over so she can go on vacation once in a while.

Certainly, not every Artisan shares the same vision. But whatever her particular wish list might look like, it probably doesn't include dreams of prestige, elevated social standing, or embarrassments of riches. The Artisan is connected to more basic goals like comfort, stability, and security.

SOME ARGUMENTS FOR INVESTING

Artisans can be uncomfortable doing anything more creative with their money than stashing it in CDs, money market accounts, and/or IRAs. Are you one of these cautious creatures who shy away from making serious investments? If so, perhaps the following facts will give you a nudge in the right financial direction.

• Family-centric Artisans are deeply committed to their children's futures. That means college, and those costs can be staggering. American Express Financial Advisors, in its *Guide to Financial Well Being,* does the math: If you've had a baby within the last five years, his or her undergraduate education will run you anywhere from $89,000 to $264,000. Saving money in an interest-bearing account is not the way to cover those expenses; sound investments are called for.

• Too many married women — not only Artisans — rely on their husbands to watch over family finances. While this might work in the short term (if the marriage is healthy), it can be devastating with advancing years. At the age of sixty-five, women outnumber men three to two. At eighty-five there are five women for every two men. Odds are great that you'll outlive your husband, at which point you will not only inherit the job of family CFO but will also have to provide for yourself for the rest of your life. Considering that life expectancy is increasing rapidly, a woman widowed at age sixty-seven could very well be on her own for another thirty years. To make matters worse, statistics released by PaineWebber found that one out of five investors have neither a will nor a written financial plan that specifically deals with a surviving spouse.

• If you're single or without husbandly benefits, beware. The U.S. Department of Labor reports that only 38 percent of female retirees receive pension benefits, and only 21 percent receive health coverage that can be continued for life. In 1996, 13.6 percent of women age sixty-five and over lived below the poverty level, compared with 6.8 percent of men in the same age group — that's 2.5 million women vis-à-vis 912,000 men.

• Shelley Schlossberg, CFP, of PaineWebber, has a reminder: Women still earn about one-quarter less than men do. "They also often take time away from their careers to raise children and care for elderly parents," she notes in Paine Webber's *Women & Investing,* "so they may have less money in traditional pension and Social Security funds." The general rule of thumb is that you will need approximately 75 percent of your pre-retirement income to maintain your present standard of living once you retire. "Social Security and your pension plan will probably provide less than half of that amount," says Schlossberg, and adds that the situation "could worsen in the future."

Earthly Pursuits

> I've been in trailers and penthouses and everyone wants the same thing—and that's peace of mind.
>
> —NAOMI JUDD

The Artisan is not on this earth to take, but to share. Of the four types, she is most aware of her place in the community and in the ecosystem. She is pained by wastefulness and believes in sharing the wealth on every level. Rather than looking for superfluous financial gains, she tries to utilize her energies in ways that will do the most good. Yes, she is committed to sustaining herself and her family. But she also wants to save the planet, right wrongs, create opportunities, and work toward common goals that will benefit everyone, in her time and in generations to come.

Claire Criscuolo, vegetarian guru and owner of Claire's Corner Copia in New Haven, Connecticut, is one Artisan who sees her company as part of a whole. Over the years, her restaurant has been a steady contributor to an astounding number of local organizations, for one simple reason: Claire believes in spreading her good fortune around. "It's not that I don't want to be rich," she says. "I just don't want others to be poor. I remember dropping toys off to a shelter once, and seeing this little kid and his mother, and they had no sheets on their bed. I was going home to my nice Laura Ashley sheets, and I was sick with the thought. My husband and I immediately ran out and bought sheets for the shelter."

It's just one example of the heartfelt generosity that the Criscuolos are known for. "At the rate I give money away I don't have to worry about being rich," Claire laughs. "But do you really need forty pairs of shoes? I'm very glad that I don't."

Artisans with minimal resources are also known to respond to the call of the less fortunate. Ayéssa Rourke, for instance, who makes a modest living from her job at the L.A. Zoo, has "several charities that I don't consider luxuries. Nature Conservancy, World Wildlife Fund, National Wildlife Federation. I just give every year no matter what."

Cents and Sensibility

Artisans want to answer to their hearts as well as their heads. But even the purest intentions can be muddied by reality. So when times get tough, the Artisan does what she has to do to keep the lights on. She may have to battle her own ambivalence about the working world, but ultimately she's a realist with a grounded sense of what it takes to get along.

That means making money and making the money work. Artisans are, in fact, excellent money managers. It is in their nature to budget themselves and stay right on top of income versus expenditures. Rarely do Artisans overspend; in fact, they can make do with very little. Artisans wouldn't consider getting a new car if the old one was still mechanically sound; they'd gladly re-heel a favorite pair of shoes instead of retiring them, and absolutely see the wisdom of libraries versus bookstores (unlike Visionaries, who would much rather own a book than borrow it).

Cherie Whaples-Elliott (Artisan, Adventurer) is just getting started with her antiques appraisal business, and she doesn't mind the up-front financial sacrifice. "I make hardly any money at this point but I love it," she says. "I'm packing this experience in a suitcase." She and her husband rise to the challenge of living with less, and do it with cheer. "People who make $50,000 a year and say they don't have any money are full of it—they just don't know how to manage their money," she asserts. "We're careful. We made all of $30,000 last year but we bought a house and completely renovated it, using our own four hands."

Some Artisans keep an extra-close watch on finances because they can't stand owing money. To these Artisans, debt is like indentured servitude—they cannot feel free with unpaid balances hanging over their heads. Of course, that concern varies from person to person. There are those who will fret desperately over $20 borrowed from a friend, but will let Citibank twist in the wind.

Artisans vs. Money

It's better to have a rich soul than to be rich.

—OLGA KORBUT

Many an Artisan dislikes thinking about, talking about, or handling money. Some have such an aversion to financial dealings that they'd almost rather be poor.

Lisa Somers, a modest "mompreneur," is one Artisan who has an uncomfortable relationship with money, which developed early in life. "I come from a fairly wealthy family," she explains. "My grandparents were well-off, and my dad grew up in a household where money replaced affection. His parents never said 'I love you,' they just gave him money. Which had a great impact on him. As a dad he was hard to talk to, but our contract was that if we needed something, we had to go to him. He wasn't allowing us to love him or talk to him outside of the realm of needing

FINANCIAL ADVICE FOR ARTISANS

• **TAKE CONTROL OF YOUR EARNINGS.** Do you blithely agree to standard payroll deduction packages offered by your company? Do you faithfully follow your banker's advice? Are your investments entirely handled by your husband? Sorry, not good enough. Your financial health is way too important to pawn off on faceless institutions, one-size-fits-all advisors, or relatives, no matter how much you trust them. You've got to become an educated, active participant — your own Chief Financial Officer. (See "Some Arguments for Investing" on page 183 for a taste of what can happen if you don't.) Does the thought of making financial decisions give you the willies? Read on.

• **OVERCOME YOUR FEAR OF MONEY.** If you're intimidated by all things Wall Street (as Suze Orman once was), get help. First, read a book or two about the basics of investing. Second, find an investment counselor with a good reputation that will take time to explain everything in terms you understand and get you started at a pace that you're comfortable with. Learning about investments is like learning to use a computer: it's best to start slowly, and though it may be confusing at first, once you get the hang of it you can become a pro in no time. It can even be fun and rewarding, in more ways than one.

• **AND SPEAKING OF COMPUTERS . . .** the archetypal Artisan is resistant to new technology. While it's okay to avoid microwave ovens and insist on driving standard-transmission cars, any woman who still can't use a computer is handicapping herself. Finances and investments can be swiftly and easily tracked on a home computer. It's become a tool that nobody — not even Artisans — can afford to be without.

• **ASK FOR WHAT YOU'RE WORTH.** Artisans typically aren't very good at asking for salaries, fees, and raises. Here's some time-honored advice: When entering any kind of pay-setting negotiation, arm yourself with what's called "objective criteria." This is data, researched by you, that shows what your kind of work is currently fetching in the marketplace. If you're a freelance graphic designer, for instance, get hold of the *Graphic Artists Guild Handbook of Pricing & Ethical Guidelines* (10th edition, Northlight Books), which spells out accepted industry fees for hundreds of graphics jobs, from menu design to national ad campaigns. Use it to help determine a price, then bring it to your meeting in case you need to defend your proposed fee.

If you're negotiating a salary, check out job banks or recruitment sites on the Internet to see what other companies are offering. Print out the appropriate page and take it with you. With objective criteria in hand, negotiations are no longer about what you want, what you need, or what you're "worth." They're simply about the fair market value of the work. Which can take the guilt, fear, and worry out of virtually any monetary discussion.

- **MAKE FRIENDS WITH DEBT.** Living in the black is noble and easy on the nerves, but if you want to do something grand like start a business or buy a franchise, loans are a fact of life. Smart borrowing is nothing to be wary of: everybody wins, including the lender, the economy, your employees, and you.
- **SPEND SOME MONEY ON YOUR OUTER SELF.** Artisans tend to put their loved ones' needs before their own. Many are also more concerned with their inner beauty than with their appearance. While this might put the Artisan a little closer to heaven, it can also tempt her to get by with clothes that have seen better days, and she can end up making a poor impression in business situations.

  If you're guilty of cutting corners when it comes to your wardrobe and your grooming, stop that right now. Go get a great haircut. Buy some new shoes and an outfit that you absolutely love (sure, you can buy it at on off-price retailer—who's to know?). And don't think that your professional style has to include power suits and shining pumps. Loose, flowing layers can make for a perfectly appropriate business wardrobe that's perfectly comfortable.
- **KNOW THE VALUE OF YOUR TIME.** Figure it out. Is your time worth, say, $60 an hour? Put a price on it. Then ask yourself, when you're following your Artisan work ethic and doing things like preparing your taxes, retiling your bathroom floor, and changing the oil in your car, if such jobs are worth your time. Sure, Artisans are capable, but that doesn't mean they have to do everything themselves. Time is money, and so is energy. Open your checkbook and hire a tax preparer, an errand-runner, a household helper, and assign yourself to the things you want to do and the things you get paid to do. Your mind, your body, and your work will be better for it.

money. Even asking him for five dollars to go to the movies killed me. In my own little-girl way I knew it hurt him. I knew he was repeating negative patterns."

Lisa came to believe that money stood in the way of happiness, communication, and even love. "To this day it's hard for me to ask for money in any situation," she says.

Ayéssa, L.A. zookeeper, is not motivated by money—but she does respect it. "I'm always concerned that I pay my bills before they're due," she says. "I'd like to have a little bit more than I have now, but I definitely wouldn't want to be a multimillionaire. I think when you have a certain amount of money, you become a commodity. God, what a pain."

Some Artisans, especially those who grew up in financially deprived circumstances, feel alienated from that mythical sector known as "people with money." Suze Orman had that problem. In *The 9 Steps to Financial Freedom* she describes her early days as a stockbroker at Merrill Lynch: "Taking that job was breaking away from everything I had ever known. I was so out of my league. The most I had ever made before was $400 a month as a waitress. . . . I'd go to work with all these men in their pin-striped three-piece suits. When everyone else would go to lunch at their fancy restaurants, I'd get in my car and go to Taco Bell. It was the only part of the day when I felt comfortable in my surroundings."

Orman eventually conquered her fear of money. It required a long and painful personal journey, but she ultimately developed a fruitful, rewarding relationship with her financial self. The lesson she learned was that abundance is a state of mind: "It takes both money and spiritual understanding to sustain us."

What Artisans Want

> Earth's crammed with heaven.
>
> —ELIZABETH BARRETT BROWNING

The importance of Artisan homeownership cannot be emphasized enough. The Artisan's eye is focused on a future that includes a wonderful place to live and the promise of weekends spent digging in the dirt, patching up the roof, or painting the attic room. But even a one-room apartment will sustain her, as long as she owns it and can call it home.

When an Artisan's salary isn't high enough to put her real estate dreams within reach, she can become unhappy and unmotivated. Which is why some Artisan freelancers, entrepreneurs, and part-timers give up their flexible schedules and squeeze themselves into the pumps and pantyhose of the corporate world. The trade-off isn't perfect, but it works: though she may have to endure eight daily hours in a windowless office, she can at least depend on regular paychecks—as well as a 401(k) plan, or perhaps a yearly bonus. With a predictable income in place, the Artisan can set a realistic future date upon which her dreams can be hitched.

The Artisan's perfect world includes a loving family, a nice home, a healthy body, and a career that is a reflection of her truest self. But if it comes down to a choice between those four elements, the dream career will no doubt be sacrificed for a job that supports the other three.

The Idealist and Money:
Making It, and Making It Behave

Investing is crucial for everyone, but for women in particular.
I'm really against being dependent upon anybody when it comes
to your finances.

— CATHY CLAY, FLOOR OFFICIAL, PACIFIC EXCHANGE

The very first bankers were probably Idealists. In fact, the whole concept of investing was probably an Idealist invention. Idealists have a real feeling not only for making money, but for making money perform. Rarely impulsive or frivolous, many of them start contributing to a retirement fund while still in their twenties, and are conscious of what their dollars are doing at all times.

Idealists see far into the future (unlike Adventurers, who believe life is short). They're interested in long-term growth and make provisions for that time when they no longer have a steady income stream.

"I have the same goal that a lot of people have," says Susan Hanlon, a Massachusetts-based engineer. "That is, when I retire I want to have the lifestyle I have now. And if you don't think about it now, you're not going to have it. You need to plan for it and you need to save for it. A big revelation for me was that my 401(k) savings plan was for my retirement—not for a rainy day, or a down payment on a house. Retirement is what it's for. That's what it's all about."

True Idealists take control of their money and pay attention not only to the big picture, but to day-to-day maintenance. They make a plan and stick with it, and are usually scrupulous about going over their financial statements, analyzing their expenditures, and keeping up a constant system of checks and balances. To the Idealist, such routines are as important as exercising regularly or having her teeth cleaned twice a year. Well-tended finances are part of what makes the Idealist's world go 'round.

Get Smart

You know all those books about overseas investments, Wall Street secrets, understanding mutual funds, and winning in the investment game? Idealists read them. What's more, they act on what they learn. They rely on solid, time-tested information to guide them through jungles of investment options. Once they've gathered all the data they can get their hands on, they take only moderate risks and tend to construct portfolios of diversified products that offer slow, steady growth.

FINANCIAL ADVICE FOR IDEALISTS

- **TRY TO MAINTAIN A BALANCE BETWEEN WHAT YOU LOVE TO DO AND WHAT YOUR PROJECTED FINANCIAL NEEDS ARE.** Idealists can find themselves trapped in jobs they despise because they have a pension plan that kicks in after ten years, or they're counting on a severance package, etc. Though it might make financial sense for you to stay, look into your soul, and figure out if it's time for you to bust out of equity jail. Remember: You might be able to negotiate a new package with a new employer in which you lose nothing financially and gain a better life.
- **DON'T WAIT TOO LONG TO MAKE A MOVE.** Idealists are so methodical that, when it comes to making investments, they're liable to comparison-shop their way right out of good opportunities. Not everything is based on logic or hard data; sometimes, intuition is part of the formula. Learn to trust yourself and to take calculated risks once in a while.
- **LET THE INTERNET BE YOUR FINANCIAL PLAYGROUND.** Many Idealists enjoy the challenges — and the rewards — of investing. And finances have never been more exciting than they are now, thanks to the multitude of Web sites dedicated to the almighty dollar. So go surfing, and splash around in vast oceans of advice, insights, statistics, and forecasts.
- **HAVE SOME FUN WITH YOUR MONEY.** Inside every Idealist is a tiny Ebenezer Scrooge, busily acquiring wealth and not enjoying it. Don't let Scrooge take over! Take a tip from those successful Idealists who have a ball with their money by indulging in hobbies that also happen to be good investments. Buy some art that thrills you; blow a stack of bills on a hand-written score by Gershwin; start collecting original Eames furniture.
- **SHARE THE WEALTH.** Speaking of Ebenezer Scrooge . . . remember to put a percentage of your profits toward good works in the community. For ideas on how to go about reaping the joy that giving brings, see page 278.

This is not to suggest that Idealists are prone to act as their own brokers or investment agents. Their usual M.O. is to educate themselves, then do intensified research about financial counselors. They are far too realistic to believe that they could do a better job than a professional with fifteen years of experience. Yet they make their choices carefully, and, even if they have the utmost respect for their portfolio manager, they don't simply go along with what is suggested. They check it out for themselves and only make a move if they feel totally informed and secure about the decision.

Idealists take the same approach when they're shopping for major purchases. In fact, they are such methodical consumers that they can drive Adventurers crazy. "Comparison" is the Idealist's middle name, and she will take all the time in the world (and test the patience of many salespeople) before making a decision. This is because Idealists have a wide streak of perfectionism, and really suffer when they make mistakes. They want to know what they're getting, where the money is coming from, and how something like a car lease or an addition to the house will impact their financial landscape for years to come.

The Idealist's concern with fiscal responsibility flies in the face of popular myths about women and money. No one knows this better than Cathy Clay, a market maker and floor manager for Timber Hill, LLC, and a floor official for the Pacific Exchange in San Francisco. "You know those stupid myths, about how women are not good with money, that they spend too much and that they don't invest smartly? That's completely false," she told *Bust* magazine. "During my years as a financial planner, I worked with women who were very concerned about what they did with their money and how they invested it. Many times, they were more savvy than their husbands or other men."

Susan Hanlon is one Idealist who is at odds with her husband when it comes to financial practices. "I rarely carry more than forty dollars in my wallet," she says. "It drives my husband crazy, he's got two hundred dollars in his wallet all the time. He's impulsive, and I'm a planner. I just can't take that much money out of my checking account for no reason. It's my own way of regulating what's going out the door." Susan's regulations are pretty effective: "I've never crossed that line where I have a bill I can't pay," she says. "I only bounced a check once, and it wasn't my fault."

Ask and Ye Shall Receive

Idealists usually know what their contributions are worth and what the market will bear, so when it comes to asking for money they tend to handle it better than Artisans and Adventurers do. Sometimes, however, it's a learned skill.

Meg Brazill, who spent the early part of her working years being underpaid by nonprofit arts organizations, remembers when she took the ask-what-you're-worth leap. "I had moved to L.A. and found a job at a college, heading up a one-year project. It was my first job out of New York and not directly in the arts, and I thought, okay, I should be paid what I deserve. I didn't have any real measure, I had been working for organizations where you're paid in tickets, and you get to rub elbows with artists and have an interesting social life. So I came up with a figure—it wasn't an outrageous sum of money, but I felt like it was more than they wanted to pay—and I also asked for a bunch of benefits. I got it all, and I thought, this is kind of a neat thing."

Meg was empowered enough that, at her next job, she successfully negotiated a starting salary that was significantly more than what she had been offered, and by then she had also learned the power of perks—including getting her company to pay for university courses. From there, she took another great leap within her company and moved from being an assistant in a large department to being the director. "Suddenly I was making twice as much money as I'd made just a few years before," she recalls. "But there is a satisfaction equation that doesn't have much relationship to the money at all. You can't go around being miserable and thinking about how much you're making—in the meantime you could be giving away the best times of your life."

The Survival Instinct

> Nothing induces me to read a novel except when I have to make money by writing about it. I detest them.
>
> —VIRGINIA WOOLF

Meg Brazill's "satisfaction equation" might beat in the deepest heart of Idealists. And yet, of all the types, Idealists are best equipped to take on jobs because they need the money—or because it forms a bridge toward their ultimate career goal. Idealists are, after all, in it for the long run. They're also practical, and realistic about what it takes to get along. Most of all, they don't want to be financially dependent.

"What drove me to make money in the first place," says engineer Susan Hanlon, "was to be able to take care of myself. Period. I still worry about that. I always feel I need to survive, not rely on somebody else. That means I have to make money."

A casual survey of Idealist women reveals that a surprising number of them make more money than their husbands or significant others. And it doesn't seem to be a problem. These women take responsibility for their own needs, and just keep on following the route that they've mapped out for themselves. Many of them don't have a greedy bone in their bodies, and though they might surround themselves with beautifully designed objects, high-end computer equipment, and a bitchin' little sports car, Idealists don't base their self-worth on what they've acquired. Rather, like a pack of Virginia Woolfs, they believe that women need money, and a room of their own. Make that a *tidy* room of their own.

Adventurers and Money:
A Match Made in Hell

> When I am an old woman I shall wear purple
> With a red hat which doesn't go, and doesn't suit me.
> And I shall spend my pension on brandy and summer gloves
> And satin sandals, and say we've no money for butter.
>
> **— JENNY JOSEPH, WARNING**

Adventurers live in the moment. Sensible budgets and conservative savings plans are too boring for them. They can't resist buying summer gloves and satin sandals—even if it means they'll be left with no money for basics. The Adventurer doesn't wait to be old before she'll wear purple. She wears purple every day.

In the galaxy of Adventurers, there are those who relish putting their money into high-risk investments, and those who would bet their house on a new enterprise. There is the woman who spends her last dime getting herself across the country because she is sure that life will be better there. Some Adventurers pursue two or more careers at the same time; others make abrupt career changes every few years. It doesn't matter if the numbers are all wrong or the risks are dangerously high. The true Adventurer believes that if she's vigorously pursuing her passion, then the money will follow.

Frisky and Risky

> I can't stand having an opportunity and not taking advantage of it. It's the thrill of adventure that keeps me going.
>
> **— STEFANIE POWERS, ACTRESS**

Adventurers are gamblers at heart. They like the rush of winning against the odds, and would rather make a killing in one fell swoop than follow a conservative program of savings and investments.

History is peppered with stories of Adventurer women who have taken great risks. One wild tale from the Sixties is about four American musicians who were stranded in Puerto Rico. Having run out of money and places to stay, they hocked their equipment, which only brought in $50. So one of the musicians, a teenager named Michelle Phillips, walked into a casino with the money and bet it all on one roll of the dice at the craps table. She won. So she threw the dice again. And again. Twelve times in a row she bet her winnings, and twelve times she won. Legend has it that by the time she walked away from the table, the whole place was screaming,

FINANCIAL ADVICE FOR ADVENTURERS

• TRY TO CURB YOUR LOVE OF RISK. Adventurers are vulnerable to high-stakes gambles and get-rich-quick schemes. Those temptations are everywhere, including the stock market. Remember the golden rule: If it sounds too good to be true, it probably is.

• GET HELP. Unless you're that rare Adventurer who loves managing money, surround yourself with an army of financial professionals — first and foremost an accountant. At the very least, buy some financial management software and let it work for you.

• HAVE FUN. When it comes to building a personal portfolio, investment clubs are a great option for Adventurers, because they combine investing with something Adventurers are very good at: socializing.

• GO AUTOMATIC. If you're on a payroll, make arrangements for regular deductions to be taken from your check and squirreled away in a 401(k) plan.

• LOOK AT THE BIG PICTURE. If you're a freelancer or a small business owner, make a business plan — even if you've been running your enterprise without one forever. This will frame your financial life and help you look at your worth not from job to job but over the course of five, ten, or fifteen years. It will also help you direct your energies toward big goals, not small ones like this month's rent. A business plan will give you a clear picture of how much you need to be making every week in order to make the profits you need, and might reveal expenditures that you could live without.

• DON'T FOOL YOURSELF. When you get a check for a freelance job, immediately take 20 percent off the top and set it aside for your quarterly taxes. Many Adventurers, when presented with lump sums, start thinking they're millionaires, and are in great danger of spending it on ultimately foolish things. And don't forget to make maximum annual contributions to an IRA.

• DON'T BURDEN YOURSELF. Because Adventurers tend to spiral in and out of jobs (or even entire careers), it's smart for them to keep their basic living expenses to a minimum. If you're a homeowner, try to arrange for small monthly mortgage payments spread out over a long period of time. Such an arrangement will definitely cost you more money in the long run, but it will offer you more financial flexibility in the short term, and leave you more cash to do Adventurish things, such as taking off to explore the Andes for a month. Likewise, renters should avoid burdening themselves with high rent. It's better for Adventurers to get a cheap apartment in a so-so neighborhood and fix it up than having a big nut every month. Adventurers abhor being enslaved by anyone or anything, including rent.

• PUT AWAY YOUR PLASTIC. Avoid credit card and debit card expenditures whenever possible. Adventurers do well with checkbooks because they can get an at-a-glance idea of how much money they really have.

Also, checkbooks provide freelance Adventurers with a good record of expenses. Conversely, credit card statements are less easy to keep track of, and they also need to be paid every month. Unlike Idealists, voted most-likely-to-pay-the-full-balance-on-their-credit-cards, Adventurers are tempted to pay the minimum balance in order to keep themselves more liquid.

"Go, Blondie, go!" She had compiled enough money to fly herself and her three friends back to New York—first class—buy all new equipment, and form a group: The Mamas and the Papas.

Many Adventurer entrepreneurs will bet the proverbial farm on a venture they believe in. When the risks pay off, it's wonderful. When they don't, the Adventurer can find herself in serious financial trouble. Adventurers are always walking a line between wealth and poverty; usually it's only hard-won experience that will teach her to take calculated risks and to maintain a financial cushion.

Carol Bellamy, executive director of UNICEF, makes the distinction between gambling and risk-taking in an interview in *Fifty on Fifty:* "Risk-taking is setting up everything, except there is one unpredictable aspect to what you're doing, so you still have to take that one leap. Gambling is setting up nothing. I'm a risk-taker, not a gambler."

Earn and Burn

In finances, as in other areas of their lives, most Adventurers are excellent short-term planners and poor long-term planners. They want instant gratification—or at least, gratification that's within sight. They can't stand sweating the small stuff and they're embarrassed by people who do. An Adventurer, splitting a check at a restaurant with three friends, would rather just pick up the whole tab than sit there while her friends poke at a miniature calculator, trying to figure out how much each of them owes.

A perfect illustration of the Adventurer-money relationship can be seen in the life of Lauren Caldwell, a New York City stylist who props TV commercials, creates settings for photo shoots, masterminds store displays, and designs packaging for cosmetics companies. Even when she's not on a job, Lauren constantly scans the city for things that startle, surprise, or amuse her. She can leave her apartment in the morning to run a simple errand and return with an armload of strange flowers, a pair of silver clogs, bags of vintage beads, a pile of magazines, and a set of handmade dinner plates. These unplanned shopping sprees are part of Lauren's artistic process. She's compelled to bring interesting things home and play with them—and that's one of the reasons she's such a good stylist.

However, the combination of an unsteady freelance income and constant shopping has been, at various times in Lauren's life, a recipe for financial disaster. More than once she has found herself in her beautiful apartment, surrounded by beautiful things, scrounging through old purses for enough change to buy herself a diet Coke. Like so many Adventurers (and many freelancers) before her, Lauren fell into a "feast or famine" pattern. Elated and exhausted after a demanding job, and presented with a nice fat check, she'd allow herself special indulgences, and often burn through her profits too soon.

This Adventurer spending pattern is much like a classic story taught in Anthropology 101 about the tribe that could no longer depend on a hunting-and-gathering means of existence and was forced to shift to an agricultural way of life. The first year, the tribe planted and harvested crops but didn't have a system for preserving or storing food over the winter. When the next planting season came around, they were on the verge of starvation; when seedlings started to sprout, the whole tribe swarmed the fields and stuffed themselves with the tiny plants. Within a day they were again faced with starvation. Eventually, the tribe could not sustain itself and was wiped out.

In anthropology class, the lesson learned has to do with the disasters that can happen when you mess with people's (and animals') natural habitats. In Adventurer land, the lesson is about finding a balance between moderation and excess. It's a tricky situation because many Adventurers are their own product. If what they bring to the market is an ability to capture the latest trends and tastes, then they have to keep themselves right in the center of things. In the competitive world of New York City stylists, for example, it is important to eat at the newest restaurants, dance at the hottest clubs, and shop the top boutiques in order to stay ahead of an ever-evolving culture. Unfortunately, even top-tier freelancers can find themselves with dry spells in which the money flows out of their bank accounts and none flows in.

The solution, it would seem, is simple: Create a fall-back position—a well-structured savings plan, say, or a permanent part-time job that covers the rent. Another answer would be to ask for more money per job. This would be a matter of studying the numbers and figuring out how much money you would need to cover the lean times as well as the flush.

Ah, but there's the catch: Adventurers resist sensible solutions. Many of them firmly believe that, at some point in their careers, they will be catapulted into a position where they'll no longer have to worry about something as dull as money.

Lauren Caldwell, who is a thoroughly modern girl, solved her problem in an old-fashioned way: she now hands her checks over to her Idealist husband. He manages her finances, and helps her keep her expenditures within reasonable boundaries. Her solution is a fine example of how two different types—in this case, the free-spirited Adventurer and the "numbers first" Idealist—can complement each other. Lauren's husband reaps the benefits of her social and artistic buzz-making, yet he anchors their lifestyle with rock-solid financial planning.

Fear of Finances

Some Adventurers are convinced that they're hopeless when it comes to handling money. Because they're action-oriented and love the heat of the moment, they tend to neglect details like paying the bills on time. As a result, many Adventurers have terrible credit ratings that haunt them when they try to get loans or increase their credit card limits.

What is perhaps more damaging, however, is that the Adventurer can lose confidence in herself and give up trying to make sense of her finances. When an Adventurer falls into a pattern of check-chasing—racing toward her next dollar and running from creditors—it's difficult for her to make smart decisions, and that can lead to a vicious circle in which no financial progress is made.

There is a solution to the Adventurer's money problem, however, and it hinges on another Adventurer personality trait: Adventurers are project-oriented. They do well in jobs that have concrete parameters (i.e., deadlines) and love to meet challenges—even if those challenges involve money. Lauren Caldwell, for instance, is very good at staying within project budgets. When an art director asks her to decorate a set and spend a maximum of $1,000, she'll manage to create something that looks as if it cost $10,000—and still have a few bucks left over. What trips up the Adventurer is managing money over the long term. So the answer is to set up a series of short-term financial goals that allow her to see results quickly. Again, this should be done with the help of an accountant, a financial planner, or even a credit counselor.

7

Playing Well with Others

In order for sound to exist, there needs to be a sender and a receiver. That basic truth is at the heart of the classic brainteaser: "If a tree falls in the forest, and there's no one there to hear it, does it make a sound?" The answer, theoretically, is no. Though the setup itself is flawed—who can imagine a forest without raccoons, deer, birds, bats, or at the very least, insects?—it's based in scientific fact. Sound is nothing but invisible waves in the air until a creature with ears receives it, translates it, and gives it meaning.

Among humans, the sender-receiver formula gets a bit more complicated. Have you ever attended a lecture that was way over your head? There's the nice professor at the podium, making references to books that you've never read and quoting scholars you've never heard of in order to support a theory that you can't even frame in reality, much less grasp and appreciate. The people in the seats to your left and your right are nodding sagely, and afterward they raise their hands and ask pertinent questions. You sit there like one of Charlie Brown's classmates, hearing your version of "Wa wa watta wa." There's definitely a sender at the front of the room. You know this because you can see and hear him/her. You're just not programmed to receive the message. The result? No communication. A tree may be falling, but you can't identify that sound.

In business, the connection between senders and receivers is a two-way street. If you are a Visionary CEO, you could make a motivational speech to your assembled employees that was so profound it would make Shakespeare cry. But your Idealist staffers might walk away feeling frustrated and confused, looking at the notes they diligently took and wondering what's expected of them.

Perhaps you're an Adventurer saleswoman, painting castles in the sky and building up your product to mythic proportions. Yet your Artisan client, instead of being enchanted, is getting more and more nervous, shrinking in her seat and thinking, "This is too much. I only wanted something simple."

Here's the point: When you're negotiating, selling, or just trying to get a point across, self-expression is only half of the equation. You need to build a sympathetic bridge between yourself and your receiver—who, by natural law, must complete the circle of communication.

And what if you're on the receiving end? Well, we're all on the receiving end, every waking moment of our lives. Listening is not a passive activity. It should engage every fiber of our being, to the extent that we hear much more than what's being said. We should listen to the whole forest and know when trees are in trouble, long before they fall.

Communication in the Age of Information

Madame C.J. Walker, the country's first self-made female millionaire, started her empire nearly one hundred years ago by selling beauty products door-to-door. That sales technique was a major component of her success: she was connecting with customers at a time when there was no television, no regular radio broadcasts, few cars, and a scant number of phone lines. Her target market consisted of black women, whose primary source of product information was the newspaper—if they were lucky enough to have learned to read.

Since Madame Walker's day, telegrams and tabloids have given way to fax machines, beepers, cell phones, voice mail, e-mail, cable TV, satellite hookups, video conferencing, laser imaging, digital cameras, and the World Wide Web.

Yet one thing has remained the same: we still communicate with words and pictures. The impact of a beautifully written letter is as potent as it's ever been, and the seductiveness of a compelling image combined with thrilling language has never diminished. Great speeches are still made; heartfelt conversations are still cherished; and the business of the world is still conducted via memos, messages, spreadsheets, written proposals, and signed contracts.

No matter how efficient its tools may be, good communication is still dependent on one person: you. You are your sender and your receiver. Only you can listen and respond, get your messages across, and absorb messages in return.

Today's businesswoman has got to synthesize tremendous amounts of information in order to stay on top of the market; on a more intimate scale, she's got to look in the eyes of an employee and perceive much more than what his or her words are stating.

Communication is both powerful and fragile. It can start wars, and it can also stop them. In business, the wrong signals can cause a deal to fall apart in an instant, just as the right words can seal it.

Talking the Talk

The spoken language of business is a whole study unto itself. Whether you work alone or with a whole posse of personalities, the following tips will help you improve communications.

• **Listen empathically.** Listening is an art; when you get inside someone else's head and really hear what that person is saying, you not only build the foundation of a good relationship but you learn in the process. Deborah Triant, CEO and president of Check Point Software Technologies, Inc., said it beautifully in *Fast Company*: "I often wonder why schools emphasize debating. Why not have listening classes as well? Debating is easy; listening with an open mind is not." She warns against taking the lead in decision-making sessions: "Stating your opinion first will short-change the discussion process and taint what you hear later."

• **Avoid declarations.** It might be dramatic to state, "Corporation X doesn't stand a chance," but it's smarter to say, "In my opinion, Corporation X doesn't stand a chance." Speaking in absolutes is dangerous because it invites argument, inhibits a free exchange of opinions, and can be intimidating. Modifiers such as "Correct me if I'm wrong, but . . ." and "If memory serves, I do believe . . ." are hallmarks of good participatory dialogue.

Likewise, if someone has broken his word to you, don't say, "You're untrustworthy." Say, "I feel let down." If a supplier has delivered shoddy merchandise, don't point a finger and declare, "This workmanship is terrible." Instead try, "I'm disappointed in the quality of these goods." It's far more constructive to open lines of communication than to put people on the defensive.

• **Become an expert apologizer.** Early feminists had a saying: "When it rains at a picnic, women apologize." Such knee-jerk fault-taking has no

the visionary as good communicator . . . has a
talent for making elegant and sometimes elaborate presentations to get her
point across. She gives a lot of thought to formal discussions, speaks her
mind clearly and with authority, and sets strong boundaries — no "over-the-
shoulder" talks for her.

the visionary as poor communicator . . . will
write a memo when a simple conversation would do. Artisans and Adventurers can be put off by this practice, because they work on being personable and approachable. Visionaries are not likely to share decision-making
processes and have a low tolerance for others' problems — especially personal problems.

the artisan as good communicator . . . involves
everybody in discussions. She's an excellent listener and lets people know
that their input is valuable. The Artisan gives full weight to personal
issues — she'll spend as much time on a big meeting as an employee
review — and wants to make everybody feel at home.

the artisan as poor communicator . . . is uncom-
fortable with confrontation and doesn't want to be the bearer of bad news.
She can be overwhelmed by others' strong personalities; in those circumstances, it can be a struggle for her to speak her mind.

the idealist as good communicator . . . gets right
to the point and is highly accurate. The title "Information Officer" could
apply to most Idealists. They keep precise records and excel at separating
people problems from business problems.

the idealist as poor communicator . . . can be
out of touch with the emotional impact of decisions, and lack the tools
necessary to smooth out emotionally charged situations. Because they
focus on details, Idealists can sometimes lose sight of the big picture and
get hung up on minutiae.

the adventurer as good communicator . . .
can get people excited about projects and is especially good at brainstorming. Adventurers tend to share everything — information, gossip, power,
time — and are adept at having fun while getting work done.

the adventurer as poor communicator . . .
can change directions so often that others can't keep up. The Adventurer
resists etching anything in stone, and the fluidity of her thought processes
can result in confusion and frustration in others — and sometimes, a
chaotic work environment.

place in business. However, when you make a mistake, step on toes, put your foot in your mouth, or screw up, apologies are called for. A good apology can be a sincere "I'm sorry," spoken face to face, or an elaborate gesture involving flowers and handwritten notes. Letitia Baldrige, in her *New Complete Guide to Executive Manners,* says that both spoken and written apologies are necessary for big gaffes, and that sending gifts is also sometimes appropriate.

• **Admit you don't know everything.** If someone is talking over your head, it's folly to sit there with a frozen smile on your face, nodding in fake comprehension. You're not *supposed* to know everything! Swallow your pride and ask to be enlightened. People are flattered and pleased when they can share their expertise with a new initiate, and you benefit from new-found knowledge.

• **Acknowledge others' emotions.** The best managers always monitor the emotional temperature of their team. If someone's unhappy, acknowledge it, talk about it, place a value on it.

• **Don't react to outbursts.** Everybody gets hot under the collar once in a while. But you preserve that person's dignity—who is, after all, out of control—and defuse a potentially explosive situation by remaining calm and focusing on the underlying issues.

• **Know how to deliver bad news.** Be clear, be simple, be direct. Focus on the message; let it be known that it's not personal but a matter of business. You might want to deliver bad news off-site; once you've dropped the bomb, allow the message to sink in, and be prepared to calmly handle any emotional fallout.

• **Be lavish with praise.** People need to hear that they're doing well. When that quiet, trusty associate storms into your office with a laundry list of not-very-convincing complaints, check yourself: Have you made it clear that this person is appreciated, and that he or she is a crucial member of the organization? In companies that don't have regular performance reviews, it's easy to forget to give applause where it's due. Be generous with your time and attention, and grease wheels before they squeak.

• **Don't make assumptions.** It's never productive to speculate on the motives and intents of other people. Whenever possible, go to the source and let people speak for themselves.

• **Be real.** People intuitively know when you're telling the whole truth. And the truth when exposed is far easier for people to handle than cover-ups. In their book *Driving Fear Out of the Workplace,* authors Dan Oestreich and Kathleen Ryan note, "It's a huge relief to no longer give life to a lie. Nothing can move forward unless it's seen in a truthful light." If

LISTENING IN ON AN INTUITIVE MEETING

THE VISIONARY:"Okay, people, let's focus. We have a lot of territory to cover and only a limited amount of time. Forget reading the minutes. Let's go right to strategies."

THE ARTISAN:"Before we start, you should all know that our receptionist Tina's grandfather passed away. I'm circulating a sympathy card for all of us to sign."

THE IDEALIST:"I have exactly four points to cover. It should take about twenty minutes. I'll be handing out printed materials for reference."

THE ADVENTURER (ARRIVING LATE):"Does anybody mind if I go first? I just have a few talking points, then I have to leave early 'cause I have that wingding going on this afternoon."

all is not well with you, your organization, or a key associate, pretending that there is nothing wrong only causes speculation and anxiety.

• **Be real, but . . .** Don't unload your fears, self-doubts, or anger on your subordinates. For professional worries, seek out a trusted colleague or mentor and discuss them in private before considering "going public" with them. For personal problems, get a good counselor.

• **Be positive.** Cheerfulness, according to the *I Ching,* is one of the important qualities of leadership. And considering that powerful leaders have consulted the *I Ching* for centuries, you might want to take the advice to heart. If cheerfulness is not in your nature, at least be positive. Chronic complainers are wolf-criers: when a legitimate problem does come up, it's hard to get people to pay attention.

• **Bring your whole self to work.** As Hatim Tyabji, CEO of VeriFone, once said, "Business is personal. People commit themselves to other people, not to organizations."

Intuitive Communication
How to Talk to a Visionary

DON'T subject her to chatter about what was on TV last night or how the avocados at the Stop & Shop were so unripe that your guacamole was ruined. She's probably not interested.

DO share industry gossip and any developments that involve current projects.

DON'T enter a Visionary's space uninvited.

DO give her a call or send her an e-mail to set up a time to talk with her.

DON'T e-mail her jokes or "cute stories."

DO engage her in witty dialogue. Visionaries love discussion and debate, and many have a wicked, delicious sense of humor.

DON'T use e-mail when a letter is more appropriate—such as when you're suggesting a new policy or lodging a serious complaint. And handwrite personal correspondence—when you're thanking her for a wedding gift, for instance, or congratulating her on a promotion.

DO use your spell-check when writing to a Visionary. Many are turned off by poor grammar and spelling.

DON'T try to rush a Visionary, and avoid pushiness—it's insulting to her. Visionaries might choose to interpret ASAP as "put this on the bottom of the pile."

DO trust that when a Visionary says she'll do something, it will get done—and done well.

DON'T take a "victim" stance when approaching a Visionary with a problem. Rather than feeling sorry for you, the Visionary will probably perceive you as weak.

DO be willing to stand up to the Visionary when necessary. It's one way to earn her respect.

DON'T seek out Visionaries when you need a shoulder to cry on.

DO seek out Visionaries when you need a powerful mentor or hard-core advice.

How to Talk to an Artisan

DON'T confront or corner an Artisan. It's unnecessary and will put her on the defensive.

DO engage the Artisan in open, easy dialogue, giving her plenty of time to explore her own feelings on a subject.

DON'T launch immediately into business mode upon first meeting or greeting an Artisan. Make pleasant, personal conversation and give her a few minutes to get comfortable.

DO be extra clear when explaining or describing something to her. Artisans appreciate instruction and direction; it's better to overexplain than to underexplain things to them. Putting it in writing as a follow-up is also recommended.

DON'T let her be outshouted by more aggressive types. The Artisan doesn't tend to speak forcefully, so if you're running a meeting, make an extra effort to give her a share of the floor.

DO listen to her concerns. Artisans are terribly sensitive to stress and strife; even if you can't do much about her problem, it will make her feel better to talk about it.

DON'T take the Artisan's modesty at face value. It's a nice quality, but there really is an ego in there, and it needs to be fed.

DO be generous with praise. Artisans need to hear that they've done a good job, even if they're the boss and you're the employee. If you really want to thank an Artisan for a job well done, do something personal for her: take her to lunch, buy her a beautiful plant, or make a donation to her favorite charity.

DON'T ask an Artisan to make a presentation in front of a large group.

DO ask an Artisan to reach out to a troubled co-worker or to orient a new employee.

How to Talk to an Idealist

DON'T be casual with facts. Even if you're just telling an amusing story, Idealists will pick up on "fudged" details and are likely to confront you with them—or worse, question your credibility.

DO be sharp and accurate—make sure you know what you're talking about, whether you're making a formal presentation or shooting the breeze.

DON'T give an Idealist elaborate, sensory-based explanations or directions. Too much peripheral detail is distracting to Idealists, and they'll have to mentally edit out decorative language to get to the essential information.

DO be succinct. If you're giving Idealists travel directions, for instance, forget "Take the State Street exit and go right, past Dunkin' Donuts, through a stop sign, then up the hill and look for a big yellow house and take a right and that's Clark Street. . . ." Keep it to, "Exit 4, right on Humphrey, go a half-mile, right on Clark." Just the facts, ma'am.

DON'T ask an Idealist to make snap decisions or immediate judgment calls. Idealists don't operate on impulse; they want to make informed decisions that are based on evidence, not random hunches.

DO count on Idealists to be the voice of reason when emotions run high.

DON'T casually throw out ideas or suggestions to Idealists. They tend to think like scientists and might give equal weight to everything that comes up—they don't automatically know whether to run with something or chuck it in the circular file.

DO give them specific—preferably written—assignments and job descriptions.

DON'T ask Idealists to "sell" a project to investors or potential clients.

DO invite Idealists to talk about their work; many have a gift for explaining complex procedures in terms that even schoolchildren can understand.

DON'T underestimate the Idealist's capacity for fun. Many have a gift for the absurd, and especially love brilliantly conceived pranks.

DO share amusing e-mails and good jokes with Idealists. You just might make their day.

How to Talk to an Adventurer

DON'T be dull or dry. If you're making a presentation to an Adventurer, stick to the entertaining bits. Nitty-gritty details can be handed over in document form to be reviewed later.

DO be spectacular. Adventurers want to be wowed.

DON'T ask Adventurers to recite facts and figures.

DO invite Adventurers to make pitches, proposals, and sales presentations in which they can turn facts and figures into high drama.

DON'T give the Adventurer too much guidance or direction. When something is overexplained to her, she loses interest. She wants to apply her unique sensibilities to a project and make it her own.

DO give Adventurers clear deadlines, budgets, and parameters.

DON'T nag, pester, or push an Adventurer. Repeated follow-up calls are offensive to her, as are multiple requests for progress reports.

DO allow Adventurers enough space to get their work done. Adventurers work like artists, and take their processes very seriously.

DON'T try to hard-sell an Adventurer on an idea or a concept. The Adventurer is stubbornly autonomous and may fight something simply because she's being pressured to accept it.

DO involve Adventurers in brainstorming sessions, whether they're casual discussions or formal meetings.

DON'T expect to have a strictly business relationship with an Adventurer.

DO expect to have a boundary-free relationship. When given the chance, Adventurers toss protocol aside; their one-on-one meetings are more like two friends getting down than two professionals discussing business.

The Intuitive Negotiator

In the movie *Clueless* (which was a retelling of Jane Austin's *Emma*), the teenage protagonist improves all of her grades—after she's gotten her report card—through the art of negotiation. When she presents her newly upgraded marks to her lawyer dad, who taught her the tricks in the first place, he says, "Honey, I couldn't be more proud if you'd earned the grades yourself."

Women who don't regularly wheel and deal may shy from formal negotiations, fearing that they'll be eaten alive. Yet everybody negotiates in day-to-day life, whether it's getting a better price at the car dealership or bribing your son to mow the lawn. Some women have native talents when it comes to negotiation, but whether you're a natural-born shark or more of a dolphin, you're doing yourself a disservice if you don't acquaint yourself with a few classic negotiating techniques.

Each of the following strategies is more thoroughly outlined in *Getting to Yes,* by Roger Fisher and William Ury—the standard manual of successful negotiating.

1. Don't bargain over positions. You're at a yard sale and see a vintage mantel clock for $25. You approach the owner and tell her you want the clock but only have a $20 bill and can't possibly spend any more. What you have just done is called "taking a position." Why is this so wrong? Because you've cut off your options. In the course of haggling, you'll likely end up defending your position and losing sight of what both you and the seller really want, that is, a mutually agreeable price.

For example: What if the seller tells you that the clock belongs to a friend, and the friend won't let it go for less than $23? The seller, whether she's telling the truth or not, has herself just copped an ironclad position (as far as you know). In order to save face, you'll either argue with her (probably fruitlessly), walk away from the sale, or come up with some embarrassing ruse like "accidentally" finding more money in your wallet. And even if you do get the clock for $20, you've got to take it and leave, because you no longer have the option of spying a great chair and buying that, too—unless you don't mind turning yourself into a liar.

Most negotiations, big or small, fall apart when egos enter into the picture. Rather than working to overcome problems, people develop a "win at any cost" attitude, as each defends his or her position. Negotiations are not contests in which there can be only one victor. Negotiations are about finding solutions that both sides can agree on. When one or both parties take a position, bargaining becomes inefficient, the ultimate goal gets lost in the shuffle, and relationships can be damaged.

2. Separate the people from the problem. You're a manager. You're approached one afternoon by an employee who complains that her office-mate, Ms. Smith, is constantly interrupting her and ruining her concentration. Rather than calling Smith into the office and telling her to cut it out, you sit back and ask yourself: Is the policy of teaming people in cubicles a bad idea for those who need a quiet environment?

Congratulations. What you've just accomplished is a fine example of separating the people from the problem. It would have been quick and easy to reprimand Ms. Smith, but by doing so you would have created a short-term solution at best, and, at worst, caused further resentment between the two officemates.

When difficulties arise, it's always best to focus on the job, the organization, the project, or the company rather than the individuals who are struggling to make it work. After all, jobs don't have feelings, and it's usually the job that's causing the problem.

3. Focus on interests. Let's say your software company wants a certain top designer to create a series of Web sites. She's interested, but is asking a fee that outpaces your budget. Rather than hammer each other over the numbers, find out why that specific sum is so important to her. You might learn that she'll have to hire a full-time nanny in order to show up at your office eight hours a day for six months, as you've requested. This opens the door to other solutions, such as providing her with the equipment she'll need to work at home.

By focusing on interests, rather than fixating on numbers, negotiators can work toward finding creative solutions.

4. Use objective criteria. Points numbered 1, 2, and 3 don't have much bite without this. In fact, maybe it should be number one, because it calls for setting standards.

Just as it's more efficient and effective to focus on problems rather than people, "objective criteria" such as well-researched reports, statistics, and

INTUITIVE DECISION-MAKING

The VISIONARY meditates on decisions . . . resists others' opinions . . . needs to be left alone to sort things out . . . then makes strong and swift declarations.

The ARTISAN likes to talk to lots of people before going forward . . . seeks feedback from teachers and mentors . . . tries to please everybody . . . and prefers not to cast her decisions in stone.

The IDEALIST tries to find logical solutions . . . gathers hard data and statistics, does the math . . . can be stymied when there's not a clear choice . . . and likes information and numbers to lead the process.

The ADVENTURER goes by her gut . . . likes inventing creative solutions to problems . . . might "throw a dart" when there's not an obvious best choice . . . and has no problem changing her mind even after the decision is made.

government standards are superb platforms from which to launch fruitful discussions.

Objective criteria take the "I" out of negotiations, and is as useful in high-stakes encounters as it is in day-to-day transactions. An antiquarian bookseller, for instance, can justify her pricing of a rare volume by referencing recent auction prices at Sotheby's. When applying for a loan at a bank, a small-business owner might strengthen her case by presenting success stories of similar ventures in the area.

Easy access to the Internet has made the use of objective criteria more convenient than ever. There's no excuse not to enter a negotiation armed with up-to-the-minute comparative materials; with facts and figures in hand, negotiations can be about what the market will bear, rather than what you or the other parties want. This is how most attorneys build their cases, and you should, too.

The Art of Leadership

Management requires concrete skills. With a combination of good information, planning, organization, and control, you and just about everyone you know could learn how to manage budgets, payroll, agendas, employee insurance policies, or virtually any nuts-and-bolts business task.

When it comes to managing people, however, concrete skills are not enough. To effectively head up a team of any size, a person must be a motivator, an empath, a peacemaker, a cheerleader, a nurturer, a coach, a futurist, a philosopher, a psychologist, a mind reader, a speech-maker, a disciplinarian, a mommy, a role model, and much more. In short, she must be a leader.

What's the difference between a leader and a manager? According to Andrew J. DuBrin, professor of business management at the Rochester Institute of Technology, management focuses on maintaining equilibrium within a company, while leadership strives to accomplish change. He makes this distinction: "An effective leader inspires people to work hard to improve profits; an effective manager makes sure people are adequately paid for their efforts."

Leadership isn't much good without management, and vice versa. A brilliant leader who can excite clients and inspire her team is useless if she can't deliver on her vision. Ideas and insights might pave the way toward greatness, but the bread and butter of business is still about meeting deadlines, staying within budgets, and keeping the doors open.

As the world of business is vast and rapidly evolving, so the details of operations change with every job and every passing year (just ask anyone who learned to set type by hand). But leadership skills are forever. It is the wise woman who cultivates her inner leader, whether she's heading up a multinational corporation or keeping track of two preschoolers.

What Makes a Leader?

Leadership starts with personal vision. It is brewed in that deep pool where passion, belief, and inner truths dwell. To be a great leader you must commit to greatness; you've got to engage your whole self and be willing to stand tall in the face of adversity. Leaders see beyond petty side issues like office politics, financial speed bumps, and difficult co-workers. They are not distracted by trying to protect their own image or ego.

There is no faking true leadership. If you're an Artisan who's attuned to nature, for example, there's no way you could take a job at the nuclear power plant and motivate your team to sidestep Department of Environmental Protection regulations, no matter how much you needed the money. In the role of commissioner of state parks, however, you'd probably be a veritable font of energy and courage. Your oneness with your assignment would, in turn, excite others and make them want to do their best for you.

Which is to say that, first and foremost, you can't be a great leader if you don't believe in what you're doing.

We hope, if you've been reading this book carefully, that you're already well on your way toward aligning your truest self with your truest work.

Good Bosses *vs.* Bad Bosses

Many corporate dollars have been poured into studies that ask employees, What makes a good boss?

Such studies are, by nature, somewhat superficial (how deep can you get with multiple-choice questions?) Still, results have tended to be quite consistent. Here is an overview of sterling leadership, gleaned from various polls and surveys:

- Good bosses allow for open communication on all levels.
- Good bosses emphasize autonomy and responsibility, and trust their employees' judgment.
- Good bosses respect the fact that employees have a life beyond the office, and work to create solutions for those with family problems or extenuating circumstances.
- Good bosses take responsibility for their own mistakes.

- Good bosses foster employees' sense of personal investment in the company by giving them personal encouragement and feedback, and offering opportunities for learning and advancement.
- Good bosses appreciate and reward employees' efforts.

Bad bosses have been the subject of intense study by Harvey Hornstein, author of *Brutal Bosses and Their Prey*. He's divided lousy leaders into six subdivisions that side by side sound like a gallery of villains worthy of a *Batman* sequel.

- **The Conqueror** never lets people forget who's in charge. In asserting her authority, she will verbally "beat up" anyone who poses a threat.

- **The Performer** takes it personally when someone's star shines brighter than hers. One of her tricks is to put criticisms or negative performance reviews in writing, without giving the victim a chance to respond. She tends to surround herself with yes-men (or yes-women).

- **The Manipulator** wants to come off smelling like a rose, even if it means taking credit for others' work or pinning her failures on team members.

- **The Dehumanizer** views employees as mere cogs in a wheel, and therefore has little or no consideration for their feelings or needs.

- **The Blamer** washes her hands of problems. When others get stuck with the fallout, she'll insist they "deserve" the bad consequences.

- **The Rationalizer** passes off her abusive behavior as "doing what's best for the company" and convinces herself that "somebody had to do it."

A Guide to Intuitive Leadership
The Visionary Leader

Leadership comes naturally to most Visionaries. They relish the opportunity to plan grand projects, map out strategies, and recruit talented people. Visionaries have a knack for assembling teams and can beautifully communicate ideas to every contributor.

As a leader, the Visionary positions herself as supreme authority. She is protective of her power and is careful not to give team members too much free rein. She can be demanding and even critical, but the successful Visionary inspires devotion and is committed not only to her own excellence but to developing others' potential.

It's not surprising that the Visionary leader tends to be intolerant of others' weaknesses and doesn't like hearing excuses of any kind. She refuses to let team members' personal problems become her problem; as such, she might gain a reputation for being tough or even heartless. The fact is, she's committed to success and wants every one of her people to be key players—not just along for the ride.

When team loyalty is in place, Visionaries can be fiercely protective of their charges, and will even take on their own bosses if they believe company policies are flawed or injustices are being done.

Advice for Visionary Leaders

- Remember that leaders are essentially servants. You're only as successful as each member of your team.
- Resist the temptation to be a micromanager. Author Andrew J. DuBrin explains that micromanagement can disempower team members and knock the motivation right out of them. If you solicit daily progress reports from each team member, require team members to submit a written report of what they learned at seminars, ask for the raw data behind reports, request that the font on a report be changed, conduct daily staff meetings before the start of each work day, or accompany each team member when he or she visits a client for the first time, you're probably guilty of micromanagement.
- Just because you can do something better yourself, doesn't mean you should. Your job is to teach as well as to lead. If a team member hands in a sloppy report, for instance, your first impulse might be to take a few hours and fix it. A better strategy, though it may take more time and effort on your part, is to have a meeting with the author and go over ways to make it better, then hand it back for a rewrite. As Mort Meyerson, CEO of Ross Perot's Perot Systems, told *Fast Company* magazine: "I don't *have* to know everything. I don't *have* to have all the customer contacts. I don't *have* to make all the decisions. In fact, in the new world of business, it can't be me, it shouldn't be me, and my job is to prevent it from being me."
- Pay attention to the morale of your team. You might want to assign a go-between—preferably an Artisan—to act as a human barometer and report to you on the overall emotional health of the group. If morale is low and motivation is slack, you'll need to fix the problem from the inside. Because Visionaries are intense and energetic, they have the tendency to drive their teams to the point of burnout. Winning-at-any-cost is an outdated notion that simply doesn't fly in today's employee-driven workplace.

The Artisan Leader

"Good corporate culture, in its purest sense, and at its most successful, has the look and feel of something organic and uncontrived, something that just exists." So writes entrepreneur Jennifer Lawton on EntreWorld.org, the Web site for the Kauffman Center for Entrepreneurial Leadership. Like many Artisans, she practices what could be called "invisible leadership," in which the team is hugely empowered and the leader serves as little more than a facilitator—or so it seems.

As leaders Artisans tend not to impose their will, but to explore and nurture others' interests and talents in order to establish a productive and happy group with a common goal. The Artisan style of leadership is beautifully described by Laura Ashley biographer Anne Sebba: "Her employees wanted to perform well to please her. She did not say much but always had time to listen. She could delegate if necessary, but worked hard herself. . . . One of Laura's great strengths was her ability always to work on a human level."

In virtually every role in life, the Artisan considers the whole person. She is sensitive to others' health, stress thresholds, relationships, hot buttons, home life, professional experience, pet projects, and pet peeves. She likes to match assignments to individuals, and also to create a team that functions like a nondysfunctional family. Such an approach isn't always efficient, but the Artisan is a bridge-builder whose greater purpose is to forge lasting alliances in and out of the office.

Benevolent by nature, Artisans often refrain from giving orders. They would rather make requests or ask for favors and are so democratic that when it comes to assigning unpleasant tasks, they'll first do it themselves so that the job won't seem degrading. As restaurateur Claire Criscuolo says, "Some people have been shocked to see me scraping butter off the dining room floor, and have said, 'Don't you have employees?' I'm the first one cleaning, as it should be—it's my restaurant."

Though their acute empathy sometimes gets in the way of productivity, Artisans can be effective and beloved leaders—unless they're in charge of an impatient Visionary or an ambitious Idealist, both of whom could perceive the Artisan's soft touch as weakness. A powerhouse Visionary could easily challenge the Artisan's authority, which is the kind of situation that an Artisan dreads and doesn't have natural defenses against.

Advice for Artisan Leaders

- Know that most people respond well to demanding assignments, as long as the goal can be reasonably accomplished with a little extra effort. Challenge is stimulating, and accomplishment is a true reward. When assigning a project, don't think of it as an imposition or an inconvenience. You've chosen that person to execute an important task (which is flattering) and you're giving that person an opportunity for personal and professional growth.

- Delegate responsibilities, and resist the temptation to shield others from dull or unpleasant tasks by doing them yourself. Assign yourself missions that only you can accomplish.
- Though it may be comfortable to put decisions to a vote, use democracy sparingly. When the will of the group is allowed to take over, it could compromise your vision.
- Try to keep your emotions separate from your business decisions. Artisans are so sympathetic to underdogs that they run the risk of making excuses for underachieving team members. Give extra attention where it's needed, but remember: There's a fine line between tenderness and rot. Don't kill your team's motivation and direction, not to mention your own goals, with kindness.
- Maintain a professional distance. As an Artisan, you might get personally involved with your people to the extent that you're playing marriage counselor, matchmaker, health advisor, and/or surrogate mother. Even in small companies, too much personal involvement is dangerous, as it can cloud your judgment and turn professional issues into personal ones.

The Idealist Leader

The Idealist leader puts her faith in strong, proven ideas, then relies on logical steps to deliver her project and her team to success. She organizes her group with military precision, assigning jobs, goals, and deadlines that have all been worked out ahead of time. Her approach is 100 percent sensible, but she can sometimes be guilty of ignoring the more human aspects of leadership.

An Idealist can be passionately committed to her goals and feel deeply connected to her team, yet shy away from displays of enthusiasm, which can seem stagy, or worse, phony to her. She might be downright embarrassed by the thought of giving pep talks or pitching a jazzy concept to others. It's not just stage fright (though that may be a factor). It's because Idealists have such respect for the integrity of a well-developed idea that they want the concept to speak for itself, without any help from pompoms or brass bands.

Unlike the other three types, the Idealist resists gilding the lily. Her best, strongest, most honest self is simple and clear; her talent as a leader involves streamlining tasks so that the straightest possible line between two points can be achieved. Such an approach can seem like nirvana to other Idealists and might also appeal to a good number of Artisans. But to Visionaries, who want to bring their own intelligence and style to a project, and Adventurers, who thrive on creative experimentation, it can be a real turnoff.

Idealists, to their credit, are able to remove their egos from business situations and focus on the project at hand rather than personal glory or status. Like Artisans, they recognize that the whole of the team is greater than the sum of its parts. But unlike Artisans, who nurture individuals and foster productive relationships, Idealists are prone to seeing team members as parts in a machine. True, each member is valuable—after all, a machine won't function if it's missing key elements—but the Idealist leader might overlook the emotional needs of individual team members. As a result, she could find herself with a lackluster, unmotivated group. To her, a job well done is a huge reward unto itself, so she may not automatically understand others' craving for personal attention and encouragement.

The archetypal Idealist relies on rules and standards to keep chaos at bay. As a leader she is always one step ahead, and the decisions she makes are based on sturdy data, not conjecture. She steers a sound ship, and her chances for success are extremely high—as long as she (or a partner) cultivates a sensitive, empathic touch.

Advice for Idealist Leaders

- Before creating ironclad strategies and procedures, gather opinions from people of all levels in every related department and consider them carefully. Their ideas might throw a wrench into your elegant solutions, but that's what innovation is all about, right?
- Beyond regular performance reviews and annual bonuses, make it a point to personally thank team members who have gone the extra mile—and do it in a timely manner, that is, when they've finished a particularly demanding project. Extra points if you give them an unscheduled reward, like a day off with pay or a gift certificate to a swank resort.
- Place a value on others' feedback, even if it seems superfluous to you. For instance, if a team member comments that your annual shareholders' report is "visually boring," give her a chance to spruce it up. You'll strengthen her loyalty, open lines of communication with other employees, and might even impress your shareholders.
- Bend the rules now and then for the sake of a happy, productive team. Have your people put in late hours on a project? Give them a half-

day Friday or allow them to come in late, when appropriate.
- If, when speaking in front of groups, you're about as relaxed and char-ismatic as a telephone pole, get yourself a coach. Public speaking is a skill that can be learned. Even if your audience is rarely larger than five co-workers, it's worth mastering.
- Don't fall into the micromanagement trap (see "Advice for Visionary Leaders," page 212).

The Adventurer Leader

Charismatic, innovative, and entertaining, the Adventurer leader excels at getting others excited about projects and visions. She is a creative thinker who relishes unconventional solutions to problems; in fact, she often positions herself (and her team) as deviant, or, at the very least, alterna-tive to the status quo. Like the folks at Apple Computer, she aspires to "think different."

One excellent example of Adventurer leadership is the story of Paula Wynne, who took a job as a copy editor at a weekly newspaper. Within days of starting, it became clear that her team—consisting of entry-level editorial assistants and college interns—had dismal research skills. So she organized a field trip to a nearby library and gave each team member a spe-cific assignment involving doughnuts. One person had to research the ori-gins of doughnuts, another had to find out which commercial bakery sold the most doughnuts the previous year, and so on. She gave them two hours to come up with the answers, after which they were to meet in the library's central court. There, Paula was waiting with doughnuts and coffee. In typ-ical Adventurer fashion the day was both educational and lots of fun.

When the Adventurer succeeds, the results can be spectacular, and she's usually generous about sharing credit (and profit) where it's due. But her grand schemes can just as easily be undone by poor planning. She is prone to bite off more than she can chew; her ideas are sometimes impractical, or so complicated that they're inscrutable to clients and/or consumers. Adventurer leaders are most successful when they themselves have a leader who will keep them on course.

The Adventurer is good at recognizing and showcasing others' talents. Though her "whatever works" style can make Idealists nervous, she brings everyone into the fold and can make every person on her team feel special. Chances are she'll initiate social activities within the group and will be especially solicitous toward those who are enthusiastic about her ideas. When someone questions her vision, however, watch out: She can become defensive. In fact, while the average Adventurer is highly sensitive to others' words, reactions, and body language, she sometimes doesn't "hear" feedback or concerns. Rather, she concentrates on winning people over to her way of thinking. Adventurers don't take criticism well, no matter how powerful they might be.

Finally, Adventurers are rebels at the core, even when they themselves are the authority that those bumper stickers urge us to question. Extreme Adventurers might refuse to respect seniority within their group, or ignore standard company guidelines, or deliberately go against established policies—and drag their team members along for the bumpy ride. On the plus side, it's never "business as usual" with Adventurers. They possess all the qualities necessary to create exciting changes.

Match the Quote with the Boss:

AN EASY QUIZ

1. "Wait till you hear what's going on. You won't *believe* it! It will blow your mind!"

2. "Let's all take a deep breath and slow down."

3. "Your report looked fine. I made some edits and suggestions; as soon as they're integrated, I think we're well on our way."

4. "I'm sorry you've all had to put in so many hours on this project. As a reward, everyone's invited to my house for a home-cooked meal."

5. "I've asked Accounting to compare our figures with last year's and print out a complete analysis. It will be e-mailed to each of you in an attachment."

6. "Of course we're going to make this deadline. We're the best."

7. "I've gotten clearance from Security to have Monday's staff meeting on the roof. Won't that be fun?"

8. "Before you bring any suggestions to the table, make sure they comply with OPEC regulations."

9. "I notice that some of you aren't recycling your business papers. To make it easier for you, I've had special pink boxes placed in each department."

10. "Spell-check, people . . . it's there for a reason! Use it!"

ANSWERS: 1. Adventurer **2.** Artisan **3.** Visionary **4.** Artisan **5.** Idealist **6.** Visionary **7.** Adventurer **8.** Idealist **9.** Artisan **10.** Visionary

Advice for Adventurer Leaders

- Solicit and respect your team members' opinions and contributions. As an Adventurer you might have the energy and flamboyance needed to put a project over, but you probably don't have all the answers. Know your strengths, and allow others to contribute theirs.
- Don't attempt to reinvent the wheel. Take a tip from Idealists and see what's worked before. Though it's in your nature to buck convention, try to work within preestablished routines and to respect company policies; otherwise, you could cause confusion and resentment.
- Your job is to make things simpler, not more complicated. Keep that in mind whenever you're tempted to turn straightforward projects into Busby Berkeley productions.
- Solicit advice and guidance from people who are bigger, stronger, and more experienced than you. If you're a CEO, get yourself a mentor outside of your company to keep you balanced and grounded in reality.
- Establish a source of applause beyond your group, or even your job. As an Adventurer you crave recognition, so it can be tempting to seek approval from the people who work for you. Which is a terrible idea—you're supposed to be giving support and encouragement, not seeking it.

Intuitive Management Archetypes

The personality of the leader is always imprinted on the group. No matter what her industry might be, each leader comes to her job with a set of strengths, weaknesses, goals, and preferences that translate into a unique business model. Often you can identify a Visionary, Artisan, Idealist, or Adventurer by how her group functions. Following are the archetypal models.

Visionary: The Monarchy

- Visionary positioned as absolute authority
- Visionary works toward creating "elite group" mentality; wants her team to be the best
- Meetings, including brainstorming sessions, are formalized; Visionary doesn't maintain an open-door policy
- Visionary wants to see her original vision carried out, with others' ideas integrated into product only after careful consideration
- Less time given to planning, more time given to execution

- Visionary interested in progress, but not necessarily process; she doesn't care how it gets done, as long as it's done well and on time
- High emphasis on quality of work, especially final details
- Slackers and slowpokes swiftly replaced
- Deadlines are nonnegotiable

Artisan: **The Tribe**

- Artisan positioned as group facilitator
- Emphasis on team members' input and ideas; Artisan encourages interaction within the group
- Decisions often put to vote
- Artisan goes out of her way to accommodate others' needs and preferences
- Artisan keeps her door open, "visits" team members regularly, and is available to hear feedback, problems, observations, etc.
- Artisan works side by side with group and takes on unpleasant tasks when necessary
- Artisan rewards good performance and gives credit to group and individuals in group

Idealist: **The Military**

- Idealist positioned as captain
- Emphasis on research and planning; steps and strategies are mapped out in detail before proceeding
- Idealist creates well-defined jobs and assigns specific tasks according to group members' expertise
- Goals, budgets, and schedules are written in stone
- Procedures, including written progress reports, are formalized
- Idealist wants group to think like a team, not as individuals
- Thoroughness, accuracy, and efficiency are valued

Adventurer: **The Coterie**

- Adventurer positioned as ringleader
- Emphasis on brainstorming, invention, innovation
- Job titles and task parameters loosely defined
- Interested in new ways of doing things versus standard procedures
- Meetings and progress reports are informal
- Personal and social interaction encouraged within the group
- Hands-off management style
- Adventurer infuses group with enthusiasm and high spirits
- Risk-taking is rewarded

Managing the Intuitive Employee

Sometimes, a leader is fortunate enough to choose her own team. Usually, however, she inherits a gallery of personalities. By becoming a student of the Intuitive System, you can get a bead on your employees' types and have a secret box of tools that will help you bring out their best.

The Visionary employee craves leadership opportunities. She takes her assignments very seriously and, no matter how challenging the project might be, will do whatever it takes to deliver a brilliant performance. If she's strong-headed and opinionated, don't go up against her; rather, court her and her talents. The Visionary does her best work when she can conceive and complete a project from beginning to end, but can be problematic when teamed with others who are less driven than she. Furnish her with plenty of resources—an expense account will be especially appreciated—and avoid overmanaging her. Too much supervision is insulting to her and can undermine her motivation. Remember that a Visionary, well-handled, can be a huge asset to any team. Reward her by parading her accomplishments in front of the company's CEO. Extra credit for helping her map her career path within the organization.

The Artisan employee needs direction, clear job descriptions, support, and encouragement. She's extremely responsible and so hard-working that she can make even Visionaries look like slackers, but she may be uncomfortable taking the reins and making judgment calls. Avoid placing her in stressful situations, such as making presentations to clients. Likewise, don't isolate her and ask her to complete a project on her own. When creating subgroups, pair her with aggressive Visionaries or hotheaded Adventurers. She will serve as a grounding device and keep projects on track. Check in frequently with Artisans; always let them know that they're appreciated; and be sure to tap into the Artisan's natural talent as a diplomat.

The Idealist employee is methodical. She wants all systems in place before proceeding, and so may take what seems like an inordinate amount of time setting up a project. But it will pay off: chances are she'll produce rock-solid results backed up with reams of reliable data, and will perform above and beyond expectations. The Idealist is most comfortable when she knows exactly what is expected of her, now and in the future; give her clear goals, explain procedures carefully, and set up a regular schedule of progress reports and reviews. The Idealist likes structure, and may resent haphazard plans or sloppy scheduling. Like Artisans, Idealists shouldn't be asked to stand and deliver in front of a crowd. Also, keep in mind that Idealists relish learning opportunities; include them in as many seminars, conferences, and courses as you can.

The Adventurer employee is a wild card whose tasks should be matched with her talents. She is motivated by situations in which she can display heroism; the phrase "It can't be done" is like a written invitation to her. Most Adventurers prefer difficult, dramatic tasks to simple ones. Adventurers tend to infuse assignments with personality; any task that requires originality, innovation, and creative problem-solving is irresistible to them. Unlike Artisans, they resent direct instruction and coaching. They do relish varied experiences, however, and welcome any chance to work in different departments or take on experimental assignments. Put her on short-term, start-up projects, and be sure to pair her with an Artisan or an Idealist, so that she stays focused. And yes, the Adventurer is a natural performer. She can definitely put on a show and pitch her ideas before the masses.

How to Manage Your Boss:
A Guide for Intuitive Employees

So you say you're always doing other people's bidding? You punch in and answer to someone else, eight (or ten) hours a day? You and millions of other women, toots.

The Intuitive System can help you with what is perhaps one of the most daunting workplace challenges of all: managing your boss. If you've paid attention to the leadership sections of this book, you probably have a good idea of which type your boss (or bosses) most resembles.

The chart on page 222 is your guide to effective boss-wrangling. Find your type in the top row, and follow it down to your fearless leader's type, then match the number in the box to the tips that follow.

1. The Visionary-on-Visionary combo works best if your boss is older and/or more experienced than you. The Visionary can be an inspiring leader who will nudge you toward a level of greatness that even you never suspected you could reach. He or she can also hook you up with important connections and advance your career. Your sacrifice for all these rewards: Be an employee. Don't try to take over. Treat your boss like a boss. Open your ears, ask for help, be a sport, and *learn.*

2. As an Artisan, you probably do everything for your boss, from running errands to overseeing complicated events. Don't let her run you ragged—stand up for yourself, when you need to. Visionaries can overwork others and not even know it. Worse, some are masters of intimidation whose tricks work beautifully on defenseless Artisans. Remember that the quality Visionaries most admire in others is bravery. As long as you

BOSS-WRANGLING	Visionary Employee	Artisan Employee	Idealist Employee	Adventurer Employee
Visionary Boss	1	2	3	4
Artisan Boss	5	6	7	8
Idealist Boss	9	10	11	12
Adventurer Boss	13	14	15	16

stand your ground, the Artisan/Visionary combo can be productive and even pleasant.

3. You, Ms. Idealist, can get along perfectly well with your Visionary boss—as long as she understands your talents and utilizes them appropriately. When she has you analyzing production problems or creating budgets, all is well. When she asks you to take clients to lunch and pitch concepts, things could get uncomfortable. Ask your boss for clear assignments and sturdy job parameters, and know exactly what's expected of you before launching into any new project.

4. As long as your boss isn't a dictator, you Adventurer types can thrive under Visionary leadership. The Visionary probably recognizes and appreciates your talents, and could help you grow or even steer you toward greatness. Approach each new challenge like a student, keep your ego out of it, give her your all, and never forget to respect her authority and her privacy.

5. Miss Visionary Employee, you will probably be challenged by your Artisan boss to do something that is not in your nature: slow down. She likes to consider all angles of a project before proceeding and will probably benefit from your superior strategic skills and networking abilities—as long as you're not too impatient to do things her way. Remember that Artisan bosses need recognition just as much as Artisan employees do. Let her know you appreciate her.

6. Artisan bosses and Artisan employees can easily become best of buddies. Which could be a problem when the going gets tense. Beware of passive-aggressive behavior on both your parts, for example, not speaking up if something bothers you in hopes that the other person will read your mind, calling in sick as a form of silent protest, or doing things to keep the peace rather than doing things to be productive. It might be up to you to be the Great Communicator and to gently bring up unpleasant subjects when necessary.

7. You probably adore your Artisan boss, and she probably adores you. Idealists and Artisans can form lasting alliances that are more like supportive friendships than boss-employee relationships. On the other hand, if your politics don't jibe with your Artisan boss's politics (say, if you're a member of the NRA and she's a gun control activist), there might be nothing but trouble between the two of you. Try to keep your personal beliefs out of the office, and just enjoy being a member of the Mutual Respect Club.

8. As an Adventurer, you probably entertain your Artisan boss no end. But be aware that Artisans don't always speak up when things are not well. So even while she's laughing at your jokes, she's quietly keeping an eye on your job performance and may be dropping hints that whiz right by you. When you work for an Artisan you need to be a self-starter and to keep tabs on your own productivity—otherwise you might get an unpleasant surprise.

9. If your Idealist boss has the foresight to give you autonomy over your projects, and avoids micromanaging your Visionary efforts, you can shine in this arrangement. Be sure to keep her posted on all new developments and to check with her before making decisions. If you keep her well inside the loop, she'll probably feel confident enough to give you more and more freedom and responsibility.

10. Artisans are warm and fuzzy. Idealists are not. The Artisan can be upset or even offended by the Idealist's taciturn ways. Don't take it personally; rather, use your people skills to help make your office a more human and more humane place to work. Note, too, that some Artisans can see right through Idealists and can form warm, relaxed, and supportive working relationships with them. Give it a chance.

11. Some Idealists see eye to eye on so many things, they can practically finish each other's sentences. Others can be competitive and constantly watch-dog each other, looking for mistakes and trip-ups. Idealists get along best when each has a different area of expertise; then they can rely on each other rather than getting in each other's way.

12. If you want to be popular (as many Adventurers do), don't look to the Idealist boss to feed your need. Idealists tend to be unresponsive to anything but results, which can drive attention-hungry Adventurers crazy. The Idealist will probably insist that you stick to the bottom line and cut out the theatrics—a situation that can be deadly to your spirit. You may have to see your position under an Idealist as a stepping-stone to greater things—or at least positions that are more suited to your social, outgoing personality.

ASK AND YOU SHALL RECEIVE

From "The Worst They Can Say Is No" Department: According to a poll taken in the late 1990s, 45 percent of women who asked for a raise got it. The numbers were even more impressive for men: 59 percent of men who requested raises got them.

13. Sneer all you want. Complain to your girlfriends about what a flake your boss is. But hang in there, because the Visionary-Adventurer combo can be sublime, if you play your cards right. First and foremost: put your wish lists in writing. If you need new equipment, an assistant, a raise, or better scheduling, the Adventurer will likely never notice unless you tell her. Once presented with a piece of paper, she'll probably do all she can to accommodate you. Don't be a mercenary, however: your strategic skills and political thinking can greatly benefit an Adventurer boss, just as she can do wonderful things for you. Make it a partnership, and you'll both reap the rewards.

14. Do you sometimes wonder what your boss would do without you? Throughout her life, Artisan Laura Ashley worked closely with her husband, Bernard, an impetuous Adventurer. "As Bernard was constantly planning the next adventure, [Laura] would never deter but always encourage him," wrote her biographer Anna Sebba, "while at the same time ensuring that the necessary details were not overlooked in the excitement." Keep this in mind, ye Artisans who work for Adventurers, and you'll probably have a job forever. Also, don't expect your Adventurer boss to notice your needs. Follow the advice for box 13, and don't forget to have some fun along the way.

15. Be patient. As an Idealist, it is your job to keep your Adventurer boss from making rash decisions and going broke in the process. You don't have to get ulcers every time she announces some new, impossibly impractical idea; help her think it through, and she'll eventually see it in a clear light. Working for an Adventurer can be exasperating, but be thankful it's rarely boring.

16. Have you ever seen the British sitcom *Absolutely Fabulous?* In it, a middle-aged P.R. woman jumps from one fad to another, followed around by her equally trendy and totally incompetent secretary, Bubble. It's the definitive example of the Adventurer leading the Adventurer, and the results are hilariously terrible. Adventurers should *never* work for their kind, especially as personal secretaries. But if you're in this position nonetheless, do everything you can to make like an Idealist and keep disaster at bay.

Building Your Dream Team:
A Guide to Modern Hiring

The good thing about building a staff is that, unlike your family, you get to pick who's in and who's out.

The bad thing is that the hiring process is incredibly time-consuming and, no matter how much you learn about your favorite candidates, it's always a crap shoot.

In the bad old days, recruitment happened immediately before somebody was fired, or right after somebody quit, or just as a new position was being created. The traditional M.O. was to take out a "help wanted" ad, then plow through an avalanche of résumés, looking for those candidates who seemed qualified, intelligent, talented—or, at the very least, appropriate. The process was like opening bushels of oysters in the hope of finding a few pearls.

Today, in what is decidedly a job-hunter's market, recruitment techniques are radically different. *Fluidity* is the key word, and smart companies have gone from "coincidence" hiring, that is, filling a job when it becomes available, to "continuous hiring," that is, snagging great performers whenever and however they can, even if it means creating a position for them.

The most obvious way to attract talent is to invite candidates to contact you via your Web site or to solicit résumés by posting positions on a national job bank on the Internet. But that approach is a bit too passive for the hungriest companies.

A recommended technique is to locate the best people in your field, and initiate a relationship with them via friendly correspondence. Send them press releases and newsletters so they become familiar with your company, and reach out to them with invitations to seminars and conferences. The right time to move in on a great candidate is when his or her company hits a rocky patch, or when your organization has something special to offer, such as an enticing new project.

Intuitive Recruitment:
Customizing the Bait

Let's say you've found a candidate who perfectly suits your needs and you're desperate to hire. What sets your company apart from the dozens of others who are also trying to romance this person? Besides corporate culture, position, location, environment, potential for growth, and salary, there is the very significant question of benefits and perks. If you have a pretty good idea of which archetype your must-have candidate most resembles, the following insights might help you create a package that seals the deal.

- **Visionaries** will likely bargain hard for the richest possible financial package, and eschew other benefits such as on-site day care or tuition reimbursement. They do like to be pampered, so company cars, concierge services, and the use of vacation properties will probably appeal to them. Also try offering stock options upon hiring; promotions given when earned or deserved rather than when yearly performance reviews allow them; and performance bonuses.

- **Artisans** are the most family-oriented of the four types. They'll likely look for flexible scheduling, child- and elder-care services, and generous maternity/paternity leaves. Artisans also appreciate relaxed dress codes as well as company-sponsored wellness and fitness programs. Because Artisans want to maximize their money, they'll probably be the first to sign on for group discounts on insurance and legal services. Also try college-planning assistance and mentoring programs.

- **Idealists** look for benefits that offer long-range rewards, including stock options, investment plans, and pension funds. Convenience is important to them, so perks such as dry-cleaning services and on-site fitness facilities will probably appeal. They're also apt to pursue advanced degrees, and therefore are likely to take advantage of tuition reimbursement programs. Also try offering savings plans that match a percentage of contributions and interest-free loans.

- **Adventurers** appreciate flexibility as much as Artisans do—but for different reasons. Telecommuting will probably entice them, and they'll bargain for all the vacation time they can get, as well as educational sabbaticals. They're turned on by performance bonuses, special incentives, and in-house awards, but tend to place less value on slow-growth advantages like stock options and retirement plans. Offer the Adventurer paid "field trips" to other branches, departments, warehouses, etc.; flexible sick day and personal day allowances; and regular companywide celebrations.

Intuitive Salesmanship

> There is no such thing as "soft sell" and "hard sell." There is only "smart sell" and "stupid sell."
>
> **— CHARLES BROWER, FIFTIES EXECUTIVE**

The first cousin to smart negotiation is the art of selling. If you're a saleswoman in any capacity, you can benefit from interpreting your customer's style and anticipating what he or she will respond to.

How to Sell to a Visionary

Visionaries are the unofficial monarchs of society. This knowledge is important in sales, because the Visionary needs to be treated as if she (or he) is the only customer in the world—or at least the most important customer in the world. In retail situations, Visionaries are the ones who want to be approached and attended to. They appreciate a salesperson's undivided attention, and they expect all of their questions—asked and implied—to be answered fully. Visionaries can be demanding clients, but they reward energetic and perceptive salespeople with repeat business. A salesperson who does extra research, phones the Visionary about new developments, or makes personal visits to the Visionary's office or home becomes a treasure forever. It might be a taxing task, but the payoff can be significant.

Visionaries don't want advice, but they do appreciate information. For example, if you're showing a Persian rug to a Visionary client, and you happen to know the history of the design, share the story. If the exact luxury coupe that the Visionary is eyeing is the favorite of a certain Nobel Prize winner, that information might stir the Visionary to covet it even more.

Visionaries are interested in quality and prestige. If you encounter a Visionary who is on a budget, try to show that person the best, most interesting item for his or her money. If you're selling real estate, avoid "handyman's specials" or "the worst house in the best neighborhood." Visionaries are not do-it-yourselfers.

Are you romancing a Visionary and want her to, say, finance your company's expansion? Then spend some money. Take her to the best restaurant you can afford. Send a car to pick her up. And mind your manners. Visionaries appreciate niceties like handwritten thank-you notes. Though most are much too smart to get into bad business deals—you can't sell a Visionary on something she doesn't want—you can lubricate the journey to "yes" with boxed roses delivered to her office.

Finally, absorb Estée Lauder's advice, who was a Visionary of the first degree: "Touch a face. Touch a hand. Say, 'This is for you, this is what I want *you* to wear.'"

Nudging the Artisan Toward "Yes"

Very few people appreciate a hard sell, and Artisans like pressure least of all. They tend to be distrustful of commerce as a whole, and many deliberately avoid showrooms or selling environments in which swarms of salespeople approach customers the minute they walk in the door. So if you're a retailer and you see someone who looks a lot like an Artisan approaching, handle her/him with care. When you greet that person and ask if there is a need for help, expect "No, just browsing" as an answer. Then gently mention any bargains, specials, or markdowns available, and offer your help if needed. This will establish the Artisan's trust: he or she will no longer believe that you are programmed to sell the most expensive thing in the store. From there, take the customer's lead, but always avoid pressure or a hard sell.

Many Artisans are "green"—they appreciate environmentally safe products. They are also community-oriented. If your company gives back a portion of its profits to, say, the local women's shelter, that will probably be a significant selling point to the Artisan. Likewise, if you're offering one-of-a-kind, handcrafted items, tell the story of who made what. Anything that promotes the health of the earth and the humans on it is likely to lure an Artisan.

It's also true that Artisans want to keep things simple. They can be easily overwhelmed or intimidated by too many details, complications, or options. They like doing business the old-fashioned way—that means if your firm's phone is answered by a human being rather than a "voice jail" system, you've already impressed them.

Enticing the Idealist

The no-nonsense Idealist thrives on hard facts and responds well to intelligent salesmanship. Like Visionaries, Idealists expect full, undivided attention from a salesperson, and will usually do a lot of research before making a major purchase. You won't just get questions, you'll get a quiz. Warning: Idealists don't have much patience for people who are not experts on what they are selling.

Idealists are usually attracted to that which is cutting-edge and top of the line. They like new trends, particularly when it comes to technology, and are especially excited when they can get their hands on a brand-new offering before anybody else does. Upgrades, add-ons, and options are all enticing to the Idealist, as long as the bells and whistles are functional rather than decorative.

Remember that Idealists love systems; as such, it's often easier to sell them a whole solution rather than a piece of a solution. For example, when an Idealist customer walks into a furniture showroom looking for a new sofa, it's possible (with the help of a savvy salesperson) that he or she will walk out with a sofa, a love seat, a cocktail table, a couple of lamps, and a rug. Buying a suite of coordinating furniture not only solves the problem of a place to sit, it solves the whole living room. The Idealist's work is done in one stop.

The same philosophy applies to major business deals. Idealists are not interested in working with people who haven't crossed every *t* and dotted every *i*. They will chase down the finest points of every deal, even if the process takes months and costs significant amounts of money. So don't bother approaching an Idealist unless all the angles are covered.

Capturing the Adventurer

Adventurers' possessions are a big part of their identities; they use them like actors use props and costumes. It's virtually impossible to predict Adventurers' desires, because they're usually not based in anything as predictable as practicality. It would be folly for a salesperson to try to talk an Adventurer into anything, or even to help with the decision-making process; even friendly nudging is likely to turn an Adventurer off.

Adventurers like to stand out from the crowd. Therefore, if you're steering an Adventurer through, say, a maze of cell phones, show him or her the extreme models—the purple handset, or the one with the ear wire, or the tiniest model available. One-of-a-kind items also have great Adventurer appeal; if anything you're selling is available in odd colors or finishes, be sure to make that known.

Looking for an impulse shopper? Look no further. If an Adventurer settles on a sale, be sure the item in question is available for immediate delivery. If you give Adventurers enough time to change their minds, they no doubt will.

For huge sales—e.g., your entire company—a multimedia approach would be your best bet. While Idealists might pour through P&L statements, Adventurers will no doubt leave the details to their advisors. They would much rather be delighted and amused by a great presentation than confronted with a slew of dry numbers and projections—no matter how exciting they may be in the abstract.

8

Changing Jobs, Changing Careers

No cohort in history has demanded as much from a career—money *and* meaning *and* a cool office—as the baby boomers and their successors.
—ANN HORNADAY, BUSINESS ANALYST

You wake up every morning with a familiar dread in the pit of your stomach. You drag yourself out of bed and munch lifelessly on breakfast cereal, mentally hexing your clients, your co-workers, and the crushing tasks that await you. In the shower, you pray for a blizzard, or maybe a case of hives—anything so you could stay home from work.

If this describes you, then you're either clinically depressed, or it's high time you reassessed your working situation.

Good news: there's never been a better time to change jobs. The federal Bureau of Labor Statistics' 1998–1999 *Occupational Outlook Handbook* forecasts 18.6 million new jobs opening up by 2006—that's a 14 percent increase since 1996. Top companies are going crazy trying to hire and keep good people, and as of early 1999, unemployment was down to 4.5 percent. "If you can heal people, resolve conflicts, or tell a good story," reported the *Utne Reader* in 1999, "a good job is probably waiting."

But before we get into what you might do with the rest of your life, let's review the possible reasons why you're so miserable in the first place.

• **Bad boss.** According to Harvey Hornstein, Columbia psychology professor and author of *Brutal Bosses and Their Prey,* an average of one in five people gets abused by their boss on any given day. Over a lifetime, more than 90 percent of employees find themselves on the wrong end of brutal bossing. Hornstein found rotten bosses on factory floors, executive suites, and everywhere in between—and there were no discernible differences along gender lines, either.

• **Meaningless or unchallenging work.** If you're upset about feeling like a wage slave, you're not alone. For the past number of years there has been a groundswell of people looking for real meaning in the workplace. "The most discouraging aspect of our jobs is that they seem to accomplish little of lasting value," writes Andrew Kimbrell in the *Utne Reader.* "Studies consistently show that as many as 80 percent of workers in our society feel their jobs, however fast and furious, are 'meaningless.' . . . We all deserve to be involved in work to which we have been called by our passions and beliefs."

Ann Hornaday hones the point in *Fast Company:* "Values-driven work doesn't always (or even usually) translate into politics or social change— you know, the young investment banker who decides to join a Greenpeace flotilla. It's more about the experience of work and whether it meets your personal needs and professional expectations."

In other words, don't hide your light under a barrel. If you love being part of a humming beehive of activity, yet you work alone most of the time, make a change. If your best talents involve conceiving projects and taking them to completion, but your present job has you doing piecework, you owe it to yourself to take your energies elsewhere. Ann Moore, President of People, Inc., says it best, and her words bear repeating: "Something is wrong with your work if you don't get a rush—that wave of pure joy. If you don't get it, you need to change jobs."

• **Lack of opportunity for advancement.** There's less talk about the "glass ceiling" these days, but that doesn't mean it's gone away. According to Catalyst, a research firm that focuses on females in the workplace, about half of women executives feel that they're held back from top management spots. The culprits they name are male stereotyping and preconceptions of women, 52 percent; exclusion from informal networks of communication, 49 percent; and lack of significant general management/line experience, 47 percent.

A 1997 study of female high-tech employees, conducted by Women in Technology International, showed similar results. Many said that they were frustrated by the "old boys' club" attitude of science and technology firms. Respondents said their ideas had been repeatedly stolen by male co-workers, and that they were often excluded from key meetings and brainstorming sessions.

• **Not enough flexibility.** Guilty moms, unite: 70 percent of parents believe that they don't spend enough time with their children, according to the Families and Work Institute.

As our Adventurer/Artisan friend Cherie Whaples-Elliott says, "I'd rather make a pittance and be flexible. I don't care, everydayness is wonderful. What good is money if you don't enjoy yourself?"

• **Not enough money.** Women still only earn about 75 cents to a man's dollar. But that's not the half of it: we live in a time when the rich keep getting richer and the poor keep getting poorer. In the early 1970s, the average CEO's salary was 41 times higher than that of the average American worker. In the years 1992 to 1994, it was 225 times higher.

Cost of living is brutal, and in order to support yourself, your family, and your future, a certain financial "breaking point" must be reached. Requirements vary with geography and certainly with circumstances (number of children, spouse's salary, etc.). But considering the opportunities that exist for ambitious women right now, there is virtually no reason to slug away in a job that offers numbing work, bad management, no personal rewards, little opportunity for advancement, and inadequate pay.

Or any combination of the above.

Why You *Should* Leave

Women who were raised with a hard-core work ethic, or who pride themselves on sticking it out in times of adversity, or who are hell-bent on a predetermined career path, may all shy away from taking the job-change leap. Ditto women who are supporting families.

Granted, it takes a tremendous amount of energy to catapult yourself into the job market, especially when your present job is sucking the life out of you. But there are good reasons to call upon your deepest strengths and improve your lot.

• **You've only got one soul.** "Not being who you are at work drains a lot of your energy," says Eunice Azzani in *Fast Company* magazine. Azzani is vice president and partner in the San Francisco office of Korn/Ferry International, the world's top executive search firm. "Too often, we think of our jobs and our careers as being the same thing. They're not. Jobs are given and jobs are taken away. . . . But your career belongs to you. You get to decide everything about it: where you go, what you do, whom you work with." Azzani advises sitting down and listening to yourself, and taking your time about it. "If you get in touch with what moves you, you'll find a job that reinforces the good stuff about you."

• **You're in a position of strength.** As an employed person, you're now in a terrific position to hone your desires and do your homework. You have the luxury of researching attractive careers, locating a few dream jobs, accessing your skills, and determining standard salaries—and turning down any job that doesn't ring your chimes.

- **You could win valuable prizes.** Changing jobs virtually assures an increase in salary. According to superagent Leigh Steinberg, "No matter how happy you are at your current company, moving laterally to another company almost always produces better financial results than staying where you are and moving vertically. The reason is simple: Someone is competing financially to get you."

Gordon Miller, a Denver-based career coach, promotes "strategic job-jumping." Miller himself changed jobs four times in five years in the late 1990s, got "huge" promotions, and tripled his pay. Why? "Because most companies no longer think long term," explains Miller on the woman.com Web site. "They are under immense pressure from owners and stockholders to produce NOW. . . . They want people who solve problems and create value immediately and they are willing to pay for it." Since few companies can guarantee job security, they're not all that worried about employees who change jobs frequently.

- **The future is now.** There's an awful lot of speculation about the future job market. One intriguing theory is that, ten years from now, nearly half the U.S. workforce will be "contract employees"—that is, people who are hired on a project-by-project basis. Gordon Miller sees it coming. "More and more companies are 'outsourcing' significant pieces of their workforce," he notes, "so they can stay flexible and fluid in these very competitive times. The good news is that we, the workers, can prosper in all these paradigm shifts." That means taking on the juicy projects we want, commanding high hourly wages, and being able to take control of our schedules.

When you think about a working world that revolves around your special talents and your special needs, instead of some company's idea of a prefab job, it seems entirely sane to pursue those passions that were once pooh-poohed by your high school guidance counselor. Increasingly, we live in a world of specialists and niche markets. In fact, the advent of e-commerce has prompted some of the best marketing minds in the country to declare that everything's a niche market.

- **Old rules are old.** Seasoned interviewers know good people when they see them. They look for energy, motivation, intelligence. Most of all, they look for candidates who get it. If your personal qualities promise to be a great asset to a company, you may only need a night course or two to put you up to speed. To a progressive company, agile thinking, global understanding, and a proven ability to pinch-hit may be more valuable than years of dogged service to an old-time autocrat.

WHAT'S YOUR EXPIRATION DATE?

Certain jobs tend to foster more loyalty than others. Here's the average number of years people in different industries stick with one employer:

Retail	1.9
Entertainment/Recreation	1.9
Social Services	2.8
Health Industries (except hospitals)	2.9
Education	3.8
Banking/Finance	3.9
Insurance	4.2
Real Estate	4.2
Hospitals	5.2
Manufacturing	5.4
Government	6.9

Not mentioned is the field of publishing, which one wag of our acquaintance calls the Roach Motel of career choices: "Women can get in, but they can't get out."

Finally, if you're still worried that you can't rise up to meet your dreams and compete with groomed-to-zoom B-school graduates, listen to business analyst Jon Spayde's philosophy in the *Utne Reader*: "So what if you didn't go to Harvard? You can go to the library, get on the Net, use the phone, and build as good a network as they've got. And you're probably hungrier and tougher than they are. Go for it."

What Are You Doing the Rest of Your Life?

Maybe you're just starting out, graduating from college or high school or technical school, ready to find your truest path in the working world. Maybe the whole world is laid out before you, glittering with opportunity like stars in a Montana sky.

Or maybe you're just ready to make a change.

Lots of women do it. They're chugging along, thinking that ennui and work go hand in hand, and then, something changes. They've taken a course that has inspired them, or they have discovered a hidden talent within themselves. Perhaps they've just been divorced, or the kids have all gone off to college. Whatever their circumstances, women have made radical career changes and either shifted direction or started over at a time when they least expected to.

The DOL Says, Go for It

Though its language may be stuffy, the U.S. Department of Labor is enthusiastic about women's increasingly diverse and important role in the workplace at large. "Women have a huge stake in the current and future job market," it reports. "Women's labor force growth is expected to increase at a faster rate than men's—16.6 percent between 1994 and 2005 as compared with 8.5 percent for men." The DOL estimates that 17 million new jobs will open up between now and 2005. "Many of these new opportunities will be in areas we would never have anticipated 20, or even 10 years ago. Occupations that used to offer solid careers are in decline, while positions once unheard of are now among the fastest growing."

According to the DOL, the speediest growth is happening in services; retail trade; government industries; health services, including home health care; and computer-related industries.

So where do you fit in? At a time when women are straddling centuries of tradition and a brave new world, it's not all that surprising that the top four occupations for women have remained pretty stable over the years. Number one is secretary. Then comes cashier, manager/administrator, and registered nurse. The fastest-growing, highest-paying occupations, however, all of which require a bachelor's degree or more, have changed drastically since your mother's day. They are:

1. Lawyers
2. Physicians
3. Systems analysts
4. Computer engineers
5. Management analysts
6. Residential counselors
7. Secondary school teachers
8. Special education teachers
9. Writers and editors
10. Personnel specialists
11. Designers
12. Artists
13. Social workers

Have You Considered "Firefighter"?

The DOL keeps track of occupations in which fewer than 25 percent of positions are filled by women. It calls them "nontraditional" occupations. Through grants and other incentives, our government encourages employers to hire women to fill some of these jobs. The DOL tracks close to 100 nontraditional occupations; a few stand out as interesting options for various types.

For Visionaries
Non-retail sales (commodities, etc.)
Boat and motor vehicle sales
Funeral director

For Artisans
Podiatrist (only 1 in 10 are women)
Forester
Farmer
Fisherperson
Agricultural supervisor
Groundskeeper
Upholsterer

For Idealists
Airline pilot (in 1997, of 120,000 U.S. airline pilots,
    only 1,000 were women)
Architect
Mechanical engineer
Construction inspector
Surveyor

For Adventurers
Firefighter
Sheriff
Announcer
Private detective

Finding a New Job
Job hunting has never been easier. Thanks to the Internet you can, in the privacy of your own home, access thousands of employment opportunities; network with others in your field; take career aptitude tests; hook up with a recruiter; register with job banks; learn how to write an effective résumé; and send your résumés out to potential employers.

It's like a career counselor in a box . . . almost.

21st-Century Career Counseling

Living, breathing career counselors are indispensable if you're unsure about your truest career path or want to make a radical change. According to a Gallup survey prepared for the National Career Development Association, more than 72 percent of employed people said that if they had to do it all over again, they'd have gotten more information about career options, while fewer than 36 percent said they started their present career because they made a conscious choice or followed a definite plan.

Personal career counselors are becoming as common as personal trainers, personal shoppers, and personal identification numbers. Their role in the service galaxy is no longer strictly about helping clients find a job, but helping guide clients through years and years of career growth. Like HMOs, the new breed of career counselors take a "wellness" approach. As such, counselor-client relationships continue over the long term—just like one's relationship with a financial advisor. Some tips:

- Experts say the best time to contact a counselor is when you feel the slightest stirrings of restlessness—or, in the worst-case scenario, when you get a hunch that you or your job might be eliminated. Don't wait until you're desperately unhappy or about to be laid off, and definitely don't wait until after you've quit your job.
- Find a counselor who's right for you. If you're an artistic Adventurer, for instance, don't go to someone who is corporate-oriented. If you don't know where to start your search, call the National Board for Certified Counselors at 800-398-5389.
- Invest some serious time and money into the project. At $75–$150 an hour, career counseling isn't cheap. But plan on scheduling at least four sessions in order to get to the bottom of your hopes and dreams. Your counselor will probably give you lots of tests, ask you provocative questions, and make suggestions you never would have come up with on your own. In fact, it might be the best investment you ever made.

Get Thee to a Recruiter

While you're getting in touch with your career chakra, browse the Internet and find yourself a recruiter. These employee-employer matchmakers, commonly known as headhunters, traditionally seek out desirable candidates for corporate clients. But headhunters aren't just for corporations anymore, and you certainly don't have to wait for them to come to you.

Recruitment Web sites are all over the Net, and they want to add gogetters like you to their rosters. Recruiters specialize in every major industry you can think of, including finance, health care, education, and technology. There are even recruiters who specialize in finding creative freelancers to work on short-term projects.

If you can impress the right recruiter, you'll have set your job hunt into fast forward. And remember: You don't pay recruiters. They're paid by the company that hires you.

A Mecca for Do-It-Yourselfers

With or without a career counselor and a recruitment firm on your side, you should take a look at a few of the many job-hunt sites on the Internet. The U.S. Department of Labor lists literally thousands of opportunities, while smaller sites dedicated to women in business, professional organizations, and employment in general are also ripe with offerings.

So, go shopping. A selected list of job hunt Web sites are listed in the Resource section at the end of this book.

The Intuitive Job Finder
If You're a Visionary, Look For:

- A leader you respect and admire.
- A position that offers autonomy, staff support, and dedicated administrative help.
- An extremely competitive salary with plenty of benefits and bonuses built in.
- Attractive headquarters with an air of formality.
- An office with a door that closes.

And keep in mind: Many Visionaries like a bit of prestige with their nine-to-five. Jobs that offer first-class travel, box seats, or tickets to the Inaugural Ball are probably more attractive than those that don't.

If You're an Artisan, Look For:

- Flexibility. Your best bets are companies that will let you work at home part-time (telecommuting), work a "compressed" week, or choose your own hours.
- Great benefits. Though salary is important, also seek out terrific health insurance and family-friendly perks such as on-site child care, elder care options, sick-child care, personal days, etc.
- A casual, friendly workplace. Avoid any company that doesn't allow easy circulation between colleagues, has strict workplace rules, or enforces a conservative dress code.

And keep in mind: Women-owned businesses are more likely, overall, to offer flextime.

If You're an Idealist, Look For:

- A stable, well-structured company with a proven track record and clear objectives.
- A job that offers learning opportunities, either through on-site training or tuition-paid course work.
- Built-in performance reviews with structured raises and bonuses.
- Lifetime benefits that include a solid retirement plan, such as a pension.

And keep in mind: Government jobs or positions within university systems are good choices for Idealists, because they're set up for the long term.

KNOW YOUR JOB LINGO

TWO-COMMA SALARY: The preferred way to describe a seven-figure income.

EXPLODING OFFER: A pressure tactic in which potential employers tell job candidates that they must accept an offer right away.

SLAMMING: If an employer suddenly changes the terms of a job offer, you've just been slammed. It's a technique intended to eliminate candidates.

TENT POLE: Someone who is so crucial to a company that he or she keeps it standing—figuratively, anyway.

FRONT-LINERS: Employees who deal directly with the public—salespeople, receptionists, etc.

MCJOB: Any meaningless, low-paying job that's comparable to working at McDonald's.

RECEPTION ENGINEER: Receptionist. Strictly tongue-in-cheek.

TWINK: Inexperienced Internet user.

CYBERAGENTS: Agents who negotiate employment deals for computer software developers.

PIRANHA POOLS: Companies with bad working environments.

DOT COM: An Internet company.

HOBBY: A small subsidiary of a larger company.

E-LANCER: A freelancer who conducts most of her business on line or via e-mail.

JOB MONKEY: Someone who works short-term or seasonal jobs.

INCUBATOR: A substructure, usually operated by a university, corporation, or government, that houses, nurtures, and advances start-up companies.

SO MANY BRIDESMAIDS, SO FEW BRIDES

Though recent years have proven to be a job-hunter's market, the demand for good jobs always outstrips supply. In 1998, the average company selected for *Fortune*'s "100 Best Companies to Work For" received an astonishing 19,000 job applications. How many of these applicants were hired? Only 724.

If You're an Adventurer, Look For:

- A position that offers short-term projects and plenty of variety.
- A workplace that emphasizes interaction between colleagues and departments and has a social environment.
- A job that lets you be a self-starter and express your individuality. Avoid getting yourself into a spot where you'll be subject to micromanagement or constant inspection.
- Benefits that don't lock you into the long term. Pension plans aren't for you.

And keep in mind: You might be better off working as a subcontractor rather than being on a company payroll. Jump on any opportunity to be an "intrapreneur," that is, to run a separate start-up company within a parent company.

WHAT TO ASK FOR

Congratulations. You've survived the résumé writing, the phone calls, the interviews. Now it's time to put a price on your head. Here are some helpful hints to put you over the final job-hunt hurdle.

- At one time a formula for determining your target salary was to take your age and add three zeros to it. That formula is now old and dusty. These days, in order to maintain a middle-class lifestyle, you've got to take your age, add three zeros, then multiply by four. Example: If you're thirty-five years old, you must earn $140,000 per year in order to have a nice house in a good neighborhood, pay your bills and taxes, maintain an appropriate lifestyle, and put two kids through a name-brand university. If you're forty-five, prepare to ask for a salary of $180,000.
- If you're changing jobs, get a 10 to 20 percent salary increase over your last position, and don't sacrifice it for vague promises of advancement.
- Ask about a signing bonus. In 1998, more than half of large companies offered them, and most were in the $2,000 to $5,000 range. Whether they're paid on the day you start or deferred for a year, they're a nice perk.

- Try to advance the date of your first salary review.
- Check out stock options, both at your old company and your new one. According to *U.S. News & World Report,* start-up firms are often cash poor, and might offer stock options to make up for modest pay and fringe benefits. "The upside is that you'll get stock at a bargain price if the firm and its shares prosper; the downside is that you assume more risk."
- Before you make a move, be sure of what you're leaving behind. Does your current firm offer deferred incentives? Stock options may need to be exercised before you leave, but exercising them might subject you to an agreement that limits whom you can work for.
- Don't expect a contract, but do ask for a letter detailing your agreement and any promises that were made for you.
- If you've got weeks of vacation time built up at your old firm, see if your new one can match it. If you're getting less time, figure the loss into your salary and make sure you're not losing money.
- Remember that window offices, laptop computers, and benefits can be negotiated.
- Rule of thumb: Older employees do well with pension plans because benefits are typically based on the final three to five years of average income. Younger employees do better with 401(k) plans because it's easier to take the money along when you switch jobs.
- Company-paid moving is a high priority for most job hunters with families. Also ask about transporting your cars; prolonging the time you have to move; and help with finding your spouse a job in the new area.
- Finally, do all your negotiating at once. You may be tempted to put off seemingly insignificant requests, such as vacation time, until after you've reached an agreement, but by then it may be too late to make any changes.

Making a Business:

The Intuitive Entrepreneur

With the burst of women-owned businesses and the number of women in high-profile executive positions, the women's business market is no longer a niche—it's as much a part of the landscape . . . as Wall Street is.

—JOLENE SYKES, PUBLISHER OF *FORTUNE*

An entrepreneurial spirit is blazing across the country. All around us, individuals are launching multinational corporations, technology firms, manufacturing companies, franchises, restaurants, agencies, stores, and services. And women are leading the trend. According to the National Foundation for Women Business Owners, females are starting businesses at nearly twice the national average. A significant number of new ventures are being launched by women of color, whose rate of business ownership grew by 153 percent from 1987 to 1996—triple the growth rate of new U.S. businesses overall. As of 1999 there were 9.1 million women-owned companies in the United States, employing about 27.5 million people and generating some $3.7 trillion in sales annually.

Why the boom? For one thing, the traditional corporate structure is rapidly changing. In olden days, giant companies made it their business to be self-contained. For example, Ford Motor Company's plant in Rouge, Michigan, not only assembled cars but also operated a steel mill to make car bodies and a glass factory to make windshields.

In the 1980s, when lean-and-mean companies started nipping at the heels of lumbering, top-heavy firms, it became clear that the old boys needed to go on a diet. Why not have small, specialized companies take over jobs that had nothing to do with the corporation's product or identity? After considerable soul-searching, certain big corporations determined that payroll could be handled better and/or less expensively by out-side specialists. Then they found out that advertising, janitorial services, property management, and a whole slew of other tasks were also ripe for jobbing out.

What resulted was a movement toward fluid, adaptable corporations that hired services as they needed them. Other considerations, such as the expense of employee benefits, also contributed to the shift. In any case we now have a business landscape in which small-scope companies play an enormous role. They provide crucial support systems not only to major corporations, but also to individuals who, due to the general decline of the traditional nuclear family, increasingly hire helpers to perform tasks that relatives might once have done.

Enter the entrepreneurs. Enter the women who are smart enough to match their talents with today's opportunities.

The Bail-Outs

For the purposes of study, experts have divided female business launchers into two categories: start-up entrepreneurs, who create their own compa-nies right out of the gate, and "bail-out" entrepreneurs, who leave the cor-porate world to set out on their own.

Nearly half of women who started a business in the past twenty years were top executives or were at the pinnacle of their corporate careers when they went solo; in fact, the number of bail-out entrepreneurs is growing so rapidly that corporations are scrambling for ways to keep their female tal-ent from jumping ship.

"Companies absolutely need to work on stemming the defections," reported *Fortune* in 1998. How? "By accepting women on their own terms. . . . By letting women be pioneers within corporate walls. . . . By raising women's confidence not with affirmative action programs but with truly gender-blind hiring." Easier said than done, apparently.

According to a study sponsored in part by the National Association of Women Business Owners, 44 percent of women bailed out of the nine-to-five life and started a business for the most basic of entrepreneurial rea-sons: they had a great idea. About 30 percent from the private sector and 16 percent from the public sector defected because they couldn't get ahead (there's that glass ceiling). Eleven percent of women said they were seek-ing greater challenges, while 9 percent became entrepreneurs after losing their jobs due to downsizing.

Apparently, these refugees from the corporate world put a great value on freedom. More than 60 percent of former desk jockeys told pollsters that nothing would induce them to return to corporate life, not even more money or flexibility.

Figures suggest that women start their own businesses because they're seeking personal growth and self-determination—wealth and power are secondary concerns, at best. In their 1997 book *Women Entrepreneurs: Moving Beyond the Glass Ceiling,* Dorothy P. Moore and E. Holly Buttner asked women why they left organizations to start a business. Their answers, by rank:

1. **Launching out was the only way to advance myself.**
2. **To create a work environment more consistent with my values.**
3. **To be on the ground floor of a new and exciting business venture in which I am in charge.**
4. **To regain the feeling of excitement about my work.**
5. **To balance family and work.**
6. **To become an entrepreneur.**

Hearing the Call

Gail Blanke is CEO of Lifedesigns, a company that empowers women and helps them act on their dreams. She founded the firm after developing the Women of Enterprise Awards program at Avon Products, Inc. On the National Association for Female Executives (NAFE) Web site she states, "I noticed, year after year, that the extraordinary winners had fought their way back from tremendous adversity." Blanke saw women who had overcome poverty, illness, and abusive situations to triumph in the business world. "What occurred to me was: What about the rest of us who don't have these disadvantages? What are we waiting for?"

In Lifedesigns workshops, Blanke helps women transform their lives with the simplest of tools: soul-searching, encouragement, empowerment, and support. Says Blanke, "Most of us are walking around in straitjackets. We have bought into a number of barriers in terms of why we can't live a life or have a career that absolutely thrills us." Blanke has discovered that when women closely examine those assumptions and barriers, they learn that many of them aren't real. "When you can open yourself up to what would be possible, it's stunning the amount of energy you have to create breakthroughs in your life. We see it in every single workshop."

There's no question that the time is ripe for women to create their own opportunities. In addition to feeding herself and her family, women entrepreneurs can rewrite the rules of business to suit their truest interests.

Do You Have What It Takes
to Be an Entrepreneur?

The U.S. Small Business Administration is worried about you. It wants to make sure that you're really cut out to be an entrepreneur, and so has dedicated a page on its Web site that reviews key questions you should ask yourself before diving into business ownership. Consider the following:

• **Are you a self-starter?** It will be up to you—not someone else telling you—to develop projects, organize your time, and follow through on details.

• **How well do you get along with different personalities?** Business owners need to develop working relationships with a variety of people, including customers, vendors, staff, bankers, and professionals such as lawyers, accountants, or consultants. Can you deal with a demanding client, an unreliable vendor, or cranky staff person in the best interest of your business?

• **How good are you at making decisions?** Small-business owners are required to make decisions constantly, often quickly, under pressure, and independently.

• **Do you have the physical and emotional stamina to run a business?** Business ownership can be challenging. Can you face twelve-hour work days six or seven days a week?

• **How well do you plan and organize?** Research indicates that many business failures could have been avoided through better planning. Good organization—of financials, inventory, schedules, production—can help avoid many pitfalls.

• **Is your drive strong enough to maintain your motivation?** Running a business can wear you down. Some business owners feel burned out by having to carry all the responsibility on their shoulders. Strong motivation can make the business succeed and will help you survive slowdowns as well as periods of burnout.

• **How will the business affect your family?** The first few years of business start-up can be hard on family life. The strain of an unsupportive spouse may be hard to balance against the demands of starting a business. There also may be financial difficulties until the business becomes profitable, which could take months or years. You may have to adjust to a lower standard of living or put family assets at risk.

The Visionary Entrepreneur

Look into your mind's eye and imagine an entrepreneurial story. It probably starts with a person, a product, and a dream, right? You picture a slow, lonely beginning with lots of sacrifices and false starts. Then come a few good breaks, and gradually a story of success unfolds against a background of relentless work.

Well, erase that image right now. The Visionary entrepreneur is not the kind of woman to start small and put her life on hold while she's waiting for business to take off. She is much more likely to launch a venture off a previously established platform. She may bail out of a corporate situation, taking clients with her, or become a consultant to companies with which she already has a relationship. She might even be paid to start a business by a group of backers. Once established, the Visionary entrepreneur is not content to keep things simple: she is an empire builder who always looks for ways to make her business bigger, better, and more profitable.

Of the four types, Visionaries are the most likely to outgrow their corporate parents; therefore, many of them fall under the category of bail-out entrepreneur. Chemistry is important: Visionaries find it difficult, even under the best circumstances, to have a boss. If they're asked to answer to someone they perceive as weak or unintelligent, the situation can become unbearable. In most Visionary bail-outs, the Visionary has become frustrated because her company isn't supporting her ideas and talents. She comes to see that she can do for herself what she's been doing for others, and reap the benefits.

Once on the entrepreneurial path, Visionaries tend to position themselves not just as leaders but as figureheads. This is one reason why the Visionary entrepreneur is so hell-bent on success: her reputation and, in some cases, whole identity, are at stake; in fact, many Visionary enterprises are extensions of their leaders' personalities. While Idealists might shudder at such a thought, the Visionary likes it just fine. In fact, many Visionaries believe it's the key to their success.

Visionaries want attractive offices, beautiful letterhead, top-notch equipment, and a well-rounded support staff right out of the gate. Obviously, such a nicely feathered nest doesn't come cheap. Strong financial backing is crucial to the Visionary's success, and the smart entrepreneur will secure plenty of funds before she opens for business.

As a leader, the Visionary is a strategist who is constantly planning her company's next steps. She avoids getting involved in the minutiae of day-to-day business, so she needs strong operational systems in place—and someone to run them. Idealists and Artisans make great partners for Visionaries, because both types tend to be steady and methodical, and will free the Visionary to think of bigger things than preparing payroll or paying the bills on time.

Visionaries need little help when it comes to sales and marketing, however. Most Visionaries are their own best P.R. agents. They understand the importance of networking and will put their connections to good use.

It should be noted that there are start-up Visionaries who begin with a single idea and build a business from scratch. But these Visionaries usually become entrepreneurs because they have limited opportunities, and must start a business in order to support the lifestyle of their dreams. Yet even Visionaries who start with $100 and a notion are attracted to so-called glamour industries like fashion, publishing, marketing, luxury retail, advertising, public relations, and the arts.

Within the huge scope of Visionary entrepreneurship are general subgroups, which follow.

Four Kinds of Visionary Entrepreneurs

1. The Take-the-Ball-and-Run-with-It Entrepreneur. This bail-out Visionary usually starts her business out of frustration. When her bosses repeatedly ignore her ideas or refuse to improve an aspect of the company, she is compelled to go into business for herself—often in direct competition with her former employer.

Maryles Casto fits this category. A one-time flight attendant, she became a star agent in a large travel firm. Casto took pride in her ability to handle huge, complex arrangements for corporate clients, and would chase down the smallest details of an itinerary to ensure that business trips were trouble-free. Then Casto's employers started lowering their standards of service in order to save money. They loaded her up with more clients than she could handle, and effectively sabotaged her ability to do her job.

Casto quit and, in 1974, started her own agency. Not surprisingly, a number of the accounts she'd served via her former employer chose to go with her. It wasn't an entirely smooth transition: initially she had a business partner who didn't have the sky's-the-limit ambition that Casto did. Casto bought her out, and today Casto Travel, Inc., employs more than 200 people in offices across the country and boasts such clients as Apple Computer.

2. The Statement-of-Style Entrepreneur. Many entrepreneurs have a need to express themselves through their work. This is very much the case for Visionaries, who are compelled to put their distinctive stamp on all aspects of business. Obviously, in order to do this effectively she's got to own the business in the first place.

Sometimes, the Statement-of-Style Entrepreneur is born when a Visionary in a position of power has style clashes with others in charge. Elizabeth Arden and Hattie Carnegie started their retail empires this way; each woman broke away from a partner to take over the reins on her own.

Vera Wang's career has been relatively free of clashes, but she, too, qualifies as a Statement-of-Style Entrepreneur. Wang, who has no formal design training, was an editor at *Vogue* for seventeen years before becoming design director for Ralph Lauren. Her entrepreneurial spirit woke up in 1989 when she was planning her wedding and couldn't find a dress to suit her. She recalls, "There was one basic look at the time: frou-frou." She eventually ordered an elaborate beaded dress that cost $10,000—and even then, she didn't really like it.

Wang left Ralph Lauren because she wanted to start a family. But it wasn't long before she opened her own boutique. At first she only carried other designers' gowns, but as it was with her wedding dress, Wang wasn't entirely satisfied with what was available. She started designing her own gowns, and within seven years had become the most influential bridal and formal wear designer in the country. Today, Wang's creations are as recognizable as the stars who wear them.

Though fashion mavens are the most visible of the bunch, Statement-of-Style Entrepreneurs can be found in virtually every industry. Jennie Grossinger, for instance, built up her family's resort in the Catskill Mountains and had such a personal touch—and flair for publicity—that during the '50s and '60s she was the best-known hotelkeeper in America. In the early '90s Frances Lear launched *Lear,* a magazine for "women who weren't born yesterday" that reflected her own ageless style. Joan Rivers, a lifelong collector of fine jewels, produces a line of costume jewelry that appeals to her own opulent tastes but is priced for Middle America.

Note: If you know of a company named after its founder, and especially if that company's logo is based on the founder's signature, it's almost certain it was started by a Statement-of-Style Visionary.

3. The Knowledge-Is-Power Entrepreneur. It's not unusual for entrepreneurs to be eponymous with their product. But the Knowledge-Is-Power Entrepreneur places a different twist on that formula: she puts her talent, know-how, and personality into one salable package and becomes a consultant.

Debra Benton, president of Benton Management Resources, Inc., has a distinctly Visionary consulting firm: she makes executives of large international companies look good. Her Executive Presence program takes her all over the world to coach managers and CEOs in the nuances of dress, presentation, etiquette, and the like. She's coached clients to meet and work with every American president since Carter, has prepped people for job interviews with Donald Trump, and has even prepared clients to testify before Senate hearings.

The Visionary is wonderfully suited to the role of independent consultant, for a number of reasons. First and foremost is the fact that she gets to be her own boss and exercise total control over all aspects of the business. Second, she gets to use her talent for making presentations. The archetypal Visionary has a gift for communication and visual display; when the product she's presenting is herself, she can truly shine. The third good reason is that consultants don't see the same faces every day. That not only keeps the Visionary on her toes, but it also keeps her away from the "familiarity breeds contempt" syndrome that she's so susceptible to. And finally, though it may seem frivolous to other types, most Visionaries love to dress up, travel, eat in fine restaurants, and stay in great hotels—all of which are perks of the high-priced consultant.

4. The Profit-In-My-Pocket Entrepreneur. You've spent years pouring your heart and soul into your job. You've taken on huge responsibilities and pulled off major coups. Along the way you've gotten pats on the back and regular raises, but then one day you get a glimpse of what your boss is earning. The disparity between that paycheck and your paycheck makes you sick.

If this describes you, you might be on the verge of becoming a Profit-in-My-Pocket Entrepreneur. These Visionaries are finished sharing the wealth; they want to do for themselves that they've been doing for others, and to profit handsomely from it. If it means competing with their former employers, that's okay; they've paid their dues and are ready to cash in.

The Artisan Entrepreneur

You know the fairy-tale entrepreneur who bakes a really good muffin one day, then bakes a few more for her friends and family, and ten years later is running a multimillion-dollar muffin franchise? That's the Artisan.

Quite unlike the methodical Idealist, who plans every inch of her business before she makes a move, the Artisan often becomes an entrepreneur by accident. Starting with a solid idea or product, she lets consumer response lead her to business success. Along the way she works like crazy and takes all the help she can get.

Of course, that's only one example of the Artisan's entrepreneurial spirit. Many Artisans are quite deliberate in following their dreams to fruition. Some start their own businesses because they don't like their other options, and a great many become entrepreneurs because their jobs aren't giving them what they need.

What do Artisans need? For one thing, flexibility. When an Artisan breaks out of her nine-to-five shackles to go solo, it's often because she wants a better balance in her life. Owning her own business means she can spend mornings in her garden and afternoons with her kids, and still make a living. For some Artisans the impulse goes even deeper: business owner-ship is part of a quest for meaning, for finding fulfilling work that is healthy for the body, mind, and spirit, as well as the ecology and the com-munity at large.

Artisans are generally happiest with concrete rather than abstract products—that is, they'd rather provide food, shelter, care, or objects than sell information systems or financial products.

Whatever her chosen field, the move to an entrepreneurial life is, for the Artisan, often accompanied by exhilaration and fear. Artisans worry that they'll be unable to pay their creditors, their financiers, and their employ-ees. They fret over the possibility of big tragedies, like earthquakes, and major inconveniences, like unreliable suppliers. This anxiety factor is what leads many entrepreneurial Artisans to start businesses on a small scale. Rather than mapping out a long-term business plan, some Artisans take baby steps into entrepreneurship, and adopt a "wait and see" stance.

Entrepreneurial Artisans who suffer from fear-of-finances do best when they partner with another type. A Visionary would be the best choice, because Visionaries are brave, business-savvy, and great at selling ideas to investors. With the right support systems in place, the Artisan is free to shine. She'll bring to the table an artful touch, a dedication to social causes, a humanitarian approach to problems, and a wicked work ethic that will make everybody else look like bums. She'll probably also employ people she likes, and build a company that is not only a pleasure to work for and with but is also a positive presence in the community.

Four Kinds of Artisan Entrepreneurs

1. The Accidental Entrepreneur. The classic Artisan enterprise starts modestly with a simple product made with love. "Hey," says a friend or two or twenty, "you make the best pickles/oven mitts/handmade paper/ shampoo I've ever seen!" The seeds are planted, and the Artisan is cajoled into bringing her creation to market.

It's a story as old as commerce itself, and has come to fruition in such modern-day success stories as Mrs. Field's Cookies, Anne Robinson's Windham Hill Records, and Dineh Mohajer's Hard Candy nail polishes. Also known as "kitchen-table start-ups," these ventures usually have a long gestation period, as the Artisan polls family and friends to find out how she really feels about going into business for herself. When she decides to move ahead, the Artisan typically takes those very same family and friends along for the ride, employing them in any way she can. Working in a grass-roots fashion, customer by customer, she slowly builds her good idea into a viable enterprise.

Usually, the Accidental Entrepreneur's business begins as a one-person, at-home affair. It isn't until she's swamped with work that she'll hire her first employee; her home will be bursting at the seams before she considers moving into a "real" office. The Accidental Entrepreneur doesn't bet on future success. She waits for growth to happen, then builds systems to accommodate it. Many Accidental ventures thrive for years without ever having a business plan in place; though this isn't always the smartest way to grow a business (just ask an Idealist), the Artisan's comfort level is very important to her—she's leery of investing in something she's not 100 percent sure of.

2. The Soul-of-Integrity Entrepreneur. Whether she's a refugee from a giant corporation or recently sprung from art school, the Soul-of-Integrity Artisan seeks to make a business that she can believe in. She wants to support herself, but money is a secondary concern; it's much more important for her to love her life and to do work that matters. So she'll peddle her hand-thrown pots at crafts fairs, or sacrifice a steady salary in order to establish a battered women's shelter, or create a wonderful company that puts people before profits.

Profit isn't out of the question, however. Judy Wicks, for instance, runs the famous White Dog Café in Philadelphia. It's a top-rated, organically oriented restaurant that's been drawing crowds and critical raves for years. But that's not the half of it: Wicks's café is also a center where public discussion forums, lectures, and storytelling sessions are held. It's the headquarters for the Philadelphia Sister Restaurant program, which promotes interchange between diverse neighborhoods; a mentoring program that offers internships to inner-city high school kids; and a project called "Table for Six Billion, Please!" that fosters international dialogue and cultural exchange via connections with restaurants in Vietnam, Nicaragua, Lithuania, and Cuba.

Bettina Richards is one Soul-of-Integrity Entrepreneur who started off in a very un-Artisan career as an artist-and-repertory executive for various big-name record companies. If you're not sure what an A&R person does, think of any rock and roll movie you've ever seen. You know the calloused record company guy who sits behind a desk and, after hearing three notes of a song, yells, "Next!"? That was Bettina Richards's job. And she didn't like it one bit. She felt that her favorite bands were ignored if they didn't make best-selling CDs, and talented musicians were discouraged for no good reason.

So in 1992 Richards started Thrill Jockey Records—what's known in the business as an "indie" label. She signs on bands she likes and doesn't try to run their careers. After a record breaks even, she gives the artists 50 percent of the cut—very generous, by industry standards. Her contracts are often literally handshakes, and she doesn't attach a career-long cut on a band's profits. Her unorthodox approach seems to be working: by late '98 Thrill Jockey's eclectic artists had recorded some sixty albums, all but three of which broke even or made money. Which, when you consider that the record industry at large takes a loss on about 85 percent of their releases, is pretty impressive.

Richards isn't rich, and neither are her bands, but that's not the point. "I want my company to stay in business and do well," she told the *New York Times*. "But the creative stuff was always the motivation. . . . It wasn't, 'I see a way to make money better.' It was, 'I can make this artist's experience better.' This is a lot of work, but it never feels like a job."

Soul-of-Integrity Entrepreneurs are not always profitable, and many have had marginal existences in which poverty was a constant threat. But others, like Laura Ashley, held on to their beliefs and became millionaires.

3. The Home-Centric Entrepreneur. A great many Artisans put their families' needs above all else. The challenge of maintaining a structured work life as well as a happy home can become too much for them, especially when kids are involved. The answer? Be your own boss.

A home-based business allows the Artisan to twist, stretch, and compress her working hours to fit her family life. At one time, such ventures were limited to spare-time activities like throwing Tupperware parties or stuffing envelopes, but no more. Today there are more than 3.5 million home businesses in the United States owned by women, which employ about 14 million people. What's more, full-time home business owners have incomes 20 percent higher than households in general, and about 11 percent pull down more than $100,000 per year.

The personal computer has been a fabulous tool for entrepreneurs of all stripes. It has allowed writers, designers, specialty retailers, travel agents, and a host of other ambitious women to earn a living without ever changing out of their bunny slippers. Since a good number of Artisans are technology-shy, making friends with PCs can be a challenge. But once that hurdle is cleared a whole world of home-based opportunities await.

Consider the story of Jeanne Cavadini, an Artisan who has run a successful vintage clothing and jewelry boutique since 1981. For years, Jeanne insisted that she was hopeless when it came to computers. Then, in 1998, her ten-year-old son—after much cajoling and wheedling on his part— finally taught her the basics of computing. In time she got on the Internet and discovered eBay, an on-line auction house, where the same kind of merchandise she sold in her shop was going for prices that made her head spin.

THE ARTISAN'S EMOTIONAL TIME LINE

Every good businesswoman needs a plan that includes financial projections. But you, as an Artisan, need more: you also need an emotional projection. So while you're crunching numbers and doing market research, try the following:

1. On a large sheet of paper, make a time line. Start on the far left with a notch indicating the age you are now. Make a brief note about your present circumstances, e.g., where you live, how much money you're making, your marital status, ages of your children, etc.

2. Divide the rest of the time line into ten-year increments, ending at the age of one hundred (why not be optimistic?).

3. Fill in each ten-year space with your projected emotional requirements. Look inside yourself and imagine what will be most meaningful to you at each phase. Between the ages of thirty and forty, would you like to have a baby? Three babies? In your mid-forties, do you see yourself owning a big country house with lots of bedrooms and plenty of land? At fifty-five, would you like to have enough wealth to abandon the business world and become a watercolorist? In your sixties, would you like to travel the world, doing volunteer work in impoverished countries?

4. When you've completed your personal time line, go back and fill in the dollar amounts that you think each evolutionary leap will require. Then, take another look at your business plan and make sure that you're setting yourself up for a life well lived, now and in the future.

Jeanne's competitive spirit kicked in. She signed on to eBay as a merchant, learned to use a scanner, downloaded photos of select pieces of her inventory, and put them up for auction. She couldn't believe the results: costume jewelry that had been languishing in her store for eight years was suddenly being sold for three times its asking price. "I thought to myself, why am I paying rent and keeping shop hours? I realized I could stay home, take the write-off, be there when my son came home, do laundry, and work at the same time," says Jeanne. In 1999 she closed her shop in order to concentrate on clients in California, Guam, Argentina, Sweden, Italy, Japan, and everywhere in between.

On the low-tech side of home-based businesses are service industries, which are increasingly lucrative and are expected to become even more important in the future. Portrait photographers, massage therapists, tailors, furniture refinishers, tutors, counselors, and herbalists can all work at home, given the space. Businesses that require some traveling but can be run from a home office include garden and landscape design, home inspection, commercial and specialty cleaning services, public relations, and event planning. Artisans can consider becoming personal trainers, yoga teachers, physical therapists, Lamaze instructors, or dog groomers. Virtually any caretaker or teacher can become an independent agent, set up cozy headquarters in a spare room, and make her own way in the open market.

4. The Quest-for-a-Better-Life Entrepreneur. These Artisans tend to be high on ambition and low on corporate-level qualifications. They're not interested in expensive, time-consuming options like business school: the Better-Life Entrepreneurs seek lucrative ventures that require hard work, dedication, and common sense.

Though they could come up with their own ideas and run with them, these Artisans are more likely to reduce their risks and buy a franchise with a proven track record. Training is part of the package so there's no need for previous experience; in fact, studies show that a majority of women entrepreneurs start businesses that are unrelated to their previous jobs.

Franchise opportunities are everywhere these days. On beyond obvious choices like Taco Bell and KFC, both of which rank in the top ten of *Entrepreneur*'s best 500 franchises for 1999, are distinctly Artisan-like businesses such as Yogen Früz Worldwide (#1); Miracle Ear Hearing Systems (#32); Big Apple Bagels (#85); Once Upon a Child (#109); Gymboree (#135); Great American Cookies (#168); Nursefinders (#229); Women's Health Boutique (#255); and Great Earth Vitamins (#394). Other hot franchise options include senior care services, bakeries, holiday decorating companies, and woodworking supply stores.

With an investment as low as $2,300 or as high as $4.5 million, the Better-Life Entrepreneur can own a business that will probably provide nicely for her family over the course of her working life, and beyond.

The Idealist Entrepreneur

Unlike Visionaries and Adventurers, most Idealists are not interested in personal glory. The Idealist entrepreneur is perfectly happy to keep a low profile and to start a business that might be virtually invisible to people outside of her direct industry.

When an Idealist decides to leave the security of a job and set off on her own, she makes sure that there's a very good reason to gamble on herself. Idealists are by-the-book types who follow proven formulas for success. The risks they take are thoroughly calculated, backed up by solid business plans that include market research, financial forecasts, growth strategies, and exit strategies.

Putting together a business plan or a financial proposal is not a stumbling block for the Idealist, as it can be for other types. Her major handicap comes in making in-person pitches to potential investors; therefore, she is wise to partner with a Visionary or an Adventurer. These more flamboyant types are perfect for handling public relations, advertising, sales, and, especially, presentations to angels, venture capitalists, loan officers, and other strangers.

The Idealist entrepreneur's great advantage in business is that her venture is probably not a vehicle for self-expression. Anyone who is able to keep her ego out of her business is blessed with clarity. Success becomes a formula, and decisions are made based on what's best for the business, rather than what's best for the self-image of those involved. In this way, the Idealist can build a company on a foundation of consistency and quality.

Four Kinds of Idealist Entrepreneurs

1. The Inventing Entrepreneur. This Idealist entrepreneur might come up with a better, more efficient, less expensive way to get something done. She might invent a gadget, a process, a formula, or a new use for available materials. Or she might, like Joanna Lau, figure out a new approach to an old problem.

Lau, you'll recall, was working with a company that manufactured circuit and control boards. When one of its divisions that was losing money was put up for sale, she analyzed the system they were running and saw that it was obsolete. She put together a plan to bring it up to speed, got her financing together, and bought it. That once-failing plant is now a multimillion-dollar company.

Like Lau, many an Idealist entrepreneur is born because her corporate superiors don't recognize, act on, and/or reward her good ideas. When the opportunity for success presents itself, she carefully plans her future and coolly sidesteps others who don't recognize her vision.

Other Inventing-Entrepreneur Idealists aren't involved with a parent company at all. They independently invent something new, and then either develop it, patent it and take it to market, or sell it outright. Don't start envisioning nutty professors running experiments in their basements: Inventing-Entrepreneur Idealists almost always identify a gap in the marketplace and then create something to fill it.

Shirley Crouch and Jo Waldron invented an astounding product: a device that allows people with as much as 99 percent hearing loss to hear clearly over the phone. The two women, both severely hearing-impaired themselves, once owned a company that ran job fairs for people with disabilities. In the course of their work they were so frustrated by their difficulty in using phones that they tackled the problem head-on. Though neither had a technical background, in less than a year they invented the Hearing Aid Telephone Interconnect System (HATIS), which interacts with conventional hearing aids to create a magnetic field that realizes the full range of sound without distortion. Though the women have had difficulty bringing their product to its largest potential market, they continue to invent, and have now created HATIS units that work with stereos and televisions, and a device that picks up "environmental" sounds such as those at movies, concerts, and meetings.

In spite of the old cliché about inventors building a better mousetrap, Idealists aren't usually drawn to consumer goods. It is more within their nature to develop patented processes that address industrial, chemical, technical, or financial challenges.

2. The Fill-in-the-Gap Entrepreneur. Like the Inventing Entrepreneur, the Fill-in-the-Gap Entrepreneur recognizes a void in the existing marketplace, then finds a way to fill the space.

Sandra Ramsey Hale and Joan Marie Rowland started San Simeon Custom Homes because they were dismayed at the business practices of building contractors. As interior designers, the two were intimately familiar with the discrepancy between what new home buyers were promised and what was delivered—and how confusing pricing could be. Their company offers "cost plus" construction, and much more, including a multitude of design options. Started in 1996 with backing from a satisfied customer, their 1999 sales projections reached $5 million.

Opportunity-seeking Idealists don't necessarily need to have expertise in their chosen business. Back in 1977, Joan Cable was working as an insurance broker on Long Island. One of her clients owned an unprofitable beauty salon and, in anticipation of closing down, canceled her policy. Cable, who has never been a beautician and doesn't even do her own hair, took a look at the business and was convinced she could make it work. So she bought the salon for $1,000, introduced a seven-day workweek, offered cut-rate prices, and made a practice of distributing price-off coupons. It worked. Three years later Cable went the franchise route; as of 1998, Lemon Tree Haircutters, Inc., was a 91-unit operation with some $15 million in sales.

Franchises are a great option for Idealists who notice markets that aren't being served. The advantage to a franchise is that it's a prefab package with built-in business practices, support systems, training, name recognition, signage, and even stationery. The Idealist, upon recognizing an unmet need in her community's business landscape, could open a franchise and either choose to run it herself or have somebody else cover day-to-day operations.

Some of the best new franchises, according to *Entrepreneur*, are in the fields of electrical contracting, home inspection, auto repair, cleaning services, and courier services. Any one of these could appeal to Idealists, as might a women's fitness center and the Mad Science Group, a children's science activity franchise.

3. The Free-Agent Entrepreneur. The phrase "intellectual property" gets tossed around when people talk about patents and copyrights. But the number of Idealists who have regular streaks of brilliance could be considered "intellectual property" in and of themselves. When the Idealist in a corporate setting starts getting a hunch that she is the source from which a great number of useful ideas flow, it may be time for her to take her show on the road.

It's not unheard of for Idealists to break free from their corporate parents and sell themselves back to the company as independent consultants, analysts, forecasters, or contractors. It's a brave move, but it makes more and more sense in today's business climate. By setting herself up as a stand-alone entity, the Idealist is free to set her own fees and, more important, build a business by servicing a number of clients instead of just one.

4. The-PC-Is-My-Oyster Entrepreneur. Overall, women are adapting to new technology faster than men. More women business owners have Web sites, use the Internet to do business research, and communicate via e-mail than men who own their businesses.

And, since a great many Idealists are miles ahead of their Visionary/Artisan/Adventurer sisters, technology-wise, that adds up to some serious computer literacy. These skills put them at the fore of a modern frontier. Place an Idealist in a room with a good computer system for three months, and chances are she'll be creating Web sites, building servers, and inventing communication systems in no time. And she'll probably be making piles of money while she's at it.

The time is right for women to start their own technology firms, especially since investors are keenly interested in cyberbusinesses. Katrina Garnett, for instance, started CrossWorlds Software with $45 million raised from Intel, Compaq, SAP, Manugistics, JD Edwards, and Ernst & Young. Her product, United Application Architecture, does nothing less than unite the operations of global enterprises. Her motto? "Aim high—then deliver."

Idealists who don't want to aim quite so high can tap into untold opportunities for home-based, Internet-dependent businesses. Financial advisors, day traders, researchers, insurance agents, industrial designers, stockbrokers, and yes, software designers need little more than a high-end PC, a great brain, and an ergonomically correct chair to start their own businesses at home.

The Adventurer Entrepreneur

[Starting my business] was like jumping off the diving board and
inventing the water on the way down.

— GAIL BLANKE, CEO, LIFEDESIGNS

Most Adventurers have what it takes to be entrepreneurs. They live for
risks; they're very good at drumming up excitement and promoting themselves; they can rally others around their cause; and they have lively imag-
inations that can see the possibilities in all things.

The Adventurer's entrepreneurial M.O. is to develop her own talents
and interests, and then find a way to run with them, right to Millionaire's
Acres. She wants to burst on the scene, make an impact, and see her name
in whatever version of bright lights her industry has to offer.

When starting a business, as in other aspects of her life, the Adventurer
has little patience for methodical planning. She is apt to have a dream, jump
right in, and let the details work themselves out later. Her best shots at success happen when she partners with an Idealist, an Artisan, or a Visionary,
who can keep the business running smoothly while she goes flying around,
making connections, and opening new doors.

The Adventurer, with her maverick energies, is good at launching start-
ups, and can put a business on a map in no time. However, once the business settles into a slow-growth routine, the Adventurer gets restless and
distracted. As such, many Adventurers either choose to go on the hit-and-
split program or keep themselves fluid by being a one-woman operation.
In this way, the Adventurer entrepreneur also preserves the all-important
freedom to change her mind.

Four Kinds of Adventurer Entrepreneurs

1. The Self-as-Product Entrepreneur. Lots of talented people—musicians, artists, actors, choreographers, etc.—are their own product. Some
are entertainers (comediennes, Elvis impersonators, torch singers) while
others fall into the category of talent-for-hire, e.g., mural painters, disc
jockeys, and models. When they're successful, Self-as-Product businesses
grow according to need, in much the same way corporations do. The entrepreneur may start with little more than a telephone and a headshot, then
eventually take on an agent, a manager, an attorney, an accountant, a personal assistant, and a roadie or two.

The Adventurer's talent for self-promotion can sometimes turn her into
a Self-as-Product Entrepreneur. The late Florence Griffith Joyner, for
instance, became a household name and a highly sought-after spokes-

woman not only because of her athletic prowess but because of her unforgettable style—as well as that nickname, Flo-Jo.

In some cases, the Self-as-Product Entrepreneur isn't technically selling herself, but becomes inseparable from her product because it's such a direct expression of her personality. When we buy Susan Powter's workout programs, we're not just purchasing an aerobics tape, we're buying into her whole story, her persona. Same goes for Betsey Johnson. She's a fashion designer with a famous face who not only wears her own clothes but actually *looks* like her own clothes. She's high-spirited and flamboyant; those qualities seem to be sewn right into Betsey Johnson Spandex.

2. The Eat-My-Dust Entrepreneur. Corporate life is generally not for Adventurers, except as a kind of training ground—an "earn as you learn" program. Most Adventurers can't be contained within strictly drawn job titles and hierarchical structures. If an Adventurer is required to put in a certain number of years before she can advance through the ranks, she'll likely leapfrog right out of the system long before her term is up and elect herself CEO of her own firm. Thus, the Eat-My-Dust Entrepreneur is born.

3. The Over-the-Top Entrepreneur. This Adventurer knows a lot about dreams, and works like a maniac to make good on her wishes. Sure, the same could be said of many entrepreneurs, no matter what their type. What separates the Over-the-Top Entrepreneur from those who have an idea and run with it is the nature of the idea itself.

Adventurers are pioneers who delight in accomplishing things that make the world a more interesting place. An Over-the-Top Entrepreneur wouldn't be satisfied opening a mere restaurant; she'd rather start a blistering-hot dance club that was the talk of the gossip columns. These entrepreneurial types might launch a travel company that brings groups through rarely visited areas of the world, or an irreverent magazine that serves as a mouthpiece for mad geniuses and pundits-in-training.

Whatever her business, Over-the-Top Entrepreneurs are not motivated by money. They may seek to make a living, but more important, they want to make a splash, and see their dreams become reality.

4. The Hit-and-Split Entrepreneur. She has many careers throughout her lifetime. She follows her dreams wherever they take her, even as they evolve and change, and never lets herself get stale, bored, or played-out.

Barbara Smith is one Adventurer who wears a string of successes like a glittering necklace. You may know her as host of the TV show *B. Smith with Style*. Or you might be familiar with her big-city restaurants called B. Smith's. She's also an author and a lecturer, but before all that, she was TWA's first African-American ground hostess. Then she was a high-fashion model who appeared on a record five *Essence* covers and was the first black model to grace the cover of *Mademoiselle*. As if that isn't enough, she has also been a cabaret singer and a producer of plays.

It is very Adventurer to throw oneself heart and soul into a project, then move on. It is in this spirit that some entrepreneurs start a business or a self-propelled career, get it going, then sell the company, diversify, or set their sights on another, more interesting prospect on the horizon.

The Business Plan and How to Work It

The U.S. Small Business Administration says that starting a business is like starting a chess game: it requires "decisive and correct opening moves."

It's good advice, whether you're a methodical Idealist or an emotional Artisan. Perhaps the most important key to a strong start and a successful future can be found in that complex bit of paperwork known as the business plan.

"The process of developing a business plan will help you think through some important issues," counsels the SBA. That's putting it mildly: the typical small-business plan is about twenty pages long and represents as many as twelve months of research, soul-searching, networking, and sweat. Though it's a flexible document that will change as your business grows, your initial business plan is no less than an entire career worked out on paper. It's a blueprint, a proposal for potential lenders to scrutinize, and a map against which you will gauge your success for years to come.

Jennifer Lawton has a lot to say about business plans. She and her partners started a technology company, Net Daemons Associates, without a plan. It was an easy launch—a large-company spin-off with plenty of built-in customers. But when business skyrocketed and Lawton had to "explain" company strategy and philosophy to a growing group of managers, a plan became essential.

"If you aren't sure of your goal, particularly at the beginning, it's OK not to have a road map," she advises on EntreWorld.org. "Overplanning up front can sometimes put the focus on the wrong area at the expense of the right area." On the other hand, she notes, "If you feel that a lot is out of control and you don't know whether you are doing well or not, it's time for a plan." Lawton also says that it's never too late to write a business plan, even if you've been in the game for years. "Look at it as a way to uncover untapped opportunities," she advises.

To create a business plan, Lawton and her associates used a plan-writing software program. She admits that it wasn't a perfect fit, but it gave them a good framework to work within. "We're partial to logic and readability; our plan is open, clear, concise, witty, and easy to take in." Her advice: "Use the format that works for you."

Business Plan Basics

A business plan is a hard-core projection that details how your business will be operated, managed, and capitalized. If you're starting a business and need financing, your business plan will serve as bait to potential investors, who will go over it with the proverbial fine-toothed comb. As such, it's got to be smart, thorough, and as reality-based as possible.

The following outline of a typical plan can be adapted to your specific business.

1. Summary statement. This is an at-a-glance overview of your business and its goals. Short, concise, and attractive, it will be the most "markety" segment of your plan.

2. Description. This section should outline the history of your business (if applicable); describe its ownership and legal structure; list the skills and experience you bring to the business; state the track records of your management team members; and discuss the advantages you and your business have over your competitors.

3. Market analysis. Here you discuss the products or services you offer; identify the customer demand for your product/service; identify your market, its size and locations; and describe your pricing strategy. Marketing plans, sales strategies, and market data all belong in this section.

4. Financials. First, explain your source and the amount of your initial equity capital. Then, make up a monthly operating budget for the first year you will be in business and develop an expected return on investment and monthly cash flow for that same time frame. Investors will want to see projected income statements and balance sheets for a two-year period. You should also discuss your break-even point; explain your personal balance sheet and method of compensation; discuss who will maintain your accounting records and how they will be kept; and provide "what if" statements that address alternative approaches to any problem that may develop. When you're looking for investors, indicate that you have evaluated the risks associated with your venture and finish up with the all-important Funding Request and Return—that's the part where you come right out and ask for money. The American Express Small Business Exchange suggests the following format for a Funding Request and Return:

a. State the amount of funding and the type (debt or equity) of investment you seek.

b. Provide a breakdown of how the money will be applied. Discuss what effect the capital will have on the business's potential to grow and profit, when the money is needed, and what investment has already been made in the company.

c. Describe what investors will receive in return for their capital. "Be as clear as you can in this section both about the potential upside and the potential downside of investing in your business," advises Amex. If the company founders have invested in the company, include this in your statement.

d. Create an exit plan for your investors. A cash-out option in five years or assurance that the company will become a strong candidate for a purchase or an IPO (Initial Public Offering) are what many venture capitalists and lenders will insist upon.

5. Operations. How will your business be managed on a day-to-day basis? All elements that relate to taking care of business should be addressed, including hiring and personnel procedures; insurance, lease, or rent agreements; how you plan to acquire and maintain necessary equipment; and how you plan to produce and deliver your products and services.

6. Concluding statement. Some professionals say that if you have an opening summary statement, you don't need a concluding statement. The choice is yours. The concluding statement allows you to make a final impression, to recap your goals and objectives, and to express your commitment to the success of your business.

The above bare-bones outline only hints at the complexity of business plan writing. To learn more, get yourself a good book. Business wizard Mark Albion recommends *Growing a Business* by Paul Hawken (Fireside); you might also check out *Anatomy of a Business Plan* by Linda Pinson and Jerry Jinnett (Dearborn Trade).

Tips for Intuitives

When writing a business plan, **Visionaries** should take care not to be overly confident. Much of a plan involves financial projections; in their eagerness to impress potential investors, they might be unrealistically optimistic about the future. This can cause headaches down the road, as investors point to her original plan and say, "So, hotshot, where's the $17 million we were supposed to have earned by now?" Another tip for Visionaries: Avoid obsessing about the look of your plan. You may be tempted to hire a graphic designer and go all out with bindings and type-faces, but unless the nature of your business calls for high-end visuals, you'll be wasting your money. Investors will be focusing on numbers, and anyway, you'll be putting your business plan through countless revisions as you go along.

Two pieces of advice for **Artisans:** First, if your picture of the future isn't easily captured with stats and studies, create an "emotional time line" for yourself (see page 253). This will help you gauge your personal goals against your business goals. Second, if you're looking for funding, be brave. The Artisan's low threshold for risk makes her inclined to hold back or even undersell her concepts. "Don't be penny-wise and pound-foolish by asking for less money than you think you'll need because you think it will help you get the money," stresses the American Express Small Business Exchange. "It may be better to ask for more than to have to go back to your financial resources when you've run out of cash." And think big: the median amount of venture capitalist investment is $6 to $7 million.

Idealists are excellent planners who grasp the technical aspects of a business plan better than anybody. But good numbers are only half the battle. The successful business plan needs to be both warm and cool, a place where math and passion live side by side. When writing your plan, let your energy and excitement come shining through in your summary statement and/or your concluding statement. Also, avoid streamlining your plan too much. You want it to be accessible not only to investors but to others in your company, including the nontechnical players.

Adventurers' inclinations are to resist formulaic devices like business plans. But perhaps Adventurers will lend an ear to a "reluctant artiste-preneur" named Princess Superstar: "[The business plan] is the the most unglamorous, annoying, un-artistic thing that we who adore music and the arts HAVE to do in order to really get ahead." Superstar founded a record label, called A Big Rich Major Label, on the strength of a well-organized business plan, and lived to tell about it. Her irreverent guide to business planning, published in *Bust* magazine, includes tips like "Talk a lot about new technology and the Internet, and how you are planning to use it. Investors foam at the mouth for that crap." Her most powerful advice is about putting the plan over and getting the green. "Investors are looking for a strong management team and a 'spark of passion' from the leader of the project. This is a good thing for us artists, because we tend to have natural charisma. . . . But the bottom line is that they, like us, want to make money, so be prepared to have a strong plan to back up the sparks."

Getting Bucks for Your Biz

> I used to think an investor was like a magic fairy wearing an outfit made of crinkly $100 bills who floated in and poured money down my throat, and then magically disappeared.
>
> — **PRINCESS SUPERSTAR, MUSIC PRODUCER**

Once your entrepreneurial dream is sussed out on paper and you're so excited you could burst, it's time for what is perhaps the most demanding start-up task of all: financing your business.

Maybe you're acquainted with a posse of millionaires who believe unequivocally in your genius. Excellent: you won't have to worry about credit cards, relatives, nervous friends, loan officers, or venture capital firms. If you're like most entrepreneurs, however, you'll have to take huge amounts of time away from your primary interest—creating a product or service, and thus a business—and focus on raising funds for your venture. It's a complex, often lonely odyssey that requires tons of networking, lots of financial savvy, tough calls, tenacity, and guts you never knew you had.

Guts are a key ingredient. A study for Babson College found out that the ultimate size a business reaches appears to be determined by the amount of funding at start-up. Big cash infusions up front mean greater chances of real growth in the future; unfortunately, other studies have found that women entrepreneurs are less likely than men to seek capital, and when they do seek it, they ask for less.

According to Babson researchers, "Having capital to grow and expand business operations, preferably through commercial business loans and private sources, contributes significantly to the high performance of women-owned businesses."

The SBA puts it more simply: "One of the leading causes of business failure is insufficient start-up capital."

So how much is sufficient? That's a complicated question and depends on the size of your company, its projected growth, and its operating costs. A simple rule is that you'll need enough capital to take care of your building and equipment needs and to cover operating expenses for at least a year, including salaries and money to repay your loans. You should have already estimated your cash flow needs via your business plan; once a grand total is reached, you'll need to cover at least 25 percent of that figure with your own money before approaching outside investors.

Then, heed the words of Renee Courington, a California-based entrepreneur who started a computer support services company: "Understand it's going to take ten times the amount of money to start a business as you think, and ten times as much time as you think to start to see a revenue stream coming in."

Sources of Funding

There are so many options for funding a new business that they can't all be covered here. One excellent place to learn the basics of business financing is the U.S. Small Business Administration. Even if your business isn't all that small, the SBA's Web site provides a good primer for neophytes (www.sba.gov). More experienced capital seekers can log on to www.vfinance.com to explore venture capital firms; or check the Resource Guide, beginning on page 289.

Intuitive Financing

Visionaries are often success machines, but they tend to resent being personally beholden to anyone. If you're a Visionary and are thinking of soliciting funds from an angel or a venture capitalist, remember that these investors will have every right to question your business practices and complain about your expenditures. When it comes from taking loans from your mother, your brother-in-law, and/or your dear Aunt Pearl, stop and think: Do you want them to raise eyebrows every time you show up in a new blouse? Unless you're positive you can pay them back right on schedule, don't go there. Perhaps the best arrangement for the Visionary is a silent partnership in which a single, noncontrolling investor backs the Visionary's dream and comes up with funds as needed. Note to Visionaries: You won't like it when loan officers and potential backers start probing into your personal credit history and quizzing you about your background. Sure, it's not polite, but try to keep your feathers smooth and focus on the prize.

Artisans might be tempted to collect a number of small, painless loans from their closest circle of relatives and friends. Then they might die a thousand guilt-induced deaths when business is going poorly. It is in the Artisan's nature to work herself half to death just to pay back personal loans, even when it's clear that bankruptcy would be a better option. If you're an Artisan, stick with bank loans, or better yet, find angel investors who will serve not only as benefactors but advisors. Note to Artisans: Since your type is notoriously uncomfortable asking for money, you're in danger of undervaluing yourself and your company. Get a hardheaded Visionary or a numbers-first Idealist on your team. They'll convince you to ask for more, then help you get it. You may also want to recruit an Adventurer to take care of schmoozing and oozing charm.

RULE-OF-THUMB PARTNERSHIPS

GOOD MATCHES
Visionary + Idealist
Adventurer + Artisan
Idealist + Adventurer
Artisan + Visionary

LESS PERFECT MATCHES
Visionary + Adventurer
Artisan + Idealist

MATCHES TO AVOID
Visionary + Visionary
Artisan + Artisan
Idealist + Idealist
Adventurer + Adventurer

If you're an **Idealist,** you could probably make loan arrangements in your sleep. Your business plans are meticulous and your extensive research into loan and investment options will serve you well. Because you are dispassionate and are rarely clouded by delusions of grandeur, you clearly see the science of risk versus returns. Chances are you'll find great backers and cut great deals—as long as you have either an Adventurer or a Visionary to help you sell your idea to potential lenders or investors. Most Idealists don't like the showbiz part of business, and that's necessary if you're selling to investors who are out for excitement, or bankers who like a little schmaltz with their numbers. Note: Of all the types, Idealists are best suited to borrow money from relatives or close friends. Another note: Get used to the idea of selling yourself to money people who care about profits, but don't fully appreciate the product. It's frustrating, but it comes with the territory.

If you're an **Adventurer** with a hunch and a go-for-broke idea, don't even think about risking your loved ones' hard-earned money. "Disposable income" too often translates into "disposable relationship." Adventurers aren't very good at sticking with long-term payback plans and should probably avoid bank loans; they're much better suited to equity arrangements in which angels or venture capitalists get a piece of the action. When preparing a business plan and/or a proposal to investors, Adventurers should definitely partner with another type who can go over the numbers with a fine-toothed comb and keep projections accurate and realistic. Visionaries, Idealists, and Artisans are all useful during investor presentations, since Adventurers might have nervous breakdowns when asked to defend minute financial details.

Much Ado About Something
Marketing for Intuitives

Every company, whether it's two hundred years old or just hatched yesterday, is as unique as a fern frond, a footprint, an ancient oak. But no matter what its mission or history, its growth is always dependent on that sweet-smelling business fertilizer known as marketing.

Some marketing strategies are tiny. A freelance designer, for instance, may need little more than a portfolio and a clean shirt to market herself effectively. More advanced marketing schemes take four elements into consideration: product, price, place, and promotion. The first three elements require lots of research in order to figure out what your company will put out, what it will cost, how much consumers will pay for it, and where it will be distributed. The fourth point is much more creative: it involves sexy projects like advertising, public relations, press relations, and the publicity stunts that go along with them.

Start-ups usually begin with a "whatever works" marketing approach. Founders do all the selling and are out there chatting up the company, networking, making calls and connections. At some point in a company's growth, a sales staff is usually developed. Then comes a formal department that takes over the company's sales and marketing; divisions within that department may or may not include marketing research and monitoring, customer service, sales, and advertising and promotion.

Even if you're a one-woman enterprise, your business needs the exposure that good marketing brings. Contrary to neophytes' beliefs, marketing is not all about snagging sales. Though it's nice when marketing efforts translate into profits, it's more accurate (and productive) to think of marketing as fresh air, sunshine, and pollination for your business—if you can bear the outdoorsy metaphor.

An ongoing marketing effort not only makes others aware of your products or services, it also keeps you in touch with new ideas, innovations, market shifts, opportunities for growth, and, of course, potential clients. If you work alone, it has the added benefit of getting you out of the office, where you're always in danger of breathing in too many of your own fumes and losing perspective.

The Visionary Marketing Maven

• Good Visionary marketing begins on the phone. When launching a new venture, the best place for you to find support and valuable leads is among people who already know and respect you. Practice a few good lines in advance, so you can get to your point quickly, concisely, and with charm. Then pick up that receiver and work your connections.

• Network, network, network. Join professional organizations, both local and national. Don't stop at groups directly related to your industry; hook up with the National Association of Women Business Owners, the National Association of Professional Saleswomen, the Better Business

Bureau et al. Check out your college alumni association, and crawl all over related Web sites. As a Visionary you'll probably stop one step short of actually signing into chat rooms, but you can still broadcast your business wishes on electronic bulletin boards.

• When you're ready to hang out your shingle, put together a killer mailing list—even if you have to buy it—and send out announcements. Spend some money; your Visionary sensibilities should be reflected in the quality of the mailing. Scribble a personal note on announcements that are going to clients you particularly covet.

• If you have an advertising budget, earmark plenty of funds for talent. A savvy media person will do much more for you than ads turned out by a friend who knows Quark and places them willy-nilly in local papers.

• The term "publicity stunt" may turn you off, but consider the concept behind the language. A brilliant marketing move can put a company on the map, as evidenced by designer Vera Wang in 1994. That was the year she became a household name and a media darling after designing Nancy Kerrigan's skating costumes for the Winter Olympics. Wang herself was once a figure skater, an Olympic hopeful in 1968. She insists she dressed Kerrigan only because she wanted to make an artistic contribution to the sport. Whatever her intentions, the world was treated to a showcase of Wang's talents, and a design star was born.

The Artisan in the Public Eye

• The best advice for Artisan entrepreneurs is: Get a mentor. Even better, get two or six or ten mentors. Just make sure that at least one of them has tons of marketing know-how and can help you showcase your stuff to your best potential audience. Finding such a mentor is a job in itself; if you already have someone in mind, it's a matter of gathering up your courage and approaching him or her. If you have no idea where to start, contact your local Small Business Administration. The seasoned folks there can steer you toward formal mentoring programs.

• If you're a true Artisan, you probably shudder at the idea of schmoozing. And you're probably committed to "green" business practices and community involvement. The solution? Get involved with organizations that you believe in, like PETA or NOW, and let local members know about your new venture. They'll probably be eager to do business with a socially conscious company, and you'll value them as people and as customers.

• List your company in Co-op America's National Green Pages. For details on how to do this, see page 278.

• Partner with a nonprofit organization, and keep in mind that your goal, besides doing good, is to get exposure. Example: Let's say your company makes organic dog biscuits. You can quietly donate broken biscuits to the local animal shelter all year and not say a word. But when the shelter holds its annual Poochies on Parade fund-raising event, it's time for you to stand up and be noticed. Arrange to hand out free biscuits to participating dogs; have a banner with your company's name flown over the parade route; and get your name mentioned as a sponsor in press releases and media coverage. It won't cost the shelter a thing, and it will be a great marketing move for you—especially if the dogs are crazy for the biscuits. (For other win/win strategies, see chapter 10, "Women Giving Back.")

• Target your market as precisely as possible. Niche marketing is the talk of the town these days; some experts, in light of the Internet's influence, have declared that all markets are niche markets. It's a philosophy that suits Artisans just fine, since many of them believe in the power of personal touch and build their businesses one customer at a time. Lisa Somers is one such Artisan; her company, Bosom Buddy, rents out breast pumps to new mothers, and provides instruction, supplies, and support (sometimes in the middle of the night). She finds that her best marketing tool is the local Lamaze class, where she gives demonstrations to each new group of parents-to-be. She doesn't make an out-and-out sales pitch, but the women in the class feel connected to her, and she to them   which translates into new business.

Idealists in Touch

• The Idealist doesn't like to leave anything to chance and is least likely to build her business on personality. Your best approach to marketing success is to find out what the people want. This means research, and lots of it. Get your hands on surveys, polls, and projections, and generate a few studies of your own. Let these be your guide on how best to reach your potential market.

• Make the Internet your new best friend. Create a terrific Web site for your company, and use it not only to generate excitement about your venture but to get feedback from interested visitors. You might consider luring new clients with a "loss leader," that is, a promotional offer that costs you money but has the potential to build a loyal client base.

• Partner with an organization that already has a solid marketing campaign. Depending on your product and your business vision, you could form an alliance that frees you of marketing responsibilities. For instance, if you manufacture microfiber fabrics, you might work out a deal with a fashion design company in which they agree to include your logo on their hang tags and mention your product in their print advertising.

• Maintain close relationships with professional organizations, and get involved with industry events, including trade shows. If your field lends itself to conferences and seminars, do what you can to create a high profile for yourself, whether that means becoming a sponsor, serving on a panel, or being a presenter.

The Attention-Getting Adventurer

• As an Adventurer, you're great at chatting up ideas. Like the Visionary, your best launching pad is the telephone, which you should use not only to put out feelers but to make dates to meet for coffee, lunch, or drinks. In one-on-one settings you can really shine and can stir up all kinds of support with the sheer power of your enthusiasm. Note: Don't forget to listen, take notes, and follow up.

• Get yourself a great press list, and make well-placed calls or send out press releases whenever you can. Spend some money up front to have professional photographs taken of you, your products, your building . . . whatever's appropriate. Good photos are always in demand by newspaper and magazine editors—and so are good stories.

• When you're ready to open your new business, have a Grand Opening party. Invite everybody who has helped you or might help you down the road, and make sure to get plenty of media coverage.

• And speaking of media coverage, no one loves a good publicity stunt like the Adventurer does. Though you may not go quite to the extreme of hiring a plane to trail a banner, there are lots of ways to get attention. The legendary New York nightclub Area once printed party invitations on individually wrapped slices of Kraft American Cheesefood, and sent them through the mail. The U.S. Post Office tried to sue, accusing the club of mailing perishables. When the case went to court, however, Area proved that the slices did not meet the official definition of "perishable." The whole incident created lots of delicious publicity and only boosted excitement about the club.

• Marketing can be almost too much fun for Adventurers. They're always in danger of overlooking its ultimate goal, which is to get results. Example: One Adventurer we know was making a pitch for a freelance styling job. The project was a book about color. Rather than do her usual portfolio presentation, she created a small book of her own that utilized collage and paint to tell a "color story" on every page. The client thought it was gorgeous, but our friend didn't get the job. Why? Because the presentation showed that she had a fabulous eye for color and a great imagination, but it didn't show she could be a good photo stylist.

10

Women Giving Back

All that is not given is lost.

It seems inevitable that at some point in every businesswoman's life, she catches a glimpse of the fabric of the universe and realizes she's not alone. Her successes are easing the way for future generations of women and of businesspeople in general; the products she creates, the work she completes, the connections she makes, the boost she gives to others—all of it matters. And when a woman sees her place in the warp and weft of evolution, when she recognizes that her actions make a difference, she is, if she's a person of conscience, compelled to take the power she's earned and turn it deliberately toward the positive.

These aren't just romantic words; huge numbers of women are giving back to their communities. As of 1998, 78 percent of women business owners spent time volunteering, compared to 48 percent of all adults and 56 percent of all business owners in the United States. Studies have shown that consumers prefer doing business with socially responsible companies, but such statistics don't seem to drive today's philanthropists: as restaurateur/cookbook author Claire Criscuolo says, "It's a perk to give back. It's a benefit. You feel so good to be able to help, and I like having that reputation. People probably know us more for our community work than for our food."

How women give back is a matter of degrees, and also a matter of priorities. Ann Moore, president and CEO of People, Inc., puts her company's muscle behind a number of charitable organizations, including the Pediatric AIDS Foundation. Supermodel Lauren Hutton campaigns for breast cancer research and is also dedicated to preserving coral reefs and endangered sea life via her work with the Environmental Protection Agency.

Then there's Regina Simmons-Mullings, a customer service rep for a New England utility company who volunteers once a week at a drug rehab facility. She once lived in poverty and struggled with being a single mother; her goal as a volunteer is simply to show those in rehab that someone cares. "I want them to see that it can happen," she told the *New Haven Register* of her work. "That you can make a change for yourself."

According to the National Foundation for Women Business Owners, most female CEOs (and/or their companies) are dedicated to community-related charities. In descending order, they contribute to educational causes, religious charities, health- or disease-related groups, and arts organizations. But whether they're raising millions for medical research, volunteering every Sunday at a soup kitchen, or planting trees in their neighborhood, working women of America are making life better for everyone.

Intuitive Sharing

> **Your giving can be for the good of your business, too — and even that type of giving is better than doing nothing at all.**
> **— GUN DENHART, FOUNDER, HANNA ANDERSSON CORP.**

Philanthropy is a state of mind. The woman who hires a promising yet underqualified candidate is no less charitable than the one who organizes a benefit ball; she who drops off canned goods during food drives is exercising the same do-good muscle as the one whose company pledges $3 million to help save the public library. There are many ways to share wealth, and many kinds of wealth to share.

Intuitively speaking, certain styles of giving seem to be suited to each type. It's tough to predict a perfect fit, however: more often than not, an individual becomes dedicated to a cause because it has stirred her on a purely emotional level. Charitable giving is, after all, a form of love, and so defies logic and rules.

The Philanthropic Visionary

The archetypal Visionary is not one to volunteer in a homeless shelter or visit shut-ins. She does her part by joining boards of directors of nonprofit organizations, supporting the arts, getting involved with benefit events, or making gifts to her alumni association. At the backbone of many charitable groups is an army of Visionaries, each doing her part by organizing events, writing checks, or donating goods to good causes.

There is often a give-and-take aspect to the Visionary's contributions; she will likely get involved with organizations in which she can not only help others but also make professional and personal contacts. This isn't to say that the Visionary is selfish; she just likes to maximize her time, and she also likes to be associated with winners.

Some Visionaries are well into their forties before they connect with a good cause. Usually, these Visionary women started with very little and fought hard for every advancement in their professional lives; thus, they've tended to focus on urgent career challenges rather than the needs of those outside their immediate circle.

Elizabeth Taylor is one example of a Visionary who took up a cause in later life. Legend has it that she went to visit her friend Rock Hudson when he was dying of AIDS, and was so moved by his going public with his diagnosis that she promised him she'd fight for AIDS awareness for the rest of her life.

Not every successful Visionary becomes a philanthropist. Some jump into the political arena. This should be no surprise, as the archetypal Visionary is well suited to the role of congresswoman, diplomat, lobbyist, campaign manager, or political fund-raiser. Bernadette Castro, for instance, was president and CEO of Castro Convertibles until she became a candidate for the U.S. Senate in 1994 at the age of fifty. Today she's commissioner of New York State Parks, Recreation and Historic Preservation.

Visionaries tend to be dedicated to literacy, education, and the arts and are more likely to be involved with established charities than grass-roots movements. You'll find them associated with public libraries, universities, dance troupes, and orchestras. What you might not notice is that Visionaries also quietly acquire highly personal and private causes. A Visionary might "adopt" a favorite niece or disadvantaged neighbor-child, and regularly lavish her with gifts and outings. She might donate loads of books to the nearest public school; as a boss, she could very well be the anonymous benefactor who slips $100 bills into her team-members' Christmas paychecks, after it's been announced that there will be no holiday bonuses that year.

How Visionaries Can Give Back

- Volunteer for leadership positions on nonprofit directory boards. As a Visionary, your talents are better suited to organizing volunteer operations than being a front-line worker.
- Contribute your talents, e.g., writing or graphic design, to help promote fund-raising events.

- Attend benefit events whenever you can. Buy those tickets to gala fund-raisers; spend your money on promotional products that promise a kickback to worthy causes.
- Do you need a caterer for your son's graduation party, a landscaper to take control of your lawn, or an accountant to make sense of your taxes? Hire local, independent companies whenever possible. Putting money into your community is a form of socially responsible spending that has significant, long-lasting benefits.

How Visionary Business Owners Can Give Back

- Look at charitable alliances as "strategic partnerships." The Visionary boutique owner, for instance, can host a benefit fashion show, while the Visionary restaurateur can donate her space for fund-raising events—thus gaining good visibility and good P.R.
- Donate your products to charitable auctions or raffles. If you're a jeweler, for instance, you might gain new customers by placing, say, a particularly gorgeous necklace in a silent auction for your city's symphony orchestra. If you match your target client base with the event in question, it can serve as terrific advertising for you while servicing a greater cause.
- Offer your company's services or commodities. Your magazine might be able to contribute a page of advertising for a fund-raising event in exchange for a page of advertising in the event's printed program. You might invite the stylists in your salon to volunteer for "haircuts for charity" events; these fund-raisers offer $10 haircuts on a given day, with proceeds going to a good cause. Or, arrange to have samples of your newest moisturizer included in the "loot bag" handed out to runners at a fund-raising road race, and get your company promoted as a corporate sponsor.
- Participate in government programs that offer tangible benefits. By joining in a "welfare-to-work" program, for example, you might be able to train people who will become valuable employees in your organization.

The All-for-One Artisan

Artisans are such natural sharers that they can barely have a job without giving back to others in some way.

The business world is bursting with stories of Artisans' generosity. Gun Denhart started the Hanna Andersson Corporation in Portland, Oregon, after she couldn't find the kind of soft, all-cotton baby clothes she'd known in her native Sweden. A few years after launching her first catalog in 1983, she started Hanna Downs, which took back used Hanna Andersson cloth-ing from customers and donated them to charity. By 1998, approximately one million Hanna Downs were distributed to kids in need, and the com-pany had added nine more charitable programs, providing everything from kids' summertime recreation to education for homeless children.

Artisans aren't only kind to strangers; they also take care of their own. Way back in 1939, Margaret Rudkin was so grateful to a publicist who convinced *Reader's Digest* to run the story of her fledgling company, Pep-peridge Farm, that she gave him a 5 percent share in the company. By 1960, the gift was worth more than $1 million.

When it comes to social responsibility, few business owners can hold a candle to Anita Roddick, founder and CEO of the Body Shop. Besides being militantly against using animals for testing, many of her company's body-and-soul products are based in something called "Community Trade." For these items, Roddick uses products or key ingredients sourced from communities in need around the world. In this way, she keeps local industries afloat and showcases their goods in a global market.

Lora Lee Stephens started Sunorganic Farm in California for the most personal of reasons: three of her sisters were diagnosed with breast cancer. Having researched the negative health effects of pesticides and chemicals, she was determined to produce untainted foods. Her company, started in 1997, is now a thriving fruit and vegetable wholesaler, and also distributes products like organically grown wheatgrass directly to cancer centers.

Artisans are hands-on women who are truly gifted when it comes to one-on-one relating; they are a mighty force of good in hospitals, hospices, shelters, rehab centers, crisis hotlines, women's shelters, children's chari-ties, geriatric facilities, and animal rescue groups. Leave it to the Artisan to take in foster children or adopt babies from impoverished countries; she'll nurture a fallen bird back to health, deliver hot soup to a friend with the flu, run in the Race for the Cure, and sew a patch for the AIDS quilt, all in a fortnight. She prefers to donate her energy rather than her money, and that's how it should be: after all, Artisans show love by doing.

How Artisans Can Give Back

- Volunteer with vigor. The more intimate your volunteer work, the better; you're a woman who can hold a hand and lend an ear when it's
  needed most. As a Red Cross volunteer, you can provide care and
  comfort to people whose homes have been wiped out by natural
  disasters; as a Meals-on-Wheels worker, you can bring sustenance
  and companionship to those whose lives have been compromised by
  ill health. The Visionary may organize a charity ball to benefit Big

Sisters, but the Artisan would rather *be* a Big Sister. Share your special gift.

- Get political. If it weren't for Artisans, there probably wouldn't be any such thing as a grass-roots political organization. When you see something you don't approve of, make a big noise. Artisans have saved historic buildings, ecologically significant wetlands, and entire animal species by making their voices heard.
- Consider teaching. If you doubt you're qualified, think again: there are classes in mothering for teenage girls, English language programs for inmates, nutritional cooking courses for families on public assistance. You could help a recent immigrant prepare for her written driver's license test. In fact, you probably have many talents that you take for granted that could translate into survival skills for others in need.

How Artisan Business Owners Can Give Back

- Develop a relationship with a community-based organization and get your employees involved. If, for instance, you choose to help sponsor a nonprofit summer camp for underprivileged kids, don't just raise funds: offer your workers paid days to volunteer there.
- Identify untapped resources in your company, and make them work for others. Is your office building empty every night? Maybe the Literacy Volunteers of America can use it as a classroom for evening courses. Does your catering company end up with loads of unserved food after certain events? Deliver it to a local soup kitchen, food pantry, or homeless shelter.
- Integrate social responsibility into your overall business plan. Beyond doing no harm, get proactive and try doing some good. Adopt a "seventh-generation" philosophy—that is, consider the impact of your decisions on seven future generations, with a special eye toward environmental issues. Utilize local products and hire local talent; consider the needs of your community and rise up to meet them, whether that involves something simple, like hiring high school kids over the summer, or something complicated, like reviving an indigenous industry.
- Think globally, act locally. Plant trees on your business's block. Start a local merchants' association. Launch a clean water/clean air initiative. Reach out to other businesses and form a cooperative.
- Donate portions of profits or sales of a specific item to a favorite cause.
- Remember that charity begins at home—or, in your case, in the workplace. Take a good look at your workers' needs. Would on-site health care be appropriate? If a number of your employees are car-

ing for their aging parents, could they benefit from an adult day care program? Think of wellness, housing, education, recreation, transportation, nutrition, spiritual needs, and more. Then try to provide whatever you can to make your company truly humane.

The Idealistic Idealist

"My skin bristles when I see . . . people attend glamorous charity functions, all dressed to kill in ball gowns and dripping with jewelry. To me, that's a big-city, old-money type of giving. Starting something that's truly effective—for profit or not for profit—is hard work." So says Katrina Garnett, founder and CEO of the California-based Crossworlds Software, Inc. After people kept pestering her about how few females were on her payroll, she launched the Garnett Foundation to address the underrepresentation of women in the computer industry. Her reason for not hiring more women was that there weren't enough of them with computer science or engineering degrees—and that was the target of her nonprofit enterprise. "Girls are hooked on the perception that programming is a lonely, nerdy job that involves sitting in a cubicle all day, writing code," she told *Fast Company*. "They don't realize the variety of jobs that are available in fields like business development or marketing."

In order to encourage young women to pursue careers in high-tech industries, the Garnett Foundation has initiated research that examines girls' math and science experiences and has sponsored all-girl computer camps. What has she discovered? "All that girls need is a little encouragement and access to opportunities. Then watch out."

Katrina Garnett is typical of Idealists in that her charitable works are rooted in practicality. Though there are plenty of Idealists who ally themselves with globally important causes—Amnesty International and Planned Parenthood come to mind—many aren't inspired to get involved in an immediate way unless a calling comes knocking at their door. Like Idealist entrepreneurs, Idealist philanthropists tend to identify a need and then fill it.

A great number of Idealists also invest their money responsibly. Amy L. Domini Kinder, CFA, wrote the book on socially responsible investing. Coauthor of *Investing for Good, The Social Investment Almanac,* and several other works about ethical investing, she is founder and chair of the Domini Social Equity Fund, a no-load mutual fund for social investors. Her work has been so influential that the Domini 400 Social Index, which tracks the performance of socially responsible companies, was named for her.

Idealists are nothing if not efficient. As such, those who jog for fun and fitness will likely sign up for benefit road races. Idealist business owners

GO CO-OP

As a socially responsible businesswoman, you might feel a little lonely—especially if you work in industries where "green" signifies either cash or envy. But there's a huge support group for conscious people like you: the Co-op America Business Network.

Founded in 1982 and headed by Alisa Gravitz, who holds a Harvard M.B.A. in marketing and finance, the Washington, D.C.–based nonprofit publishes *Co-op America's National Green Pages,* the largest annual directory of socially and environmentally responsible businesses in the United States. But that's not the half of it. The Green Business Program supports small start-ups with advice and publicity; the Corporate Responsibility Program helps corporations make a positive impact on the environment and the community; and the Consumer Education and Empowerment Program helps consumers use their purchasing and investing power to create "a more just and sustainable future."

Among Co-op America's many publications is *The Socially Responsible Financial Planning Guide,* which has steered a half-million investors toward profoundly wise decisions.

Ready to join 43,000 individuals and 1,400 business owners who think like you? Call 800-58-GREEN.

might sponsor scholarships that relate to their industry, or give money to research groups that focus on studies that could alter their company's direction—but not before they make damn sure that the charity in question is doing everything it claims to do. Idealists are research-oriented creatures and want to be assured that their hard work is, indeed, benefiting others.

It is not a "feel-good" payoff that Idealists seek. They are genuinely interested in making a difference and can manage to keep their egos out of it. But, like Visionaries, they're extra-satisfied when they can benefit on a professional level.

How Idealists Can Give Back

- Put your beliefs out front. Rather than jump on a popular bandwagon, get involved with something that stirs you personally. If you're impressed by a community-based effort to reintroduce bluebirds to your area, jump in; if you're concerned about low reserves at your local blood bank, make an appointment to donate your own.
- Contribute your special skills. Are you a computer wizard? Don't keep it to yourself; your expertise is probably in demand at senior centers, community colleges, or public schools. If you're a carpenter—either by trade or in your free time—your know-how could be put

to great use building sets for a local theater group or renovating homes for Habitat for Humanity.

- Join a church or synagogue, and get involved with its outreach groups.
- Become a habitual giver. Every year at the same time, choose a few charities (after making background checks, of course), and contribute as much as you can. Cynthia Katz, a retired educator, has developed a system for giving: all year long she saves the funding pleas she receives in the mail and puts them in a box. On Christmas Eve—a holiday she doesn't celebrate—she and her husband go through the box and come up with four favorites. Cynthia tries for a mix of good causes, e.g., a wildlife preservation group, a children's charity, an arts organization, and what she calls "a needy organ." "Last year it was lungs," she explains. "The year before that it was livers."

How Idealist Business Owners Can Give Back

- Hire interns, retirees, and developmentally disabled workers whenever possible.
- Do pro bono work. If you head up an accounting or law firm, offer free services to worthy clients who are financially strapped. You can use the freebie to your advantage—to break in new associates, for example—and write it off as a loss at year's end.
- Start an office-wide car-pool program—and participate in it.
- Think of unconventional ways in which your company's products or services can be useful to the community. We know of a packaging engineer who donated rolls of bubble wrap to a children's hospital; the kids had a ball popping it, and for some it was excellent physical therapy.
- Create synergistic relationships with community groups. If you run a research lab, for instance, you might consider sponsoring a science fair at the local high school or setting up a science scholarship in your company's name.

The Generous Adventurer

Adventurers enjoy interactive giving. Like Artisans, they are hands-on women who aren't likely to sit back, write a check, and leave it at that. You might find an Adventurer serving as Grand Marshal of the St. Patrick's Day Parade or working as a volunteer firefighter. She might host the kickoff party of a fund-raising event or allow herself to be "dunked" at a school carnival.

Because they're naturally generous of spirit, Adventurers think nothing of handing out dollar bills to every person on the street who asks for spare change. In fact, she'll give her money and/or her time to almost any individual or group who approaches her—whether she can afford it or not.

Most Adventurers don't have the Artisan knack for serious social work. But they're great at creating excitement around a cause and so can serve as organizers, spokespeople, and rabble-rousers. They're also perfectly happy to share whatever they've got. One Adventurer we know owns a stretch of beachfront property in an exclusive Connecticut community. Throughout the summer months, he has inner-city kids bused in to play in the sand and surf. His privacy-craving neighbors don't like it one bit, but their protests make these beach parties all the more fun for him.

Some Adventurers combine their love of travel with good works. These global volunteers might spend their vacations helping build schools, teaching, or offering medical care to people in impoverished countries. Some take time off to work on research vessels, help rebuild disaster-torn areas, or deliver supplies to refugee camps. Closer to home, they might sponsor an exchange student and promote cross-cultural ties.

One company that combines wanderlust with social responsibility is Modern Design, which produces city maps that point out environmentally significant areas, including toxic hot spots, farmers' markets, solar energy sites, bird-watching areas, and more. The Green Apple Map is an earth-first view of Manhattan; other Green Maps cover Copenhagen, San Francisco, Liverpool, Milwaukee, Kyoto, and Bombay.

How Adventurers Can Give Back

- Use your natural salesmanship to raise funds, either on a global scale or on the most basic level, such as selling raffle tickets.
- Heighten public awareness of problems or causes by issuing press releases, writing fiery letters to editors, or circulating petitions.
- Get involved in a political campaign. Personable Adventurers are great canvassers, either in person or on the phone.
- Sign up to help out at big benefit events—the Olympics, art and music festivals, regattas, and the like.
- Buy art—preferably local art. You might even become a personal benefactor to a struggling artist.
- Teach at a community college, adult education program, or after-school program. Adventurers are engaging and can be very entertaining; you'll probably excel at teaching short-term courses.

How Adventurer Business Owners Can Give Back

- Create matching-grant programs in which your company matches the amount of money raised by a community organization. Horse races are always fun for Adventurers.
- Lend your talented people out to nonprofit organizations. The United Way is one group that has an employee-sharing program, in which, say, marketing experts work half-time on projects for various United Way charities.
- Invite groups of school-age kids to tour your facility, and show them how it's done.
- Develop a relationship with a "sister company" in an emerging economic area. Exchange information and use your company's experience, power, and resources to help the distant company and its township grow.

11
Split Personalities

Generally speaking, Intuitive types are suited to industries that are harmonious with their particular working styles, business sensibilities, aesthetic preferences, etc. However, since many women are actually Intuitive hybrids—that is, they have more than one dominant personality type—they might be drawn to careers that appeal to both archetypes.

Examples:

visionary +
adventurer = wedding planner

Her Visionary side loves the music, the flowers, the table settings; her Adventurer side loves the party.

artisan +
idealist = furniture designer

As an Artisan, she has a feel for natural materials and is tuned in to the body's needs. As an Idealist she enjoys engineering and manufacturing puzzles as well as efficient, elegant solutions.

adventurer +
visionary = record executive

Her Adventurer energy is well suited to the fast-moving record biz; her Visionary streak makes her a decisive leader who can make judgment calls and stand behind them.

visionary +
idealist = **ballet dancer**

The ballet as an art form is exquisitely beautiful to many a Visionary; her inner Idealist gives her the discipline to work constantly toward perfection.

artisan +
idealist = **veterinarian**

Nobody loves animals more than the Artisan. It's her Idealist side that gets her through veterinary school and allows her to detach from emotionally charged situations, such as performing painful procedures or euthanizing a patient.

idealist +
adventurer = **airline pilot**

As an Idealist, she's perfectly suited to mastering complicated controls and coolly guiding those big birds through international skies. As an Adventurer, she loves to travel.

visionary +
artisan = **vintner**

The history, the pageantry, and the prestige of wines appeal to her Visionary sensibilities, while the grape-growing, the vine-tending, and the land ownership tickle her Artisan palette.

artisan +
adventurer = **drug counselor**

As an Artisan, she's both sympathetic and therapeutic. As an Adventurer, she's most likely to have an addictive personality and therefore be *really* sympathetic.

artisan +
idealist = **portrait photographer**

The Artisan sees beauty in all things: crying toddlers, unruly dogs, homely couples. The Idealist digs the equipment and is a monster in the darkroom.

visionary +
adventurer = **tv producer**

The Visionary knows what she wants; the Adventurer can handle the personalities and the pressure, and actually have fun with the three-ring circus of it all.

adventurer +
artisan = **art teacher**

As an Adventurer, she lives for coming up with wacky, creative projects and preaching unconventional points of view. As an Artisan, she loves interacting with students and watching them develop.

artisan +
visionary = **spa operator**

Her Artisan side welcomes guests with massages, aromatherapy treatments, and yoga, while her Visionary side offers makeovers, hairdos, and manicures.

adventurer +
artisan = **dude ranch operator**

Her Adventurer side has fun with the flow of guests, the events, the hostessing. Her Artisan side has fun with the horses.

idealist +
adventurer = **electronic games developer**

As an Idealist, her technical know-how and analytical mind make for seriously challenging games, while her Adventurer irreverence makes them seriously wild.

artisan +
visionary = **home and garden editor**

The Artisan can feather a nest like nobody's business; it is her Visionary side that turns her into a homestyle doyenne.

visionary +
idealist = **cosmetic surgeon**

Visionary aesthetics meet Idealist skills, with eternally youthful results.

Cross-Fertilization
Working Against Your Type

Are you an Artisan with a dollop of Visionary? Have you discovered yourself to be an Adventurer with Idealist tendencies, or a Visionary with sprinklings of Artisan/Idealist? Excellent. You're right in the Intuitive pocket and should be able to trace your tendencies all over this book.

Now, here's a stick in your spokes: Who you are and what you do don't always have to match, Intuitively speaking.

The fact is, you're always going to bring your style to work, no matter what you do for a living. And as long as you remain true to yourself, you can be hugely fulfilled and terribly successful in a career that doesn't, on paper, suit your Intuitive type.

It takes guts to enter an industry in which there isn't a bunch of people like you around; your language, your sensibilities, and your goals could place you in a lonely minority. However, your atypical approach probably sets you apart from the pack. If you're especially brave, you could make a unique contribution that strengthens, redefines, or even revolutionizes your industry.

How can a person thrive in a job that doesn't harmonize with her inner Intuitive qualities? Actually, it happens all the time. Some examples:

- The Idealist who works as a garden designer (a typically Artisan occupation) and creates meticulously manicured plots with clean lines and restrained color.
- The Adventurer stockbroker (working alongside wall-to-wall Idealists, no doubt) who puts together the highest-risk mutual funds that Wall Street has ever known.
- The Visionary dog groomer (a favorite occupation of Artisans) who allies herself with kennel clubs and becomes the stylist of champions.
- The Artisan software writer (interloping into the Idealist's realm) who designs exceptionally user-friendly computer programs.

Curious Career Clashes

In this age of pop culture and no privacy, we are exposed not only to bodies of work but to an intimate knowledge of the people who created the work. As such, it's pretty easy to come up with examples of famous people who seem (or seemed) to be entirely unsuited to their careers.

Think of:

- Dr. Ruth Westheimer. the Intuitive Casting Department would have placed the diminutive German therapist in a Visionary/Idealist office in a large city, where she could discreetly dispense advice to wealthy clients from good families. Instead, she's running around Hollywood like a mad Adventurer, talking about masturbation and hawking the orgasmic qualities of shampoo in TV commercials.
- Sister Wendy Beckett, who has been a nun since she was a teenager. She studied English at Oxford, taught in South Africa, and since 1970 has spent her life in seclusion—which might sound like heaven to some Visionaries. Yet, despite the fact she's myopic and epileptic, speaks with a lisp, and watched television for the first time in 1997, she became a TV star. It happened when the BBC sent her around the world to view, and comment on, the great works of art she'd been studying and writing about for years but had never seen in person. She was such a natural on camera that the crew nicknamed her "One-Take Wendy." The public fell in love with her breezy, easy style; her first show spawned sequel after sequel, as well as numerous books and international fame. Rather Adventurous of her.

- Meryl Streep, who in the Intuitive System's estimation, is every inch an Idealist. She might have donned a lab coat and worked in any branch of science that she wanted. But she chose acting, a vocation that usually requires at least a soupçon of Adventurism. Yet Streep approaches her craft like an archetypal Idealist. She does deep research, she studies accents, she historically re-creates characters from Poland, Australia, Madison County, wherever, and gets Oscar nominations all over the place.
- Tonya Harding, who grew up in a trailer that was parked in someone's driveway. It seems a minor miracle that she became an Olympic skater, but not just because of her compromised upbringing; she simply wasn't one of the sweet, innocent fairy-tale girls we'd all come to expect on Olympic ice. As a skater, she had the discipline of an Idealist and the irreverence of an Adventurer. That irreverence went too far, as we all know. But she was, and is, an unforgettable character, and forever branded a competitive edge on what had once been an excruciatingly ladylike and very Visionary sport.

Spontaneous Combustion

If you look at the above list carefully, you'll see that career-clashers seem to bring new energy to their seemingly ill-fitting fields. The same dynamic happens on the corporate level, too. Many mighty companies have burst into bloom as a result of brilliant, unpredictable cross-fertilization. Ponder the following:

- Restaurants are typically started by Artisans, Visionaries, or Adventurers. Think of places in your town: you've probably got an Artisan café that offers fresh, healthy food in a comfortable setting. Your Visionary restaurant is for special occasions, and offers upscale ambiance and fancy cuisine; the local Adventurer joint might be a novelty restaurant or pub where the atmosphere is as entertaining as the food. So, can you name an Idealist restaurant? How about McDonald's? It's built on a much-copied formula that combines easy access with a limited menu of familiar foods that are inexpensive, filling, and consistent. It's not so much a restaurant as a food-dispensing system.
- Martha Stewart creates porn for Artisans. With her books, her magazine, her TV program, and her products, she has breathed life back into the beaten-up-and-left-for-dead role of housewife, elevating the home-centric woman to the status of creative goddess. Martha gets down in the kitchen and the garden; she grows her own stuff; she rolls up her sleeves and makes gorgeous things out of simple materials. Artisans drool and

swoon, and rush off to the crafts store. But here's the kicker: Martha Stewart is a *Visionary*. Of course she is. You're not fooled by that denim shirt and those sensible shoes, are you? She's not only a take-no-prisoners businesswoman, she's also a brand, and her public persona is as carefully crafted as her garden topiary. Rumor has it that she won't allow Kmart—with which she has a major merchandising contract—to advertise in *Martha Stewart Living*. That doesn't sound very Artisan-like, does it? But the combination of Visionary drive and direction, combined with meltingly beautiful Artisan creations, has been pure dynamite on a business level—and a real pleasure for millions of home-loving consumers.

• The Gap specializes in drab, utilitarian play clothes in many sizes and styles for women, men, and children. The Gap could double as a department at Sears, except for one thing: marketing. Its airy-yet-sleek stores appeal to Artisans and Idealists. Its ads appeal to everyone, even crotchety Visionaries (who are inherently anti-mall), and individualistic Adventurers. Who among us can resist adorable young dancers performing adorable young dance routines? How can we turn away from the cutest babies in the world, staring wide-eyed against a pristine backdrop? There are virtually no words in Gap ads, but there is so much style that they make the clothes seem like acts of genius.

• Ben & Jerry were the original Artisan merchandisers, and became famous for mingling social awareness with a free-market attitude. But their products don't wear Birkenstocks. In fact, Ben & Jerry's ice cream is deeply Visionary (all that richness, all those luxury ingredients, and *so* expensive!), yet it is packaged with an extremely Adventurer sensibility. Only Adventurers would name an ice cream Chunky Monkey, Wavy Gravy, or Cherry Garcia.

The Moral of the Story

If your job, your profession, or your aspirations don't seem to groove with your Intuitive type, don't fret. Yes, there are industries that, in and of themselves, are inherently well matched to each type. But personalities and industries are like tops and trousers: they don't have to match. All they really need to do is not clash.

Intuitive-wise, it's far more important that your truest personality can live, breathe, and grow in your workplace. Such growth conditions are usually facilitated by the nature of your work environment, the types of tasks you do, and the people you work with—not the industry itself.

For example, you may be an Artisan working as a caterer. According to the Intuitive System, that job should suit you well. But if you work for a cold, hypercritical boss, have unpredictable working hours, and have to deal with extremely stressful situations, like coaxing checks out of hysterically weeping brides, you're not going to be happy.

On the other side of the coin, you might be an Artisan loan officer. Though it's not exactly in the Artisan Intuitive Career Handbook, it's possible that you work for a progressive bank in a friendly, familylike office and get real satisfaction from brokering loans for young families, first-time home buyers, and eager entrepreneurs.

You could be an Adventurer who finds deep satisfaction as an industrial designer, a Visionary who loves being a kindergarten teacher, or an Idealist who can't wait to get to work every day and make sushi.

The bottom line: If you love what you're doing, keep doing it. If you're suffering, either fix the situation or get out and do something that makes you feel good inside.

And don't forget to keep growing. The more we understand what makes us tick, the clearer our choices become. Our tasks seem easier, our best options seem obvious, and major life decisions are not a trauma but a joy. When we stop trying to fight ourselves and instead greet ourselves with open arms, we foster spiritual, emotional, and physical growth. And, as we become more alive to ourselves, we are more available to others. We can afford to have an increased appreciation of the unique talents and perspectives of the people that surround us. By embracing a language of understanding, we become better bosses, employees, entrepreneurs, mothers, daughters, wives, friends—better citizens of the world.

Resource Guide

Sources for business advice, inspiration, networking, and counseling are exploding—especially on the Internet. Here is but a small sampling of on-line destinations that promise to help women like you become more prosperous, challenged, and contented.

American Agri-Women (AAW)

11605-04 Road, Mayetta, KS 66509

www.americanagriwomen.com
e-mail: aagriwomen@aol.com.

This is a national coalition composed of farm, ranch, and agri-businesswomen's organizations that serves as a communications link. A national convention is held annually to discuss issues of mutual interest and concern.

American Association of University Women

1111 Sixteenth Street NW,
Washington, DC 20036

Phone: (800) 326-AAUW Fax: (202) 872-1425
TDD: (202) 785-7777
www.aauw.org/home.html
e-mail: info@aauw.org

AAUW is a 150,000-member national organization that lobbies and advocates for education and equity for all women and girls.

The American Chemical Society— Women Chemists

1155 Sixteenth Street NW,
Washington, DC 20036

www.acs.org/acsgen/womenscc/wccn1094.htm

This Web site features the electronic newsletter "Women Chemists." It's published twice a year and distributed by the Women Chemists Committee of the American Chemical Society.

The American Express Small Business Exchange

www.americanexpress.com/smallbusiness

This on-line "community for entrepreneurs" offers everything from advice from business experts to instructions on how to create a business plan.

American Nurses Association (ANA)

600 Maryland Avenue SW, Suite
100 W., Washington, DC 20024-2571

Phone: (800) 274-4ANA
www.nursingworld.com
e-mail: memberinfo@ana.com.

ANA is a full-service professional organization that represents the nation's 2.6 million registered nurses. It promotes the nursing profession by fostering high standards of nursing practice and lobbying Congress and regulatory agencies on health care issues.

Asian Women in Business (AWIB)

1 West 34th Street, Suite 200,
New York, NY 10001

Phone: (212) 868-1368 Fax: (212) 868-1373
www.awib.org

This nonprofit membership organization was founded in 1995 to help Asian women realize their entrepreneurial potential. Conferences, workshops, and networking opportunities are offered.

Association for Women in Computing (AWC)

www.awc-hq.org

Founded in 1978, AWC promotes the advancement of women in the computing professions and offers connections, camaraderie, and sites such as Live Wire, a directory of most-wanted computer equipment.

Association for Women in Mathematics (AWM)

4114 Computer and Space Sciences
Building, University of Maryland,
College Park, MD 20742-2461

Phone: (301) 405-7892 Fax: (301) 314-9363
www.awm-math.org
e-mail: awm@math.umd.edu

Founded in 1971, this is a nonprofit organization dedicated to encouraging women in the mathematical sciences.

Black Career Women Organization (BCW)

P.O. Box 19332,
Cincinnati, OH 45219

Phone/fax: (513) 531-1932
www.bcw.org

Conceived by black women in 1977, BCW is a nonprofit organization that serves as a nucleus of support and uses its nationwide contacts to identify and address the critical needs of black women in the workforce as it relates to career mobility and achievement.

Business and Professional Women/USA

2012 Massachusetts Avenue NW,
Washington, DC 20036

Phone: (202) 293-1100 Fax: (202) 861-0298
www.bpwusa.org
e-mail: moneill@bpwusa.org

Founded in 1919, BPW/USA is a national organization dedicated to achieving equity for all women in the workplace through advocacy, education, and information.

Catalyst

120 Wall Street, New York, NY 10005

Phone: (212) 514-7600 Fax: (212) 514-8470
www.catalystwomen.org
e-mail: info@catalystwomen.org

Catalyst is a leading nonprofit organization working to advance women in business and the professions. It offers up-to-date statistics and ongoing research studies.

Centercourt

IFX International, Inc.,
12526 High Bluff Drive, Suite 300,
San Diego, CA 92130

Phone: (858) 792-3511
www.centercourt.com

This Internet site is a resource for global franchise and business opportunities. It has a searchable database featuring information on hundreds of business opportunities, a business classified section, and information on finding legal, operational, and marketing help for the entrepreneur.

Coalition of Labor Union Women (CLUW)

661 27th Street, Oakland, CA 94612

Phone: (510) 893-8766 Fax: (510) 893-0934
www.emf.net

CLUW provides organizing, counseling, and advocacy to promote the welfare of working women through union involvement. Strike support, affirmative action, and an end to sexual harassment are highlighted.

The Company Corporation

www.corporate.com
e-mail: info@corporate.com

Since 1899, The Company Corporation has helped the legal, financial, and entrepreneurial communities with incorporation services and advice on starting and running a successful business.

Cybergrrl, Inc.

50 Broad Street, Suite 1614,
New York, NY 10004

Phone: (212) 785-1276   Fax: (212) 785-1383
www.cybergrrl.com
e-mail: info@cgim.com

Created in 1995, Cybergrrl offers access to an extensive number of Web sites "for, by and about women." Officially, it is "a Web site architecture and on-line marketing consulting firm that specializes in communicating with the female audience."

Entrepreneur's HomeOfficeMag.com

www.homeofficemag.com

This site provides useful information for the home-based business. HomeOfficeMag.com's home page offers everything from client-pleasing voice-mail tricks to advice on where to put your home office.

EntreWorld

The Ewing Marion Kauffman
Foundation, 4801 Rockhill Road,
Kansas City, MO 64110

Phone: (816) 932-1000
www.entreworld.org
e-mail: info@entreworld.org

This on-line information resource for entrepreneurs is divided into three channels: Starting Your Business, Growing Your Business, and Supporting Entrepreneurship. The site is coordinated by the Kauffman Center for Entrepreneurial Leadership and provides edited information gathered from more than 800 Web sites.

Executive Recruiters International

1545 Kingsway Court,
Trenton, MI 48183

Phone: (734) 671-6200 Fax: (734) 671-8714
www.execrecruiters.com/html
e-mail: eriinc@execrecruiters.com

ERI is a global recruiting company that specializes primarily in the automotive industry.

FeMiNa

www.femina.com

Created in 1995 by Cybergrrl, Inc., the site provides women with a comprehensive, searchable directory of links to female-friendly sites.

Financial Women International (FWI)

www.fwi.org

In 1921, FWI was known as the National Association of Bank Women. Today, nearly 6,500 financial services professionals from the United States, Bermuda, Canada, Japan, Mexico, and Russia benefit from FWI's advocacy, seminars, and products.

The International Alliance (TIA)

P.O. Box 1119, Sparks-Glencoe,
Baltimore, MD 21152

Phone: (410) 472-4221 Fax: (410) 472-920
www.t-i-a.com
e-mail: info@t-i-a.com

TIA serves worldwide as the umbrella organization that unites, supports, and promotes professional and executive women and their networks in the business, not-for-profit, and government sectors. Opportunities abound.

Internets

305 Vineyard Town Center,
Morgan Hill, CA 95037

Phone: (800) 831-1113 Fax: (408) 842-3211
www.internets.com/women.htm
e-mail: www.internets.com

This "women's search engines" site gives an extensive listing of topics and Web sites of specific interest to women, from "Bridges, A Journal for Jewish Feminists" to mothers struggling with their child's chronic bed-wetting.

ivillage: The Women's Network

www.ivillage.com/work

This Web site specializes in information for women who want to start or who already operate an at-home business. Channels include the "Mompreneur of the Month," expert advice, career astrology, and on-line business courses.

The National Association for Female Executives (NAFE)

Phone: (800) 634-6233
e-mail: nafe@nafe.com

Established in 1972, NAFE is the largest businesswomen's association in the United States. Its mission is to empower its 150,000 members through education, networking, and public advocacy and to provide services and resources to help women achieve career success and financial security.

National Association of Women Business Owners (NAWBO)

www.nawbo.org

NAWBO is the only dues-based national organization that represents women entrepreneurs in all types of business. As of 1999 it had 75 chapters in the United States and abroad. The group seeks to strengthen its members' wealth capacity, create innovative changes in the business culture, build strategic alliances, and transform public policy.

The National Foundation for Women Business Owners (NFWBO)

1100 Wayne Avenue, Suite 830,
Silver Spring, MD 20910-5603

Phone: (301) 495-4975 Fax: (301) 495-4979
e-mail: NFWBO@worldnet.att.net
www.nfwbo.org

The NFWBO is the premier source of information and statistics on women business owners and their enterprises worldwide.

9to5, National Association of Working Women (NAWW)

231 West Wisconsin Avenue, Suite 900, Milwaukee, WI 53203-2308

Phone: (414) 274-0925 Fax: (414) 272-2870
www.feminist.com/9to5.htm
e-mail: NAWW9to5@execpc.com

NAWW is the largest membership organization of working women in the country. Founded in 1973 by a group of Boston clerical workers, the association has been in the forefront in the fight for family and medical leave on the state and national level.

Nolo Press

950 Parker Street, Berkeley, CA 94710

Phone: (510) 549-1976 Fax: (800) 645-0895
www.nolo.com
e-mail: libs@nolo.com

The mission of Nolo is to provide consumers with understandable, accurate legal information and tools they can use to take charge of their own legal affairs. The company also sells legal forms, books, and software.

Smallbizsearch.com

This site contains a searchable database for the small-business owner. The site also offers "Tips for the Day," such as making the most of management, how to write a business plan, and much more.

The Small Business Marketing Letter

www.smallbizhelp.net/marketing.htm

For new and existing small-business owners, the electronic "Small Business Marketing Letter" offers vast information about what's happening in direct marketing today and how to apply it to increase your own business's profits.

Society of Women Engineers

120 Wall Street, 11th Floor, New York, NY 10005-3902

Phone: (212) 509-9577
www.swe.org
e-mail: hq@swe.org

SWE is a nonprofit educational and service organization of graduate engineers and those with equivalent engineering experience. Founded in 1950, the society's mission is to stimulate women to achieve full potential in careers as engineers and leaders.

SuccessTalk

www.successtalk.com

This site offers inspiration and advice to women who want to achieve success in all walks of life. It features WiseWoman Quotes, a SuccessTalk newsletter, a Women's Mentoring Scholarship, and Success Coaching.

U.S. Department of Labor— Women's Bureau

www.dol.gov/dol/wb/welcome.html
e-mail: Webmaster@dol.gov

Established in 1920, the WB is the single unit at the federal government level exclusively concerned with serving and promoting the interests of working women. Its duty is to formulate standards and policies that promote the welfare of wage-earning women, improve their working conditions, increase their efficiency, and advance their opportunities.

U.S. Small Business Administration (SBA)

Phone: (800) 697-4636 or (202) 401-9600
www.sba.gov

Established in 1953, the U.S. SBA provides financial, technical, and management assistance to help Americans start, run, and grow their own businesses.

Women Chefs Resource Center

www.chefnet.com/womenchefs
e-mail: women@chefnet.com

WCRC is an online-only home for women chefs and students. It provides an environment in which to network with other women chefs.

Women.com

www.women.com

This site's 20 channels are, of course, women-oriented and range from career advice to pregnancy issues to small-business information. It also has a "Newsstand" where the browser can click on and open any magazine from *Cosmo* to *Good Housekeeping*.

Women Construction Owners and Executives

4849 Connecticut Avenue NW, Suite 704, Washington, DC 20008-5838

Phone: (800) 788-3548 Fax: (202) 788-3548
www.wcoeusa.org

Objective: to promote the role of women in the construction industry, assist women in executive management positions, provide resources, create a legislative network, and encourage professional standards.

Women in Film (WIF)

61464 Sunset Boulevard, Suite 1080, Hollywood, CA 90028

Phone: (323) 463-6040 Fax: (323) 463-0963
www.wif.org
e-mail: membersvcs@wif.org

This professional organization was founded in 1973 to recognize, develop, and actively promote the unique visions of women in the global communications industry.

Women in Technology International (WITI)

14622 Ventura Boulevard, #1022, Sherman Oaks, CA 91403

Phone: (818) 990-6705 Fax: (818) 906-3299
www.witi.com

The WITI Foundation is dedicated to advancing women in technology, increasing the number of women in executive roles in technology, helping women become more financially independent and technology-literate, and encouraging young women to choose careers in science and technology.

Women of NASA

http://quest.arc.nasa.gov/women/intro.html
e-mail: tkrieg@quest.arc.nasa.gov

This site was established as a resource to encourage young women to pursue careers in math, science, and technology. It also showcases outstanding women in these fields.

The Women's Council of Realtors® (WCR)

www.wcr.org
e-mail: wcrweb@wcr.org

WCR is a nationwide organization established in 1938 consisting of real estate professionals to create career opportunities, promote success strategies, and inspire leadership and individual achievement in the real estate field.

www.EntrepreneurMag.com

EntrepreneurMag is a resource site containing a veritable library of information for the small-business owner.

www.feminist.com/career.htm

Offers extensive and impressive listings and links to women's career and professional organizations.

www.firstunion.com/smallbusiness

This is the First Union Bank Web site devoted to helping people grow a successful business. The site contains information on everything from creating a business plan to finding appropriate loans.

www.monster.com

Phone: (800) MONSTER

Monster.com is a leading global on-line network that connects potential employees with career opportunities. For job-seekers and employers alike.

WWWomen.com

www.wwwomen.com

This mother-lode-of-a-resource directory offers more than 1,000 significant links to sites for ambitious women, including BridgesOnline.com, a job-matching service for candidates and employers.

www.vfinance.com

Provides information on more than 200 venture capital firms, as well as news updates about the industry.

www.womenconnect.com

This Web site claims to be the most popular on-line destination for business and professional women. It offers thousands of pages of information, from daily women-related news to directories of women-owned businesses and organizations.

Notes

Quotations and general biographical information were taken from the following reference works:

Concise Columbia Encyclopedia. New York: Avon, 1983.

Fifty on Fifty: Wisdom, Inspiration, and Reflections on Women's Lives Well Lived. By Bonnie Miller Rubin. New York: Warner Books, 1998.

Great Lives from History—American Women Series III. Ed. Frank Magill. Englewood Cliffs, NJ: Salem Press, 1995.

Hell's Belles. By Seale Ballenger. New York: MJF Books, 1997.

The New International Dictionary of Quotations. Ed. Margaret Miner and Hugh N. Rawson. New York: Signet, 1994.

The Oxford Dictionary of Quotations, Third Edition. Oxford, England: Oxford University Press, 1980.

The Quotable Woman. Philadelphia: Running Press, 1991.

The Reader's Quotation Book. Ed. Steven Gilbar. New York: Penguin Books, 1990.

"Remarkable American Women: 1776-1976," *Life* magazine special report, 1976.

An Uncommon Scold. Ed. Abby Adams. New York: Simon & Schuster, 1989.

Untamed Tongues: Wild Quotes from Wild Women. Autumn Stephens. Berkeley, CA: Conari Press, 1983.

Webster's II New Riverside Desk Quotations. Ed. James B. Simpson. Boston: Houghton Mifflin Company, 1992.

Webster's Dictionary of American Women. New York: Smithmark Publishers in cooperation with Merriam-Webster, 1996.

The Words of a Woman: A Literary Mosaic. By Christine Mary McGinley. New York: Crown Publishers, 1999.

Words on Women: Quotes by Famous Americans. Ed. Evelyn L. Beilenson and Sharon Melnick. White Plains, NY: Peter Pauper Press, 1987.

The Wordsworth Dictionary of Film Quotations. Ed. Tony Crawley. Hertfordshire, England: Wordsworth Editions, Ltd., 1994.

INTRODUCTION

p. 7, p. 8, stats about women-owned firms: "Key Facts About Women-Owned Businesses," © National Foundation for Women Business Owners (NFWBO), 1999, www.nfwbo.org.

p. 7, stats about women's earnings; **p. 8,** "The advice is not about . . .": Betsy Morris, "Tales of the Trailblazers: *Fortune* Revisits Harvard's Women MBAs of 1973," *Fortune,* 12 October 1998, pp. 114–122.

p. 7, stats about women's earnings: April L. Butcher, "Women Need Financial and Networking Skills to Control Their Economic Growth," *Babson Entrepreneurial Review,* spring/summer 1998, p. 10.

p. 7, census figures: Andrew Kimbrell, "Breaking the Job Lock," *Utne Reader,* January–February 1999, pp. 47–49.

p. 7, quotes from Darla Moore and Sherry Lansing, and **p. 8,** "tend to bring their whole . . .": Patricia Sellers, "The 50 Most Powerful Women in American Business," *Fortune,* 12 October 1998, pp. 76–98.

p. 7, on Carly Fiorina: Carly Fiorina biography, Hewlett-Packard Web site, www.hp.com © 1999.

2 THE VISIONARY

Inside the Visionary Mind

p. 21, Nancy Friday quote: Betty Boob, "Our Gal Friday," *Bust*, summer/fall 1998, pp. 70–73.

p. 22, Gloria Allred quote: Bonnie Miller Rubin, *Fifty on Fifty: Wisdom, Inspiration, and Reflections on Women's Lives Well Lived* (New York: Warner Books, 1998), p. 1.

p. 28, "I've seen the best feminist minds...": Elaine Showalter, "The Professor Wore Prada," *Vogue*, quoted in *Bust*, summer/fall 1998, p. 9.

On Madame C.J. Walker

p. 29, Susan McHenry, "Madame C.J. Walker, Historic Entrepreneur," Women's Wire, www.womenswire.com, posted 1/29/97.

"Remarkable American Women: 1776–1976", *Life* magazine special report, 1976.

On Hattie Carnegie

p. 31 "I've had three husbands . . ."; **p. 32,** "Working with her is like . . .": Hambla Bauer, "Hot Fashions by Hattie," *Collier's*, 16 April 1949, pp. 26–70.

p. 32, "We've made three wedding dresses . . ."; **p. 33,** "Hattie Carnegie, Inc., . . .": Russell Maloney, "Hattie Carnegie," *Life*, 12 November 1945.

p. 33, on FIT's retrospective of her work. "From Henrietta Königeiser to Hattie Carnegie: An Austrian Immigrant's Success Story," Austrian Information Web site, www.austria.org/mar96/hattie.htm.

On Elizabeth Arden

p. 33, "There's only one Elizabeth . . .": Alfred Allen Lewis and Constance Woodworth, *Miss Elizabeth Arden: An Unretouched Portrait* (New York: Coward, McCann & Geoghegan, 1972), p. 22.

p. 33, "She not only wanted . . .": Richard Gheman, *Cosmopolitan*, June 1956, quoted in Marjorie Dent Candee, ed., *Current Biography* (New York: H.W. Wilson Company, 1957).

p. 34, "From the first she was . . .": "Profiles: Luxury, Inc.," *The New Yorker*, 31 March 1934, pp. 23–24.

p. 34, ". . . erratic, unpredictable, vague . . .": Elizabeth Arden quote: "I Am a Famous Woman in This Industry," *Fortune*, October 1938, p. 152.

p. 34, "Dear, never forget . . . ," Elizabeth Arden quote: *Webster's II New Riverside Desk Quotations* (New York: Houghton Mifflin, 1992), 103:9.

The Visionary at Work

p. 35, "Stick to three concepts . . .": Roberta Vasko Kraus of the Center for Creative Leadership, *Working Woman*, October 1998, p. 59.

p. 36: "No matter how bad . . ."; and **p. 37,** "Success at work . . .": Letitia Baldrige, *Letitia Baldrige's New Complete Guide to Executive Manners* (New York: Rawson Associates, 1993), p. 4.

p. 39, "On the home front . . .": Fran Rodgers, "The Entrepreneurial Balancing Act: Making the Best of a Good Thing," www.EntreWorld.org, A World of Resources for Entrepreneurs, the Kauffman Center for Entrepreneurial Leadership, May 1997.

p. 43, "Surviving disaster . . .": Lesley Stahl quote: "Up Close and Personal," *Marie Claire*, October 1998, p. 88.

On Rose Marie Bravo

p. 48, ". . . revered on Seventh Avenue"; **p. 50,** "Her Rolodex . . .": Laura Bird, "Saks President Bravo Quits Chain to Take Chief's Job at Burberrys," *Wall Street Journal*, 5 September 1997, p. B8.

p. 48, ". . . a brand name herself in the fashion world"; details about Bravo's salary; "Where she used to pick . . ."; **p. 49,** "Look for the Burberry plaid . . .": Lauren Goldstein, "Dressing Up an Old Brand," *Fortune*, 9 November 1998, p. 154.

p. 50, on Bravo's move to Burberry; **p. 51,** on Burberry's history: "Saks Fifth Avenue President Joins Burberrys," *New York Times*, 5 September 1997, p. D2.

On Lois Silverman

pp. 51–55, Josh Hyatt, "A Woman Leader, a Woman's Touch," *Boston Globe*, 6 March 1996. "Lois Silverman," *Boston Business Journal*, 1–7 September 1995.

Advice for Visionaries

p. 56: "Forget *Atlas Shrugged* . . .": Barnett Helzberg Jr., "Mentoring Is for Entrepreneurs, Too," www.EntreWorld.org, A World of Resources for Entrepreneurs, the Kauffman Center for Entrepreneurial Leadership, August 1997.

3 THE ARTISAN

Inside the Artisan Mind

p. 58, on Shamita Das Dasgupta: Carolyn Jones, *The Family of Women: Voices Across the Generations* (New York: Abbeville Press, 1999), p. 68.

On Margaret Rudkin

p. 66, "There was no planning . . ."; "whimsical idea"; "We started our country life . . ."; **p. 67,** ". . . should have been sent to the Smithsonian . . ."; **p. 68,** "At one time, ten members . . .": Margaret Rudkin, *The Margaret Rudkin Pepperidge Farm Cookbook* (New York: Athenaeum, 1963).

p. 67, "I was forty . . .": Mark Zullo, Bill Hartigan, *Success After 40* (Kansas City, MO: Andrews and McMeel, 1996), pp. 125–128.

p. 67, on Rudkin's New York press: *Great Lives from History—American Women Series III,* ed. Frank Magill (Englewood Cliffs, NJ: Salem Press, 1995), pp. 1561–1564.

p. 68, on the sale of Pepperidge Farm: Constance L. Hays, "Will Goldfish Tactics Help Campbell's Soups?", *New York Times*, 18 October 1998, p. B4.

On Margaret Sanger

p. 68, "The sexual impulse . . .": Margaret H. Sanger, *What Every Girl Should Know* (Belvedere Press, 1920, reprint 1980), p. 28.

p. 70, ". . . bone-heads, spineless and brainless"; **p. 70,** "Women must come to recognize . . .": Joy Johannessen, preface to Sanger's *What Every Girl Should Know*, pp. x–xii. Additional biographical information provided by Janet W. Lyon, Professor, Women's Studies, University of Illinois.

On Laura Ashley

p. 70, "I'm only interested . . ."; **p. 71,** "The minute I set eyes . . ."; **p. 71,** "I didn't set out to be Victorian"; **p. 72,** "I sensed that most people . . .";
p. 72, "She was so quiet . . ."; ". . . a kind of scrubbed . . ."; ". . . an unshakable belief . . .": Anne Sebba, *Laura Ashley: A Life by Design* (London: Weidenfeld and Nicolson, 1990), pp. 15–199.

The Artisan at Work:

p. 73, "The new psychology . . . ": Joline Godfrey, "Been There, Doing That," *Inc.*, March 1996, p. 21.

p. 74, "My greatest assets . . . ": Ann Sample, "Marsha Serlin, Scrap Metal Maven," Women's Wire, www.womenswire.com, posted 30 October 1996.

p. 74, "I view my company . . . ," Donna Karan quote: Bonnie Miller Rubin, *Fifty on Fifty: Wisdom, Inspiration, and Reflections on Women's Lives Well Lived* (New York: Warner Books, 1998), p. 85.

p. 75, "I first kick in . . . ," Deborah Triant quote: Anna Muoio, "Unit of One," *Fast Company*, October 1998, p. 98.

p. 75: "Every woman I know . . . ," Caryn Mandabach quote: Ken Auletta, "In the Company of Women," *The New Yorker*, 20 November 1998, p. 75.

p. 75, "Life is stressful . . .": Dina Tayson, "Beth Cross & Pam Parker, Equestrian Entrepreneurs," Women's Wire, www.womenswire.com, posted 9 May 1997.

p. 76, "Politics is the process . . . ," Marilyn Moats Kennedy quote: "Playing Office Politics," *Newsweek*, 195, quoted in *Webster's II New Riverside Desk Quotations*, ed. James B. Simpson (Boston: Houghton Mifflin Company, 1992), 108:9.

p. 80, "I spent four months . . . ," Christine Kealy quote: Carolyn Jones, *The Family of Women* (New York: Abbeville Press, 1999), p. 102.

p. 80, "I've had no boredom . . . ," Brenda Barnes quote: Patricia Sellers, "The 50 Most Powerful Women in American Business," *Fortune*, 12 October 1998, pp. 76–98.

p. 80, on Denise Ilitch: Colleen Mastony, "Executive moms," *Forbes*, July 1998.

Seventh Heaven

p. 76, on Kim Schaefer: "The Growing Green Marketplace: Kim Schaefer Architects," *Co-op America's National Green Pages*, 1999 ed., p. 10.

p. 76, on the 7-G approach: "Dream Job," *Working Woman*, December/January 1999, p. 16.

The Artisan as Mentor and/or Protégée

p. 77, stats on women seeking advice: "Retirement Plan Trends in the Small Business Market: A Survey of Women- and Men-Owned Firms," NFWBO Report, 1997.

p. 77, "If you get a good idea . . . ": Barnett Helzberg Jr., "Mentoring Is for Entrepreneurs, Too," www.EntreWorld.org, Kauffman Center for Entrepreneurial Leadership, August 1997.

On Anne Robinson

pp. 88 and **90,** on Windham Hill's beginnings and business practices, and **p. 91,** "Will and I didn't try . . . ": Michael Barrier, "Only the Music is in the Clouds," *Nation's Business*, November 1991, pp. 60–61.

p. 88, on Windham Hill's revenues and industry impact, and **p. 91,** company's move to a converted auto shop: Dyan Machan, "To Be Continued," *Forbes*, 2 May 1988, p. 120–121.

On Lane Nemeth

p. 94, on husband Ed: Marie-Jeanne Juilland, "Lane Nemeth, Discovery Toys," Women's Wire, www.womenswire.com, posted 27 December 1995.

p. 95, on daughter Tara, and **p. 95,** "Things are never really black and white . . . ": Lane Nemeth, "Discovering Another Way: Raising Brighter Children, While Having a Meaningful Career," book preview, web@beyondword.com, Beyond Words Publishing, Inc., ©1998. Also: Donna Fenn, "A League of Your Own," *Inc.* Online, www.inc.com, posted 1998, ©1999 Goldhirsh Group, Inc.

Advice for Artisans

p. 96, about speaking up: "Delivering Bad News, or Talking About a Problem at Work That Nobody Else Wants to Talk About," excerpted from Dan Oestreich and Kathleen Ryan, *The Courageous Messenger: How to Successfully Speak Up at Work*, in *Fast Company*, December 1998, pp. 241–242.

4 THE IDEALIST

Inside the Idealist Mind

p. 99, on Pamela Lopker: Anna Muoio, "Unit of One," *Fast Company,* October 1998, p. 94.

p. 102, on Ayn Rand: Objectivism Web site, the Ayn Rand Institute, www.aynrand.org, ©1997.

p. 104, on Annie Leibovitz: *Webster's Dictionary of American Women* (New York: Smithmark Publishers in cooperation with Merriam-Webster, 1996).

p. 104, on Abby Joseph Cohen: Patricia Sellers, "The 50 Most Powerful Women in American Business," *Fortune,* 12 October 1998, pp. 76–98.

p. 107, Lillian Hellman quote: *Webster's II New Riverside Desk Quotations,* ed. James B. Simpson (Boston: Houghton Mifflin Company, 1992).

On Christine McGaffey Frederick

p. 108, "A new concept of glory . . . ," **p. 109,** "There isn't the slightest reason in the world . . . ," **p. 109,** " . . . apply a very large share . . . ," **p. 109,** "We have more because . . . ": Christine Frederick, *Selling Mrs. Consumer* (New York: The Business Bourse, 1925).

Also: *Women in American Architecture: A Historic and Contemporary Perspective,* Susana Torre, ed. (New York: Whitney Library of Design, 1977).

On Fannie Farmer Merritt

p. 110, "Progress in civilization . . . ": *The Cook's Quotation Book,* Maria Polushin Robbins, ed. (New York: Penguin Books, 1983), p. 18.

p. 110, on Farmer's beginnings, **p. 111,** on her favorite book, and **p. 111,** "Mankind will eat to live . . . ": *Webster's Dictionary of American Women* (New York: Smithmark Publishers in cooperation with Merriam-Webster, 1996), pp. 184–185.

p. 111, "Today more than ever . . . ," James Beard quote: *The Fannie Farmer Cookbook,* Twelfth Edition, rev. by Marion Cunningham and Jeri Laber (New York: Alfred A. Knopf, 1980), p. x.

p. 111, " . . . mother of the level measurement . . . ": Susan G. Purdy, *A Piece of Cake* (New York: Collier Books, 1989), p. 13.

p. 111, " . . . by guess and by golly," "Remarkable American Women: 1776–1976," *Life* magazine special report, 1976, p. 77.

On Grace Hopper

p. 112, "Life was simple..," **p. 112,** "They told me computers . . . ," **p. 113,** "I seem to do a lot of retiring": Philip Schieber, "The Wit and Wisdom of Grace Hopper," *The OCLC Newsletter,* March/April 1987, no.167.

p. 112, " . . . to have the coefficients . . . ": Trevor Kokal and Nikki Barker, "Grace Hopper," Web biography, January 1998.

p. 113, " . . . tommyrot and nonsense," *Webster's Dictionary of American Women* (New York: Smithmark Publishers in cooperation with Merriam-Webster, 1996), p. 290.

p. 113, " . . . all the young people . . . ": The 1994 Grace Hopper Celebration of Women in Computing, conference catalog.

Idealists at Work

p. 117, Shalala quote: Bonnie Miller Rubin, *Fifty on Fifty: Wisdom, Inspiration, and Reflections on Women's Lives Well Lived* (New York: Warner Books, 1998), p. 137.

p. 120, Lesley Stahl quote: "Up Close and Personal," *Marie Claire,* October 1998, p. 88.

p. 121, Audrey MacLean quote: Mary Beth Grover, "Starting a Company Is Like Going to War," *Forbes,* 2 November 1998, p. 190.

p. 123, on Cathy Clay: Cathy Clay as told to Heather Cassell, "Bond Girl: A Lady Trader's Guide to Success on the Stock Exchange Floor," *Bust,* spring 1999, p. 48.

On Shelly Lazarus
p. 127, Lazarus as fourth most powerful: Patricia Sellers, "The 50 Most Powerful Women in American Business," *Fortune,* 12 October 1998, pp. 76–98.
Also: "Shelly Lazarus," *People,* 5 May, 1997, p. 90.
Ken Auletta, "In the Company of Women," *The New Yorker,* 20 November 1998, p. 75.

On Rev. Margaret Bullitt-Jonas
p. 133, book review: Alexandria Hall, "Pigging Out," *New York Times Book Review,* 10 January 1999, p. 10.
p. 134, "Going numb is a popular way . . . ": Karen R. Long, "Once Addicted to Food, Priest Satisfies Hunger for God," *Bakersfield Californian,* 21 January 1999.

5 THE ADVENTURER

Inside the Adventurer's Mind
p. 137, on Nellie Bly and Clare Boothe Luce: "Remarkable American Women: 1776–1976," *Life* magazine special report, 1976
p. 137, "It is vain to say . . . ," George Eliot quote: "Thoughts on the Business of Life," *Forbes,* 2 November 1998, p. 396.
p. 138, "Women have the feeling . . . ," Diane Johnson quote: *An Uncommon Scold,* ed, Abby Adams (New York: Simon & Schuster, 1989), p. 159.
p. 142, "School was hard . . . "; Cher quote: Bonnie Miller Rubin, *Fifty on Fifty: Wisdom, Inspiration, and Reflections on Women's Lives Well Lived* (New York: Warner Books, 1998), p. 25.

On Diana Vreeland
p. 144, "I'm sure I chose . . . "; **p. 145,** "I couldn't take off . . . ": Diana Vreeland, *D.V.* (New York: Da Capo Press, 1997).
p. 145, "Vreeland invented the fashion editor . . . ,"Avedon quote; **p. 146,** "Diana Vreeland's sense of style . . . ": "Diana Vreeland: Immoderate Style," report on the exhibition at the Metropolitan Museum of Art, www.costumeinstitute.org, 1993.
p. 146, "She nourishes the soul . . . ": from the intro by Mary Louise Wilson, Diana Vreeland, *D.V.* (New York: Da Capo Press, 1997).

On Clare Boothe Luce
p. 146, "What rage for fame . . .": Sylvia Jukes Morris, *Rage for Fame: The Ascent of Clare Boothe Luce* (New York: Random House, 1997).
p. 146, life "full of double dares"; **p. 147,** Dorothy Parker review; **p. 147,** H. L. Mencken commentary; **p. 148,** "If I fail . . . ": "Remarkable American Women," *Life* special report, 1976, p. 11.
p. 146, "easily the most hated woman . . ."; **p. 148,** "She had been Eisenhower's . . . ";
p. 148, "Clare was endlessly seductive . . . ": Gore Vidal, "The Woman Behind the Women," *The New Yorker,* 26 May 1997, pp. 70–75.

On Josephine Baker
p. 149: "Josephine, with those *long* black legs . . . ": Diana Vreeland, *D.V.* (New York: Da Capo Press, 1997), p. 50.
p. 151, " . . . died of joy": Alan Schroeder, "Josephine Baker," *Black Americans of Achievement* (New York: Chelsea House, 1991), pp. 111–121.

Adventurers at Work

p. 151, "Real success . . . ," Betsey Johnson quote: *1994 Current Biography Yearbook.*

p. 153, "I had no desire . . . ": Caroline Myss, *Anatomy of the Spirit: The Seven Stages of Power and Healing* (New York: Three Rivers Press, 1996).

p. 154, on Bach Nguyen: Judy Birke, "Art Links Entrepreneur, Homeland," *The New Haven Register,* 24 May 1998, p. G2.

p. 155, "I'm not going . . . ," Missy Elliot quote: Scarlett Fever, "Little Miss Strange," *Bust,* summer/fall, 1998, pp 63–64.

p. 155, "Every day I count . . . ," Dolly Parton quote: Jack Gramling, "Dolly: My Life and Other Unfinished Business," *Saturday Evening Post,* March/April 1995, p. 23.

p. 155, "I got more guts . . . ," Dolly Parton quote: Miriam Kanner, "Good Golly Miss Dolly," *Ladies' Home Journal,* January 1994, p. 82.

p. 155, "Don't wait too long . . . ," Carol Bellamy quote: Bonnie Miller Rubin, *Fifty On Fifty* (New York: Warner Books, 1998), p. 5.

p. 159, on Jill Barad: Adam Bryant, "A Toyshop That Doesn't Forget to Play," *New York Times,* 11 October 1998.

p. 159, on Tanya Styblo Beder: Anne Faircloth, "The Class of '83," *Fortune,* 12 October 1998, p. 127.

p. 160, on Barbara Waugh: Katharine Mieszkowski, "I Grew Up Thinking . . . ," *Fast Company,* December 1998, pp. 149–154.

On Laura Groppe

p. 164, "I wanted to know everything . . . , ": Silvia Sansoni, "Phat, way kewl, da bomb!," *Forbes,* 9 February 1998.

On Marilyn Carlson Nelson

p. 173, "The American way is not . . . "; **p. 174,** " . . . we are as much a technology company . . . "; Sherrie E. Zhan, "Spell Marilyn with a Capital CEO," reprint from *World Trade* in *Continental* magazine, March 1999, p. 35.

6 INTUITIVE FINANCES

p. 178, "To me, success . . . ," Carol Szatkowski quote: Susan Diesenhouse, "Blazing Gender Trails," *Boston Globe,* 6 May 1998, p. F1.

p. 179, on Mary Kay: Mark Zullo and Bill Hartigan, *Success After 40: Late Bloomers Who Made It Big* (Kansas City, MO: Andrews and McMeel, 1996), pp. 77–86.

p. 181, "With each check I wrote . . . "; **p. 188,** "Taking that job . . . ": Suze Orman, *The 9 Steps to Financial Freedom* (New York: Crown Publishers, 1997), p. 25, p. 253.

p. 182, "Money doesn't buy . . . ," Caroline Hirsch quote: Wendy Shanker, "My Funny Caroline," *Bust,* spring 1999, p. 50.

p. 183, on college costs; **p. 183,** on widowhood: American Express Financial Advisors, *Guide to Financial Well Being,* publication, March 1999.

p. 183, on wills; "They also often take care . . . ": Shelley Schlossberg, "Women and Investing," issued by PaineWebber, www.womensweb.com.

p. 183, on female retirees, U.S. Department of Labor fact sheet no. 98–2, www.dol.gov.

p. 184, "I've been in trailers . . . ," Naomi Judd quote: Bonnie Miller Rubin, *Fifty on Fifty: Wisdom, Inspiration, and Reflections on Women's Lives Well Lived,* (New York: Warner Books, 1998), p. 80.

p. 189, "Investing is crucial . . . "; **p. 191,** "You know those stupid myths . . . ": Cathy Clay as told to Heather Cassell, "Bond Girl: A Lady Trader's Guide to Success on the Stock Exchange Floor," *Bust,* spring 1999, p. 48.

p. 193, "I can't stand . . . ," Stefanie Powers quote: Bonnie Miller Rubin, *Fifty on Fifty: Wisdom, Inspiration, and Reflections on Women's Lives Well Lived*, (New York: Warner Books, 1998), p. 124.

p. 195, "Risk-taking is setting up . . . ," Carol Bellamy quote: Bonnie Miller Rubin, *Fifty on Fifty: Wisdom, Inspiration, and Reflections on Women's Lives Well Lived* (New York: Warner Books, 1998), p. 5.

7 PLAYING WELL WITH OTHERS

p. 200, "I often wonder why . . . ," Deborah Triant quote: Anna Muoio, "Unit of One," *Fast Company*, October 1998, p. 98.

p. 202, on apologies: Letitia Baldrige, *Letitia Baldrige's New Complete Guide to Executive Manners*, New York: Rawson Associates, 1993.

p. 202, "It's a huge relief . . . ": "Delivering Bad News, or Talking About a Problem at Work That Nobody Else Wants to Talk About," excerpted from Dan Oestreich and Kathleen Ryan, "*Driving Fear Out of the Workplace*," in *Fast Company*, December 1998, pp. 241–242.

p. 203, "Business is personal . . . ," Hatim Tyabji quote: William C. Taylor, "At Veri-Fone, It's a Dog's Life, and They Love It," *Fast Company's Handbook of the Business Revolution*, 1997, p. 12.

pp. 207–209, on negotiating: Roger Fisher and William Ury, *Getting to Yes: Negotiating Agreement Without Giving In*, (New York: Penguin Books, 1991).

p. 209, "An effective leader . . ."; **p. 216,** on micromanagement: Andrew J. DuBrin, *The Complete Idiot's Guide to Leadership* (New York: Alpha Books, 1998), p. 5.

p. 210, on good leadership: "Avery Salute to Success Survey," *Strive: Ideas and Solutions for Small Business Success*, First Union Bank publication, autumn 1998, p. 5.

p. 211, on bad bosses: Harvey Hornstein, *Brutal Bosses and Their Prey*, New York: Riverhead Books, 1996, excerpted in Peter Bernstein and Christopher Ma, *The Practical Guide to Practically Everything* (New York: Random House, 1997), p. 371.

p. 212, "I don't *have* to know . . . ": Mort Meyerson, "Everything I Thought I Knew About Leadership Is Wrong," *Fast Company's Handbook of the Business Revolution*, 1997, p. 9.

p. 213, "Good corporate culture . . . ": Jennifer Lawton, "The Corporate Petri dish," www.EntreWorld.org, the Kauffman Center for Entrepreneurial Leadership, January 1998.

p. 213, "Her employees wanted . . . "; **p. 224,** "As Bernard was constantly . . . ": Anne Sebba, *Laura Ashley: A Life by Design* (London: Weidenfeld and Nicolson, 1990), p. 73.

p. 224, on asking for a raise: Lutheran Brotherhood and Louis Harris and Associates study, Peter Bernstein and Christopher Ma, *The Practical Guide to Practically Everything* (New York: Random House, 1997), p. 349.

p. 225, on hiring statistics: *Strive: Ideas and Solutions for Small Business Success*, First Union Bank publication, autumn 1998, p. 8.

p. 226, on employee benefits: "100 Best Companies to Work For," *Fortune*, January 1999.

p. 227, "There is no such thing . . . ," Charles Brower quote, *Webster's II New Riverside Desk Quotations*, ed. James B. Simpson (Boston: Houghton Mifflin Company, 1992), 104:7.

p. 228, "Touch a face . . . ," Estée Lauder quote: *Webster's II New Riverside Desk Quotations*, ed. James B. Simpson (Boston: Houghton Mifflin Company, 1992), 108:15.

8 CHANGING JOBS, CHANGING CAREERS

p. 230, "No cohort in history . . . "; **p. 231,** "Values-driven work . . . ": Ann Hornaday, "How Do You Know When It's Time to Go?", *Fast Company's Handbook of the Business Revolution*, 1997, p. 34.

p. 230, "If you can heal . . . ": Brad Edmondson, "Hot Jobs," *Utne Reader*, January–February 1999, p. 59.

p. 231, about abusive bosses: Harvey Hornstein, *Brutal Bosses and Their Prey* (New York: Riverhead Books, 1997), excerpted in Peter Bernstein and Christopher Ma, *The Practical Guide to Practically Everything*, (New York: Random House, 1997), page 370.

p. 231, "The most discouraging aspect . . . ": Andrew Kimbrell, "Breaking the Job Lock," *Utne Reader*, January–February 1999, pp. 47–48.

p. 231, about women being held back in the workplace: Infobrief, "Women in Business: A Snapshot," excerpt from *The 1997 Catalyst Census of Women Corporate Officers and Top Earners of the* Fortune 500, April 1998.

p. 231, on WITI study of female high-tech employees: "Quick Guide for Women Entrepreneurs," *Entrepreneur*, January 1999, p. 26.

p. 232, on guilty-parent report by the Families and Work Institute: Debra Phillips, "The In Crowd," *Entrepreneur*, January 1999, p. 14.

p. 232, on CEO salary increases: Peter Bernstein and Christopher Ma, *The Practical Guide to Practically Everything* (New York: Random House, 1997), p. 352.

p. 232, "Not being who you are . . . ," Eunice Azzani quote: Katharine Mieszkowski, "Jobs Are Given . . . ," *Fast Company,* December 1998, p. 129.

p. 233, "No matter how happy you are . . . ," Leigh Steinberg quote, reported by Christina Novicki in *Fast Company's Handbook of the Business Revolution*, 1997, p. 46.

p. 233, " . . . most companies no longer think . . . "; "More and more companies are outsourcing . . . ": Gordon R. Miller, "Unconventional Career Paths: Your Ticket to Success in the Coming Work Place Revolution," www.WomanOf.com.

p. 234, "So what if you didn't go to Harvard? . . . ": Jon Spayde, "How to Think Outside the Cube," *Utne Reader,* January–February 1999, p. 61.

p. 234, career expiration dates: *1998–99 Occupational Outlook Handbook*, U.S. Department of Labor http://stats.bls.gov/ocohome.htm.

pp. 235–236, top careers for women: U.S. Department of Labor, "Hot Jobs for the 21st Century," fact sheet No. 97–3, May 1998, www.dol.gov.

p. 235, top careers for women: U.S. Department of Labor, "Nontraditional Occupations for Employed Women in 1997," www.dol.gov/dol/wb.

p. 237, on new breed of career counselors: Ann Hornaday, "How Do You Know When It's Time to Go?", *Fast Company's Handbook of the Business Revolution*, 1997, p. 34.

p. 239, on flextime offered by women business owners: "Key Facts About Women-Owned Businesses," National Foundation for Women Business Owners fact sheet, June 1997.

p. 240, on job applications vs. hires: Shelly Branch, "The 100 Best Companies to Work for in America," *Fortune*, 11 January 1999, p.121.

p. 241, "The upside is that . . .": Leonard Wiener, "Upward Mobility: The Ultimate Job-Hopper's Guide," *U.S. News & World Report,* 26 October 1998, pp. 64–65, 87.

9 MAKING A BUSINESS: THE INTUITIVE ENTREPRENEUR

p. 242, about women-owned firms: "Key Facts About Women-Owned Businesses," © National Foundation for Women Business Owners (NFWBO), 1999, www.nfwbo.org.

pp. 242–243, on corporate outsourcing: *Working Woman*, October 1998, p. 63.

p. 243, on bail-out entrepreneurs: Amanda Walmac, "Reality Check: Today's Entrepreneur Isn't Who You Think She Is," *Working Woman,* July–August 1998, p. 32.

p. 243, "Companies absolutely need . . . ": Patricia Sellers, "The 50 Most Powerful Women in American Business," *Fortune*, 12 October 1998, p. 98.

p. 243, on why women bail out of corporate life: Promotion for Women's Economic Summit 1998, www.womenconnect.com/summit98.

pp. 243–244, on not returning to corporate life, and why women start businesses: Barbara C. Lyon, *Women-Owned Businesses Accelerating Into the 21st Century: An Independent Learning Project,* master's degree thesis, Cambridge College, Cambridge, MA, 1998.

p. 244, motivations for starting a business: Dorothy P. Moore and E. Holly Buttner, *Women Entrepreneurs: Moving Beyond the Glass Ceiling* (Thousand Oaks, CA: Sage Publications, 1997), p. 23.

p. 244, on Gail Blanke: Catherine Cartwright, "Designing Woman: Gail Blanke Jumped the Corporate Ship to Start a Company Dedicated to Helping Women Live Their Dreams," National Association for Female Executives (NAFE) Web site, www.nafe.com.

p. 245, on what it takes to be an entrepreneur: U.S. Small Business Administration, www.sba.gov.

The Visionary Entrepreneur

p. 248, on Debra Benton: biography from materials on Women In Technology (WITI) Third Annual Hall of Fame and Second Annual CEO Recognition Awards presentation, 25 June 1998.

The Artisan Entrepreneur

p. 251, on Judy Wicks: *Social Venture Network Member Directory,* 1998.

p. 251, on Bettina Richards: Jon Pareles, "It's Her Label and She'll Sign Who She Wants To," *New York Times,* 23 September 1998, special "Entrepreneurs" section, p. 11.

p. 252, stats on home-based businesses: "Key Facts About Women-Owned Businesses," fact sheet, National Foundation for Women Business Owners, June 1997.

p. 254, on franchises: *Entrepreneur* 20th Annual Franchise 500, January 1999, pp. 209–295.

p. 254, on franchises: "New Attitude: The Nation's Top 50 New Franchises," *Entrepreneur,* April 1999, pp. 150–153.

The Idealist Entrepreneur

p. 255, on Shirley Crouch and Jo Waldron: Amanda Walmac, "Sound Ideas," *Working Woman,* December–January 1999, pp. 36–37.

p. 256, on Sandra Ramsey Hale and Joan Marie Rowland; on women's use of technology: Amanda Walmac, "Reality Check," *Working Woman,* July–August 1998, p. 36.

p. 256, on new franchises: "New Attitude: The Nation's Top 50 New Franchises," *Entrepreneur,* April 1999, p. 150.

p. 256, on Joan Cable: Cara Trager, "Women Entrepreneurs," *Distinction,* special women's issue, 1998, pp. 56–58.

p. 257, on Katrina Garnett: program for Women In Technology (WITI) Third Annual Hall of Fame and Second Annual CEO Recognition Awards presentation, 25 June 1998.

The Adventurer Entrepreneur

p. 258, "[Starting my business] was like . . . ,"; on Gail Blanke: Catherine Cartwright, "Designing Woman," National Association for Female Executives (NAFE) Web site, www.nafe.com.

p. 259, on Barbara Smith: Cara Trager, "Women Entrepreneurs," *Distinction,* special women's issue, 1998, pp. 56–58.

The Business Plan and How to Work It

p. 260, "If you aren't sure of your goal . . . ": Jennifer Lawton, "The Just-Right Business Plan," www.EntreWorld.org, the Kauffman Center for Entrepreneurial Leadership.

p. 261, on Funding Request and Return; **p. 263,** on Artisan comfort levels: American Express Small Business Exchange Information and Resources, www.americanexpress.com /smallbusiness.

pp. 261–262, U.S. Small Business Administration Tool Kit for Start-Ups, www.sba.gov.

pp. 263–264, "[The business plan] is the most unglamorous . . . ": Princess Superstar, "Taking Care of Business: How to Write a Business Plan, for the Reluctant Artistepreneur," *Bust,* spring 1999, pp. 79–81.

Getting Bucks for Your Biz

p. 264, "I used to think an investor . . . ": Princess Superstar, "Taking Care of Business: How to Write a Business Plan, for the Reluctant Artistepreneur," *Bust,* spring 1999, pp. 79–81.

p. 264, funding at start-up: Kathleen R. Allen and Nancy M. Carter, Babson College's *Frontiers of Entrepreneurship Research*, 1996.

p. 264, "One of the leading causes . . . ": U.S. Small Business Administration Tool Kit for Start-Ups, www.sba.gov.

pp. 264–265, "Understand it's going to take . . . ," Renee Courington quote: "Quick Guide for Women Entrepreneurs," *Entrepreneur*, January 1999, p. 26.

Marketing for Intuitives

p. 267, about marketing departments within a company: Andrew J. Sherman, *The Complete Guide to Running and Growing Your Business* (New York: Times Business, Random House, 1997), p. 322.

p. 268, about Vera Wang: Ann Sample, "Vera Wang, Designer to the Stars," www.womensweb.com, posted 26 June 1996.

10 WOMEN GIVING BACK

p. 271, about women business owners volunteering; **p. 272,** about their chosen charities: National Foundation of Women Business Owners (NFWBO), research highlights, December 1998.

p. 271, on consumers prefering socially responsible companies; "I want them to see . . . ," Regina Simmons-Mullings quote: Wayne Travers, *New Haven Register*, 16 May 1999, p. F1.

p. 272, "Your giving can be . . . ," Gun Denhart quote: "Unit of One," Anna Muoio, ed., *Fast Company*, December 1998, p. 92.

p. 273, on Bernadette Castro: Cara Trager, "Women Entrepreneurs," *Distinction,* special women's issue 1998, p. 46.

p. 274, on Gun Denhart: Hanna Andersson Web site, www.hannaandersson.com.

p. 275, on Lora Lee Stephens: "The Growing Green Marketplace: Sunorganic Farm," *Co-op America's National Green Pages,* 1999, p. 15.

p. 277, "My skin bristles when I see . . . ," Katrina Garnett quote: "Unit of One," Anna Muoio, ed., *Fast Company*, December 1998, p. 100.

p. 277, about Amy L. Domini Kinder: "Responsible Investing: Funds with Impressive Results," *Co-op America Quarterly*, spring 1998, p. 13.

p. 278, on Co-op America Business Network: Brandi Clark, Co-op America fact sheet, 1999.

p. 279, on Cynthia Katz: Letters to the Editor, *CT Life,* January 1997, p. 5.

p. 280, on Modern Design Co.: "On the Green Map," *Co-op America Quarterly*, no. 47, p. 26.

Bibliography

Access to Capital and Credit: Recommendations for Growing Women's Businesses. Report of the National Women's Business Council, Washington, D.C., 1997.

Access to Credit: A Guide for Lenders and Women Owners of Small Businesses. Report of the Federal Reserve Bank of Chicago and Women's Business Development Center, Chicago, 1996.

Letitia Baldrige. *Letitia Baldrige's New Complete Guide to Executive Manners.* New York, Rawson Associates, 1993.

Renee Baron. *What Type Am I?: Discover Who You Really Are.* New York, Penguin Books, 1998.

Lisa Berger. *Feathering Your Nest: The Retirement Planner.* New York, Workman Publishing, 1993.

Jeff Berner. *The Joy of Working from Home: Making a Life While Making a Living.* San Francisco, Berrett-Koehler Publishers, 1994.

Caroline Bird. *Lives of Our Own: Secrets of Salty Old Women.* Boston, Houghton Mifflin Company, 1995.

Robert Bolton and Dorothy Grover Bolton. *People Styles at Work: Making Bad Relationships Good and Good Relationships Better.* New York, Amacom, 1996.

Mark Bryan, Julia Cameron, Catherine Allen. *The Artist's Way at Work: Riding the Dragon.* New York, William Morrow and Company, Inc., 1998.

Andrew J. DuBrin. *The Complete Idiot's Guide to Leadership.* New York, Alpha Books, 1998.

Clarissa Pinkola Estés. *Women Who Run with the Wolves.* New York, Ballantine Books, 1995.

Roger Fisher and William Ury. *Getting to Yes: Negotiating Agreement Without Giving In.* New York, Penguin Books, 1991.

Michael E. Gerber. *The E Myth Revisited.* New York, HarperBusiness, 1995.

Geoffrey James. *Success Secrets from Silicon Valley: How to Make Your Teams More Effective.* New York, Times Business/Random House, 1998.

Carolyn Jones. *The Family of Women: Voices Across the Generations.* New York, Abbeville Press, 1999.

Jon R. Katzenbach. *Real Change Leaders: How You Can Create Growth and High Performance at Your Company.* New York, Times Business/Random House, 1995.

Gail Kuenstler. *The Career Atlas: How to Find a Good Job When Good Jobs Are Hard to Find.* New Jersey, Career Press, 1996.

Frank N. Magill, ed. *Great Lives from History: American Women Series III.* Englewood Cliffs, NJ, Salem Press, 1995.

Steve Mariotti. *The Young Entrepreneur's Guide to Starting and Running a Business.* New York, Times Business/Random House, 1996.

Dorothy P. Moore and E. Holly Buttner. *Women Entrepreneurs: Moving Beyond the Glass Ceiling.* Thousand Oaks, CA, Sage Publications, 1997.

Caroline Myss. *Anatomy of the Spirit: The Seven Stages of Power and Healing.* New York, Three Rivers Press, 1996.

Suze Orman. *The 9 Steps to Financial Freedom.* New York, Crown Publishers, 1997.

Tom Peters. *The Circle of Innovation: You Can't Shrink Your Way to Greatness.* New York, Alfred A. Knopf, 1997.

Tom Peters. *The Pursuit of WOW!: Every Person's Guide to Topsy-Turvy Times.* New York, Vintage Books, 1994.

Lisa Angowski Rogak. *100 Best Retirement Businesses*. Dover, N.H., Upstart Publishing Company, 1994.

Bonnie Miller Rubin. *Fifty on Fifty: Wisdom, Inspiration, and Reflections on Women's Lives Well Lived*. New York, Warner Books, 1998.

Andrew J. Sherman. *The Complete Guide to Running and Growing Your Business*. New York, Times Business/Random House, 1997.

Adrian J. Slywotzky and David J. Morrison. *The Profit Zone: How Strategic Business Design Will Lead You to Tomorrow's Profits*. New York, Times Business, Random House, 1997.

Jennifer Starr and Marcia Yudkin. *Women Entrepreneurs: A Review of Current Research*, special report. Center for Research on Women, Wellesley, MA, Wellesley College, 1996.

John Tarrant. *Perks and Parachutes*. New York, Times Business/Random House, 1997.

Paul D. Tieger and Barbara Barron-Tieger. *Do What You Are*, Second Edition. Boston, MA, Little, Brown and Company, 1995.

Webster's Dictionary of American Women. New York: Smithmark Publishers in cooperation with Merriam-Webster, 1996.

Barbara J. Winter. *Making a Living Without a Job*. New York, Bantam Books, 1993.

Allan Zullo and Bill Hartigan. *Success After 40: Late Bloomers Who Made It Big*. Kansas City, MO, Andrews and McMeel, 1996.

Index

a